WISE
WOMEN

WISE WOMEN

Over Two Thousand Years of
Spiritual Writing by Women

EDITED BY

SUSAN CAHILL

W.W. NORTON & COMPANY • NEW YORK • LONDON

The text of this book is composed in Electra with the display set in Centaur.
Composition and manufacturing by the Haddon Craftsmen, Inc.
Book design by Jam Design

Library of Congress Cataloging-in-Publication Data

Wise women : over two thousand years of spiritual writing by women / edited by Susan Cahill.
p.   cm.
Includes bibliographical references and index.
ISBN 0-393-03946-3
1. Women and religion.   2. Spiritual life.   3. Women—Religious
life.   I. Cahill, Susan Neunzig.
BL45.W55   1996
200′.82—dc20   95-40575
CIP

ISBN 0-393-31679-3 pbk.

W.W. Norton & Company, Inc., 500 Fifth Avenue, New York, N.Y. 10110   http://web.wwnorton.com
W.W. Norton & Company Ltd., 10 Coptic Street, London WC1A 1PU

2 3 4 5 6 7 8 9 0

For my son,
Joseph Neunzig Cahill

ACKNOWLEDGMENTS

Many people have contributed their own special wisdom to this collection. I am grateful to the memory of my mother, Florence Splain Neunzig, whose invocation of Eleanor Roosevelt as our household's matron saint influenced my sense of what a wise woman was (and was not): She was courageous and practical; she did not keep safely quiet. I revere, too, the memory of Miriam Luisi Pollock, a philosopher whose scholarship on the passionate intellectual independence of medieval women, especially Catherine of Siena and Teresa of Avila, and on the convergences between medieval and modern world views anticipated the perspectives of contemporary feminist theology and history. My friend Renée Wiener, Viennese exile and resistance fighter, has lived the wisdom of the stories of Ruth and Naomi and the fierce loyalty of Judith. Other friends have led me to writers and points of view I might have missed on my own: The novelist Elizabeth Cullinan introduced me to the writing of Patricia Hampl; Sister Jane Clary of the Order of St. Ursula, to Kathleen Norris; my husband, Tom Cahill, to the narratives of Etty Hillesum and Rigoberta Menchu; Susanne Stubbs of Madonna House in Combemere, Ontario, sent me the poetry of Catherine de Vinck; Tillie Olsen in twenty years of correspondence has led me to more writers than any one volume could represent. Kathy Splain, a teacher of meditation, of the Sri Chinmoy community, provided insight into the Hindu and Buddhist mystic traditions. The writings of the Benedictine Joan Chittister as well as feminist scholars Rosemary Radford Ruether, Beverly Wildung Harrison, and Jean Bethke Elshtain are important voices within a wisdom tradition grounded in social justice. The staffs of the research division of the New York Public Library and of

Fordham University's Duane Library, especially Milica Radjenovic Gasparevic, facilitated the pursuit of these resources.

Finally, I express my warm appreciation to my agent, Lois Wallace, for her support; to my editor at Norton, Mary Cunnane, whose valuable suggestions and enthusiasm sustained this project from beginning to end; to Amy Cherry for overseeing the paperback edition; and to Evan Gaffney for the elegance of the cover design.

CONTENTS

THE NINETEENTH CENTURY

THE TWENTIETH CENTURY

I. VOICES OF FAITH, IMAGINATION, AND PROTEST

II. NEW INSIGHTS: THE GOODS OF THE SPIRIT
ACCORDING TO SHAMANS, SCHOLARS, WITCHES, AND THEOLOGIANS

INTRODUCTION

P ERHAPS BECAUSE IT has been women's task throughout history "to go on believing in life when there was almost no hope," in the words of Margaret Mead, women have sought and cultivated the goods of the spirit out of a practical need for meaning. The varieties of significance they have intuited amid vast fields of lived experience have illumined their understanding and shaped the strategies of the journey, making the hard going sometimes easier, sometimes blessed, more promising than opaque. And meaning, the traveler's sustaining wisdom, is its own reward. A destination, in the country of solidarities.

The lights of wisdom — the truth of things — that radiate from the actual, often dense circumstances of life have inspired many writing women to transform their understanding and intuitions into language. As the voices of *Wise Women* confirm, the goods of the spirit and the perceptions of wisdom are mutually generative: Wise love, generous action, practical vision, a belief in the reality of the invisible are the core truths of many of the narratives represented in this collection.

A significant portion of writing by women seems not to fit with philosopher Charles Taylor's observation that "We tend in our culture to stifle the spirit." Rather, the women in this book have let it play. Reading their accounts of desire for the harmonies and illuminations of love, of resistance of the spirit crushers, of the revelatory silences of interior space enlarges our sense of the spiritual foundations of all our cultures, a generative force in history that a neglected body of women's writing evokes with passionate conviction.

Women have always found the world of the spirit compelling for a number of reasons. One is their historical exclusion from the full exercise of their spiritual identities within religious institutions; that injustice raises consciousness is a cliché by now, however true it is. Related to the gender exclusiveness of religious institutions is the paradoxical fact that spirituality itself is a fertile source of feminist consciousness and human liberation, though some cultural theorists ignore it. And as many historians have pointed out, religious institutions, despite their petrified official hierarchies, have provided abundant opportunities for women's self-authorization and -actualization. In spite of themselves, these institutions have nurtured the love of freedom and goodness and justice within their own hidebound bodies.

In America, for instance, the historic freedom movements of abolitionism, women's suffrage, and civil rights had their roots, for blacks and whites, in the Hebrew and Christian Scriptures and their respective spiritual communities. The women's movement of the last third of the twentieth century has heightened a simultaneous awareness of spirituality as an empowering force of women's self-understanding and of religious hierarchies that continue to practice an exclusive and sexist politics. As a consequence, women today, realizing the complexity and contradictions of their spiritual legacies, are at once rereading, rejecting, and reinventing their religious ideologies and rituals. Some of the best examples of this vitality appear in *Wise Women*. The writings produced by this critique demonstrate the same independent and countercultural judgment that has made women's writing on spirituality so distinctive and resoundingly clear and in the course of centuries has cost not a few their security and their lives.

The power and beauty of women's witness to a spiritual dimension of experience, of a world beyond the single separative self, resonate through centuries of writing. In this anthology, trying to represent a plurality of testimonies, I have included essays, poems, prayers, journal writings, stories, and memoirs that articulate a dynamic pattern of spiritual experience and growth: the self made larger by being open to and moving toward—as the unorthodox William James called it in *The Varieties of Religious Experience*—"the More," "transmundane energies, God, if you will . . . *something* larger than ourselves." In *The Shaking of the Foundations* theologian Paul Tillich defines the spiritual dimension this way: "There is a grace in life. Otherwise we could not live." Receptivity to the fact or possibility of mystery, to a something larger, makes the difference, I think, between a graciousness, a hospitality of consciousness, and a tone-deaf tendentiousness. Theologian Elizabeth Johnson's description of God in *She Who Is* as "relational aliveness," a masculine/feminine force of mutuality, implies openheartedness and change as signs of the presence of a holy spirit. Historian

Gerda Lerner in *The Creation of Feminist Consciousness* explores the connection—of such keen interest at this cultural moment—between "women's search for the Divine and through it women's search for full humanity, transcending differences of class, race and religion." The search and demand for individual and universal justice expressed in many of the following pieces embody that connection; as the theologian Judith Plaskow asserts, politics can be the flip side of a living spiritual experience.

Approximately ninety writings in *Wise Women* address various aspects of the spiritual life: mystical or visionary experience; love of God, of nature, of all creation; anger against the destruction of life on earth, the body of God and Goddess; desire for union with God; desire for healing; prayer; silence; the experience of emptiness, loss, and death; suffering and injustice; a vision of social justice; the primacy of conscience; spirit, theistic and nontheistic (some call it a presence) as the source of women's sense of meaning, of courage, of commitment to work for social change and human rights; friendship; freedom and the responsibilities of community—the core themes of human experience that also mark the shadowed valleys and luminous peaks of the hidden territory of the spirit. Women ponder and define these sacred spaces according to the roles they fulfill, the work they do—"the multiplicity of the lived and the real," to use the words of Germaine Brée. The focus of women's lives directs their gaze and explains the fruits of their contemplation; women's wisdom writings come out of the particular grounds of a gendered experience.

Women have recorded a spirituality beyond the boundaries of self and family in every century, within every religious tradition, and beyond the distinct traditions. My selections of texts and contexts reflect those backgrounds that have had the strongest influence on American spiritual consciousness. Clearly, Judaism and Protestant and Catholic Christianity, and the alternative versions of these traditions, dominate our spiritual heritage in all its variety: African American, Latin American, Jewish, Irish, Italian, and so on. To represent America's always diversifying cultural identity, I have included voices of Native American and Goddess spirituality, of Islam, Hinduism, Buddhism, and Taoism. Within the predominant spiritual traditions, however, there is no uniformity. As religious historian Ninian Smart states, "Even if for some purposes it is useful to talk about Christianity or Buddhism, it is in fact more realistic to speak of Christianities and Buddhisms. Each has more than fifty-seven varieties."

The varieties of spiritual experience demonstrate a range of moral and ethical behavior that the writings of this collection describe, especially in the selections from the nineteenth and twentieth centuries, when women's dissent from the cultural status quo took a public and activist form. These behaviors—signs of profound conversion in some lives—include the making of art, especially literature, an experience of discovering possible sources of meaning; public work—writing and politics, for example—on behalf of the enslaved, the poor, the dispossessed, and the environment; and resistance, feminist, political, theological, of the oppressions that violate the dignity that religious people as well as the descendants of the Enlightenment and contemporary agnostics believe is the natural right of all created beings. Judith Plaskow calls this praxis by its Hebrew name— *tikkun*—meaning "the repair of the world." Ninian Smart designates the things people do because they believe in doing them as the concern of the modern study of religion. From this stance, belief systems such as feminism and democracy belong as much to this subject as do the various religious traditions. Again, the nonsectarian William James: "[T]here is no one specific and essential kind of religious object, and no one specific and essential kind of religious act."

What is common to many of the writers in this book, despite their eclectic responses to the call of conscience, is a desire to resolve—or a refusal to admit—the old dualisms of patriarchal religion: between self and other, body and soul, male and female, the sacred and the secular, God the Father and God the Mother. The failures of history point up the obfuscating and nullifying effects of such bifurcations and abstractions on the work of building an earth fit for human beings. The voice that speaks in the Hebrew Bible's Book of Proverbs (see page 32) as well as in E. M. Broner's version of the same text (see page 36) rings with the corrective of practical common sense that is key to the wisdom of women. The wise pragmatic writings of Florence Nightingale (see page 143), Eleanor Roosevelt (see page 171), Florida Scott-Maxwell (see page 168), and Natalia Ginzburg (see page 200) support the point. These extraordinary and down-to-earth women also show that worldly cynicism and wisdom, worldly and otherworldly, speak radically different languages. In the interests of getting results and of protecting the life of the community, many women who seek the fairness of the polity and a unity of heart and mind acknowledge no difference between spirituality and politics. Sandra Cisneros, echoing a number of the voices in this collection, says she sees "the spiritual and political in some ways being the same thing."

Life schematized according to the dichotomies I have mentioned and the isolating individualism that is this mindset's emotional consequence contrasts with the desire for unitive experience voiced by women mystics and prophets of every cultural period. Their writings about wanting and meeting and knowing the presence of the divine person, the ground of being, Divine Love, are often erotic cries of the heart. From Eros, the God/Goddess of Love, the timeless source of mystical longing, comes the sensory language of mysticism and its imagery of touching, dancing, arousal, penetration, ecstasy, suckling, satisfaction. Though contemporary women writers are now addressing the erotic configuration of spirituality (in this book there are the writings of Audre Lorde—see page 238—and Carter Heyward—see page 315), women mystics—Hindu, Sufi, Jewish, Christian—have had the experience of mutual longing and love between creator and creature at the center of their spirituality and theology since ancient times.

The contents of *Wise Women* reveal this and other thematic continuities throughout centuries of oral and recorded narratives of women's spiritual lives. Organizing this experience according to chronology best suits the purposes of presenting an overview of common grounds as well as showing some of the changes that mark this selective history of women's spirituality. Whereas the references of Western medieval and early modern women are mainstream Christian or, in the cases of the Quakers and Shakers, alternative Christian, many of the twentieth-century voices resonate beyond the boundaries of denominational identities, or some—Diana Eck (see page 341), Rigoberta Menchu (see page 295)—blend the tones of several spiritualities, demonstrating the syncretism of contemporary religious experience. The embodied, earthly holiness/wholeness celebrated in the writings by Tillie Olsen, Denise Levertov, and Marge Piercy marks a strong and prevailing current of women's spirituality from every historical period. Some writers—Patricia Hampl (see page 264), Starhawk (see page 307)— blend rhetorical modes as well as spiritual influences, using autobiography, travel writing, theology, and cultural theory to shape their narratives. No matter what a writer's historical period or spiritual tradition—and many evoke no particular religious background—the wise women of this book, from the medieval mystic Hildegard of Bingen to the contemporary African American poet Rita Dove to Buddhist shaman Joan Halifax, are visionaries who imagine and love a creative presence inspiriting the heart of reality.

A few points regarding the contents of the main sections.

The opening section, "Testimonies of Ancient Cultures," includes selections about the myths and cults of the mother goddess Ishtar in Babylonia and Isis in Egypt. These texts record an originally oral tradition; the narrators are male or anonymous scribes writing about female goddesses of wisdom and fertility who were worshiped over the course of many millennia. The first stone image of the mother goddess, or the Great Mother, according to historian Werner Forman, comes from Czechoslovakia and dates to 20,000 B.C. The study of goddess-based religion has been important to contemporary feminist spirituality, including witchcraft, as scholars have sought to retrieve and refashion nonpatriarchal mythologies and rituals. Though archaeologists, anthropologists, and historians challenge their scholarship, the effect of such studies as Marija Gimbutas's *The Language of the Goddess* and Riane Eisler's *The Chalice and the Blade* has been to support the belief that knowledge of the goddess religion of the past encourages the possibility of a sexually egalitarian, peaceful, and earth-centered future.

Like Ishtar and Isis, the Jewish women of the ancient world—Ruth and Naomi and Judith, to name a few, and the feminine wisdom texts of the Old Testament, and Mary of the New Testament—come to us not in their own words but through their interpreters and translators, whom we either know or presume to have been males. In these instances and in the bits that are extant from ancient India—the words of Buddhist nuns—and from Greece—the words of Sappho and Sophocles's character of Antigone—the stories and words of these women have influenced later writers and the configuration of later spiritualities. Joan Erikson presents in *Saint Francis et His Four Ladies* some symbols that join the ancient mother goddesses of the Mediterranean world and Christianity's Mary: Both Isis and Aphrodite were "ladies of the rose," symbol of beauty, love, and wisdom; the rose, from the earliest Christian art, was used as a symbol of the wise and mysterious Virgin, Bride, and Mother. Esther Harding in *Woman's Mysteries* connects the statues of Isis representing her as a mother nursing her child Horus with the statues of the Virgin Mary and the suckling infant Jesus. Across a much wider time frame, the biblical Judith shows up as an icon of courage in the life story of Rigoberta Menchu, a late-twentieth-century leader of Indian resistance in Guatemala. The love between the biblical Ruth and Naomi figures as emblematic healing in the narrative of African American poet June Jordan's battle with cancer. The evidence of the cross-fertilization of spiritual traditions is vast, indicating, it seems to me, a generic spirituality of one universal loving power at the heart of the world.

"The Middle Ages" section includes a majority of Catholic Christian mystics-scholars-nuns; the visionary poetry of Hindu, Chinese, and Sufi women is also represented. As scholar Anne Fremantle explains, "As in Europe, so also in Islam, side by side with the theoretical philosophers were . . . the mystics, who agreed with St. Augustine that 'to Him Who is everywhere present, one comes by love and not by sail' nor even by thought." Like their Western sisters who suffered the wrath of the Inquisition, the Sufis (from *suf*, the white woolen gown they wore) were persecuted by the more orthodox Muslims. The female mysticism of both Eastern and Western cultures signals the erotic contours of religious ecstasy that I mentioned previously. Dancing, for example, is a figure of mystical encounter in both the Eastern and Western poetic imagination; both Shiva and the Christian God are Lords of the Dance.

The Western writers of this period also invoke an androgynous God, a loving father and mother. (Benedictine medievalist Jean Leclercq and scholar Caroline Bynum point out that recognition of the maternal aspect of God is a long tradition, expressed in the words of Isaiah, of Jesus, of Augustine, Anselm, Mechthild, the author of the *Ancrene Riwle*, St. Brigid of Sweden, and St. Catherine of Siena. "Mother Jesus" did not originate in the Middle Ages with Julian of Norwich.) In her exemplary study *Jesus as Mother: Studies in the Spirituality of the High Middle Ages* Caroline Bynum gives the women's writing of this period a new reading, one so richly nuanced that it resonates in our responses to the spirituality of contemporary writers. In his study of the thirteenth-century mystic Hadewijch, *Hadewijch and Her Sisters: Other Ways of Loving and Knowing*, Giles Milhaven sifts the common ground joining medieval women writers and such writers from our own day as Naomi Goldenberg, Susan Griffin, Beverly Wildung Harrison, Carter Heyward (see page 315), Mary Hunt, Audre Lorde (see page 238), Adrienne Rich, Rosemary Ruether (see page 254), and Haunani-Kay Trask. (In both historical periods women concerned with matters of spirit have incurred the censure of their established churches. In our own time, as in the Middle Ages, as Peter Dronke writes in *Women Writers of the Middle Ages*, "the spirit of such women was not crushed. However savagely the authoritarian church tried to suppress them, their beliefs lived on irresistibly. . . . [S]uch testimonies remain a wonder and an inspiration.") A particularly interesting angle of the new medieval studies is the study of the Beguines, those communities of thirteenth-century women (represented here by Mechthild of Magdeburg—see page 64), who lived mostly in the Low Countries, choosing to lead lives of contemplation, poverty, and service of the sick, without taking vows as nuns. The beguinages, along with the female monastic communities that many scholars have studied, were the first communities of women writers.

In "The Early Modern Period" section, the Protestant backlash against the high ecstasies of the Middle Ages and the Catholic backlash against the reform in the modes of Inquisition and a piety bent on outdoing John Calvin in otherworldliness are the contexts of the sixteenth, seventeenth, and eighteenth-century writer-nuns, mystics, and poets, as well as a Jewish widow (Glückel of Hameln) writing the meaning of life for her children; an obedient Puritan housewife (Anne Bradstreet) writing her own survival in the wilderness and a moral legacy for her children; and a renegade preacher (Anne Hutchinson) declaring her insubordinate conscience before Puritan magistrates. Hutchinson's allegiance to her conscience, despite the consequences, signaled the fault lines created beneath patriarchal religion by the conflation of a democratic ideal and a biblical faith based on the Pauline text "In Christ there is neither Jew nor Greek, slave nor free, male nor female, but you are all one in Christ Jesus" (Galatians 3:27–29). Alternative Christianities, such as Quakerism and Shakerism, and eventually the liberation movements of the nineteenth and twentieth centuries, refusing to participate in ecclesiastical systems of class distinctions and racial and gender discrimination, took their original cue from St. Paul in this radical voicing of the Christian call. They took literally the elimination of all culturally constructed distinctions and the vision of a truly universal community of love.

Writings from "The Nineteenth Century" (for example, the Grimké sisters, Florence Nightingale, Elizabeth Cady Stanton) continue to show the grounding of reform—the practical wisdom of political and social action—in consciences formed within various spiritual traditions. Other writers (Christina Rossetti, Emily Dickinson) reflect an increasingly interiorized spirituality as they retreat from the world of social relationships into their private domestic chambers, exclaustrated mystical brides-nuns without monasteries. This pattern of spirituality, showing a division between a radical commitment to social justice and a fiercely solitary spiritual life, continues into the present, defining some of the tension between the spirituality of social justice and a strand of New Age religion that focuses on the healthcare of the soul.

"The Twentieth Century" section—only Part I is arranged chronologically—is the longest in the anthology because the eclectic spiritual identities of our own time have written the most prolific records. And, too, many powerful accounts must be omitted for the sake of achieving a reasonable book length. (To name the omissions is to voice sore regrets; perhaps they might figure in a second volume.) The horrors of the century contextualize some of the strongest examples of modern wisdom literature: The Holocaust informs the diaries of Etty Hillesum; the racism of the American South provokes Marian Wright Edelman's letter to her children; the chemical and ideological destruction of life on earth inspires at once the prophetic Nos and visionary affirmations of the earth's sacredness by Willa Cather, Paula Gunn Allen, Marge Piercy, and Joan Halifax; the spiritual maiming done by other competitive materialisms arouses the moral force of Natalia Ginzburg's superb essay. Individual writers from Europe and the Middle East, from North, Latin, and Native America, articulate strategies of survival and the meanings they have constructed in the face of personal and collective suffering; theirs is the wisdom-in-the-making inspired by the patient living out of seemingly meaningless or miserable or ordinary circumstances (the difficult lives of Nancy Mairs and Anne Lamott come to mind here). Like the writing self, the making of wisdom—growing up, asking questions, developing insight, empathy, and a sense of complexity—is an open-ended process, never complete. Lucille Clifton puts her finger on a most fertile source of wisdom. Acknowledging that she, like everybody else, has had a difficult life, she names her saving grace: "But I was blessed with a sense of humor."

The concluding selections in Part II of "The Twentieth Century" (which are not arranged chronologically) exemplify the eclectic thought of contemporary feminist theologians and cross-cultural scholars of religion, science, linguistics, and politics. Their work of reimagining and widening inherited spiritual affiliations comes across with a vigor that colors the prospect of the coming century with hope. The contemporary scholarship on women's spirituality from many diverse perspectives is now so vast and immensely interesting that this final section of the book could in itself take on the length of a complete text.

Until our own time women's voices have been largely left out of the conversation about spirituality. Throughout the history of Christianity, for example, men have dominated systematic theology and philosophy; although women are the most important figures in the history of devotion, that angle on religious experience has been ignored or regarded as of minor interest. In this anthology my purpose has been to highlight some writers whose voices on the goods of the spirit have been neglected (Rabi'a, Mirabai, Natalia Ginzburg, Iris Origo) while choosing writers of the greatest power so that we can enjoy reading women voicing the resonances of wisdom on a subject with which they have an ancient intimacy. Again some words of William James are to the point: ". . . more life, a larger, richer, more satisfying life, is, in the last analysis the end of religion. The love of life, at any and every level of development, is the religious impulse." Taking care of life on many fronts and designing a sense of purpose in the process might be called the wisdom impulse.

The contents of *Wise Women* reflect a wide range of cultural backgrounds, as I have mentioned, and of social roles: mystics, scholars, saints (both "working saints," to use Ruskin's phrase, and the reclusive kind), shamans, mothers, wives, witches, professional writers, intellectuals, rebels, politicians. Across this spectrum, unifying chords of emotional and moral courage and ethical conviction resound. Throughout history the spiritual dimension of culture has been more of a liberating than a repressive force for women, a catalyst, a call to agency. Women historians have begun to name the diverse effects of this spiritual energy. This collection, literary, historical, religious, offers ample evidence of the active voices of free spirits, women who strike us, miraculously in some cases, as more compassionate agents than passive victims, despite the centuries of circumstance and custom stacked against them. Reminding us of what has been and is now possible, their writings are a wisely practical and visionary legacy.

Testimonies of
Ancient
Cultures

THE NEAR EAST

V ISUAL IMAGES OF a goddess that have been found from the Pyrenees
to Siberia are thought to be at least twenty thousand years old. They are
made of stone, bone, and ivory, many with lunar notations, many depicting pregnancy. As British writer Angela Tilby states in *Soul: God, Self, and
the New Cosmology* (see page 367), "many researchers believe that these
goddess figures may point to a universal religion in which the creative
source of life is imaged as a mother." The myth of a universal mother/moon
goddess seems to have weakened in the five thousand years before the
Christian era, but as the following texts from this period indicate, worship
of the multifaceted power of the feminine was a main current of the spirituality of the ancient Near East.

ISHTAR
(c. 3000 B.C.–?)

The Great Mother goddess of Mesopotamia—the Tigris and Euphrates
river valley—was worshiped under the name of Ishtar in Babylonia and
of Inanna in the Near Eastern dynasties of Sumeria, Akkadia, and
Assyria. The various names under which Ishtar was worshiped in
mysterious temple rituals all referred to the Magna Dea of the East, the
many-breasted goddess who gave the gift of fertility and, as Queen of the
Underworld (aka the Terrible Mother and Destroyer of Life), presided
over storms and war. The ever-changing goddess was also feared/revered
as the source of immortality, the hope of life after death. The following

selections are taken from a hymn sung in her honor, found on one of
the "Seven Tablets of Creation" (seventh century B.C.), though the
hymn is much older.

Hymn in Praise of the Goddess Ishtar of Babylonia

I pray unto thee, Lady of Ladies, Goddess of Goddesses!
O Ishtar, Queen of all peoples, directress of mankind!
O Irnini, thou art raised on high, mistress of the spirits of
    heaven;
Thou art mighty, thou hast sovereign power, exalted is thy
    name!
Thou art the light of heaven and earth, O valiant daughter of
    the Moon-god.
        Ruler of weapons, arbitress of the battle!
        Framer of all decrees, wearer of the crown of dominion!
O Lady, majestic is thy rank, over all the gods it is exalted!
Thou art the cause of lamentation, thou sowest hostility among
    brethren who are at peace;
Thou art the bestower of strength! (friendship)
Thou art strong, O Lady of Victory, thou canst violently attain
    my desire!
O Gutira who are girt with battle, who art clothed with terror,
Thou wieldest the sceptre and the decision, the control of earth
    and heaven!
Holy chambers, shrines, divine dwellings and temples worship
    thee!
Where is thy name not (heard)? Where is thy decree not
    (obeyed)?

              *   *   *

At the thought of thy name the heaven and earth quake.
The gods tremble, and the spirits of the earth falter.
Mankind payeth homage to thy mighty name,
For thou art great, thou art exalted.
All mankind, the whole human race, boweth down before thy
    power.
Thou judgest the cause of men with justice and righteousness;
Thou lookest with mercy on the violent man, and thou settest
    right the unruly every morning.
How long wilt thou tarry, O Lady of Heaven and earth, Shep
    herdess of those that dwell in human habitations?

How long wilt thou tarry, O Lady, whose feet are unwearied,
   whose knees have not lost their vigour?
How long wilt thou tarry, O Lady of all fights and of all battles?
O thou glorious one, that ragest among the spirits of heaven,
   that subduest angry gods,
Thou hast power over all princes, that controllest the sceptre
   of kings,
That openest the bonds of all handmaids,
That art raised on high, that art firmly established, O valiant
Ishtar, great is thy might
Bright torch of heaven and earth, light of all dwellings.

*   *   *

O goddess of men, O goddess of women, thou whose counsel
   none may learn,
Where thou lookest in pity, the dead man lives again, the sick
   is healed,
The afflicted is saved from his affliction, when he beholdest thy
   face!
I, thy servant, sorrowful, sighing, and in distress cry unto thee.
Look upon me, O my Lady, and accept my supplication,
      Truly pity me and hearken unto my prayer!
Cry unto me "It is enough!" and let thy spirit be appeased!
How long shall my body lament, which is full of restlessness and
   confusion?
How long shall my heart be afflicted, which is full of sorrow and
   sighing?

*   *   *

Let my prayer and my supplication come unto thee,
And let thy great mercy be upon me.
That those who behold me in the street may magnify thy name,
And that I may glorify thy godhead and thy might before man
   kind!
      Ishtar is exalted! Ishtar is Queen!
     My Lady is exalted! My Lady is Queen!
Irnini, the valiant daughter of the Moon-god hath not a rival.

*   *   *

O exalted Ishtar, that givest light unto the (four) quarters of
   the world!

ISIS
(c. 3100 B.C.–?)

Isis, the goddess-queen of the Egyptian civilization of the Nile river valley, was worshiped, like Ishtar of Mesopotamia, as having power over life and death; she was prayed to as a divine source of fertility in life and of an afterlife in death. "Mighty Isis" was also worshiped as the protector of her brother, Osiris, and the mother of their child, Horus. According to religion scholar Serinity Young, the magical powers associated with the name of Isis led to depictions of her as the goddess of wisdom. Her cult spread beyond Egypt to Athens and Rome, where she was especially revered by women. The selection that follows here is taken from a second-century narrative, *The Golden Ass* by Apuleius, a Roman writer from North Africa, who after his conversion to the cult of Isis, became one of her priests. In this scene he is dreaming of the goddess, whose restorative powers, he believed, could transform him from beast to man.

Isis, Queen of Heaven

Not long afterwards I awoke in sudden terror. A dazzling full moon was rising from the sea. It is at this secret hour that the Moon-goddess, sole sovereign of mankind, is possessed of her greatest power and majesty. She is the shining deity by whose divine influence not only all beasts, wild and tame, but all inanimate things as well, are invigorated; whose ebbs and flows control the rhythm of all bodies whatsoever, whether in the air, on earth, or below the sea. Of this I was well aware, and therefore resolved to address the visible image of the goddess, imploring her help; for Fortune seemed at last to have made up her mind that I had suffered enough and to be offering me a hope of release.

Jumping up and shaking off my drowsiness, I went down to the sea to purify myself by bathing in it. Seven times I dipped my head under the waves — seven, according to the divine philosopher Pythagoras, is a number that suits all religious occasions — and with joyful eagerness, though tears were running down my hairy face, I offered this soundless prayer to the supreme Goddess:

"Blessed Queen of Heaven, whether you are pleased to be known as Ceres, the original harvest mother who in joy at the finding of your lost daughter Proserpine abolished the rude acorn diet of our forefathers and gave them bread raised from the fertile soil of Eleusis; or whether as celestial Venus, now adored at sea-girt Paphos, who at the time of the first Creation coupled the sexes in mutual love and so contrived that man should continue to propagate his kind for ever; or whether as Artemis, the physician sister of Phoebus Apollo, reliever of the birth pangs of women, and now adored in the ancient shrine at Ephesus; or whether as dread Proserpine to whom the owl cries at night, whose triple face is potent against the malice of ghosts, keeping them imprisoned below earth; you who wander through many sacred groves and are propitiated with many different rites—you whose womanly light illuminates the walls of every city, whose misty radiance nurses the happy seeds under the soil, you who control the wandering course of the sun and the very power of his rays—I beseech you, by whatever name, in whatever aspect, with whatever ceremonies you deign to be invoked, have mercy on me in my extreme distress, restore my shattered fortune, grant me repose and peace after this long sequence of miseries. End my sufferings and perils, rid me of this hateful four-footed disguise, return me to my family, make me Lucius once more. But if I have offended some god of unappeasable cruelty who is bent on making life impossible for me, at least grant me one sure gift, the gift of death."

When I had finished my prayer and poured out the full bitterness of my oppressed heart, I returned to my sandy hollow, where once more sleep overcame me. I had scarcely closed my eyes before the apparition of a woman began to rise from the middle of the sea with so lovely a face that the gods themselves would have fallen down in adoration of it. First the head, then the whole shining body gradually emerged and stood before me poised on the surface of the waves. Yes, I will try to describe this transcendent vision, for though human speech is poor and limited, the Goddess herself will perhaps inspire me with poetic imagery sufficient to convey some slight inkling of what I saw.

Her long thick hair fell in tapering ringlets on her lovely neck, and was crowned with an intricate chaplet in which was woven every kind of flower. Just above her brow shone a round disc, like a mirror, or like the bright face of the moon, which told me who she was. Vipers rising from the left-hand and right-hand partings of her hair supported this disc, with ears of corn bristling beside them. Her many-coloured robe was of finest linen; part was glistening white, part crocus-yellow, part glowing red and along the entire hem a woven bordure of flowers and fruit clung swaying in the breeze. But what caught and held my eye more than anything else was the deep black lustre of her mantle. She wore it slung across her body from the right hip to the left shoulder, where it was caught in a knot resembling the boss of a shield; but part of it hung in innumerable folds, the tasselled fringe quivering. It was embroidered with glittering stars on the hem and everywhere else, and in the middle beamed a full and fiery moon.

In her right hand she held a bronze rattle, of the sort used to frighten away the God of the Sirocco; its narrow rim was curved like a sword-belt and three little rods, which sang shrilly when she shook the handle, passed horizontally through it. A boat-shaped gold dish hung from her left hand, and along the upper surface of the handle writhed an asp with puffed throat and head raised ready to strike. On her divine feet were slippers of palm leaves, the emblem of victory.

All the perfumes of Arabia floated into my nostrils as the Goddess deigned to address me: "You see me here, Lucius, in answer to your prayer. I am Nature, the universal Mother, mistress of all the elements, primordial child of time, sovereign of all things spiritual, queen of the dead, queen also of the immortals, the single manifestation of all gods and goddesses that are. My nod governs the shining heights of Heaven, the wholesome sea-breezes, the lamentable silences of the world below. Though I am worshipped in many aspects, known by countless names, and propitiated with all manner of different rites, yet the whole round earth venerates me. The primeval Phrygians call me Pessinuntica, Mother of the gods; the Athenians, sprung from their own soil, call me Cecropian Artemis; for the islanders of Cyprus I am Paphian Aphrodite; for the archers of Crete I am Dictynna; for the trilingual Sicilians, Stygian Proserpine; and for the Eleusinians their ancient Mother of the Corn.

"Some know me as Juno, some as Bellona of the Battles; others as Hecate, others again as Rhamnubia, but both races of Aethiopians, whose lands the morning sun first shines upon, and the Egyptians who excel in ancient learning and worship me with ceremonies proper to my godhead, call me by my true name, namely, Queen Isis. I have come in pity of your plight, I have come to favour and aid you. Weep no more, lament no longer; the hour of deliverance, shone over by my watchful light, is at hand."

NORTH AMERICAN INDIAN

U NLIKE THE CREATION stories of Judaism and Christianity, the emergence stories of North American Indians reject notions of human apartness and superiority over the natural world. People did not originate in a protoworld (like Eden), but rather in the womb of the Earth Mother, from which they were called out into the daylight of their Sun Father. According to scholar Andrew Wiget, in American Indian mythology "the earth is Mother not metaphorically but actually," and all life—human, animal, plant, and mineral—is born from within her. Her spiritual role was to establish harmony among all the orders of creation. As the following passage from the *Book of the Hopi* indicates, Spider Woman, the universal source of life within the Hopi creation story, exemplifies the core belief of American Indian spirituality: All the world was sacred or potentially sacred. Other tribes gave the incarnations of First Woman different names, such as Clan Mother, Brave-Hearted Woman, Early Morning Woman, Grandmother Turtle, Rainwater Woman, Corn Mother. Each one embodied the creative wisdom of a polytheistic cosmos. These beliefs are known today through the literary transcriptions of an ancient oral tradition made in the nineteenth and twentieth centuries by anthropologists and ethnographers.

SPIDER WOMAN
(3500 B.C.?–   )

The Creation of Spider Woman

Sótuknang went to the universe wherein was that to be Tokpela, the First
World, and out of it he created her who was to remain on that earth and
be his helper. Her name was Kókyangwúti, Spider Woman.

When she awoke to life and received her name, she asked, "Why am I
here?"

"Look about you," answered Sótuknang. "Here is this earth we have created. It has shape and substance, direction and time, a beginning and an
end. But there is no life upon it. We see no joyful movement. We hear no
joyful sound. What is life without sound and movement? So you have been
given the power to help us create this life. You have been given the knowledge, wisdom, and love to bless all the beings you create. That is why you
are here."

Following his instructions, Spider Woman took some earth, mixed with
it some *túchvala* (liquid from mouth: saliva), and molded it into two beings. Then she covered them with a cape made of white substance which
was the creative wisdom itself, and sang the Creation Song over them.
When she uncovered them the two beings, twins, sat up and asked, "Who
are we? Why are we here?"

To the one on the right Spider Woman said, "You are Pöqánghoya and
you are to help keep this world in order when life is put upon it. Go now
around all the world and put you hands upon the earth so that it will become fully solidified. This is your duty."

Spider Woman then said to the twin on the left, "You are Palöngawhoya
and you are to help keep this world in order when life is put upon it. This
is your duty now: go about all the world and send out sound so that it may
be heard throughout all the land. When this is heard you will also be known
as 'Echo,' for all sound echoes the creator."

*   *   *

She then created from the earth trees, bushes, plants, flowers, all kinds of
seed-bearers and nut-bearers to clothe the earth, giving to each a life and
name. In the same manner she created all kinds of birds and animals—

molding them out of earth, covering them with her white-substance cape, and singing over them. Some she placed to her right, some to her left, others before and behind her, indicating how they should spread to all four corners of the earth to live.

Sótuknang was happy, seeing how beautiful it all was—the land, the plants, the birds and animals, and the power working through them all. Joyfully he said to Taiowa, "Come see what our world looks like now!"

"It is very good," said Taiowa. "It is ready now for human life, the final touch to complete my plan."

So Spider Woman gathered earth, this time of four colors, yellow, red, white, and black; mixed with *túchvala,* the liquid of her mouth; molded them; and covered them with her white-substance cape which was the creative wisdom itself. As before, she sang over them the Creation Song, and when she uncovered them these forms were human beings in the image of Sótuknang. Then she created four other beings after her own form. They were *wúti,* female partners, for the first four male beings.

When Spider Woman uncovered them the forms came to life. This was at the time of the dark purple light, Qoyangnuptu, the first phase of the dawn of Creation, which first reveals the mystery of man's creation.

They soon awakened and began to move, but there was still a dampness on their foreheads and a soft spot on their heads. This was at the time of the yellow light, Síkangnuqua, the second phase of the dawn of Creation, when the breath of life entered man.

In a short time the sun appeared above the horizon, drying the dampness on their foreheads and hardening the soft spot on their heads. This was the time of the red light, Tálawva, the third phase of the dawn of Creation, when man, fully formed and firmed, proudly faced his Creator.

"That is the Sun," said Spider woman. "You are meeting your Father the Creator for the first time. You must always remember and observe these three phases of your Creation. This time of the three lights, the dark purple, the yellow, and the red reveal in turn the mystery, the breath of life, and warmth of love. These comprise the Creator's plan of life for you as sung over you in the Song of Creation. . . ."

JUDAISM

―――――――――――――― 🔲🔲🔲 ――――――――――――――

THE MOTHER GODDESS of the Near East was gradually replaced with a Father God who became the patriarchal God of the Israelites, the Christians, and the Muslims, the focus of male-dominant theologies.

The feminine was not completely suppressed in Judaism, however. It figures in the notion of Shekhinah as the female aspect of God or the name for the manifestation of the sacred presence on earth in the cloud and fire over the Ark of the Covenant, the burning bush, and Mount Sinai. It appears, too in the figure of Hokhmah, the Hebrew embodiment of Wisdom—like the Greek Sophia, feminine in gender—whose female voice is heard in the Wisdom literature of the Bible, excerpted in the following pages.

Biblical scholar Phyllis Bird, in her essay "Images of Women in the Old Testament," points out that "no single statement can be formulated concerning *the* image of woman in the Old Testament." Instead, in texts spanning close to a millennium in their dates of composition (Twelfth to Third century B.C.), there is a "plurality of conception." The creation story of Genesis is only one part of a much longer and complex interaction of God with his creation. (And Genesis becomes the focus of feminist writers' and theologians' reinventions of the biblical legacy in the twentieth-century section of this book.)

The following pages present selective evidence of the Hebrew Bible's diverse conceptions of the wisdom of women.

THE STORY OF RUTH AND NAOMI

According to the editors of *Reading Ruth: Contemporary Women Reclaim a Sacred Story*, "If we understand Torah, the gift of God 'who brought you out of the land of Egypt,' as directed centrally to the sustenance and liberation from suffering of . . . 'the stranger, the orphan, and the widow'—then the Book of Ruth . . . speaks to the essence of Torah. Its women characters challenge the Jewish world to live up to Torah ideals . . . and make manifest . . . what sort of people Torah is supposed to create." The Book of Ruth, which follows here, shows the centrality of friendship to women's spirituality. A quintessential woman's story, it continues to shape the wisdom of women as the piece by June Jordan in "The Twentieth Century" section of this book (see page 247) demonstrates so beautifully.

From the Book of Ruth

I :

1 In the days when the Judges were governing, a famine occurred in the country and a certain man from Bethlehem of Judah went—he, his wife and his two sons—to live in the Plains of Moab. The man was called Elimelech, his wife Naomi and his two sons Mahlon and Chilion; they were Ephrathites from Bethlehem of Judah. Going to the Plains of Moab, they settled there. Elimelech, Naomi's husband, died, and she and her two sons were left. These married Moabite women: one was called Orpah and the other Ruth. They lived there for about ten years. Mahlon and Chilion then both died too, and Naomi was thus bereft of her two sons and her husband. She then decided to come back from the Plains of Moab with her daughters-in-law, having heard in the Plains of Moab that God had visited his people and given them food. So, with her daughters-in-law, she left the place where she was living and they took the road back to Judah.

Naomi said to her two daughters-in-law, "Go back, each of you to your mother's house. May Yahweh show you faithful love, as you have done to those who have died and to me. Yahweh grant that you may each find happiness with a husband!" She then kissed them, but they began weeping loudly, and said, "No, we shall go back with you to your people." "Go home, daughters," Naomi replied. "Why come with me? Have I any more sons in my womb to make husbands for you? Go home, daughters, go, for I am now too old to marry again. Even if I said, 'I still have a hope: I shall take a husband this very night and shall bear more sons,' would you be prepared to wait for them until they were grown up? Would you refuse to marry for their sake? No, daughters, I am bitterly sorry for your sakes that the hand of Yahweh should have been raised against me." They started weeping loudly all over again; Orpah then kissed her mother-in-law and went back to her people. But Ruth stayed with her.

Naomi then said, "Look, your sister-in-law has gone back to her people and to her god. Go home, too; follow your sister-in-law."

But Ruth said, "Do not press me to leave you and to stop going with you, for

> wherever you go, I shall go,
> wherever you live, I shall live.
> Your people will be my people,
> and your God will be my God.
>
> Where you die, I shall die
> and there I shall be buried.
> Let Yahweh bring unnameable ills on me
> and worse ills, too,
> if anything but death
> should part me from you!"

Seeing that Ruth was determined to go with her, Naomi said no more.

The two of them went on until they came to Bethlehem. Their arrival set the whole town astir, and the women said, "Can this be Naomi?" To this she replied, "Do not call me Naomi, call me Mara, for Shaddai has made my lot bitter.

> I departed full,
> and Yahweh has brought me home empty.
> Why, then, call me Naomi,
> since Yahweh has pronounced against me
> and Shaddai has made me wretched?"

This was how Naomi came home with her daughter-in-law, Ruth the Moabitess, on returning from the Plains of Moab. They arrived in Bethlehem at the beginning of the barley harvest.

II: RUTH IN THE FIELDS OF BOAZ

2 Naomi had a kinsman on her husband's side, well-to-do and of Elimelech's clan. His name was Boaz.

Ruth the Moabitess said to Naomi, "Let me go into the fields and glean ears of corn in the footsteps of some man who will look on me with favour." She replied, "Go, daughter." So she set out and went to glean in the fields behind the reapers. Chance led her to a plot of land belonging to Boaz of Elimelech's clan. Boaz, as it happened, had just come from Bethlehem. "Yahweh be with you!" he said to the reapers. "Yahweh bless you!" they replied. Boaz said to a servant of his who was in charge of the reapers, "To whom does this young woman belong?" And the servant in charge of the reapers replied, "The girl is the Moabitess, the one who came back with Naomi from the Plains of Moab. She said, 'Please let me glean and pick up what falls from the sheaves behind the reapers.' Thus she came, and here she stayed, with hardly a rest from morning until now."

Boaz said to Ruth, "Listen to me, daughter. You must not go gleaning in any other field. You must not go away from here. Stay close to my workwomen. Keep your eyes on whatever part of the field they are reaping and follow behind. I have forbidden my men to molest you. And if you are thirsty, go to the pitchers and drink what the servants have drawn." Ruth fell on her face, prostrated herself and said, "How have I attracted your favour, for you to notice me, who am only a foreigner?" Boaz replied, "I have been told all about the way you have behaved to your mother-in-law since your husband's death, and how you left your own father and mother and the land where you were born to come to a people of whom you previously knew nothing. May Yahweh repay you for what you have done, and may you be richly rewarded by Yahweh, the God of Israel, under whose wings you have come for refuge!" She said, "My lord, I hope you will always look on me with favour! You have comforted and encouraged me, though I am not even the equal of one of your work-women."

When it was time to eat, Boaz said to her, "Come and eat some of this bread and dip your piece in the vinegar." Ruth sat down beside the reapers and Boaz made a heap of roasted grain for her; she ate till her hunger was satisfied, and she had some left over. When she had got up to glean, Boaz gave orders to his work-people, "Let her glean among the sheaves themselves. Do not molest her. And be sure you pull a few ears of corn out of the bundles and drop them. Let her glean them, and do not scold her." So she gleaned in the field till evening. Then she beat out what she had gleaned and it came to about a bushel of barley.

Taking it with her, she went back to the town. Her mother-in-law saw what she had gleaned. Ruth also took out what she had kept after eating all she wanted, and gave that to her. Her mother-in-law said, "Where have you been gleaning today? Where have you been working? Blessed be the man who took notice of you!" Ruth told her mother-in-law in whose field she had been working. "The name of the man with whom I have been working today," she said, "is Boaz." Naomi said to her daughter-in-law, "May he be blessed by Yahweh who does not withhold his faithful love from living or dead! This man," Naomi added, "is a close relation of ours. He is one of those who have the right of redemption over us." Ruth the Moabitess said to her mother-in-law, "He also said, 'Stay with my work-people until they have finished my whole harvest.'" Naomi said to Ruth, her daughter-in-law, "It is better for you, daughter, to go with his work-women than to go to some other field where you might be ill-treated." So she stayed with Boaz's work-women, and gleaned until the barley and wheat harvests were finished. And she went on living with her mother-in-law.

III: BOAZ SLEEPS

3 Her mother-in-law Naomi then said, "Daughter, is it not my duty to see you happily settled? And Boaz, the man with whose work-women you were, is he not our kinsman? Tonight he will be winnowing the barley on the threshing-floor. So wash and perfume yourself, put on your cloak and go down to the threshing-floor. Don't let him recognise you while he is still eating and drinking. But when he lies down, take note where he lies, then go and turn back the covering at his feet and lie down yourself. He will tell you what to do." Ruth said, "I shall do everything you tell me."

So she went down to the threshing-floor and did everything her mother-in-law had told her. When Boaz had finished eating and drinking, he went off happily and lay down beside the pile of barley. Ruth then quietly went, turned back the covering at his feet and lay down. In the middle of the night, he woke up with a shock and looked about him; and there lying at his feet was a woman. "Who are you?" he said; and she replied, "I am your servant Ruth. Spread the skirt of your cloak over your servant for you have the right of redemption over me." "May Yahweh bless you, daughter," he said, "for this second act of faithful love of yours is greater than the first, since you have not run after young men, poor or rich. Don't be afraid, daughter, I shall do everything you ask, since the people at the gate of my town all know that you are a woman of great worth. But, though it is true that I have the right of redemption over you, you have a kinsman closer than myself. Stay here for tonight and, in the morning, if he wishes to exercise his right over you, very well, let him redeem you. But if he does not wish to do so, then as Yahweh lives, I shall redeem you. Lie here till morning." So she lay at his feet till morning, but got up before the hour when one man can recognise another; and he thought, "It must not be known that this woman came to the threshing-floor." He then said, "Let me have the cloak you are wearing, hold it out!" She held it out while he put six measures of barley into it and then loaded it on to her; and off she went to the town.

When Ruth got home, her mother-in-law asked her, "How did things go with you, daughter?" She then told her everything that the man had done for her. He gave me these six measures of barley and said, "You must not go home empty-handed to your mother-in-law.' " Naomi said, "Do nothing, daughter, until you see how things have gone; I am sure he will not rest until he has settled the matter this very day."

IV: BOAZ MARRIES RUTH

4 Boaz, meanwhile, had gone up to the gate and sat down, and the relative of whom he had spoken then came by. Boaz said to him, "Here my friend, come and sit down"; the man came and sat down. Boaz then picked out ten of the town's elders and said, "Sit down here"; they sat down. Boaz then said to the man who had the right of redemption, "Naomi, who has come back from the Plains of Moab, is selling the piece of land that belonged to our brother, Elimelech. I thought I should tell you about this and say, 'Acquire it in the presence of the men who are sitting here and in the presence of the elders of my people. If you want to use your right of redemption, redeem it; if you do not, tell me so that I know, for I am the only person to redeem it besides yourself, and I myself come after you.' " The man said, "I am willing to redeem it." Boaz then said, "The day you acquire the field from Naomi, you also acquire Ruth the Moabitess, the wife of the man who has died, to perpetuate the dead man's name in his inheritance." The man with the right of redemption then said, "I cannot use my right of redemption without jeopardising my own inheritance. Since I cannot use my right of redemption, exercise the right yourself."

Now, in former times, it was the custom in Israel to confirm a transaction in matters of redemption or inheritance by one of the parties taking off his sandal and giving it to the other. This was how agreements were ratified in Israel. So, when the man with the right of redemption said to Boaz, "Acquire it for yourself," he took off his sandal.

Boaz then said to the elders and all the people there, "Today you are witnesses that from Naomi I acquire everything that used to belong to Elimelech, and everything that used to belong to Mahlon and Chilion and that I am also acquiring Ruth the Moabitess, Mahlon's widow, to be my wife, to perpetuate the dead man's name in his inheritance, so that the dead man's name will not be lost among his brothers and at the gate of his town. Today you are witnesses to this." All the people at the gate said, "We are witnesses"; and the elders said, "May Yahweh make the woman about to enter your family like Rachel and Leah who together built up the House of Israel.

> Grow mighty in Ephrathah,
> be renowned in Bethlehem!

And through the children Yahweh will give you by this young woman, may your family be like the family of Perez, "whom Tamar bore to Judah."

So Boaz took Ruth and she became his wife. And when they came together, Yahweh made her conceive and she bore a son. And the women said to Naomi, "Blessed be Yahweh who has not left you today without anyone to redeem you. May his name be praised in Israel! The child will be a comfort to you and the prop of your old age, for he has been born to the daughter-in-law who loves you and is more to you than seven sons." And Naomi, taking the child, held him to her breast; and she it was who looked after him.

And the women of the neighbourhood gave him a name. "A son," they said, "has been born to Naomi," and they called him Obed. This was the father of Jesse, the father of David.

THE STORY OF JUDITH AND HOLOFERNES

The biblical portrait of Judith has the complexity and emotion of a great literary creation. She also has the courage and wisdom of a prophet. Michelangelo painted her story into a corner spandrel of the Sistine Chapel, but as Judy Chicago points out, in men's pictures, Judith's gory deed is not shown and she is depicted as standing by passively. The woman artist Artemisia Gentileschi (1597–1651), on the other hand, did many paintings on the theme of "Judith Beheading Holofernes" in which Judith herself, true to the original story which follows here, decapitates the tyrant. Rigoberta Menchu, the Indian freedom fighter of Guatemala (see page 295), writes in her autobiography that the women rebels of her country took Judith as their model of self-defense in the fighting of a just war.

From The Book of Judith

II. BETHULIA UNDER SIEGE

The Campaign against Israel

7 The following day Holofernes issued orders to his whole army and to the whole host of auxiliaries who had joined him to break camp and march on Bethulia, to occupy the mountain passes and so open the campaign against the Israelites. The troops broke camp that same day. The actual fighting force numbered one hundred and twenty thousand infantry and twelve thousand cavalry, not to mention the baggage train with the vast number of men on foot concerned with that. They penetrated the valley in the neighbourhood of Bethulia, near the spring, and deployed on a wide front from Dothan to Balbaim and, in depth, from Bethulia to Cyamon, which faces on Esdraelon. When the Israelites saw this horde, they were all appalled and said to each other, 'Now they will lick the whole country clean. Not even the loftiest peaks, the gorges or the hills will be able to stand the weight of them.' Each man snatched up his arms; they lit beacons on their towers and spent the whole night on watch.

On the second day Holofernes deployed his entire cavalry in sight of the Israelites in Bethulia. He reconnoitred the slopes leading up to the town, located the water-points, seized them and posted pickets over them and returned to the main body. The chiefs of the sons of Esau, the leaders of the Moabites and the generals of the coastal district then came to him and said, "If our master will please listen to us, his forces will not sustain a single wound. The Israelites do not rely so much on their spears as on the height of the mountains where they live. And admittedly it is not at all easy to scale these heights of theirs.

"This being the case, master, do not engage them in a pitched battle, and then you will not lose a single man. Stay in camp, keep all your troops there too, while your servants seize the spring which rises at the foot of the mountain, since that is what provides the population of Bethulia with their water supply. Thirst will then force them to surrender their town. Meanwhile, we and our men will climb the nearest mountain tops and form advance posts there to prevent anyone from leaving the town. Hunger will waste them with their wives and children, and before the sword can reach them they will already be lying in the streets outside their houses. And you will make them pay dearly for their defiance and their refusal to meet you peaceably."

Their words pleased Holofernes as well as all his officers and he decided to do as they suggested. Accordingly a troop of Moabites moved forward with a further five thousand Assyrians. They penetrated the valley and seized the Israelites' waterpoints and springs. Meanwhile the Edomites and Ammonites went and took up positions in the highlands opposite Dothan, sending some of their men to the south-east opposite Egrebel, near Chous on the wadi Mochmur. The rest of the Assyrian army took up positions in the plain, covering every inch of the earth; their tents and equipment made an immense encampment, so vast were their numbers.

The Israelites called on the Lord their God, dispirited because the enemy had surrounded them and cut all line of retreat. For thirty-four days the Assyrian army, infantry, chariots, cavalrymen, had them surrounded. Every water jar the inhabitants of Bethulia had was empty, their wells were drying up; on no day could a man quench his thirst, since their water was rationed. Their little children pined away, the women and young men grew weak with thirst; they collapsed in the streets and gateways of the town; they had no strength left.

Young men, women, children, the whole people thronged clamouring round Uzziah and the chief men of the town, shouting in the presence of the assembled elders, "May God be judge between you and us! For you have done us great harm, by not suing for peace with the Assyrians. And now there is no one to help us. God has delivered us into their hands to be prostrated before them in thirst and utter helplessness. Call them in at once; hand the whole town over to be sacked by Holofernes' men and all his army. After all, we should be much better off as their booty than we are now; no doubt we shall be enslaved, but at least we shall be alive and not see our little ones dying before our eyes or our wives and children perishing. By heaven and earth and by our God, the Lord of our fathers who is punishing us for our sins and the sins of our ancestors, we implore you to take this course now, today." Bitter lamentations rose from the whole assembly, and they all cried loudly to the Lord God.

Then Uzziah spoke to them, "Take heart, brothers! Let us hold out five days more. By then the Lord our God will take pity on us, for he will not desert us altogether. At the end of this time, if there is no help forthcoming, I will do as you have said." With that he dismissed the people to their various quarters. The men went to man the walls and towers of the town, sending the women and children home. The town was full of despondency.

III. JUDITH

A *Portrait of Judith*

8 Judith was informed at the time of what had happened. She was the daughter of Merari son of Ox, son of Joseph, son of Oziel, son of Elkiah, son of Ananias, son of Gideon, son of Raphaim, son of Ahitub, son of Elijah, son of Hilkiah, son of Eliab, son of Nathanael, son of Salamiel, son of Sarasadai, son of Israel. Her husband Manasseh, of her own tribe and family, had died at the time of barley harvest. He was supervising the men as they bound up the sheaves in the field when he caught sunstroke and had to take to his bed. He died in Bethulia, his home town, and was buried with his ancestors in the field that lies between Dothan and Balamon. As a widow, Judith stayed inside her home for three years and four months. She had had an upper room built for herself on the roof. She wore sackcloth round her waist and dressed in widow's weeds. She fasted every day of her widowhood except for the sabbath eve, the sabbath itself, the eve of New Moon, the feast of New Moon and the festival days of the House of Israel. Now, she was very beautiful, charming to see. Her husband Manasseh had left her gold and silver, menservants and maidservants, cattle and lands; and she lived among all her possessions without anyone finding a word to say against her, so devoutly did she fear God.

Judith and the Elders

Hearing how the water shortage had demoralised the people and how they had complained bitterly to the headman of the town, and being also told what Uzziah had said to them and how he had given them his oath to surrender the town to the Assyrians in five days' time, Judith immediately sent her woman of affairs who managed her property to summon Chabris and Charmis, two elders of the town. When these came in she said:

"Listen to me, leaders of the people of Bethulia. You were wrong to speak to the people as you did today and to bind yourself by oath, in defiance of God, to surrender the town to our enemies if the Lord did not come to your help within a set number of days. Who are you, to put God to the test today, you, out of all mankind, to set yourselves above him? You of all people to put the Lord Almighty to the test! You do not understand anything, and never will. If you cannot sound the depths of the heart of man or unravel the arguments of his mind, how can you fathom the God who made all things, or sound his mind or unravel his purposes? No, brothers, do not provoke the anger of the Lord our God. Although it may not be his will to help us within the next five days, he has the power to protect us for as many days as he pleases, just as he has the power to destroy us before our enemies. But you have no right to demand guarantees where the designs of the Lord our God are concerned. For God is not to be coerced as man is, nor is he, like mere man, to be cajoled. Rather, as we wait patiently for him to save, let us plead with him to help us. He will hear our voice if such is his good pleasure.

"And indeed of recent times and still today there never has been one tribe of ours, or family, or village, or town that has worshipped gods made with human hands, as once was done, and that was the reason why our ancestors were delivered over to sword and sack, and perished in misery at the hands of our enemies. We for our part acknowledge no other God than him; and so we may hope he will not look on us disdainfully or desert our nation.

"If indeed they capture us, as you expect, then all Judaea will be captured too, and our holy places plundered, and we shall answer with our blood for their profanation. The slaughter of our brothers, the exile of our country, the unpeopling of our heritage, will recoil on our own heads among the nations whose slaves we will become, and our new masters will look down on us as an outrage and a disgrace; for our surrender will not reinstate us in their favour; no, the Lord our God will make it a thing to be ashamed of. So now, brothers, let us set an example to our brothers, since their lives depend on us and our most sacred possessions—Temple and altar—rest on us.

"All this being so, let us rather give thanks to the Lord our God who, as he tested our ancestors, is now testing us. Remember how he treated Abraham, all the ordeals of Isaac, all that happened to Jacob in Syrian Mesopotamia while he kept the sheep of Laban, his mother's brother. For as these ordeals were intended by him to search their hearts, so now this is not vengeance God exacts against us, but a warning inflicted by the Lord on those who are near his heart."

Uzziah replied, "Everything you have said has been spoken from sincerity of heart and no one will contradict a word of it. Not that today is the first time your wisdom has been displayed; from your earliest years all the people have known how shrewd you are and of how sound a heart. But, parched with thirst, the people forced us to act as we had promised them and to bind ourselves by an inviolable oath. You are a devout woman; pray to the Lord, then, to send us a downpour to fill our cisterns, so that our faintness may pass."

Judith replied, "Listen to me. I intend to do something, the memory of which will be handed down to the children of our race from age to age. Tonight you must be at the gate of the town. I shall make my way out with my attendant. Before the time fixed by you for surrendering the town to our enemies, the Lord will make use of me to rescue Israel. You must not ask what I intend to do; I will not tell you until I have done it." Uzziah and the chief man said, "Go in peace. May the Lord show you a way to take revenge on our enemies." And leaving the upper room they went back to their posts.

Judith's Prayer

9 Judith threw herself face to the ground, scattered ashes on her head, uncovered the sackcloth she was wearing and cried loudly to the Lord. At the same time in Jerusalem the evening incense was being offered in the Temple of God. Judith said:

> "Lord, God of my father Simeon,
> you armed him with a sword to take vengeance on the foreigners
> who had undone a virgin's girdle to her shame,
> laid bare her thigh to her confusion,
> violated her womb to her dishonour,
> since though you said, "This must not be," they did it.
> For this you handed their leaders over to slaughter,
> their bed, defiled by their deceit, to blood.
> You struck the slaves down with the chiefs
> and the chiefs with their servants.
> You left their wives to be carried off,
> their daughters to be taken captive,
> and their spoils to be shared out
> among the sons you loved,
> who had been so zealous for you,
> had loathed the stain put on their blood
> and called on you for help.
>
> "God, my God,
> now hear this widow too;
> for you have made the past,
> and what is happening now, and what will follow.
> What is, what will be, you have planned;
> what has been, you designed.
> Your purposes stood forward;
> 'See, we are here!' they said.
> For all of your ways are prepared
> and your judgements delivered with foreknowledge.

"See the Assyrians, boasting in their army,
glorying in their horses and their riders,
exulting in the strength of their infantry.
Trust as they may in shield and spear,
in bow and sling,
in you they have not recognised
the Lord, the shatterer of war;
yours alone the title of Lord.

"Break their violence with your might,
in your anger bring down their strength.
For they plan to profane your holy places,
to defile the tabernacle, the resting place of your glorious name,
and to throw down with iron the horn of your altar.
Observe their arrogance,
send your fury on their heads,
give the needful courage
to this widow's hand.
By guile of my lips
strike slave down with master,
and master with his servant.
Break their pride
by a woman's hand.

"Your strength does not lie in numbers,
nor your might in violent men;
since you are the God of the humble,
the help of the oppressed,
the support of the weak,
the refuge of the forsaken,
the saviour of the despairing.

"Please, please, God of my father,
God of the heritage of Israel,
Master of heaven and earth,
Creator of the waters,
King of your whole creation,
hear my prayer.
Give me a beguiling tongue
to wound and kill
those who have formed such cruel designs
against your covenant,

against your holy dwelling place,
against Mount Zion,
against the house belonging to your sons.
And demonstrate to every nation, every tribe,
that you are Yahweh, God almighty, all-powerful,
and that the race of Israel
has you for sole protector."

IV. JUDITH AND HOLOFERNES

Judith Goes to the Camp of Holofernes

10 Thus Judith called on the God of Israel. When she had finished praying, she rose from where she lay, summoned her attendant and went down into the rooms which she used on sabbath days and feasts. There she removed the sackcloth she was wearing and, taking off her widow's dress, she washed all over, anointed herself with costly perfumes, dressed her hair, wrapped a turban round it and put on the dress she used to wear on joyful occasions when her husband Manasseh was alive. She put sandals on her feet, put on her necklaces, bracelets, rings, earrings and all her jewelery, and made herself beautiful enough to catch the eye of every man who saw her. Then she handed her attendant a skin of wine and a flask of oil, filled a bag with barley girdle cakes, cakes of dried fruit and pure loaves, and wrapping all these provisions up gave them to her as well. They then went out, making for the town gate of Bethulia. There they found Uzziah waiting with the two elders of the town, Chabris and Charmis. When they saw Judith, her face so changed and her clothes so different, they were lost in admiration of her beauty. They said to her:

> "May the God of our ancestors keep you in his favour!
> May he grant your purposes fulfilment
> to the glory of the sons of Israel,
> to the greater glory of Jerusalem!"

Judith worshipped God, and then she said, "Have the town gate opened for me so that I can go out and make all your wishes come true." They did as she asked and gave orders to the young men to open the gate for her. This done, Judith went out accompanied by her maid, while the men of the town watched her all the way down the mountain and across the valley, until they lost sight of her.

As the women were making straight through the valley, an advance unit of Assyrians intercepted them, and seizing Judith began questioning her.

"Which side are you on? Where do you come from? Where are you going?" "I am a daughter of the Hebrews," she replied, "and I am fleeing from them since they will soon be your prey. I am on my way to see Holofernes, the general of your army, to give him trustworthy information. I will show him the road to take if he wants to capture all the highlands without losing one man or one life." As the men listened to what she was saying, they stared in astonishment at the sight of such a beautiful woman. "It will prove the saving of you," they said to her, "coming down to see our master of your own accord. You had better go to his tent; some of our men will escort you and hand you over to him. Once you are in his presence do not be afraid. Tell him what you have just told us and you will be well treated." They then detailed a hundred of their men as escort for herself and her attendant, and these led them to the tent of Holofernes.

News of her coming had already spread through the tents, and there was a general stir in the camp. She was still outside the tent of Holofernes waiting to be announced, when a crowd began forming round her. They were immensely impressed by her beauty and impressed with the Israelites because of her. "Who could despise a people having women like this?" they kept saying. "Better not leave one man of them alive; let any go and they would twist the whole world round their fingers!"

Then the bodyguard and adjutants of Holofernes came out and led Judith into the tent. Holofernes was resting on his bed under a canopy of purple and gold studded with emeralds and precious stones. The men announced her and he came out to the open part of the tent, with silver torches carried before him. When Judith confronted the general and his adjutant, the beauty of her face astonished them all. She fell on her face and did homage to him, but his servants raised her from the ground.

The First Meeting of Judith with Holofernes

11 "Courage, woman," Holofernes said, "do not be afraid. I have never hurt anyone who chose to serve Nebuchadnezzar, king of the whole world. Even now, if your nation of mountain dwellers had not insulted me, I would not have raised a spear against them. This was their fault, not mine. But tell me, why have you fled from them and come to us? . . . Anyhow, this will prove the saving of you. Courage! You will live through this night, and many after. No one shall hurt you. No, you shall be treated as well as all those are who serve my lord King Nebuchadnezzar."

Judith said, "Please listen favourably to what your slave has to say. Permit your servant to speak in your presence. I will speak no word of a lie in my lord's presence tonight. You have only to follow your servant's advice and God will bring your work to a successful conclusion; in what my lord undertakes he shall not fail. Long life to Nebuchadnezzar, king of the whole world, who has sent you to set every living soul to rights; may his power endure! Since, thanks to you, he is served not only by men, but through your compulsion the wild animals themselves, the cattle, and the birds of the air are to live in the service of Nebuchadnezzar and his whole House.

"We have indeed heard of your genius and adroitness of mind. It is known everywhere in the world that throughout the empire you have no rival for ability, wealth of experience and brilliance in waging war. We have also heard what Achior said in his speech to your council. The men of Bethulia having spared him, he has told them everything that he said to you. Now, master and lord, do not disregard what he said; keep it in your mind, since it is true; our nation will not be punished, the sword will indeed have no power over them, unless they sin against their God. But as it is, my lord need expect no repulse or setback, since death is about to fall on their heads, for sin has gained a hold over them, provoking the anger of their God each time that they commit it. As they are short of food and their water is giving out, they have resolved to fall back on their cattle and decided to make use of all the things that God has, by his laws, forbidden them to eat. Not only have they made up their minds to eat the first-fruits of corn and the tithes of wine and oil, though these have been consecrated by them and set apart for the priests who serve in Jerusalem in the presence of our God and may not, lawfully, even be touched by the people, but they have even sent men to Jerusalem—where the inhabitants are doing much the same—to bring them back authorisation from the Council of Elders. Now this will be the outcome: when the permission arrives and they act on it, that very day they shall be delivered over to you for destruction.

"When I, your servant, came to know all this, I fled from them. God has sent me to do things with you at which the world will be astonished when it hears. Your servant is a devout woman; she honours the God of heaven day and night. I therefore propose, my lord, to stay with you. I, your servant, will go out every night into the valley and pray to God to let me know when they have committed their sin. I will then come and tell you, so that you can march out with your whole army; and none of them will be able to resist you. I will be your guide right across Judaea until you reach Jerusalem; there I will enthrone you in the very middle of the city. Then you shall lead them like sheep and never a dog dare open its mouth to bark at you. Foreknowledge tells me this; this has been foretold to me and I have been sent to reveal it to you."

Her words pleased Holofernes and all his adjutants. Full of admiration at her wisdom they exclaimed, "There is no woman like her from one end of the earth to the other, so lovely of face and so wise of speech!" Holofernes said, "God has done well to send you ahead of your people. Strength will be ours, and ruin theirs who have insulted my lord. As for you, you are as beautiful as you are eloquent; if you do as you have promised, your god shall be my god, and you yourself shall make your home in the palace of King Nebuchadnezzar and be famous throughout the world."

12 With that he had her brought in to where his silver dinner service was already laid, and had his own food served to her and his own wine poured out for her. But Judith said, "I would rather not eat this, in case I incur some fault. What I have brought will be enough for me." "Suppose your provisions run out," Holofernes asked, "how could we get more of the same sort? We have no one belonging to your race here." "Never fear, my lord," Judith answered, "the Lord will have used me to accomplish his plan, before your servant has finished these provisions." Then the adjutants of Holofernes took her to a tent where she slept till midnight. A little before the morning watch she rose. She had already sent this request to Holofernes, "Let my lord kindly give orders for your servant to be allowed to go out and pray," and Holofernes had ordered his guards not to prevent her. She stayed in the camp for three days; she went out each night to the valley of Bethulia and washed at the spring where the picket had been posted. As she came up again she prayed to the Lord God of Israel to guide her in her plan to relieve the children of her people. Having purified herself, she would return and stay in her tent until her meal was brought her in the evening.

Judith at the Banquet of Holofernes

On the fourth day Holofernes gave a banquet, inviting only his own staff and none of the other officers. He said to Bagoas, the eunuch in charge of his personal affairs, "Go and persuade that Hebrew woman you are looking after to come and join us and eat and drink in our company. We shall be disgraced if we let a woman like this go without knowing her better. If we do not seduce her, everyone will laugh at us!" Bagoas then left Holofernes and went to see Judith. "Would this young and lovely woman condescend to come to my lord?" he asked. "She shall occupy the seat of honour opposite him, drink the joyful wine with us and be treated today like one of the Assyrian ladies-in-waiting in the palace of Nebuchadnezzar." "Who am I," Judith replied, "to resist my lord? I will not hesitate to do whatever he wishes, and doing this will be my joy to my dying day."

At this she rose and put on her dress and all her feminine adornments. Her maid preceded her, and on the floor in front of Holofernes spread the fleece which Bagoas had given Judith for her daily use to lie on as she ate.

Judith entered and took her place. The heart of Holofernes was ravished at the sight; his very soul was stirred. He was seized with a violent desire to sleep with her; and indeed since the first day he saw her, he had been waiting for an opportunity to seduce her. "Drink, drink!" Holofernes said. "Enjoy yourself with us!" "I am delighted to do so, Lord, for since my birth I have never felt my life more worthwhile than today." She took what her maid had prepared, and ate and drank facing him. Holofernes was so enchanted with her that he drank far more wine than he had drunk on any other day in his life.

13 It grew late and his staff hurried away. Bagoas closed the tent from the outside, having shown out those who still lingered in his lord's presence. They went to their beds wearied with all their drinking, and Judith was left alone in the tent with Holofernes who had collapsed wine-sodden on his bed. Judith then told her maid to stay just outside the bedroom and wait for her to come out, as she did every morning. She had let it be understood she would be going out to her prayers and had also spoken of her intention to Bagoas.

By now everyone had left Holofernes and no one, either important or unimportant, was left in the bedroom. Standing beside the bed, Judith murmured to herself:

> "Lord God, to whom all strength belongs,
> prosper what my hands are now to do
> for the greater glory of Jerusalem,
> now is the time to recover your heritage
> and further my designs
> to crush the enemies arrayed against us."

With that she went up to the bedpost by Holofernes' head and took down his scimitar; coming closer to the bed she caught him by the hair and said, "Make me strong today, Lord God of Israel!" Twice she struck at the nape of his neck with all her strength and cut off his head. She then rolled his body off the bed and tore the canopy down from the bedposts. Soon after, she went out and gave the head of Holofernes to her attendant who put it in her food bag. The two then left the camp together, as they always did when they went to pray. Once they were out of the camp, they skirted the ravine, climbed the slope to Bethulia and made for the gates.

Judith Brings the Head of Holofernes to Bethulia

From a distance, Judith shouted to the guards on the gates, "Open the gate! Open! For the Lord our God is with us still, displaying his strength in Israel and his might against our enemies, as he has today!" Hearing her voice, the townsmen hurried down to the town gate and summoned the elders. Everyone, great and small, came running down, since her arrival was unexpected. They threw the gate open, welcomed the women, lit a fire to see by and crowded round them. Then Judith raised her voice and said, "Praise God! Praise him! Praise the God who has not withdrawn his mercy from the House of Israel, but has shattered our enemies by my hand tonight!" She pulled the head out of the bag and held it for them to see. "This is the head of Holofernes, general-in-chief of the Assyrian army; here is the canopy under which he lay drunk! The Lord has struck him down by the hand of a woman! Glory to the Lord who has protected me in the course I took! My face seduced him, only to his own undoing; he committed no sin with me to shame me or disgrace me."

Overcome with emotion, the people all fell on their knees and worshipped God, exclaiming as one man, "Blessings on you, O our God, for confounding your people's enemies today!" Uzziah then said to Judith:

> "May you be blessed, my daughter, by God Most High,
> beyond all women on earth;
> and may the Lord God be blessed,
> the Creator of heaven and earth,
> by whose guidance you cut off the head
> of the leader of our enemies.
> The trust you have shown
> shall not pass from the memories of men,
> but shall ever remind them
> of the power of God.
> God grant you to be always held in honour,
> and rewarded with blessings,
> since you did not consider your own life
> when our nation was brought to its knees,
> but warded off our ruin,
> walking undeterred before our God."

All the people answered, "Amen! Amen!"

Israel Gives Thanks

Joakim the high priest and the Council of Elders of Israel, who were in Jerusalem, came to gaze on the benefits that the Lord had lavished on Israel and to see Judith and congratulate her. On coming to her house they blessed her with one accord, saying:

> "You are the glory of Jerusalem!
> You are the great pride of Israel!
> You are the highest honour of our race!
>
> "By doing all this with your own hand
> you have deserved well of Israel,
> and God has approved what you have done.
>
> "May you be blessed by the Lord Almighty
> in all the days to come!"

All the people answered, "Amen!"

The people looted the camp for thirty days. They gave Judith the tent of Holofernes, all his silver plate, his divans, his drinking bowls and all his furniture. She took this, loaded her mule, harnessed her carts and heaped the things into them. All the women of Israel, hurrying to see her, formed choirs of dancers in her honour. Judith distributed branches to the women who accompanied her; she and her companions put on wreaths of olive. Then she took her place at the head of the procession and led the women as they danced. All the men of Israel, armed and garlanded, followed them, singing hymns. . . .

When they reached Jerusalem they fell on their faces before God and, once the people were purified, they offered their holocausts and voluntary offerings and gifts. All Holofernes' property given her by the people and the canopy she herself had stripped from his bed, Judith vowed to God as a dedicated offering. For three months the people gave themselves up to rejoicings in Jerusalem before the Temple, where Judith stayed with them.

Judith Lives to Old Age. Her Death

When this was over, everyone returned home. Judith went back to Bethulia and lived on her estate; as long as she lived, she enjoyed a great reputation throughout the country. She had many suitors, but all her days, from the time her husband Manasseh died and was gathered to his people, she never gave herself to another man. Her fame spread more and more the older she grew in her husband's house; she lived to the age of a hundred and five years. She emancipated her maid, then died in Bethulia and was buried in the cave where Manasseh her husband lay. The House of Israel mourned her for seven days. Before her death she had distributed her property among her own relations and those of her husband Manasseh.

Never again during the lifetime of Judith, nor indeed for long after her death, did anyone trouble the sons of Israel.

LADY WISDOM

"Lady Wisdom," the persona of the Book of Proverbs, is, according to
Jack Miles's *God: A Biography*, "a mysteriously allegorical combination
of goddess, prophetess, and angelic messenger"; she is "God's
handmaiden or consort" who describes the attributes of human decency
with a feminine common sense. She also conceives of reality as an
ontology of relationship: She remembers that in the beginning was
community, an otherness of persons within the oneness of God. Before
the creation of the skies, the earth, and the sea, she was beside him.

WISDOM SPEAKS: A WARNING TO THE HEEDLESS

Wisdom calls aloud in the streets,
    she raises her voice in the public squares;
she calls out at the street corners,
    she delivers her message at the city gates.
"You simple people, how much longer will you cling
    to your simple ways?
How much longer will mockers revel in their mocking
    and fools go on hating knowledge?
Pay attention to my warning.
    To you I will pour out my heart
    and tell you what I have to say.
Since I have called and you have refused me,
    since I have beckoned and no one has taken notice,
since you have ignored all my advice
    and rejected all my warnings,
I, for my part, shall laugh at your distress,
    I shall jeer when terror befalls you,
when terror befalls you, like a storm,
    when your distress arrives, like a whirlwind,
    when ordeal and anguish bear down on you.
Then they will call me, but I shall not answer,
    they will look eagerly for me and will not find me.
They have hated knowledge,
    they have not chosen the fear of Yahweh,

they have taken no notice of my advice,
    they have spurned all my warnings:
so they will have to eat the fruits of their own ways of life,
    and choke themselves with their own scheming.
For the errors of the simple lead to their death,
    the complacency of fools works their own ruin;
but whoever listens to me may live secure,
    will have quiet, fearing no mischance."

*   *   *

THE JOYS OF WISDOM

Blessed are those who have discovered wisdom,
    those who have acquired understanding!
Gaining her is more rewarding than silver,
    her yield is more valuable than gold.
She is beyond the price of pearls,
    nothing you could covet is her equal.
In her right hand is length of days;
    in her left hand, riches and honour.
Her ways are filled with delight,
    her paths all lead to contentment.
She is a tree of life for those who hold her fast,
    those who cling to her live happy lives.

In wisdom, Yahweh laid the earth's foundations,
    in understanding, he spread out the heavens.
Through his knowledge the depths were cleft open,
    and the clouds distil the dew.

My child, hold to sound advice and prudence,
    never let them out of sight;
they will give life to your soul
    and beauty to your neck.
You will go on your way in safety,
    your feet will not stumble.
When you go to bed, you will not be afraid,
    having gone to bed, your sleep will be sweet.
Have no fear either of sudden terror
    or of attack mounted by wicked men,
since Yahweh will be your guarantor,
    he will keep your steps from the snare.

Refuse no kindness to those who have a right to it,
    if it is in your power to perform it.
Do not say to your neighbour, "Go away! Come another time!
    I will give it you tomorrow," if you can do it now.
Do not plot harm against your neighbour
    who is living unsuspecting beside you.
Do not pick a groundless quarrel with anyone
    who has done you no harm.
Do not envy the man of violence,
    never model your conduct on his;
for the wilful wrong-doer is abhorrent to Yahweh,
    who confides only in the honest.
Yahweh's curse lies on the house of the wicked,
    but he blesses the home of the upright.
He mocks those who mock,
    but accords his favour to the humble.
Glory is the portion of the wise,
    all that fools inherit is contempt.

                    *   *   *

WISDOM AS CREATOR

"Yahweh created me, first-fruits of his fashioning,
    before the oldest of his works.
From everlasting, I was firmly set,
    from the beginning, before the earth came into being.
The deep was not, when I was born,
    nor were the springs with their abounding waters.
Before the mountains were settled,
    before the hills, I came to birth;
before he had made the earth, the countryside,
    and the first elements of the world.
When he fixed the heavens firm, I was there,
    when he drew a circle on the surface of the deep,
when he thickened the clouds above,
    when the sources of the deep began to swell,
when he assigned the sea its boundaries
    —and the waters will not encroach on the shore—
when he traced the foundations of the earth,

I was beside the master craftsman,
   delighting him day after day,
   ever at play in his presence,
at play everywhere on his earth,
   delighting to be with the children of men.

THE SUPREME INVITATION

"And now, my children, listen to me.
   Happy are those who keep my ways.
Listen to instruction and become wise,
   do not reject it.
Blessed, whoever listens to me,
   who day after day keeps watch at my gates
   to guard my portals.
For whoever finds me finds life,
   and obtains the favour of Yahweh;
but whoever misses me harms himself,
   all who hate me are in love with death."

WISDOM AS HOSTESS

Wisdom has built herself a house,
   she has hewn her seven pillars,
she has slaughtered her beasts, drawn her wine,
   she has laid her table.
She had despatched her maidservants
   and proclaimed from the heights above the city,
"Who is simple? Let him come this way."
   To the fool she says,
"Come and eat my bread,
   drink the wine which I have drawn!
Leave foolishness behind and you will live,
   go forwards in the ways of perception."

From The Book of Proverbs
EISHET CHAYIL

The only description of a wife in the Bible comes from the Book of
Proverbs. This hymn to the ideal woman, "Eishet Chayil," is
traditionally read at Friday night Sabbath tables. In 1994 the scholar E.
M. Broner, author of *A Weave of Women* and many other books,
composed and read the "updated version" that follows Proverbs 31 here,
in honor of Alice Shalvi, a Jewish Orthodox feminist who was being
honored by the New Israel Fund, an organization that seeks peace and
equality in Israel.

From Proverbs 31

What a rare find is a capable wife!
Her worth is far beyond that of rubies.
Her husband puts his confidence in her,
And lacks no good thing.
She is good to him, never bad,
All the days of her life.
She looks for wool and flax,
And sets her hand to them with a will.
She is like a merchant fleet,
Bringing her food from afar.
She rises while it is still night,
And supplies provisions for her household,
The daily fare of her maids.
She sets her mind on an estate and acquires it;
She plants a vineyard by her own labors.
She girds herself with strength,
And performs her tasks with vigor.
She sees that her business thrives;
Her lamp never goes out at night.
She sets her hand to the distaff;
Her fingers work the spindle.
She gives generously to the poor;
Her hands are stretched out to the needy.
She is not worried for her household
        because of snow,
For her whole household is dressed in crimson.
She makes covers for herself;

Her clothing is linen and purple.
Her husband is prominent in the gates,
As he sits among the elders of the land.
She makes cloth and sells it,
And offers a girdle to the merchant.
She is clothed with strength and splendor;
She looks to the future cheerfully.
Her mouth is full of wisdom,
Her tongue with kindly teaching.
She oversees the activities of her household
And never eats the bread of idleness.
Her children declare her happy;
Her husband praises her,
"Many women have done well,
But you surpass them all."
Grace is deceptive,
Beauty is illusory;
It is for her fear of the LORD
That a woman is to be praised.
Extol her for the fruit of her hand,
And let her works praise her in the gates.

Proverbs 31
An updated version by E. M. Broner

Who can find a wise woman?
For her price is far above rubies.
Those in her house safely trust her
For she heeds the words of her children,
She works alongside her husband,
But outside the walls of the house,
Outside the gates of her garden,
She hears the cries in the city,
The cries of women in distress.
She is their rescuer.
She rises at dawn to organize.
She rises before light to make orderly
        the day.
She stretches out her hand to unchain
The chained woman, the women
        without recourse,

The women not paid their worth on this earth.
She taketh on the men at the gate,
The men of the law-making bodies,
The men of the Bet Din
The Judges on high.
She looks them in the eye
And says, This is unacceptable.
This is unjust.
This is cruel.
We demand a state where there is
        not religious rule.
In her household she is praised.
In the state she is extolled.
Many women have done wisely
But she excels them all.

THE SONG OF SONGS

An allegory of the mystical union of the soul with God, this poem
figures the marriage between God and Israel in the imagery of the love
uniting a husband and wife. The Songs may be interpreted as a lyrical
expression of the relationship between the individual soul, who is
personified as female, and the God of Love. The thirteenth-century
mystic Hadewijch expressed this love mysticism as the loved one
submerging in the abyss of the Beloved's wisdom: "the loved one and
the Beloved dwell one in the other . . . one sweet divine nature flows
through both."

You ravish my heart,
my sister, my promised bride,
you ravish my heart
with a single one of your glances,
with a single link of your necklace.
What spells lie in your love,
my sister, my promised bride!
How delicious is your love, more delicious than wine!
How fragrant your perfumes,

more fragrant than all spices!
Your lips, my promised bride,
distil wild honey.
Honey and milk
are under your tongue;
and the scent of your garments
is like the scent of Lebanon.

She is a garden enclosed,
my sister, my promised bride;
a garden enclosed,
a sealed fountain.
Your shoots from an orchard of pomegranate trees,
bearing most exquisite fruit:
nard and saffron,
calamus and cinnamon,
with all the incense-bearing trees;
myrrh and aloes,
with the subtlest odours.
Fountain of the garden,
well of living water,
streams flowing down from Lebanon!

BELOVED: Awake, north wind,
come, wind of the south!
Breathe over my garden,
to spread its sweet smell around.
Let my love come into his garden,
let him taste its most exquisite fruits.

LOVER: I come into my garden,
my sister, my promised bride,
I pick my myrrh and balsam,
I eat my honey and my honeycomb,
I drink my wine and my milk.

POET: Eat, friends, and drink,
drink deep, my dearest friends.

A PORTRAIT OF WISDOM

This biblical portrayal casts wisdom as a feminine spirit. The Greek term for wisdom, *sophia*, is feminine, and exegetes of the following passage (and others) have speculated that God is presenting himself here as co-creator, having conceived the world and humanity with a partner who is a feminine power or spirit, possibly *sophia*. Religion scholar Elaine Pagels explains that some gnostics believed such Wisdom texts signified that God himself was a secondary power, created by the divine Mother, the Source of life.

From The Book of Wisdom

EULOGY OF WISDOM

For within her is a spirit intelligent, holy,
unique, manifold, subtle,
mobile, incisive, unsullied,
lucid, invulnerable, benevolent, shrewd,
irresistible, beneficent, friendly to human beings,
steadfast, dependable, unperturbed,
almighty, all-surveying,
penetrating all intelligent, pure
and most subtle spirits.
For Wisdom is quicker to move than any motion;
she is so pure, she pervades and permeates all things.
She is a breath of the power of God,
pure emanation of the glory of the Almighty;
so nothing impure can find its way into her.
For she is a reflection of the eternal light,
untarnished mirror of God's active power,
and image of his goodness.

Although she is alone, she can do everything;
herself unchanging, she renews the world,
and, generation after generation, passing into holy souls,

she makes them into God's friends and prophets;
for God loves only those who dwell with Wisdom.
She is indeed more splendid than the sun,
she outshines all the constellations;
compared with light, she takes first place,
for light must yield to night,
but against Wisdom evil cannot prevail.
Strongly she reaches from one end of the world to the other
and she governs the whole world for its good.

SOLOMON'S LOVE FOR WISDOM

Wisdom I loved and searched for from my youth;
I resolved to have her as my bride,
I fell in love with her beauty.
She enhances her noble birth by sharing God's life,
for the Master of All has always loved her.
Indeed, she shares the secrets of God's knowledge,
and she chooses what he will do.
If in this life wealth is a desirable possession,
what is more wealthy than Wisdom whose work is everywhere?

BUDDHISM

BUDDHISM FINDS TRUTH and peace not in ritual observance or abstract authority but in experience. Truth must be tried out, as gold is tried by fire. The Buddhist ethos is more egalitarian than that of Hinduism and more resistant to orthodoxy of vision or practice. The earliest-known anthology of women's literature consists of the songs, excerpted here, composed by Buddhist nuns, or *theris*, collected into the *Therigatha*. The poets were contemporaries of the Buddha, though their lyrics were not written down until about 80 B.C. They testify to lives transformed by the Buddha's teaching and celebrate the spiritual freedom—nirvana—achieved by the release of the soul from some anxiety of everyday life.

THERIGATHA
(Sixth century B.C.)

Songs of the Nuns

MUTTA
[So free am I, so gloriously free]

So free am I, so gloriously free,
Free from three petty things—
From mortar, from pestle and from my twisted lord,
Freed from rebirth and death I am,
And all that has held me down
Is hurled away.

Translated by Uma Chakravarti and Kumkum Roy

UBBIRI
[O Ubbiri, who wails in the wood]

"O Ubbiri, who wails in the wood
'O Jiva! Dear daughter!'
Return to your senses. In this charnel field
Innumerable daughters, once as full of life as Jiva,
Are burnt. Which of them do you mourn?"
The hidden arrow in my heart plucked out,
The dart lodged there, removed.
The anguish of my loss,
The grief that left me faint all gone,
The yearning stilled,
To the Buddha, the Dhamma, and the Sangha
I turn, my heart now healed.

Translated by Uma Chakravarti and Kumkum Roy

SUMANGALAMATA
[A woman well set free! How free I am]

A woman well set free! How free I am,
How wonderfully free, from kitchen drudgery.
Free from the harsh grip of hunger,
And from empty cooking pots,
Free too of that unscrupulous man,
The weaver of sunshades.
Calm now, and serene I am,
All lust and hatred purged.
To the shade of the spreading trees I go
And contemplate my happiness.

Translated by Uma Chakravarti and Kumkum Roy

METTIKA
[Though I am weak and tired now]

Though I am weak and tired now,
And my youthful step long gone,
Leaning on this staff,
I climb the mountain peak.
My cloak cast off, my bowl overturned,
I sit here on this rock.
And over my spirit blows
The breath
Of liberty

GREECE

GREEK CULTURE—RELIGIOUS, political, and social—revered reason, a spiritual quality associated with males. Women were regarded as an inferior breed, irrational, good for slavery and housework. Except in the instance of Athena, wisdom was not sought within the pantheon of goddesses. There are few primary written sources from classical antiquity attesting to what women thought about life in Athenian democracy. Predating the golden age of this era is the isolated voice of Sappho, who clearly did have a mind and body of her own.

SAPPHO
(630 B.C.–570 B.C.)

Orphaned at the age of six, Sappho was married, had a daughter named Kleis, and lived most of her life in the city of Mytilene on Lesbos, an island in the Aegean off the west coast of what is now Turkey. The legends of antiquity and her poetry present her as a woman of independent mind whose erotic life centered on women. The second of the following two poems is addressed to Aphrodite, the goddess of love, beauty, and fertility. Revered throughout the Greek world and by later writers for their "fluidity, ease, grace, and melodic variety," in the words of translator Jim Powell, Sappho's poems have survived only in fragments, offering us no more than some five hundred lines.

Most beautiful of all the stars
O Hesperus, bringing everything
the bright dawn scattered:
you bring the sheep, you bring the goat,
you bring the child back to her mother.

Translated by Jim Powell

On the throne of many hues, Immortal Aphrodite,
child of Zeus, weaving wiles—I beg you
not to subdue my spirit, Queen,
with pain or sorrow

but come—if ever before
having heard my voice from far away
you listened, and leaving your father's
golden home you came

in your chariot yoked with swift, lovely
sparrows bringing you over the dark earth
thick-feathered wings swirling down
from the sky through mid-air

arriving quickly—you, Blessed One,
with a smile on your unaging face
asking again what have I suffered
and why am I calling again

and in my wild heart what did I most wish
to happen to me: "Again whom must I persuade
back into the harness of your love?
Sappho, who wrongs you?

For if she flees, soon she'll pursue,
she doesn't accept gifts, but she'll give,
if not now loving, soon she'll love
even against her will."

Come to me now again, release me from
this pain, everything my spirit longs
to have fulfilled, fulfill, and you
be my ally.

Translated by Diane J. Rayor

ANTIGONE
(from Sophocles: 496–406 B.C.)

Antigone, the heroine of Sophocles's play of the same name, the
daughter of Oedipus and Jocasta, risked—and lost—her life for the sake
of her determination to bury her brother's body. She would not obey
King Creon's order that Polyneices's body remain unburied as a
punishment for opposing Creon in battle. When Antigone is discovered
breaking the king's law to honor her brother in death, she does not
cower or equivocate. She has the courage of her heart and her integrity:
She puts Creon in his place. His law forbidding the burial of her
brother's body strikes her conscience as obscene, deserving not
compliance but defiance for its violation of God's law and the unwritten
laws of decency and humanity. Antigone's civil disobedience enacts a
spirituality of heroic resistance in the face of tyranny that appears again
and again in the narratives of *Wise Women*.

From *Antigone*

[Guard:]
And then she brought more dust
And sprinkled wine three times for her brother's
    ghost.

We ran and took her at once. She was not afraid,
Not even when we charged her with what she had
    done.
She denied nothing.
    And this was a comfort to me,
And some uneasiness: for it is a good thing
To escape from death, but it is no great pleasure
To bring death to a friend.
    Yet I always say
There is nothing so comfortable as your own safe
    skin!

CREON: [*Slowly, dangerously*]
And you, Antigonê,
You with your head hanging,—do you confess this
    thing?
ANTIGONE:
I do. I deny nothing.
CREON: [*To* SENTRY:]
You may go.

                       [*Exit* SENTRY]
                       [*To* ANTIGONE:]
Tell me, tell me briefly:
Had you heard my proclamation touching this matter?
ANTIGONE:
It was public. Could I help hearing it?
CREON:
And yet you dared defy the law.
ANTIGONE:
    I dared.
    It was not God's proclamation. That final Justice
That rules the world below makes no such laws.

Your edict, King, was strong,
But all your strength is weakness itself against
The immortal unrecorded laws of God.
They are not merely now: they were, and shall be,
Operative for ever, beyond man utterly.

I knew I must die, even without your decree:
I am only mortal. And if I must die
Now, before it is my time to die,
Surely this is no hardship: can anyone
Living, as I live, with evil all about me,
Think Death less than a friend? This death of mine
Is of no importance; but if I had left my brother
Lying in death unburied, I should have suffered.
Now I do not.
    You smile at me. Ah Creon,
Think me a fool, if you like; but it may well be
That a fool convicts me of folly.

CHORAGOS:
Like father, like daughter: both headstrong, deaf to
    reason!
She has never learned to yield.

Translated by Robert Fitzgerald and Dudley Fitts

CHRISTIANITY

———————————— 卐卐卐 ————————————

CHRISTIANITY'S EARLY MEDITERRANEAN version—before the Roman emperor Constantine legitimated a triumphal institutional variety (A.D. 313) and before Martin Luther rejected the corruption of that version and instituted Christian otherworldliness (1517)—refers to the followers of Jesus, who, they believed, was son of God and human prophet. Practicing his message of unboundaried—catholic—love and service of neighbor, especially the poor, was, in the early Christian community, the only path to the freedom of love. According to the incarnational world view of Christianity, God, in the person of Jesus and suffering humanity, is present in the embodied world and can be known through the senses and the ordinary experiences of everyday life.

MARY

Theologians ranging from the ninth-century Irishman John Scotus Erigena to the twentieth-century paleontologist Teilhard de Chardin consider the identification of God with the world through the physical/spiritual agency of the woman Mary the essence of Catholic Christian revelation. A woman of few words, Mary—Miriam, in Hebrew—the mother of Jesus, comes to us mostly from the pen of the Gospel writer Luke, who attributed to her the Magnificat, the Latin title of the song that follows here. Similar to the Hebrew Bible's songs of

Hannah and Deborah, Mary's prayer has been dismissed by feminists who saw it as part of the church's use of the cult of Mary to promote a subservient role for women. More recently, however, the Magnificat has been outlawed in parts of Latin America because it is recited within liberation movements as a prophecy of class revolution. The perception of Mary herself has undergone a similar change. Revered through centuries of masculinist theology as the Virgin–Madonna-on-a-pedestal, the contemporary Mary has a more complex identity. German theologian Dorothee Sölle (see page 324) rereads her as a figure of resistance rather than subservience. According to feminist theologian Elisabeth Schüssler Fiorenza, Mary has always represented liberation for women. In Fiorenza's words, "on an emotional, imaginative, experiential level the Catholic child experiences the love of God in the figure of a woman," an identification that, in her view, undercuts the sexism of the institution.

The Magnificat

And Mary said, "My soul magnifies the Lord, and my spirit rejoices in God my Savior, for he has looked with favor on the lowliness of his servant. Surely, from now on all generations will call me blessed; for the Mighty One has done great things for me, and holy is his name. His mercy is for those who fear him from generation to generation. He has shown strength with his arm; he has scattered the proud in the arrogance of their hearts. He has brought down the powerful from their thrones, and lifted up the lowly. He has filled the hungry with good things, and sent the rich away empty. He has helped his servant Israel, in remembrance of his mercy, according to the promise he made to our ancestors, to Abraham and to his descendants forever."

(Luke 1:46–55)

THE
MIDDLE
AGES

D ESPITE THE WEIGHT of church authority against the education of women, throughout the Middle Ages, "voluminous writing," in the words of Mary Ritter Beard's *Woman as Force in History*, "was done by women, particularly those associated with the mystics." And in all the works of making history and contributing to culture—the foundation (and reform) of monasteries and cloisters (and the scripting and decoration of manuscripts into books that went on in these communities), the foundations of beguinages and hospitals, the creation of liturgies and religious devotions, the interactions of commerce and diplomacy—women, she concludes, "displayed titanic energies."

RABI'A
(717–801)

In *Rabi'a: The Life and Work of Rabi'a and Other Women Mystics in Islam*, Islamic scholar Margaret Smith tells the little that is known about Rabi'a's life and her place within the spiritual history of Islam. Born in Basra, where she grew up as an orphan who was sold into and later freed from slavery, Rabi'a exemplifies the tradition of mysticism—Sufism— within Islam. According to her twelfth-century biographer Attar, Smith's main source, Rabi'a is the most important woman saint of Islam, "that one," according to Attar, "set apart in the seclusion of holiness, that woman . . . on fire with love and longing, . . . that woman who lost herself in union with Divine, that one accepted by men as a second spotless Mary." According to legend, when Rabi'a prayed, her head was surrounded by light, the enveloping radiance or *sakina* (derived from the Hebrew Shekhinah, the cloud of glory indicating the presence of God) of the Muslim saint, corresponding to the halo of the Christian saint. Like her Christian sister mystics, she said love was the core of the mystical union: She espoused a heavenly bridegroom and rejected earthly marriage. Of her refusal to marry, she said, "My peace, O my brothers, is in solitude, / And my Beloved is with me alway, / For His love I can find no substitute." Despite what Smith describes as the Eastern belief in the essential superiority of the male sex, Sufi leaders of Rabi'a's time acknowledged her preeminence above other Sufi teachers. Within Sufism, it is prayer that provides the best evidence of personality—not the ritual prayer but the loving conversation with God (*munajat*) that the mystic speaks out of the depths of her heart. A selection of prayers attributed to Rabi'a follows.

O my Lord, the stars are shining and the eyes of men are
closed, and kings have shut their doors
and every lover is alone with his beloved,
and here am I alone with Thee

O God, whatsoever Thou has apportioned to me of worldly things,
do Thou give that to Thy enemies;
and whatsoever Thou hast apportioned to me in the world to come,
give that to Thy friends;
for Thou sufficest me.

O God, if I worship Thee for fear of Hell,
burn me in Hell,
and if I worship Thee in hope of Paradise,
exclude me from Paradise;
but if I worship Thee for Thy own sake,
grudge me not Thy everlasting beauty.

O God, my whole occupation and all my desire in this world,
of all worldly things,
is to remember Thee,
and in the world to come,
of all things of the world to come,
is to meet Thee.
This is on my side,
as I have stated;
now do Thou whatsoever Thou wilt.

KASSIANE
(804?–?)

Born in Constantinople, Kassiane is the one woman poet who has come down to us from the Byzantine Greek. When the empress Theodora reestablished Eastern Orthodoxy as the state religion of Byzantium in 843, Kassiane became a nun. She founded a convent and, like Hildegard of Bingen two centuries later, wrote hymns for her nuns to sing. The following example, sung in the voice of the "sinful woman," is part of the Holy Week liturgy of the Eastern Orthodox Church. The hymn evokes both the Gospel story of an anonymous prostitute who showed up at the house of Simon to wash the feet of Jesus and the devotion of Mary Magdalene. First at the tomb on Easter morning, and thus the first eyewitness and messenger of the central fact of Christian revelation, the woman Mary Magdalene (and the women who accompanied her) represent the beginning of the Christian apostolic tradition. Kassiane's theme of God's mercy to sinners—as well as woman's mystical knowledge of the love of God in her body—is, as the contents of this section will show, a favorite of medieval women writers.

Mary Magdalene

Lord, this woman who fell into many sins
    perceives the God in you,
    joins the women bringing you myrrh,
    crying she brings myrrh   before your tomb.
"O what a night   what a night I've had!
    Extravagant frenzy   in a moonless gloom,
    craving the body.

Accept this spring of tears,
  you who empty seawater   from the clouds.
Bend to the pain   in my heart, you
  who made the sky bend   to your secret incarnation
  which emptied the heavens.
I will kiss your feet, wash them,
  dry them with the hair of my head, those feet whose steps
Eve heard at dusk
  in Paradise   and hid in terror.
Savior of souls   who will trace the plethora
  of my sins or the knowable chasm of your judgments?
Do not overlook me, your slave,
  in your measureless mercy."

Translated by Aliki Barnstone

HILDEGARD OF BINGEN
(1098–1179)

Born in the Rhineland of aristocratic parents, Hildegard became a
novice at seven, professed at fourteen, and abbess at thirty-eight, when
she began to record the experiences of the divine presence she had had
for years in her book *Scivias* ("One Knowing the Ways of the Lord").
Composed of three parts, which unfold visions of creation, salvation,
and the life of holiness (Book Three is excerpted here), *Scivias*,
according to the medievalist Barbara Newman, describes the divine life
with visual more than affective imagery and uses female images to
represent the world (the "cosmic egg") and the church ("mother of the
faithful"). Renowned as "the Sybil of the Rhine," Hildegard possessed an
encyclopedic learning, also writing works on mathematics, science, and
medicine and the lyrics and music for *Symphonia Armonie Celestium
Revelationum* ("Symphony of the Harmony of Celestial Revelations"), a
collection of liturgical works from which the currently popular album
Vision is taken. Unlike other mystics of the Middle Ages, she did not
display an ascetic holiness or practice in isolation. She carried on an
extensive correspondence and went on tours preaching monastic and
clerical reform (never a topic the church authorities liked to hear
addressed by women mystics), and her Benedictine monastery at
Rupertsberg, across the Nahe River from the town of Bingen, had indoor
plumbing and served good food.

From *Scivias*

VISION THIRTEEN

Symphony of the Blessed

Then I saw the lucent sky, in which I heard different kinds of music, marvellously embodying all the meanings I had heard before. I heard the praises of the joyous citizens of Heaven, steadfastly persevering in the ways of Truth; and laments calling people back to those praises and joys; and the exhortations of the virtues, spurring one another on to secure the salvation of the peoples ensnared by the Devil. And the virtues destroyed his snares, so that the faithful at last through repentance passed out of their sins and into Heaven.

And their song, like the voice of a multitude, making music in harmony praising the ranks of Heaven, had these words:

I Songs to Holy Mary

O splendid jewel, serenely infused with the Sun!
The Sun is in you as a fount from the heart of the Father;
It is His sole Word, by Whom He created the world,
The primary matter, which Eve threw into disorder.
He formed the Word in you as a human being,
And therefore you are the jewel that shines most brightly,
Through whom the Word breathed out the whole of the virtues,
As once from primary matter He made all creatures.

O sweet green branch that flowers from the stem of Jesse!
O glorious thing, that God on His fairest daughter
Looked as the eagle looks on the face of the sun!
The Most High Father sought for a Virgin's candor,
And willed that His Word should take in her His body.
For the Virgin's mind was by His mystery illumined,
And from her virginity sprang the glorious Flower. . . .

*　　*　　*

O angels with shining faces who guard the people,
O ye archangels, who take just souls into Heaven,
And you, O virtues and powers, O principalities,
Dominions and thrones, who by five are secretly counted,
And you, cherubim and seraphim, seal of God's secrets,

Praise be to you all, who behold the heart of the Father,
And see the Ancient of Days spring forth in the fountain,
And His inner power appear like a face from His heart.

*   *   *

14 The Song of Rejoicing Softens the Hard Heart and Summons the Holy Spirit

For the song of rejoicing softens hard hearts, and draws forth from them the tears of compunction, and invokes the Holy Spirit. And so *those voices you hear are like the voice of a multitude, which lifts its sound on high*; for jubilant praises, offered in simple harmony and charity, lead the faithful to that consonance in which is no discord, and make those who still live on earth sigh with heart and voice for the heavenly reward.

And their song goes through you so that you understand them perfectly; for where divine grace has worked, it banishes all dark obscurity, and makes pure and lucid those things that are obscure to the bodily senses because of the weakness of the flesh.

15 The Faithful Should Rejoice without Ceasing

Therefore, let everyone who understands God by faith faithfully offer Him tireless praises, and with joyful devotion sing to Him without ceasing. As My servant David, filled with the spirit of lofty profundity, exhorts on My behalf, saying:

16 Words of David

"Praise Him with the sound of trumpets; praise Him with psaltery and harp. Praise Him with timbrel and dance; praise Him with stringed instruments and flute. Praise Him on high-sounding cymbals; praise Him on cymbals of joy; let every spirit praise the Lord" [Psalm 150:3–5]. This is to say:

You know, adore and love God with simple mind and pure devotion. Praise Him, then, with the sound of trumpets, which is to say by the use of the reason. For when the lost angel and his consenters fell into perdition, the armies of the blessed spirits stood firm in the truth of reason, and with faithful devotion adhered to God.

And praise Him on the psaltery of deep devotion, and the honey-toned harp. For when the trumpet sounds the psaltery follows, and when the psaltery sounds the harp follows; as first the blessed angels stood fast in the love of truth, and then after the creation of Man the prophets arose with their wonderful voices, and then the apostles followed with their words of sweetness.

And praise Him with the timbrel of mortification and in the dance of exultation. For after the harp sounds, the timbrel exults, and after the timbrel, the dance; as after the apostles preached words of salvation, the martyrs endured many bodily torments for the honor of God, and then arose the truthful doctors of the priestly office.

And praise Him with the stringed instruments of human redemption and the flute of divine protection. For after the dance of joy, the voice of the stringed instruments and the flute emerge; as, after the doctors who served beatitude showed the truth, there appeared the virgins, who loved the Son of God, Who was true Man, like stringed instruments and adored Him, Who was true God, like flutes. For they believed Him to be true Man and true God. What does this mean? When the Son of God assumed flesh for human salvation, He did not lose the glory of Divinity; and so the happy virgins chose Him as their Bridegroom, and knew Him with faithful devotion as true Man in betrothal and true God in chastity.

And praise Him too on high-sounding cymbals, which is to say by loud and joyful declarations, whenever people who lay in the depths of sin are touched by divinely inspired remorse and raise themselves from those depths to the height of Heaven.

And praise Him on cymbals of joy, which is to say by statements of praise, whenever the strong virtues gain the victory and overthrow human vice, and lead people who persevere in good works and holy desires to the beatitude of the true recompense.

And so let every spirit who wills to believe in God and honor Him praise the Lord, Him Who is the Lord of all; for it is fitting that anyone who desires life should glorify Him Who is Life.

Liturgical Song

Antiphon 16: Love Overflows

Love overflows into all things,
From out of the depths to above the highest
    stars;
And so Love overflows into all best beloved,
    most loving things,
Because She has given to the highest King
The Kiss of Peace.

Translated by Barbara L. Grant

SUN BU-ER
(1124–?)

The most famous woman Taoist sage, Sun Bu-er was married and the mother of three children before devoting herself at the age of fifty-one to the full-time practice of Tao (the Way). According to religion historian Peter Occhiogrosso, by the time Sun Bu-er attracted her own following of students, Chinese religious culture was a synthesis of each of its sacred traditions, Confucianism, Taoism, and Buddhism. From the beginning of Chinese religious history, wise men and women, led by Confucius and Lao-tzu, believed that the entire universe was filled with a mystical presence, an eternal principle Lao-tzu called the Tao. The word may be translated as "Way" or "Path" but can also mean "teaching." In the sense that Tao as mystery is the Source of the universe, it is similar to the Hindu Brahman, the impersonal Absolute. Like the Brahman, the Tao is knowable only in the depths of the heart in silent meditations. The following poem reflects certain aspects of Taoist spirituality: that the cyclical changes in the human body and the cycles or seasons of the natural world are related; that the inner microcosm of the human body is related to the outer macrocosm of the world. Letting things take their course is the practical wisdom that follows from this mystical vision of reality. Not to worry, as Sun Bu-er might say.

Projecting the Spirit

There is a body outside the body,
Which has nothing to do with anything produced by magical arts.
Making this aware energy completely pervasive
Is the living, active, unified original spirit.
The bright moon congeals the gold liquid,
Blue lotus refines jade reality.
When you've cooked the marrow of the sun and moon,
The pearl is so bright you don't worry about poverty.

Translated by Thomas Cleary

MAHADEVIYAKKA
(Twelfth century)

The bhakti (devotee) poet Mahadeviyakka left her husband to wander naked in search of Siva—her "lord, white as jasmine"—covered only by her long hair. First introduced into Hinduism in the Bhagavad Gita, bhakti, an emotional and subjective expression of religious devotion offering salvation to all who feel love for God, is a more popular form of worship than orthodox Hinduism. Instead of the traditional religion of a hereditary brahman priesthood requiring religious learning, a caste system, and sacrifice, bhakti idealizes a simple cowherd such as Krishna who opens wide the door to the divine or gods such as Mahadeviyakka's Siva. Bhakti religion was important for Hindu women, according to religion scholar Serinity Young: Many important bhaktas were women, who gave other women religious role models; the typical devotee of the male gods was imagined as a female, who inspired male devotees to figure themselves as women desiring mystical union with God.

Song

> People,
> male and female,
> blush when a cloth covering their shame
> comes loose.
>   When the lord of lives
> lives drowned without a face
> in the world, how can you be modest?
> When all the world is the eye of the lord,
> onlooking everywhere, what can you
> cover and conceal?
> I love the Beautiful One
>   with no bond nor fear
>   no clan no land
>   no landmarks
>   for his beauty.
> So my lord, white as jasmine, is my husband.
> Take these husbands who die,
>   decay, and feed them
>   to your kitchen fires!

Translated by A. K. Ramanujan

MECHTHILD OF MAGDEBURG
(1207–c. 1297?)

Mechthild spent most of her life as a Beguine, a member of those communities of laywomen (beguinages) devoted to prayer, poverty, and service among the poor and sick (see page xxi). Toward the end of her life, in 1270, she entered the convent at Helfta, perhaps, as the medievalist Elizabeth Petroff suggests, under pressure from church inquisitors who disapproved of the unorthodox spirituality of her writing as well as of its criticism of clerical corruption. Helfta, the Benedictine/Cistercian monastery near Eisleben in Saxony, placed a high value on education. Under the rule of the abbess Gertrude, it was a center of learning and intense spirituality. As the social historian Caroline Bynum has documented, books were collected and studied, manuscripts copied and illustrated, and the nuns wrote their testimonies of mystical experience. There Mechthild wrote the seventh and last book of *The Flowing Light of the Godhead*, a remarkable work of religious lyrical poetry in which the divine is imagined and loved as the "lord of the dance."

From *The Flowing Light of the Godhead*

39–43. GOD ASKS THE
SOUL WHAT IT BRINGS

God:
Thou huntest sore for thy love,
What bring'st thou Me, my Queen?

Soul:
Lord! I bring Thee my treasure;
It is greater than the mountains,
Wider than the world,
Deeper than the sea,
Higher than the clouds,
More glorious than the sun,
More manifold than the stars,
It outweighs the whole earth!

God:
O thou! image of My Divine Godhead,
Enobled by My humanity,
Adorned by My Holy Spirit,—
What is thy treasure called?

Soul:
Lord! it is called my heart's desire!
I have withdrawn it from the world,
Denied it to myself and all creatures.
Now I can bear it no longer.
Where, O Lord, shall I lay it?

God:
Thy heart's desire shalt thou lay nowhere
But in mine own Divine Heart
And on My human breast.
There alone wilt thou find comfort
And be embraced by My Spirit.

44. *Of the way of love in seven things, of three
bridal robes and of the dance*

God speaks:
Ah! loving soul! wouldst thou know where thy
    way lies?

Soul:
Yes! Holy Spirit! Show it me!

Holy Spirit:
Thou must overcome the need of remorse,
the pain of penitence, the labour of
confession, the love of the world,
temptation of the devil, pride of the body,
and annihilation of self-will which drags so
many souls back that they never come to
real love. Then, when thou hast conquered
most of thine enemies, thou art so wearied,
that thou criest out—Ah! beautiful Youth!
where shall I find thee?

The Youth:
I hear a voice
Which speaks somewhat of love.
Many days have I wooed her
But never heard her voice.
Now I am moved
I must go to meet her,
She it is who bears grief and love together,
In the morning, in the dew is the intimate
   rapture
Which first penetrates the soul.

Her Waiting-Maids, The Five Senses Speak:
Lady! Thou must adorn thyself!

Soul:
Ah! Love! Whither shall I go?

The Senses:
We have heard a whisper,
The Prince comes to greet thee,
In the dew and the song of the birds!
Tarry not, Lady!

And so the soul puts on a shift of
humility, so humble that nothing could
be more humble. And over it a white
robe of chastity, so pure that she cannot
endure words or desires which might
stain it. Next she wraps herself in a
mantle of Holy Desire which she has
woven out of all the virtues.

   Thus she goes into the wood, that is
the company of holy people. The
sweetest nightingales sing there day and
night and she hears also many pure
notes of the birds of holy wisdom. But
still the youth does not come. He sends
her messengers, for she would dance. He
sends her the faith of Abraham, the
longings of the Prophets, the chaste
modesty of our Lady St. Mary, the sacred

perfection of our Lord Jesus Christ and
the whole company of His elect. Thus
there is prepared a noble Dance of
Praise. Then the Youth comes and
speaks to her—

  Maiden! thou shalt dance merrily
Even as mine elect!

Soul:
I cannot dance O Lord, unless Thou lead me.
If Thou wilt that I leap joyfully
Then must Thou Thyself first dance and sing!
  Then will I leap for love
From love to knowledge,
From knowledge to fruition,
From fruition to beyond all human sense
There will I remain
And circle evermore.

MARGUERITE PORETE
(late 1200s–1310)

At first the Beguines, to which Marguerite Porete belonged, were
praised by churchmen as communities of *mulieres sanctae* (holy
women). In time, however, their independence from the church
establishment aroused suspicion. Marguerite Porete wrote *The Mirror
of Simple Souls* between 1296 and 1306, when it was condemned and
burned by the Inquisition. As the following portion of its Prologue
shows, she claimed that the voice of Love, which dictates the
narrative, is wiser than its antagonist, the voice of Reason. Censured
from further writing or speaking about her doctrine of spiritual
eroticism and nihilism—she believed the soul could be "annihilated"
in a state of complete union with God so that it no longer needed any
clerical intermediaries—she was imprisoned in Paris for eighteen
months, during which time she did not deign to speak to her
Dominican inquisitor. Unlike Mechthild of Magdeburg (see page
64), she would not submit to the church or retreat to a convent. And
she had the audacity to claim that she spoke not in God's voice but in

her own. She was publicly burned by the Inquisition in the Place de Grève in Paris. In 1312 a church council condemned the Beguines' way of life, and though they were ordered to dissolve their communities, fringe groups of the movement remained until the French Revolution.

From the Prologue to *The Mirror of Simple Souls*

> Theologians and other clerks,
> you won't understand this book
> —however bright your wits—
> if you do not meet it humbly,
> and in this way Love and Faith
> make you surmount Reason:
> they are the mistresses of Reason's house.
>
> Reason herself proclaims to us
> in the thirteenth chapter
> of this book, unashamed,
> that Love and Faith make her live:
> she never frees herself from them—
> they have sovereignty over her,
> and she must do obeisance.
>
> So bring low your sciences
> which are founded by Reason,
> and put all your trust
> in the sciences conferred by Love,
> that are lit up by Faith—
> and then you'll understand this book,
> which by Love makes the soul live.

JULIAN OF NORWICH
(1342–c.1423)

Julian, who lived as a solitary anchoress in a cell adjoining the parish Church of St. Julian in Conisford at Norwich, England, believed she was divinely commissioned to record her visions. *Showings* (sometimes called *Revelations*), excerpted here, describes her experience of God's presence in the course of one day, May 13, 1373. Scholars interpret her claim of illiteracy as an expression of her sense of herself as a weak writer when in fact, according to her translators Edmund Colledge and James Walsh, *Showings* is "the most profound and difficult of all medieval English spiritual writings," a masterpiece of rhetorical art comparable to Chaucer's translation of Boethius's *Consolation of Philosophy*. Julian's spirituality appeals to many women because she conceives of each of the three persons in God—Father, Son, and Holy Spirit—as a nursing Mother; in their motherhood they reveal their wisdom and "lovingness." In her words:

> As truly as God is our Father, so truly is God our Mother.
> What, do you wish to know your Lord's meaning in this thing.
> Know it well, love was his meaning. . . .
> Who reveals it to you? Love. What did he reveal to you?
> Love. Why does he reveal it to you? For Love.

From *Showings*

THE FIFTY-EIGHTH CHAPTER

God the blessed Trinity, who is everlasting being, just as he is eternal from without beginning, just so was it in his eternal purpose to create human nature, which fair nature was first prepared for his own Son, the second person; and when he wished, by full agreement of the whole Trinity he created us all once. And in our creating he joined and united us to himself, and through this union we are kept as pure and as noble as we were created. By the power of that same precious union we love our Creator and delight in him, praise him and thank him and endlessly rejoice in him. And this is the work which is constantly performed in every soul which will be saved, and this is the godly will mentioned before.

And so in our making, God almighty is our loving Father, and God all wisdom is our loving Mother, with the love and the goodness of the Holy Spirit, which is all one God, one Lord. And in the joining and the union he is our very true spouse and we his beloved wife and his fair maiden, with which wife he was never displeased; for he says: I love you and you love me, and our love will never divide in two.

I contemplated the work of all the blessed Trinity, in which contemplation I saw and understood these three properties: the property of the fatherhood, and the property of the motherhood, and the property of the lordship in one God. In our almighty Father we have our protection and our bliss, as regards our natural substance, which is ours by our creation from without beginning; and in the second person, in knowledge and wisdom we have our perfection, as regards our sensuality, our restoration and our salvation, for he is our Mother, brother and saviour; and in our good Lord the Holy Spirit we have our reward and our gift for our living and our labour, endlessly surpassing all that we desire in his marvellous courtesy, out of his great plentiful grace. For all our life consists of three: In the first we have our being, and in the second we have our increasing, and in the third we have our fulfillment. The first is nature, the second is mercy, the third is grace.

As to the first, I saw and understood that the high might of the Trinity is our Father, and the deep wisdom of the Trinity is our Mother, and the great love of the Trinity is our Lord; and all these we have in nature and in our substantial creation. And furthermore I saw that the second person, who is our Mother, substantially the same beloved person, has now become our mother sensually, because we are double by God's creating, that is to say substantial and sensual. Our substance is the higher part, which we have in our Father, God almighty; and the second person of the Trinity is our Mother in nature in our substantial creation, in whom we are founded and rooted, and he is our Mother of mercy in taking our sensuality. And so our Mother is working on us in various ways, in whom our parts are kept undivided; for in our Mother Christ we profit and increase, and in mercy he reforms and restores us, and by the power of his Passion, his death and his Resurrection he unites us to our substance. So our Mother works in mercy on all his beloved children who are docile and obedient to him, and grace works with mercy, and especially in two properties, as it was shown, which working belongs to the third person, the Holy Spirit. He works, rewarding and giving. Rewarding is a gift for our confidence which the Lord makes to those who have laboured; and giving is a courteous act which he does freely, by grace, fulfilling and surpassing all that creatures deserve.

Thus in our Father, God almighty, we have our being, and in our Mother of mercy we have our reforming and our restoring, in whom our parts are united and all made perfect man, and through the rewards and the gifts of grace of the Holy Spirit we are fulfilled. And our substance is in our Father, God almighty, and our substance is in our Mother, God all wisdom, and our substance is in our Lord God, the Holy Spirit, all goodness, for our substance is whole in each person of the Trinity, who is one God. And our sensuality is only in the second person, Christ Jesus, in whom is the Father and the Holy Spirit; and in him and by him we are powerfully taken out of hell and out of the wretchedness on earth, and gloriously brought up into heaven, and blessedly united to our substance, increased in riches and nobility by all the power of Christ and by the grace and operation of the Holy Spirit.

THE FIFTY-NINTH CHAPTER

And we have all this bliss by mercy and grace, and this kind of bliss we never could have had and known, unless that property of goodness which is in God had been opposed, through which we have this bliss. For wickedness has been suffered to rise in opposition to that goodness; and the goodness of mercy and grace opposed that wickedness, and turned everything to goodness and honour for all who will be saved. For this is that property in God which opposes good to evil. So Jesus Christ, who opposes good to evil, is our true Mother. We have our being from him, where the foundation of motherhood begins, with all the sweet protection of love which endlessly follows.

As truly as God is our Father, so truly is God our Mother, and he revealed that in everything, and especially in these sweet words where he says: I am he; that is to say: I am he, the power and goodness of fatherhood; I am he, the wisdom and the lovingness of motherhood; I am he, the light and the grace which is all blessed love; I am he, the Trinity; I am he, the unity; I am he, the great supreme goodness of every kind of thing; I am he who makes you to love; I am he who makes you to long; I am he, the endless fulfilling of all true desires. For where the soul is highest, noblest, most honourable, still it is lowest, meekest and mildest.

And from this foundation in substance we have all the powers of our sensuality by the gift of nature, and by the help and the furthering of mercy and grace, without which we cannot profit. Our great Father, almighty God, who is being, knows us and loved us before time began. Out of this knowledge, in his most wonderful deep love, by the prescient eternal counsel of all the blessed Trinity, he wanted the second person to become our Mother, our brother and our saviour. From this it follows that as truly as God is our Father, so truly is God our Mother. Our Father wills, our Mother works, our good Lord the Holy Spirit confirms. And therefore it is our part to love our God in whom we have our being, reverently thanking and praising him for our creation, mightily praying to our Mother for mercy and pity, and to our Lord the Holy Spirit for help and grace. For in these three is all our life: nature, mercy and grace, of which we have mildness, patience and pity, and hatred of sin and wickedness; for the virtues must of themselves hate sin and wickedness.

And so Jesus is our true Mother in nature by our first creation, and he is our true Mother in grace by his taking our created nature. All the lovely works and all the sweet loving offices of beloved motherhood are appropriated to the second person, for in him we have this godly will, whole and safe forever, both in nature and in grace, from his own goodness proper to him.

I understand three ways of contemplating motherhood in God. The first is the foundation of our nature's creation; the second is his taking of our nature, where the motherhood of grace begins; the third is the motherhood at work. And in that, by the same grace, everything is penetrated, in length and in breadth, in height and in depth without end; and it is all one love.

But now I should say a little more about this penetration, as I understood our Lord to mean: How we are brought back by the motherhood of mercy and grace into our natural place, in which we were created by the motherhood of love, a mother's love which never leaves us.

Our Mother in nature, our Mother in grace, because he wanted altogether to become our Mother in all things, made the foundation of his work most humbly and most mildly in the maiden's womb. And he revealed that in the first revelation, when he brought that meek maiden before the eye of my understanding in the simple stature which she had when she conceived; that is to say that our great God, the supreme wisdom of all things, arrayed and prepared himself in this humble place, all ready in our poor flesh, himself to do the service and the office of motherhood in everything. The mother's service is nearest, readiest and surest: nearest because it is most natural, readiest because it is most loving, and surest because it is truest. No one ever might or could perform this office fully, except only him. We know that all our mothers bear us for pain and for death. O, what is that? But our true Mother Jesus, he alone bears us for joy and for endless life, blessed may he be. So he carries us within him in love and travail, until the full time when he wanted to suffer the sharpest thorns and cruel pains that ever were or will be, and at the last he died. And when he had finished, and had borne us so for bliss, still all this could not satisfy his wonderful love. And he revealed this in these great surpassing words of love: If I could suffer more, I would suffer more. He could not die any more, but he did not want to cease working; therefore he must needs nourish us, for the precious love of motherhood has made him our debtor.

The mother can give her child to suck of her milk, but our precious Mother Jesus can feed us with himself, and does, most courteously and most tenderly, with the blessed sacrament, which is the precious food of true life; and with all the sweet sacraments he sustains us most mercifully and graciously, and so he meant in these blessed words, where he said: I am he whom Holy Church preaches and teaches to you. That is to say: All the health and the life of the sacraments, all the power and the grace of my word, all the goodness which is ordained in Holy Church for you, I am he.

The mother can lay her child tenderly to her breast, but our tender Mother Jesus can lead us easily into his blessed breast through his sweet open side, and show us there a part of the godhead and of the joys of heaven, with inner certainty of endless bliss. And that he revealed in the tenth revelation, giving us the same understanding in these sweet words which he says: See, how I love you, looking into his blessed side, rejoicing.

This fair lovely word "mother" is so sweet and so kind in itself that it cannot truly be said of anyone or to anyone except of him and to him who is the true Mother of life and of all things. To the property of motherhood belong nature, love, wisdom and knowledge, and this is God. For though it may be so that our bodily bringing to birth is only little, humble and simple in comparison with our spiritual bringing to birth, still it is he who does it in the creatures by whom it is done. The kind, loving mother who knows and sees the need of her child guards it very tenderly, as the nature and condition of motherhood will have. And always as the child grows in age and in stature, she acts differently, but she does not change her love. And when it is even older, she allows it to be chastised to destroy its faults, so as to make the child receive virtues and grace. This work, with everything which is lovely and good, our Lord performs in those by whom it is done. So he is our Mother in nature by the operation of grace in the lower part, for love of the higher part. And he wants us to know it, for he wants to have all our love attached to him; and in this I saw that every debt which we owe by God's command to fatherhood and motherhood is fulfilled in truly loving God, which blessed love Christ works in us. And this was revealed in everything, and especially in the great bounteous words when he says: I am he whom you love.

✶   ✶   ✶

THE SIXTY-SECOND CHAPTER

For at that time he revealed our frailty and our falling, our trespasses and our humiliations, our chagrins and our burdens and all our woe, as much as it seemed to me could happen in this life. And with that he revealed his blessed power, his blessed wisdom, his blessed love, and that he protects us at such times, as tenderly and as sweetly, to his glory, and as surely to our salvation as he does when we are in the greatest consolation and comfort, and raises us to this in spirit, on high in heaven, and turns everything to his glory and to our joy without end. For his precious love, he never allows us to lose time; and all this is of the natural goodness of God by the operation of grace.

God is essence in his very nature; that is to say, that goodness which is natural is God. He is the ground, his is the substance, he is very essence or nature, and he is the true Father and the true Mother of natures. And all natures which he has made to flow out of him to work his will, they will be restored and brought back into him by the salvation of man through the operation of grace. For all natures which he has put separately in different creatures are all in man, wholly, in fulness and power, in beauty and in goodness, in kingliness and in nobility, in every manner of stateliness, preciousness and honour.

Here we can see that we are all bound to God by nature, and we are bound to God by grace. Here we can see that we do not need to seek far afield so as to know various natures, but to go to Holy Church, into our Mother's breast, that is to say into our own soul, where our Lord dwells. And there we should find everything, now in faith and understanding, and afterwards truly, in himself, clearly, in bliss.

But let no man or woman apply this particularly to himself, because it is not so. It is general, because it is our precious Mother Christ, and for him was this fair nature prepared for the honour and the nobility of man's creation, and for the joy and the bliss of man's salvation, just as he saw, knew and recognized from without beginning.

CATHERINE OF SIENA
(1347–1380)

Born Caterina di Diacomo di Benincasa in Siena, the twenty-fourth of twenty-five children, Catherine practiced contemplation in solitude throughout her youth, taking the Dominican habit when she was eighteen and experiencing her "mystical espousal" to Christ in 1368. Then she became what Suzanne Noffke, O.P., calls "a mystic activist" and leader of a group Catherine called *la bella brigata*; they served the poor and sick and dying during the plague, sharing the poverty of the people. She also acted as a peacemaker in the feud between the city-states of Italy and the papacy. The pope's return from Avignon to Rome has been attributed to her influence. Her life story is filled with legends, but she seems to have been a practical leader of charismatic force, once persuading the pope to share in her sense of sin by walking to the Vatican through the streets of Rome barefoot. Catherine thought of God as *la prima dolce Verità* (gentle first truth). God, she said, as *essa carita* — charity itself — is *pazzo d'amore* (mad with love). Her narrative *The Dialogue*, excerpted here, presents her conversation with God and his replies to her questions, which she dictated to her followers. For all her personal austerity, *The Dialogue* counsels moderation as a sign of the wisdom of love.

From *The Dialogue*

104

I have told you, dearest daughter, about two; now I will tell you about the third thing I want you to be careful of. Reprove yourself if ever the devil or your own short-sightedness should do you the disservice of making you want to force all my servants to walk by the same path you yourself follow, for this would be contrary to the teaching given you by my Truth. It often happens, when many are going the way of great penance, that some people would like to make everyone go that very same way. And if everyone does not do so, they are displeased and scandalized because they think these others are not doing the right thing. But you see how deluded they are, because it often happens that those who seem to be doing wrong because they do less penance are actually better and more virtuous, even though they do not perform such great penances, than those who are doing the grumbling.

This is why I told you earlier that if those who eat at the table of penance are not truly humble, and if their penance becomes their chief concern rather than an instrument of virtue, they will often, by this sort of grumbling, sin against their very perfection. So they should not be foolish, but should see that perfection consists not only in beating down and killing the body but in slaying the perverse selfish will. It is by this way of the will immersed in and subjected to my gentle will that you should—and I want you to—want everyone to walk.

This is the lightsome teaching of this glorious Light, by which the soul runs along in love with my Truth and clothed in him. I do not for all that despise penance, for penance is good for beating the body down when it wants to fight against the spirit. Yet I do not want you, dearest daughter, to impose this rule on everyone. For all bodies are not the same, nor do all have the same strong constitution; one is stronger than another. Also, it often happens that any number of circumstances may make it right to abandon the penance one has begun. But if you took penance as your foundation, or made it so for others, that foundation would be weak and imperfect, and the soul would be bereft of consolation and virtue.

Then, when you were deprived of the penance you had loved and taken as your foundation, you would think you had lost me. And thinking you had lost my kindness, you would become weary and very sad, bitter and confused. So you would abandon the exercises and the fervent prayer you had been accustomed to when you were doing your penance. With that penance left behind because of circumstances, prayer simply would not have the same flavor it had for you before.

All this would happen if your foundation were in your love for penance rather than in eager desire for true and solid virtue.

So you see what great evil would follow on taking penance alone for your foundation. You would foolishly fall to grumbling about my servants. And all this would bring you weariness and great bitterness. You would be putting all your effort into mere finite works for me; but I am infinite Good and I therefore require of you infinite desire.

It is right, then, that you should build your foundation by slaying and annihilating your self-will. Then, with your will subjected to mine, you would give me tender, flaming, infinite desire, seeking my honor and the salvation of souls. In this way you would feast at the table of holy desire—a desire that is never scandalized either in yourself or in your neighbors, but finds joy in everything and reaps all the different kinds of fruit that I bestow on the soul.

Not so do the wretched souls who do not follow this teaching, the gentle straight way given by my Truth. In fact, they do the opposite. They judge according to their own blindness and lame vision. They carry on like frantic fools and deprive themselves of the goods of earth as well as those of heaven. And even in this life they have a foretaste of hell.

1 0 5

Now, dearest daughter, I have satisfied your desire by clarifying what you asked me to. I have told you how you should reprove your neighbors if you would not be deluded by the devil or your own meager insight, that is, that you should reprove in general terms, not specifically, unless you have had a clear revelation from me, and humbly reprove yourself along with them.

I also told you, and I will tell you again, that nothing in the world can make it right for you to sit in judgment on the intentions of my servants, either generally or in particular, whether you find them well or ill disposed.

And I told you the reason you cannot judge, and that if you do you will be deluded in your judgment. But compassion is what you must have, you and the others, and leave the judging to me.

I told you also the teaching and principal foundation you should give to those who come to you for counsel because they want to leave behind the darkness of deadly sin and follow the path of virtue. I told you to give them as principle and foundation an affectionate love for virtue through knowledge of themselves and of my goodness for them. And they should slay and annihilate their selfish will so that in nothing will they rebel against me. And give them penance as an instrument but not as their chief concern — not equally to everyone but according to their capacity for it and what their situation will allow, this one more and this one less, depending on their ability to manage these external instruments.

I told you that it is not right for you to reprove others except in general terms in the way I explained, and this is true. But I would not because of that have you believe that when you see something that is clearly sinful you may not correct it between that person and yourself, for you may. In fact, if that person is obstinate and refuses to change, you may reveal the matter to two or three others, and if this does not help, reveal it to the mystic body of holy Church. But I told you that it is not right for you to hand anyone over merely on the basis of what you see or feel within you or even what you see externally. Unless you have clearly seen the truth or have understood it through an explicit revelation from me, you are not to reprove anyone except in the manner I have already explained. Such is the more secure way for you because the devil will not be able to deceive you by using the cloak of neighborly charity.

CHRISTINE DE PISAN
(1365–c.1429)

Born in Venice, Christine de Pisan moved as a child to France, was married at fifteen, and at the age of twenty-five was left a widow with three children, her mother, and a niece to support. They survived as a result of her becoming the first and only professional woman writer of her time. Self-taught and widely read, she wrote about moral issues and the practicalities of daily life, as the following piece from *The Treasure of the City of Ladies* (the sequel to *The Book of the City of Ladies*) shows. Her practical wisdom reflects the realism of a nonaristocratic woman who earned her own money and learned to think and act in terms of what she learned from her own experience. In a misogynist age she advised women, in the words of her translator, Sarah Lawson, "to rely on their own experience for knowledge of the feminine condition and not on the ignorant scribbles of men who could not possibly have the same accurate knowledge, no matter what the evidence of their wide reading in the works of other misogynists." Pisan was a prolific and highly praised writer in her own time, whose volumes are considered classic representations of the life of the Middle Ages. Most of her work remains untranslated.

From *The Treasure of the City of Ladies* or *The Book of the Three Virtues*

9. OF THE HABITS OF PIOUS CHARITY THAT THE GOOD PRINCESS WILL CULTIVATE.

By this path, which is Charity, the good princess will travel. But with this in mind she will do still more, as if she took to heart the speech of St. Basil when he addressed the rich man: "If you recognize and confess that temporal wealth has come to you from God, and you know very well, however, that you have received more plentifully than many others who are better than you, you would think for this reason that God, who has not divided the wealth equally, was unjust. However, this ought not to be thought at all, because He has done it so that in giving and distributing to the poor, you can deserve your wealth from God and by his long suffering the poor man can be crowned with the diadem of patience. So ensure that the bread of the hungry does not grow mouldy in your bread bin, that you do not let the side of the naked man be bitten by serpents, that you do not keep the shoes of the barefoot person locked up in your house, and that you do not have in your possession the money of the needy. For know truly that the goods of which you have such an over-abundance belong to the poor and not to you. You are a thief and you steal from God if you are able to go to the aid of your neighbour and yet you do not help him."

Therefore, the good princess, ever mindful of this principle so that she may accomplish works of mercy, although she may be well established in her grandeur, preserves the virtue of her station. She will have very good ministers around her, for although it is said of princesses that they have bad counsel or bad ministers, I believe that those who are well intentioned have counsellors who would not dare to advise them badly. The master usually seeks out servants according to the sort of person he is; they counsel him well or badly according to what they feel is his will. Therefore, this excellent lady will have servants who accord with her character. She will know that her almoner is a pious, charitable, honourable man without covetousness before she places him in such a position, not at all like some lords, who put the most thievish in positions of authority. God knows what the regime is like of some almoners of lords or prelates entrusted with this duty by that person or by someone else! She will command them to make inquiries in the town and everywhere near by and find out where the houses of the poor are: poor gentlemen or poor gentlewomen sick or fallen on hard times, poor widows, needy householders, poor maidens waiting to marry, women in childbed, students, and poverty-stricken priests or members of religious orders. By the example of my lord St. Nicholas she will secretly send gifts to these good people by her almoner, without even the poor themselves knowing who is sending them the alms. The good princess will never be ashamed to visit hospitals and the poor in all her grandeur, accompanied magnificently, as is fitting. She will speak to the poor and to the sick; she will visit their bedsides and will comfort them sweetly, making her excellent and welcome gift of alms. For poor people are much more comforted and accept with more pleasure the kind word, the visit, and the comfort of a great and powerful person than of someone else. The reason for this is that they think that all this world scorns them, and when a powerful person deigns to visit them or to comfort them they feel that they have recovered some honour, which is naturally a thing that everyone desires.

And so when the princess or great lady practises charity, she acquires greater merit than a lesser woman would in the same situation, for three principal reasons. The first is that the greater the person is and the more she humbles herself, the more her goodness increases. The second is that she gives greater aid and comfort to the poor, as has already been said. And the third, which is by no means an unimportant reason, is that she gives a good example to those who see her perform such work and with such great humility, for nothing influences the common people so much as what they see their lord and lady do. Therefore, it is a great benefit when lords and ladies and all other persons who hold positions of authority over others are well brought up, and great mischief when they are not.

Do not by any means imagine that there is a lady so great that it is shameful or in conflict with her rank for her to go herself, devoutly and humbly, on pilgrimages or to visit churches and holy places, nor that such thoughts are misguided, for if she is ashamed of doing good, she is ashamed of saving her soul.

"But," you will say to me, "how does the great lady give her alms, and those other things, if she has no money? For you said before that it is dangerous to lay up treasure." I answer that there is nothing wrong with the princess or great lady amassing treasure of money from revenue or a pension that she receives lawfully and without committing extortion, but what will she do with this treasure? She is certainly not obliged, even according to the Word of God, to give everything to the poor if she does not wish to. She can legitimately keep it for the necessities of her rank and to pay her servants, give gifts when it is appropriate and pay for what is requisitioned on her behalf. Her debts must be paid, for otherwise it would be pointless to distribute alms to others. If the good lady refrains from unnecessary things (which she can easily do if she wishes to)—from having so many gowns and jewels that she does not need—therein lies the pure and right kind of almsgiving and great merit.

Oh, how great and well advised is the lady who does this! She can be compared to the wise man who was once elected to be governor of a city. He was circumspect and noticed that several other men who had been elected to this same office had afterwards been deposed and banished, poor and deprived of all their possessions, in exile in a certain poor country where they died of starvation. He said to himself that he would provide for just such an emergency, so that in case he was sent into exile he would not die of hunger. He managed in such a way the money and wealth that came to him from his earnings and from his revenue while he was in office that after his obligations had been scrupulously met, he put all the remainder aside in a safe place. In the end what happened to the others happened to him, but the provision that he had wisely put aside saved him and kept him from need. Likewise the wealth that is tied up in needless fripperies ought to be used for giving to the poor and doing good. It is the treasure that is set aside in your holy coffer that supplies you after death and keeps you from the exile of Hell. The Gospels emphasize this fact, saying again and again, "Lay up treasures in Heaven, for alas, the only thing you take with you is this treasure." It is true, as the Holy Scriptures affirm, that the princess and all women who conscientiously lay up this kind of treasure are undoubtedly excellent managers.

To put it briefly, besides the other virtues mentioned above, this noble virtue of charity which, as I have said, will envelop the heart of the good princess, will render her of such very good will towards all people that she will imagine that everyone else is more worthy than she. Since her heart will rejoice as much at the well-being of another as at her own, she will be delighted to hear good reports about other people. To the best of her ability in all things she will give opportunities to the good to persevere and to the bad to reform.

MARGERY KEMPE
(1373–1439)

The daughter of the mayor of Lynn in Norfolk and the wife of John Kempe at twenty, Margery Kempe went mad after the birth of her first child. A vision of Christ, she said, brought her back to her senses. Subsequently she became a mystic and a pilgrim throughout Europe, also bearing thirteen more children. For her habit of public crying she was ridiculed and dismissed variously as a whore and a heretic. Medievalist Elizabeth Petroff explains that Margery's tears "are an expression of an ancient female role, that of mourner for the dead." Margery said she cried out of compassion for the suffering of others and her identification with the suffering Christ. A good storyteller, she defended herself with wit and courage against clerical attacks, as the following passage shows. At the end of her life she dictated the story of her life to scribes. *The Book of Margery Kempe,* considered the first autobiography in English, was lost for almost five hundred years, an early copy being discovered in 1934. Joan Goulianos describes the book in her *By a Woman Writt* as "a rare medieval work, a work in which a woman had described pregnancy, post-partum depression, her relations with her husband, her travels, her humiliations, her triumphs, even her times of madness." Precisely because of its "strange" contents—a record of one woman's experiences from a woman's point of view, as well as its unorthodox spirituality, a spirituality "rooted in ordinary dailyness," as Gerda Lerner puts it—scholars until recently have ridiculed it.

From *The Book of Margery Kempe*

THE TRIAL AT YORK, 1417: MARGERY ACQUITS HERSELF OF HERESY AND PROVES HERSELF THE EQUAL OF MANY CLERICS

There was a monk who was going to preach in York who had heard much slander and evil spoken about the said creature. And, when he was due to preach, there was a great crowd of people came to hear him, and she was there as well. And so, when he gave his sermon, he said some things so pointedly that people understood he meant her. Her friends who loved her were sorry and sad, but she was much the merrier, for she had something to test her patience and her charity, by which she hoped to please our Lord Christ Jesus. When the sermon was over, a doctor of divinity who loved her came to her with many other people and said, "Margery, how are you today?" "Sir," she said, "very well, praise God. I have reason to be merry and glad in my soul if I suffer anything for his love, for he suffered much more for me." Immediately afterwards a man of good will who loved her well came with his wife and several others, and led her seven miles to the Archbishop of York. They took her into a handsome room, and a clerk came, saying to the good man who had brought here there: "Sir, why have you and your wife brought this woman here? She will slip away from you and you will be embarrassed by her." The good man said: "I dare say she will stay and answer with good will."

On the next day she was taken into the Archbishop's Chapel, and many of the Archbishop's household came, despising her and calling her Lollard and heretic. And they swore many horrible oaths that she should be burned. And she replied to them through the strength of Jesus: "Sirs, I fear you shall be burnt in Hell without end unless you quit your swearing, for you do not keep the commandments of God. I would not swear as you do for all the things of this world." Then they went away as though they were ashamed. She prayed inwardly, asking to be judged that day as was most pleasing to God and good for her own soul and the best example to her fellow-Christians. Our Lord, answering her, said all would be well. At last the Archbishop came into the Chapel with his clerks and he said sharply to her: "Why do you dress in white? Are you a virgin?" Kneeling before him on her knees, she said, "No, sir, I am no virgin; I am a wife." He commanded his men to fetch a pair of fetters and said she should be fettered because she was a false heretic. And then she said, "I am no heretic, nor shall you prove me one." Then the Archbishop went away and left her standing all alone. Then she prayed for a long time to our Lord God Almighty to help her and succour her against all her enemies, spiritual and physical. And she trembled and shook so much that she wanted to hide her hands in her sleeves so no one could see. Afterwards the Archbishop came back to the Chapel with many worthy clerics, among whom were the same doctor who had examined her before and the monk who had preached against her just a little while before in York. Some people asked if she were a Christian woman or a Jew; some said she was a good woman and some said she was not.

Then the Archbishop took his seat and his clerks did so too, each according to his degree, since many people were there. And the whole time, while people were gathering together and the Archbishop was taking his seat, the said creature was standing at the back praying for help and succour against her enemies. She prayed so devoutly for so long that she melted into tears. And, finally, she began to cry so loudly that the Archbishop and his clerics and many people were astonished, for they had never heard such crying before. When her crying had passed, she came before the Archbishop and fell down on her knees, and the Archbishop said sharply to her: "Why do you weep this way, woman?" She replied, "Sir, someday you will wish you had wept as bitterly as I." And then, after the Archbishop questioned her on the Articles of our Faith, which God gave her the grace to answer well and truly and readily without any hesitation, so that the Archbishop could not find fault with her, he said to the clerics:

"She knows her Faith well enough. What shall I do with her?" The clerics said: "We know she knows the Articles of Faith, but we will not let her live among us, for the people have faith in what she says and perhaps she will mislead some of them." Then the Archbishop said to her, "I have heard evil things about you; I hear tell you are a very wicked woman." And she replied: "Sir, so I hear tell that you are a wicked man. And if you are as wicked as men say, you will never get to Heaven unless you change your ways while you are here." Then he said angrily: "Why, you wretch, what do men say about me?" She answered: "Other men, sir, can tell you well enough." Then an important cleric with a furred hood said, "Peace, speak for yourself and let him be."

Afterwards, the Archbishop said to her: "Lay your hand on the book before me and swear you will go out of my diocese as soon as you can." "No, sir," she said, "give me leave to go back to York to say goodbye to my friends." Then he gave her permission to stay for a day or two. She thought it too short a time, so she replied: "Sir, I cannot leave this diocese that fast. I must stay and speak with certain good men before I go. I must sir, with your leave, go to Bridlington and speak with my confessor, a good man, who was the confessor of the good Prior who is now canonized." Then the Archbishop said to her, "You must swear that you will not teach or challenge the people in my diocese." "No, sir, I will not swear," she said, "I shall speak of God where I want and reprove those who swear great oaths until the Pope and Holy Church ordain that no one shall be so bold as to speak about God; for God Almighty does not forbid us, sir, to speak of him. And also the Gospel mentions that when the woman heard our Lord preach, she came to him and said in a loud voice, 'Blessed be the womb that bore you and the breast that gave you suck.' Then our Lord replied, 'Truly, they are blessed who hear the word of God and keep it.' And therefore, sir, I think the Gospel gives me leave to speak of God." "Sir," said the clerics, "we know she has a devil inside her, for she speaks of the Gospel." Quickly, an important cleric brought out a book and quoted St. Paul saying that women should not preach. Answering that, she said: "I do not preach, sir, I do not use a pulpit. I rely on good words and good deeds only, and that I will continue to do as long as I live." Then the doctor who had examined her previously said, "Sir, she told the worst tales about priests that I ever heard." The Bishop commanded her to tell the tale.

"Sir, I spoke only about one priest by way of example. As I heard it, one day he wandered, lost in the woods, as God would have it for the good of his soul, until night fell. Without anywhere to stay, he found a pretty arbor, where he could rest, which had a pear tree in the middle, flourishing and covered with flowers and blossoms, which were lovely to look at. Then a bear arrived, huge and violent and ugly, and shook the pear tree so the flowers fell. Greedily, the horrible beast ate and devoured the beautiful flowers. And when he had eaten them, turning his tail to the priest, he voided them out of his hind quarters."

The priest, disgusted by this abominable sight, and confused about what it meant, wandered on his way the next day in a sad and thoughtful mood. He chanced to meet an old man, rather like a palmer or pilgrim, who asked him why he was so serious. The priest, explaining the above, said he began to dread and doubt when he saw the horrible beast defoul and devour such beautiful flowers and blossoms and then void them so horribly from his tail-end. He did not understand what it meant. Then the palmer, showing himself to be God's messenger, enlightened him.

"Priest, you yourself are the pear tree, flourishing and flowering in many ways because you say the service and minister the Sacraments. But you do it without devotion; you take little care how you say your Matins and the service, as long as you blabber it somehow to the end. You go to Mass without devotion and you have little contrition for your sins. You receive the fruit of everlasting life, the Sacrament of the Altar, in the wrong spirit. The whole day after, you waste your time; you devote yourself to buying and selling, bargaining and bartering as though you were a worldly man. You sit and drink ale, giving in to gluttony and excess, as well as to lust, through lechery and uncleanness. You break God's commandments, swearing, lying, detracting, backbiting, and sinning in other ways. Thus, your misbehavior is like the horrible bear, you devour and destroy the flowers and blossoms of virtuous living. It will be your endless damnation and a hindrance to many other men unless you receive the grace to repent and change your ways."

The Archbishop liked the story and praised it, saying it was a good story. And the cleric who had examined her earlier without the Archbishop said, "Sir, this story pierces me to the heart." The aforesaid creature said to the cleric, "There is a honorable doctor, sir, in the place where I generally live, who is a worthy cleric, and a good preacher, and who speaks out boldly against people's misbehavior and will flatter no one. He has said many times in the pulpit, "if any man is not pleased by my preaching, notice who he is, for he feels guilty." "And just so, sir," she said to the cleric, "you have responded to me, may God forgive you." The cleric did not know what he could say to her then. Afterwards, he came to her and begged forgiveness for having been against her. Also he asked her specially to pray for him.

And then immediately afterwards the Archbishop said, "Where can I find a man who will lead this woman away from here?" Quickly, many young men jumped up and every one of them said, "My Lord, I will go with her." The Archbishop answered, "You are too young; I cannot use you." Then a good, earnest man from the Archbishop's household asked what he would be given for it and where he should lead her. The Archbishop offered him five shillings and the man asked for a noble. The Archbishop answered, "I will not stake that much on her body." "Yes, good sir," said the creature, "our Lord will reward you well in return." Then the Archbishop said to the man, "See, here is five shillings. Lead her out of here immediately." Asking her to pray for him, he blessed her and let her go. Then she returned to York and was well received by many people and many worthy clerics, who rejoiced in Our Lord, who had given an unlettered woman the wit and wisdom to answer so many learned men without mistake or fault.

JOAN OF ARC
(1412–1431)

During the Hundred Years War between England and France, Joan, a sixteen-year-old peasant from a village of Domrémy, claimed to have been told by God, St. Michael, St. Catherine, and St. Margaret to drive the English out of France and see Charles, the dauphin, crowned king of France at Rheims Cathedral. Successful as a military leader, Joan was then captured by the English, who put her into the hands of the Inquisition. An ecclesiastical court tried her as a heretic and a witch. Refusing to deny her voices and visions, she was convicted as a witch and burned at the stake. In 1456 the Inquisition's condemnation was overturned; in 1920 she was canonized as a saint. In the Preface to his play *Saint Joan*, George Bernard Shaw called her "one of the first Protestant martyrs" because in her spoke "the protest of the individual soul against the interference of priest or peer between the private man and his God." There are clear parallels between the story of Joan's defiance of authority and the lives of Antigone (see page 47), Marguerite Porete (see page 67), and Anne Hutchinson (see page 97); each woman exemplifies a wisdom tradition of resistance of totalitarian aggression against the sacred space of individual conscience.

From the Transcript of the Trial of Joan of Arc

"Will you submit your actions and words to the decision of the Church?"

"My words and deeds are all in God's Hands: in all, I wait upon Him. I assure you, I would say or do nothing against the Christian Faith: in case I have done or said anything which might be on my soul and which the clergy could say was contrary to the Christian Faith established by Our Lord, I would not maintain it, and would put it away."

"Are you not willing to submit yourself in this to the order of the Church?"

"I will not answer you anything more about it now. Send me a cleric on Saturday; and, if you do not wish to come yourself, I will answer him on this, with God's help; and it shall be put in writing."

"When your Voices come, do you make obeisance to them as to a Saint?"

"Yes; and if perchance I have not done so, I have afterwards asked of them grace and pardon. I should not know how to do them such great reverence as belongs to them, for I believe firmly they are Saint Catherine and Saint Margaret. I believe the same of Saint Michael."

✳   ✳   ✳

"Will you, in respect of all your words and deeds, whether good or bad, submit yourself to the decision of our Holy Mother the Church?"

"The Church! I love it, and would wish to maintain it with all my power, for our Christian Faith; it is not I who should be prevented from going to Church and hearing Mass! As to the good deeds I have done and my coming to the King, I must wait on the King of Heaven, who sent me to Charles, King of France, son of Charles who was King of France. You will see that the French will soon gain a great victory, that God will send such great doings that nearly all the Kingdom of France will be shaken by them. I say it, so that, when it shall come to pass, it may be remembered that I said it."

"When will this happen?"

"I wait on Our Lord."

"Will you refer yourself to the decision of the Church?"

"I refer myself to God Who sent me, to Our Lady, and to all the Saints in Paradise. And in my opinion it is all one, God and the Church; and one should make no difficulty about it. Why do you make a difficulty?"

"There is a Church Triumphant in which are God and the Saints, the Angels, and the Souls of the Saved. There is another Church, the Church Militant, in which are the Pope, the Vicar of God on earth, the Cardinals, Prelates of the Church, the Clergy and all good Christians and Catholics: this Church, regularly assembled, cannot err, being ruled by the Holy Spirit. Will you refer yourself to this Church which we have thus just defined to you?"

"I came to the King of France from God, from the Blessed Virgin Mary, from all the Saints of Paradise, and the Church Victorious above, and by their command. To this Church I submit all my good deeds, all that I have done or will do. As to saying whether I will submit myself to the Church Militant, I will not now answer anything more."

"What do you say on the subject of the female attire, which is offered to you, to go and hear Mass?"

"I will not take it yet, until it shall please Our Lord. And if it should happen that I should be brought to judgment, [and that I have to divest myself in Court,] I beseech the lords of the Church to do me the grace to allow me a woman's smock and a hood for my head; I would rather die than revoke what God has made me do; and I believe firmly that God will not allow it to come to pass that I should be brought so low that I may not soon have succour from Him, and by miracle."

"As you say that you bear a man's dress by the command of God, why do you ask for a woman's smock at the point of death?"

"It will be enough for me if it be long."

"Did your Godmother who saw the fairies pass as a wise woman?"

"She was held and considered a good and honest woman, neither divineress nor sorceress."

"You said you would take a woman's dress, that you might be let go: would this please God?"

"If I had leave to go in woman's dress, I should soon put myself back in man's dress and do what God has commanded me: I have already told you so. For nothing in the world will I swear not to arm myself and put on a man's dress; I must obey the orders of Our Lord."

"What age and what dress had Saint Catherine and Saint Margaret?"

"You have had such answers as you will have from me, and none others shall you have: I have told you what I know of it for certain."

"Before today, did you believe fairies were evil spirits?"

"I know nothing about it."

THE EARLY
MODERN PERIOD:
THE SIXTEENTH,
SEVENTEENTH,
AND EIGHTEENTH
CENTURIES

AS CULTURAL HORIZONS widened onto new prospects—the possibilities of the new middle class and the mapping of new worlds of space and self—the varieties of spiritual experience changed and proliferated accordingly. Modes of spirituality began to reflect the theological reconceptualizations of ancient traditions by women believers. The consequences of their intellectual challenges—the persecution and silencing of dissenters, the formation of new denominations—began to mark religious history in Europe and America. At the same time women in uncharted and difficult worlds continued to revere their ancient spiritual traditions as resources of wisdom for themselves and the generations they had the responsibility to protect. Mystical women continued to sing and write their desire for union with the unchanging, invisible holy One. As much as the Enlightenment deified reason and empiricism and denigrated the mysterious, women continued to abide by the invisible testimony of their visions and consciences and to shape new communities of wider spiritual freedom.

MIRABAI
(1498–1565)

The best-known Indian woman poet-saint, Mirabai, like Mahadeviyakka, (see page 63), expresses the spirituality of bhaktism, a version of Hinduism stressing a passionate devotion to a personal god and a desire for mystical union. As in the Western mystical tradition, Mirabai's love for God, whom she calls both Krishna and Hari (Lord), is erotic, personal, and ecstatic. All her poems, which are intended to be sung, configure God as her beloved, her true husband. Her life story abounds with legends of her defiance of her earthly husband, of her miraculous survival of his and his family's attempts on her life, of her friendships with beggars and wandering saints, and of her running away to join a band of Krishna devotees.

> I have talked to you, talked,
>   dark Lifter of Mountains,
> About this old love,
>   from birth after birth.
> Don't go, don't,
>   Lifter of Mountains,
> Let me offer a sacrifice—myself—
>   beloved,
>   to your beautiful face.
> Come, here in the courtyard,
>   dark Lord,
> The women are singing auspicious wedding songs;
> My eyes have fashioned
>   an altar of pearl tears,
> And here is my sacrifice:
>   the body and mind
> Of Mira,
>   the servant who clings to your feet,
>   through life after life,
>   a virginal harvest for you to reap.

[Caturvedi, no. 51]

TERESA OF AVILA
(1515–1582)

Despite the Inquisition's suspicion of independent-minded religious women, of mystical women, and of ecclesiastical reformers in general, Teresa of Avila insisted on the reform of her Carmelite order and on telling the truth about the mystical experiences she was ordered to record in the *Interior Castle* (1577). Excerpted here and considered one of the most celebrated books of mystical theology in existence, the narrative imagines the soul in search of God as roaming through the rooms of its own private spiritual spaces and cultivating the preliminary stages of union with prayer, patience, and the humor for which the saint-narrator herself was known. Bernini captured her holy rapture in his famous seventeenth-century sculpture, which can be seen in a chapel of Santa Maria della Vittoria in Rome. Novelist Francine Prose describes the saint's expression in this orgasmic representation as passive and "semicomatose" when in fact she was a complex combination of mystic visionary and resilient, practical administrator.

From *Interior Castle*[1]

Few tasks which I have been commanded to undertake by obedience have been so difficult as this present one of writing about matters relating to prayer: for one reason, because I do not feel that the Lord has given me either the spirituality or the desire for it; for another, because for the last three months I have been suffering from such noises and weakness in the head that I find it troublesome to write even about necessary business. But, as I know that strength arising from obedience has a way of simplifying things which seem impossible, my will very gladly resolves to attempt this task although the prospect seems to cause my physical nature great distress; for the Lord has not given me strength enough to enable me to wrestle continually both with sickness and with occupations of many kinds without feeling a great physical strain. May He Who has helped me by doing other and more difficult things for me help also in this: in His mercy I put my trust.

I really think I have little to say that I have not already said in other books which I have been commanded to write; indeed, I am afraid that I shall do little but repeat myself, for I write as mechanically as birds taught to speak, which, knowing nothing but what is taught them and what they hear, repeat the same things again and again. If the Lord wishes me to say anything new, His Majesty will teach it me or be pleased to recall to my memory what I have said on former occasions; and I should be quite satisfied with this, for my memory is so bad that I should be delighted if I could manage to write down a few of the things which people have considered well said, so that they should not be lost. If the Lord should not grant me as much as this, I shall still be the better for having tried, even if this writing under obedience tires me and makes my head worse, and if no one finds what I say of any profit.

---

[1]As a kind of sub-title St. Teresa wrote on the back of the first page of the autograph: "This treatise, called 'Interior Castle,' was written by Teresa of Jesus, nun of Our Lady of Carmel, to her sisters and daughters the Discalced Carmelite nuns."

And so I begin to fulfil my obligation on this Day of the Holy Trinity, in the year MDLXXVII, in this convent of St. Joseph of Carmel in Toledo, where I am at this present, submitting myself as regards all that I say to the judgment of those who have commanded me to write, and who are persons of great learning. If I should say anything that is not in conformity with what is held by the Holy Roman Catholic Church, it will be through ignorance and not through malice. This may be taken as certain, and also that, through God's goodness, I am, and shall always be, as I always have been, subject to her. May He be for ever blessed and glorified. Amen.

I was told by the person who commanded me to write that, as the nuns of these convents of Our Lady of Carmel need someone to solve their difficulties concerning prayer, and as (or so it seemed to him) women best understand each other's language, and also in view of their love for me, anything I might say would be particularly useful to them. For this reason he thought that it would be rather important if I could explain things clearly to them and for this reason it is they whom I shall be addressing in what I write—and also because it seems ridiculous to think that I can be of any use to anyone else. Our Lord will be granting me a great favour if a single one of these nuns should find that my words help her to praise Him ever so little better. His Majesty well knows that I have no hope of doing more, and, if I am successful in anything that I may say, they will of course understand that it does not come from me. Their only excuse for crediting me with it could be their having as little understanding as I have ability in these matters if the Lord of His mercy does not grant it me.

CHAPTER I

Treats of the beauty and dignity of our souls; makes a comparison by the help of which this may be understood; describes the benefit which comes from understanding it and being aware of the favours which we receive from God; and shows how the door of this castle is prayer.

While I was beseeching Our Lord to-day that He would speak through me, since I could find nothing to say and had no idea how to begin to carry out the obligation laid upon me by obedience, a thought occurred to me which I will now set down, in order to have some foundation on which to build. I began to think of the soul as if it were a castle made of a single diamond or of very clear crystal, in which there are many rooms, just as in Heaven there are many mansions. Now if we think carefully over this, sisters, the soul of the righteous man is nothing but a paradise, in which, as God tells us, He takes His delight. For what do you think a room will be like which is the delight of a King so mighty, so wise, so pure and so full of all that is good? I can find nothing with which to compare the great beauty of a soul and its great capacity. In fact, however acute our intellects may be, they will no more be able to attain to a comprehension of this than to an understanding of God; for, as He Himself says, He created us in His image and likeness. Now if this is so—and it is—there is no point in our fatiguing ourselves by attempting to comprehend the beauty of this castle; for, though it is His creature, and there is therefore as much difference between it and God as between creature and Creator, the very fact that His Majesty says it is made in His image means that we can hardly form any conception of the soul's great dignity and beauty.

It is no small pity, and should cause us no little shame, that, through our own fault, we do not understand ourselves, or know who we are. Would it not be a sign of great ignorance, my daughters, if a person were asked who he was, and could not say, and had no idea who his father or his mother was, or from what country he came? Though that is great stupidity, our own is incomparably greater if we make no attempt to discover what we are, and only know that we are living in these bodies, and have a vague idea, because we have heard it and because our Faith tells us so, that we possess souls. As to what good qualities there may be in our souls, or Who dwells within them, or how precious they are—those are things which we seldom consider and so we trouble little about carefully preserving the soul's beauty. All our interest is centred in the rough setting of the diamond, and in the outer wall of the castle—that is to say, in these bodies of ours.

Let us now imagine that this castle, as I have said, contains many mansions, some above, others below, others at each side; and in the centre and midst of them all is the chiefest mansion where the most secret things pass between God and the soul. You must think over this comparison very carefully; perhaps God will be pleased to use it to show you something of the favours which He is pleased to grant to souls, and of the differences between them, so far as I have understood this to be possible, for there are so many of them that nobody can possibly understand them all, much less anyone as stupid as I. If the Lord grants you these favours, it will be a great consolation to you to know that such things are possible; and, if you never receive any, you can still praise His great goodness. For, as it does us no harm to think of the things laid up for us in Heaven, and of the joys of the blessed, but rather makes us rejoice and strive to attain those joys ourselves, just so it will do us no harm to find that it is possible in this our exile for so great a God to commune with such malodorous worms, and to love Him for His great goodness and boundless mercy. I am sure that anyone who finds it harmful to realize that it is possible for God to grant such favours during this our exile must be greatly lacking in humility and in love of his neighbour; for otherwise how could we help rejoicing that God should grant these favours to one of our brethren when this in no way hinders Him from granting them to ourselves, and that His Majesty should bestow an understanding of His greatness upon anyone soever? Sometimes He will do this only to manifest His power, as He said of the blind man to whom He gave his sight, when the Apostles asked Him if he were suffering for his own sins or for the sins of his parents. He grants these favours, then, not because those who receive them are holier than those who do not, but in order that His greatness may be made known, as we see in the case of Saint Paul and the Magdalen, and in order that we may praise Him in His creatures.

*   *   *

I am hopeful, sisters, that, not for my sake but for your sakes, He will grant me this favour, so that you may understand how important it is that no fault of yours should hinder the celebration of His Spiritual Marriage with your souls, which, as you will see, brings with it so many blessings.

*   *   *

When Our Lord is pleased to have pity upon this soul, which suffers and has suffered so much out of desire for Him, and which He has now taken spiritually to be His bride, He brings her into this Mansion of His, which is the seventh, before consummating the Spiritual Marriage. For He must needs have an abiding-place in the soul, just as He has one in Heaven, where His Majesty alone dwells: so let us call this a second Heaven. It is very important, sisters, that we should not think of the soul as of something dark. It must seem dark to most of us, as we cannot see it, for we forget that there is not only a light which we can see, but also an interior light, and so we think that within our soul there is some kind of darkness. . . . [T]his secret union takes place in the deepest centre of the soul, which must be where God Himself dwells, and I do not think there is any need of a door by which to enter it. I say there is no need of a door because all that has so far been described seems to have come through the medium of the senses and faculties and this appearance of the Humanity of the Lord must do so too. But what passes in the union of the Spiritual Marriage is very different. The Lord appears in the centre of the soul, not through an imaginary, but through an intellectual vision. . . . This instantaneous communication of God to the soul is so great a secret and so sublime a favour, and such delight is felt by the soul, that I do not know with what to compare it, beyond saying that the Lord is pleased to manifest to the soul at that moment the glory that is in Heaven, in a sublimer manner than is possible through any vision or spiritual consolation. It is impossible to say more than that, as far as one can understand, the soul (I mean the spirit of this soul) is made one with God, Who, being likewise a Spirit, has been pleased to reveal the love that He has for us by showing to certain persons the extent of that love, so that we may praise His greatness. For He has been pleased to unite Himself with His creature in such a way that they have become like two who cannot be separated from one another: even so He will not separate Himself from her.

*   *   *

This, with the passage of time, becomes more evident through its effects; for the soul clearly understands, by certain secret aspirations, that it is endowed with life by God. Very often these aspirations are so vehement that what they teach cannot possibly be doubted: though they cannot be described, the soul experiences them very forcibly. One can only say that this feeling is produced at times by certain delectable words which, it seems, the soul cannot help uttering, such as: "O life of my life, and sustenance that sustaineth me!" and things of that kind. For from those Divine breasts, where it seems that God is ever sustaining the soul, flow streams of milk, which solace all who dwell in the Castle . . .

ANNE HUTCHINSON
(1591–1643)

Like her soul sisters Antigone, Joan of Arc, and Mary Dyer, Anne Hutchinson refused the silence and submission to authority imposed by the going cultural script, suffering as a consequence excommunication from the church and banishment from the Massachusetts Bay Colony. For many years, as Amy Lang points out in *Prophetic Woman: Anne Hutchinson and the Problem of Dissent in the Literature of New England*, historians remembered her as a troublemaker, a prototypical American Jezebel; the rebellion of "goody" housewife could only be the work of the devil. On a larger canvas of American religious history, though, Hutchinson becomes a model of conscientious objection and free speech who incurred the wrath of the Puritan elders for criticizing—and walking out on—their boring sermons. Even worse, she opened her home as an alternative pulpit, her own sermons drawing a large and enthusiastic audience, male and female. Her theological differences with the clergy over the covenant of grace versus the covenant of works were real, but it was insubordination that cost her her home and family and eventually her life. The autocratic church-state was not ready for her radical spirituality, according to which, as Rosemary Keller explains, the spiritual equality of human beings before God sanctions the social equality of men and women on earth. What follows here is a partial transcript of her trial for heresy before her Puritan judges, conducted while she was late in her fifteenth pregnancy at the age of forty-five but no less possessed of the courage of her antinomian convictions.

From the Transcript of Her Trial

Mr. Winthrop, governor. Mrs. Hutchinson, you are called here as one of those that have troubled the peace of the commonwealth and the churches here; you are known to be a woman that hath had a great share in the promoting and divulging of those opinions that are causes of this trouble, and to be nearly joined not only in affinity and affection with some of those the court had taken notice of and passed censure upon, but you have spoken divers things as we have been informed very prejudicial to the honour of the churches and ministers thereof, and you have maintained a meeting and an assembly in your house that hath been condemned by the general assembly as a thing not toberable nor comely in the sight of God nor fitting for your sex, and notwithstanding that was cried down you have continued the same, therefore we have thought good to send for you to understand how things are, that if you be in an erroneous way we may reduce you that so you may become a profitable member here among us, otherwise if you be obstinate in your course that then the court may take such course that you may trouble us no further, therefore I would intreat you to express whether you do not hold and assent in practice to those opinions and factions that have been handled in court already. . . . that is to say, whether you do not justify Mr. Wheelwright's sermon and the petition.

Mrs. Hutchinson. I am called here to answer before you but I hear no things laid to my charge. . . .

Dep. Gov. I would go a little higher with Mrs. Hutchinson. About three years ago we were all in peace. Mrs. Hutchinson from that time she came hath made a disturbance, and some that came over with her in the ship did inform me what she was as soon as she was landed. I being then in place dealt with the pastor and teacher of Boston and desired them to enquire of her, and then I was satisfied that she held nothing different from us, but within half a year after, she had vented divers of her strange opinions and had made parties of the country, and at length in comes that Mr. Cotton and Mr. Vane were of her judgment, but Mr. Cotton hath cleared himself that he was not of that mind, but now it appears by this woman's meeting that Mrs. Hutchinson hath so forestalled the minds of many by their resort to her meeting that now she hath a potent party in the country. How if all these things have endangered us as from that foundation and if she in particular hath disparaged all our ministers in the land that they have preached a covenant of works, and only Mr. Cotton a covenant of grace, why this is not to be suffered, and therefore being driven to the foundation and it being found that Mrs. Hutchinson is she that hath depraved all the ministers and hath been the cause of what is fallen out, why we must take away the foundation and the building will fall.

Mrs. H. I pray Sir prove it that I said they preached nothing but a covenant of works.

Dep. Gov. Nothing but a covenant of works, why a Jesuit may preach truth sometimes.

Mrs. H. Did I ever say they preached a covenant of works then?

Dep. Gov. If they do not preach a covenant of grace clearly, then they preach a covenant of works.

Mrs. H. No Sir, one may preach a covenant of grace more clearly than another, so I said. . . .

D. Gov. When they do preach a covenant of works do they preach truth?

Mrs. H. Yes Sir, but when they preach a covenant of works for salvation, that is not truth.

*   *   *

Gov. Mrs. Hutchinson, the court you see hath laboured to bring you to acknowledge the error of your way that so you might be reduced, the time now grows late, we shall therefore give you a little more time to consider of it and therefore desire that you attend the court again in the morning.

[The next morning.]
Gov. We proceeded the last night as far as we could in hearing on this cause of Mrs. Hutchinson. There were divers things laid to her charge, her

ordinary meetings about religious exercises, her speeches in derogation of the ministers among us, and the weakening of the hands and hearts of the people towards them. Here was sufficient proof made of that which she was accused of in that point concerning the ministers and their ministry, as that they did preach a covenant of works when others did preach a covenant of grace, and that they were not able ministers of the new testament, and that they had not the seal of the spirit, and this was spoken not as was pretended out of private conference, but out of conscience and warrant from scripture alledged the fear of man is a snare and seeing God had given her a calling to it she would freely speak. Some other speeches she used, as that the letter of the scripture held forth a covenant of works; and this is offered to be proved by probable grounds. If there be any thing else that the court hath to say they may speak.

Mrs. H. The ministers come in their own cause. Now the Lord hath said that an oath is the end of all controversy; though there be a sufficient number of witnesses yet they are not according to the word, therefore I desire they may speak upon oath.

Gov. Well, it is in the liberty of the court whether they will have an oath or no and it is not in this case as in case of a jury. If they be satisfied they have sufficient matter to proceed. . . .

Mrs. H. But it being the Lord's ordinance that an oath should be the end of all strife, therefore they are to deliver what they do upon oath.

Mr. Bradstreet. Mrs. Hutchinson, these are but circumstances and adjuncts to the cause, admit they should mistake you in your speeches you would make them to sin if you urge them to swear.

Mrs. H. That is not the thing. If they accuse me I desire it may be upon oath.

*   *   *

Gov. Mr. Cotton, the court desires that you declare what you do remember of the conference which was at that time and is now in question.

Mr. Cotton. . . . the greatest passage that took impression upon me was to this purpose. The elders spoke that they had heard that she had spoken some condemning words of their ministry, and among other things they did first pray her to answer wherein she thought their ministry did differ from mine, how the comparison sprang I am ignorant, but sorry I was that any comparison should be between me and my brethren and uncomfortable it was, she told them to this purpose that they did not hold forth a covenant of grace as I did, but wherein did we differ? why she said that they did not hold forth the seal of the spirit as she doth. . . . You preach of the seal of the spirit upon a work and he upon free grace without a work or without respect to a work, he preaches the seal of the spirit upon free grace and you upon a work. I told her I was very sorry that she put comparisons between my ministry and their's for she had said more than I could myself. . . .

Dep. Gov. They affirm that Mrs. Hutchinson did say they were not able ministers of the new testament.

Mr. Cotton. I do not remember it.

Mrs. H. If you please to give me leave I shall give you the ground of what I know to be true. Being much trouble to see the falseness of the constitution of the church of England, I had like to have turned separatist; whereupon I kept a day of solemn humiliation and pondering of the thing; this scripture was brought unto me — he that denies Jesus Christ to be come in the flesh in antichrist — this I considered of and in considering found that the papists did not deny him to be come in the flesh, nor we did not deny him — who then was antichrist? Was the Turk antichrist only? The Lord knows that I could not open scripture; he must by his prophetical office open it unto me. So after that being unsatisfied in the thing, the Lord was pleased to bring this scripture out of the Hebrews. He that denied the testament denied the testator, and in this did open unto me and give me to see that those which did not teach the new covenant had the spirit of antichrist, and upon this he did discover the ministry unto me and ever since, I bless the Lord, he hath let me see which was the clear ministry and which the wrong. Since that time I confess I have been more choice and he hath let me to distinguish between the voice of my beloved and the voice of Moses, the voice of John Baptist and the voice of antichrist, for all those voices are spoken of in scripture. Now if you do condemn me for speaking what in my conscience I know to be truth I must commit myself unto the Lord.

Mr. Nowell. How do you know that that was the spirit?

Mrs. H. How did Abraham know that it was God that bid him offer his son, being a breach of the sixth commandment?

Dep. Gov. By an immediate voice.

Mrs. H. So to me by an immediate revelation.

Dep. Gov. How! an immediate revelation.

Mrs. H. By the voice of his own spirit to my soul. I will give you another scripture . . . out of Daniel chap. 7. and he and for us all, wherein he shewed me the sitting of the judgment and the standing of all high and low before the Lord and how thrones and kingdoms were cast down before him. When our teachers came to New England it was a great trouble unto me, my brother Wheelwright being put by also. I was then much troubled concerning the ministry under which I lived, and then that place in the 30th of Isaiah was brought to my mind. Though the Lord give thee bread of adversity and water of affliction yet shall not thy teachers be removed into corners any more, but thine eyes shall see thy teachers . . . this place in Daniel was brought unto me and did shew me that though I should meet with affliction yet I am the same God that delivered Daniel out of the lion's den, I will also deliver thee.—Therefore, I desire you to look to it, for you see this scripture fulfilled this day and therefore I desire you that as you tender the Lord and the church and commonwealth to consider and look what you do. You have power over my body but the Lord Jesus hath power over my body and soul, and assure yourselves thus much, you do as much as in you lies to put the Lord Jesus Christ from you, and if you go on in this course you begin you will bring a curse upon you and your posterity, and the mouth of the Lord hath spoken it. . . .

Dep. Gov. I desire Mr. Cotton to tell us whether you do approve of Mrs. Hutchinson's revelation as she hath laid them down.

Mr. Cotton. I know not whether I do understand her, but this I say, if she doth expect a deliverance in a way of providence—then I cannot deny it.

Dep. Gov. No Sir we did not speak of that.

Mr. Cotton. If it be by way of miracle then I would suspect it.

Dep. Gov. Do you believe that her revelations are true?

Mr. Cotton. That she may have some special providence of God to help her is a thing that I cannot bear witness against. . . .

Mrs. H. By a providence of God I say I expect to be delivered from some calamity that shall come to me.

*   *   *

Dep. Gov. I never saw such revelations as these among the Anabaptists, therefore am sorry that Mr. Cotton should stand to justify her. . . . I am fully persuaded that Mrs. Hutchinson is deluded by the devil, because the spirit of God speaks truth in all his servants.

Gov. I am persuaded that the revelation she brings forth is delusion.
All the court but some two or three ministers cry out, we all believe it—we all believe it. . . .

*   *   *

Gov. Well, you remember that she said but now that she should be delivered from this calamity. . . . The court hath already declared themselves satisfied concerning the things you hear, and concerning the troublesomness of her spirit and the danger of her course among us, which is not to be suffered. Therefore if it be the mind of the court that Mrs. Hutchinson for these things that appear before us is unfit for our society, and if it be the mind of the court that she shall be banished out of our liberties and imprisoned till she be sent away, let them hold up their hands.
All but three.
Those that are contrary minded hold up yours.
Mr. Coddington and Mr. Colborn, only.

Mr. Jennison. I cannot hold up my hand one way or the other, and I shall give my reason if the court require it.

Gov. Mrs. Hutchinson, the sentence of the court you hear is that you are banished from out of our jurisdiction as being a woman not fit for our society, and are to be imprisoned till the court shall send you away.

Mrs. H. I desire to know wherefore I am banished?

Gov. Say no more, the court knows wherefore and is satisfied.

ANNE BRADSTREET
(1612–1672)

Until she left England for the New World at the age of eighteen, Anne Dudley Bradstreet led a leisurely life in Lincolnshire, learning to read and write, with access to volumes of Spenser, Marlowe, Jonson, Herbert, Milton, and Shakespeare. It was her father, Thomas Dudley, and her husband, Simon Bradstreet, who undertook the Puritan errand into the wilderness with religious passion; though she loved both men, her "heart rose" against their mission. Once arrived, she bore eight children, managed the wilderness home, and wrote the poetry that reflects her spiritual doubts and fervor, her love for her family, and her conflicts about the subordinate role of women within Puritan society. She was the first poet to be published in America, and her writing became a lifelong process of self-discovery, self-clarification, and spiritual survival. The wisdom she passed on to her children, excerpted here, has the common sense of lived experience and a reflective intelligence.

From *Meditations Divine and Moral*

From the letter of dedication to her son Simon, March 20, 1664: ". . . You once desired me to leave something for you in writing that you might look upon, when you should see me no more; I could think of nothing more fit for you nor of more ease to myself than these short meditations. . . ."

1

There is no object that we see, no action that we do, no good that we enjoy, no evil that we feel or fear, but we may make some spiritual advantage of all; and he that makes such improvement is wise as well as pious.

2

Many can speak well, but few can do well. We are better scholars in the theory than the practice part, but he is a true Christian that is a proficient in both.

4

A ship that bears much sail and little or no ballast is easily overset, and that man whose head hath great abilities and his heart little or no grace is in danger of foundering.

9

Sweet words are like honey: a little may refresh, but too much gluts the stomach.

10

Diverse children have their different natures: some are like flesh which nothing but salt will keep from putrefaction, some again like tender fruits that are best preserved with sugar. Those parents are wise that can fit their nurture according to their nature.

12

Authority without wisdom is like a heavy axe without an edge: fitter to bruise than polish.

13

The reason why Christians are so loath to exchange this world for a better is because they have more sense than faith: they see what they enjoy; they do but hope for that which is to come.

19

Corn, till it have past through the mill and been ground to powder, is not fit for bread. God so deals with his servants: he grinds them with grief and pain till they turn to dust, and then are they fit manchet for his mansion.

47

A shadow in the parching sun and a shelter in a blustering storm are of all seasons the most welcome; so a faithful friend in time of adversity is of all other most comfortable.

48

There is nothing admits of more admiration than God's various dispensation of His gifts among the songs of men, betwixt whom He hath put so vast a disproportion that they scarcely seem made of the same lump or sprung out of the loins of one Adam, some set in the highest dignity that mortality is capable of, and some again so base that they are viler than the earth, some so wise and learned that they seem like angels among men, and some again so ignorant and sottish that they are more like beasts than men, some pious saints, some incarnate devils, some exceeding beautiful, and some extremely deformed, some so strong and healthful that their bones are full of marrow and their breast of milk, and some again so weak and feeble that while they live they are accounted among the dead; and no other reason can be given of all this but so it pleased Him whose will is the perfect rule of righteousness.

74

Well doth the apostle call riches "deceitful" riches, and they may truly be compared to deceitful friends who speak fair and promise much but perform nothing, and so leave those in the lurch that most relied on them; so is it with the wealth, honours, and pleasures of this world which miserably delude men and make them put great confidence in them, but when death threatens and distress lays hold upon them, they prove like the reeds of Egypt that pierce instead of supporting, like empty wells in the time of drought that those that go to find water in them return with their empty pitchers ashamed.

77

God hath by his providence so ordered that no one country hath all commodities within itself, but what it wants another shall supply that so there may be a mutual commerce through the world. As it is with countries so it is with men; there was never yet any one man that had all excellences, let his parts natural and acquired, spiritual and moral, be never so large, yet he stands in need of something which another man hath (perhaps meaner than himself) which shows us perfection is not below, as also that God will have us beholden one to another.

MARGARET FELL
(1614–1702)

The name Quakers implied trembling with awful silence in the presence of God's word. Founded in England by the mystic George Fox, the Quakers, who were also known as Friends, were from the beginning committed to causes of social justice; they themselves were persecuted for their deviation from established Christianity. When they moved to America, they were among the first of the dissenting Protestant sects to oppose slavery and war, though that is not to say there were no Quaker slaveholders or soldiers. Fox and his wife, Margaret Fell, the "mother" of the Friends, stressed seeking the "inner light" of Christ that exists equally in every human being and authorizes any Friend, male or female, to preach. Relying on the direct authority of the Holy Spirit, Quakers did not recognize ordained clergy or their sacraments; for this rejection of official clerical and civil authority the Quaker missionary Mary Dyer, a friend of Anne Hutchinson (see page 97), was hanged on Boston Common in 1660. The following excerpted document, reflecting the theology of women's equality in Christ developed in Margaret Fell's *Women's Speaking Justified, Proved and Allowed of by the Scriptures,* was sent by her daughter to the Women's Meetings in England and America, a controversial institution that gave Quaker women an official role in the government of the society. A number of nineteenth-century feminists and abolitionists, including Sarah Grimké (see page 120), Lucretia Mott, and Susan B. Anthony were Quaker ministers.

Letter to the Quaker Women's Meeting

From our Country Women's meeting in Lancashire to the Dispersed abroad, among the Women's meetings every where.

Dear Sisters,

In the blessed unity in the Spirit of grace our Souls Salute you who are sanctified in Christ Jesus, and called to be Saints. . . . Where there is neither male nor female &c. but we are all one in Christ Jesus. . . .

So here is the blessed Image of the living God, restored againe, in which he made them male and female in the beginning. . . . And he makes no difference in the seed, between the male and the female, as Christ saith, they were both the work of God in the beginning, and so in the restoration. . . .

Soe all Dear friends and sisters, make full proofe of the gift of God that is in you, and neglect it not. . . .

And also all friends, in their womens monthly, and particular Meetings, that they take special care for the poore, and for those that stands in need: that there be no want, nor suffering, for outward things, amongst the people of God, . . .

And so let Care be taken for the poore, and widdows, that hath young Children, that they be relieved, and helped, till they be able and fitt, to be put out to apprentices or servants.

And that all the sick, and weak, and Infirme, or Aged, and widdows, and fatherless, that they be looked after, and helped, and relieved in every particular meeting, either with clothes, or maintainance, or what they stand in need off. So that in all things the Lord may be glorified, and honoured, so that there be no want, nor suffering in the house of God, who loves a Chearfull giver.

So here was the womens meeting, and womens teachings of one another, so that this is no new thing, as some raw unseasoned spirits would seem to make it:

And though wee be looked upon as the weaker vessels, yet strong and powerfull is God, whose strength is made perfect in weakness, he can make us good and bold, and valliant Souldiers of Jesus Christ, if he arm us with his Armour of Light, he who respect no persons, but chuseth the weak things of this world, and foolish things to confound the wise: our sufficiency is of him, and our Armour, and strength is in him.

GLÜCKEL OF HAMELN
(1646–1724)

A German Jew from a prominent family of Hamburg, Glückel of Hameln married at fourteen, had twelve children, and, after her husband's death, continued his business and remarried. She began to write her memoirs at the age of forty-six as a way of offering her children advice on how to live wisely and well. Not published until 1896, her writing is a useful source of information about Jewish culture in the towns of seventeenth-century Berlin. As the following passage shows, the source of the wisdom Glückel passed on to her children is the tradition of Judaism in all its powerful and ethical dimension. Like Natalia Ginzburg, (see page 200), Glückel of Hameln highlights spiritual values as essential to the survival of the human spirit and of any civilization worth the name. Her identification of the quintessential sacred text— "Thou shalt love thy neighbour as thyself"—underscores the core truth of Jewish morality on which the philosopher Martin Buber has based his existentialism. "Man is a creature of the 'between,' " he writes, "of the happening between man and man." Human beings find meaning in the movement toward and within "the life of dialogue," in the mutual experience of "the kernel of the Torah" with which Jewish mothers since ancient times have, like Glückel of Hameln, nourished the spirits of their children.

From the Memoirs

In my great grief and for my heart's ease I begin this book in the year of Creation 5451—God soon rejoice us and send us His redeemer soon. Amen. With the help of God, I began writing this, my dear children, upon the death of your good father in the hope of distracting my soul from the burdens laid upon it, and the bitter thought that we have lost our faithful shepherd. In this way I have managed to live through many wakeful nights, and springing from my bed have shortened the sleepless hours.

I do not intend, my dear children, to compose and write for you a book of morals. Such I could not write, and our wise men have already written many. Moreover, we have our holy Torah in which we may find and learn all that we need for our journey through this world to the world to come. Of our beloved Torah we may seize hold. . . . We sinful men are in the world as if swimming in the sea and in danger of being drowned. But our great, merciful and kind God, in his great mercy, has thrown ropes into the sea that we may take hold of them and be saved. These are our holy Torah where is written what are the rewards and punishments for good and evil deeds. . . .

I pray you this, my children: be patient, when the Lord, may He be praised, sends you a punishment, accept it with patience and do not cease to pray to Him; perhaps He will have mercy upon you. . . . Therefore, my dear children, whatever you lose, have patience, for nothing is our own, everything is only a loan. . . . We men have been created for nothing else but to serve God and to keep His commandments and to obey the Torah, for "He is thy life, and the length of thy life."

The kernel of the Torah is: "Thou shalt love thy neighbour as thyself." But in our days we seldom find it so, and few are they who love their fellowmen with all their heart. On the contrary, if a man can contrive to ruin his neighbour nothing pleases him more. . . .

The best thing for you, my children, is to serve God from your heart without falsehood or deception, not giving out to people that you are one thing while, God forbid, in your heart you are another. Say your prayers with awe and devotion. During the time for prayers do not stand about and talk of other things. While prayers are being offered to the Creator of the world, hold it a great sin to engage another man in talk about an entirely different mater—shall God Almighty be kept waiting until you have finished your business?

Moreover, set aside a fixed time for the study of the Torah, as best you know how. Then diligently go about your business, for providing your wife and children with a decent livelihood is likewise a mitzwah—the command of God and the duty of man. We should, I say, put ourselves to great pains for our children, for on this the world is built. . . .

SOR JUANA INÉS DE LA CRUZ
(1651–1695)

Well educated as a child in Mexico (New Spain), Juana Ramírez de Asbaje grew up with the freedom to explore her grandfather's library. As a teenager she proposed to disguise herself as a man in order to be admitted to university studies. Instead she joined a convent in Mexico City as the only institution available to women to offer the possibility of an intellectual life. Though much of her life, like her writing, is surrounded with mystery, records show that as a nun she studied, read, performed scientific experiments, published poems and essays, and kept up a wide correspondence with the world. Her prolific artistic and intellectual life did not escape the notice of the Inquisition. Its suspicion of scholarly and mystical women in particular kept clerical inquisitors busy investigating, silencing, and purging the likes of Sor Juana until 1826, the date of the last recorded execution for heresy. In 1692, after a lengthy investigation, Juana made a confession, the archbishop in charge of her case forcing her to sign (in her own blood, according to legend) a profession of faith, a renunciation of her art, and a renewal of her vows. Her library was confiscated. Octavio Paz has written at length about the poet-nun of New Spain, the first great poet born in the New World. Margaret Sayers Peden did the first complete English translation of Sor Juana's masterpiece, *A Woman of Genius: The Intellectual Autobiography of Sor Juana Inés de la Cruz*, a major declaration of women's intellectual freedom entitled *La Respuesta a Sor Filotea* when it was published in Spain in 1701.

Divine Love

En que expresa los efectos del amor divino,
y propone morir amante,
a pesar de todo riesgo

   Traigo conmigo un cuidado,
y tan esquivo que creo
que, aunque sé sentirlo tanto,
aun yo misma no lo siento.

In which she expresses the effects of Divine Love
and proposes to die loving,
despite the risk

   There's something disturbing me,
so subtle, to be sure,
It's love, but love, for once,
that though I feel it keenly,

Es amor; pero es amor
que, faltándole lo ciego,
los ojos que tiene, son
para darle más tormento.

El término no es *a quo*,
que causa el pesar que veo:
que siendo el término el bien,
todo el dolor es el medio.

Si es lícito, y aun debido
este cariño que tengo,
¿por qué me han de dar castigo
porque pago lo que debo?

¡Oh cuánta fineza, oh cuántos
cariños he visto tiernos!
Que amor que se tiene en Dios
es calidad sin opuestos.

De lo lícito no puede
hacer contrarios conceptos,
con que es amor que al olvido
no puede vivir expuesto.

Yo me acuerdo, ¡oh nunca fuera!,
que he querido en otro tiempo
lo que pasó de locura
y lo que excedió de extremo;

mas como era amor bastardo,
y de contrarios compuesto,
fue fácil desvanecerse
de achaque de su ser mesmo.

Mas ahora, ¡ay de mi!, está
tan en su natural centro,
que la virtud y razón
son quien aviva su incendio.

Quien tal oyere, dirá
que, si es así, ¿por qué peno?
Mas mi corazón ansioso
dirá que por eso mesmo.

¡Oh humana flaqueza nuestra,
a donde el más puro afecto
aun no sabe desnudarse
del natural sentimiento!

Tan precisa es la apetencia
que a ser amados tenemos,

it's not hard to endure.
without a blindfold—whence
whoever sees his eyes,
feels torture the more intense.

It's not from their terminus a quo
that my sufferings arise,
for their terminus is the Good;
it's in distance that suffering lies.

If this emotion of mine
is proper—indeed, is love's due—
why must I be chastised
for paying what I owe?

Oh, all the consideration,
the tenderness I have seen:
when love is placed in God,
nothing else can intervene.

From what is legitimate
it cannot deviate;
no risk of being forgotten
need it ever contemplate.

I recall—were it not so—
a time when the love I knew
went far beyond madness even,
reached excesses known to few,

but being a bastard love,
built on warring tensions,
it simply fell apart
from its own dissensions.

But oh, being now directed
to the goal true lovers know,
through virtue and reason alone
it must stronger and stronger grow.

Therefore one might inquire
why it is I still languish.
My troubled heart would reply:
what makes my joy makes my anguish.

Yes, from human weakness,
in the midst of purest affection,
we still remain a prey
to natural dejection.

To see our love returned
is so insistent a craving

que, aun sabiendo que no sirve,
nunca dejarla sabemos.

Que corresponda a mi amor,
nada añade; mas no puedo,
por más que lo solicito,
dejar yo de apetecerlo.

Si es delito, ya lo digo;
si es culpa, ya la confieso;
mas no puedo arrepentirme,
por más que hacerlo pretendo.

Bien ha visto, quien penetra
lo interior de mis secretos,
que yo misma estoy formando
los dolores que padezco.

Bien sabe que soy yo misma
verdugo de mis deseos,
pues muertos entre mis ansias,
tienen sepulcro en mi pecho.

Muero, ¿quién lo creerá?, a manos
de la cosa que más quiero,
y el motivo de matarme
es el amor que le tengo.

Así alimentando, triste,
la vida con el veneno,
la misma muerte que vivo
es la vida con que muero.

Pero valor, corazón:
porque en tan dulce tormento,
en medio de cualquier suerte
no dejar de amar protesto.

that even when out of place,
we still find it enslaving.

It means nothing in this instance
that my love be reciprocated;
yet no matter how hard I try,
the need persists unabated.

If this is a sin, I confess it,
if a crime, I must avow it;
the one thing I cannot do
is repent and disallow it.

The one who has power to probe
the secrets of my breast,
has seen that I am the cause
of my suffering and distress.

Well he knows that I myself
have put my desires to death—
my worries smother them,
their tomb is my own breast.

I die (who would believe it?)
at the hands of what I love best.
What is it puts me to death?
The very love I profess.

Thus, with deadly poison
I keep my life alive:
the very death I live
is the life of which I die.

Still, take courage, heart:
when torture becomes so sweet,
whatever may be my lot,
from love I'll not retreat.

SIDQI
(d. 1703)

The daughter of Qamr Muhammad, a seventeenth-century scholar of
Constantinople, Sidqi was one of the most important Sufi poets of the
Turks. Following the Sufi tradition, she lived a celibate life. Her two
major poems, *The Treasury of Lights* and *The Collection of Information*,

reflect the mysticism and pantheism of the later Sufis. The ghazel that follows here reflects the Sufi poets' use of the metaphor of wine to describe the soul's intoxication with God.

Ghazel

He who union with the Lord gains, more delight
    desireth not!
He who looks on charms of fair one, other sight
    desireth not.
Pang of love is lover's solace, eagerly he seeks therefor,
Joys he in it, balm or salve for yonder blight, desireth not.
Paradise he longs not after, nor doth aught
    beside regard;
Bower and Garden, Mead, and Youth, and Húrí bright,
    desireth not.
From the hand of Power Unbounded draineth he the
    Wine of Life,
Aye inebriate with Knowledge, learning's light,
    desireth not.
He who loves the Lord is monarch of an empire, such
    that he—
King of Inward Mysteries—Sulymán's might,
    desireth not.
Thou art Sultan of my heart, aye, Soul of my soul e'en
    art Thou;
Thou art Soul enow, and Sidqí other plight
    desireth not.

ANN LEE
(1736–1784)

Founder of the Shakers, the most important of the sectarian offspring of the Quakers, Mother Ann Lee led her disciples from Manchester, England, to New York in 1774. The Shakers' theology began with two visions Ann Lee had while in jail in England for profaning the Sabbath. (The Shakers—unlike the Puritans, who forbade "sinful song and dance"—chanted, shouted, sang, shook, laughed, and gyrated in dances that were part of their daily worship.) Her prison revelations showed her God as both male and female, father and mother; Sophia, Holy Wisdom of the Bible, was the female element of God. The second vision convinced her that sexual relations were evil; like Catherine of Siena, Teresa of Avila, and many Sufi and Hindi mystics, she believed that union with God could occur only through celibacy. In the American colonies she also forbade the private ownership of property, the bearing of arms, and inequality between men and women. A charismatic preacher, she encouraged simple living in her egalitarian communities: no frills in clothing, furniture, or food. For refusing to take a loyalty oath and for the ecstatic worship services of her converts, she was jailed during the American Revolution on suspicion of spying and witchcraft. Released, she preached forgiveness: "You can never enter into the Kingdom of God with hardness against anyone, for God is love, and if you love God you will love one another." The Shaker Bible, a portion of which follows here, presents her faith in an androgynous God, a loving mother and father to all her/his creation.

"SIMPLE GIFTS," A SHAKER HYMN

> 'Tis the gift to be simple,
> 'Tis the gift to be free,
> 'Tis the gift to come down where we ought to be,
> And when we find ourselves in the place that's right
> 'Twill be in the valley of love and delight.

From the Shaker Bible

THE ORDER OF DEITY, MALE AND FEMALE, IN WHOSE IMAGE MAN WAS CREATED.

All who profess the Christian name, mutually believe in *one God*, the eternal *Father*, the Creator of heaven and earth; the original Father of spirits, of angels, and of men. They also believe in the first begotten *Son* of God in man; the Saviour of the world; the Redeemer of men. By the Son, the *true* being and *true character* of the Father, was first revealed: and, the existence of the Son, while it proved the existence of the *Eternal Father*, proved also the existence of the *Eternal Mother*.

Neither argument, nor illustration, would seem necessary to prove this! For, without both a *father* and *mother*, there can be neither son nor daughter; either natural or spiritual, visible or invisible! The visible order of *male* and *female*, by which all animated creation exists, proves the existence of the order, in the invisible world, from which our existence is primarily derived. *"For the invisible things of God, from the creation of the world are clearly seen, being understood by the things that are made, even his eternal Power and Divinity; so that they are without excuse:* because that when they knew God, they glorified him not as God."

For "God said, *Let us make man in our image, after our likeness.*" "So God created man; *male and female* created he them, in his own image, and after his own likeness." To whom did God say, "Let US make man in OUR image?" Was it to the Son the Father spoke, as the divines (so called) have long taught, and still teach? How then came man to be created male and female? *father* and *son* are not male and female; but *father* and *mother* are male and female, as likewise are *son* and *daughter*. It was in this order that man was created. It was the order that existed in Deity, and superior spiritual intelligences before him, even *"before the world was;"* and in the image and after the likeness of which he was made, and placed as a probationer on the earth.

But it was not the Son with whom the Father spoke or counselled; or with any other being, angel or spirit, save only with the Eternal *Mother;* even *Divine Wisdom;* the Mother of all celestial beings! It was the *Eternal Two* who thus counselled together, and said, *"Let US make man in our image, after our likeness."* This is the same Eternal Mother who was with the Father, whom the *"Lord possessed in the beginning of his way, before his works of old; even from everlasting, before ever the earth was."*

And this was, and is, the voice of the Eternal Mother, through the inspiration of her holy spirit: When the Lord prepared the heavens, I was there: When he appointed the foundations of the earth, then I was by him as one brought up with him; and I was daily his delight, rejoicing always before him. Now, therefore, hearken unto me, my children; for blessed are they that keep my ways."

Thus we may see the true order and origin of our existence, descending through proper mediations, not only in the state of innocent nature, but in the state of grace; proceeding from an Eternal *Parentage;* the Eternal Two, as distinctly Two, as *Power* and *Wisdom* are Two; and as the *Father* and *Mother* are two; yet immutably, unchangeably, *One Spirit:* One in *Essence* and in *substance,* One in *love* and in *design;* and so of the whole spiritual relationship in the new creation and household of God, *Father* and *Mother, Son* and *Daughter, Brother* and *Sister, Parents* and *Children;* of which the order in the natural creation is a similitude.

THE
NINETEENTH
CENTURY

D ESCRIPTIONS OF THIS period often focus on its expressions of doubt, despair, and alienation from the new and the big everything— cities, factories, immigrant populations. Often men of privilege—Tennyson, Mill, Arnold—are quoted to support this response to the century of which Marx wrote, "All that is solid melts into air." The determinisms of Darwinism, Marxism, and Freudianism offered explanations but few solutions to the ordinary lives being destroyed by the exploitative processes of economic individualism and industrial capitalism.

In the same century, however, the voices of prophets, male and female, called for reform and solidarity with, among others, the suffering populations of slaves, women, the sick. Some of the strongest cries—and action— came from women represented in the following section, who in a number of cases, acted on their own, outside the precincts of hidebound do-nothing institutions. In every case a spiritual tradition was one profound source of their subjectivity and their sense of moral and political justice. As their contemporary Walt Whitman writes in *Democratic Vistas*, "At the core of democracy, finally, is the religious element."

The lives and writings of the nineteenth-century women that follow here demonstrate that the wisdom found in spiritual experience is at its best when, to paraphrase theologian David Tracy, it is a form of resistance.

THE GRIMKÉ SISTERS

Sarah (1792–1873) and Angelina (1805–1879) Grimké grew up in South Carolina, in an Episcopalian slaveholding family. Both sisters rebelled against their background, leaving Charleston for Philadelphia, where they became Quakers and active abolitionists and feminists. They were eloquent lecturers and writers, despite harsh criticism each received for her defiance of racial and gender boundaries. Historian Gerda Lerner's *The Grimké Sisters from South Carolina: Rebels against Slavery* (1967) describes their conversions to public resistance of the evil of America's "peculiar institution."

For addressing "promiscuous" congregations (assemblies composed of both men and women) the Grimkés were condemned by a pastoral letter of the Congregational clery of Massachusetts. Sarah's response to the attack follows.

From Sarah Moore Grimké's *Letters on the Equality of the Sexes and the Condition of Woman Addressed to Mary S. Parker, president of the Boston Female Anti-Slavery Society* (1838)

In examining this important subject, I shall depend solely on the Bible to designate the sphere of woman, because I believe almost every thing that has been written on this subject, has been the result of a misconception of the simple truths revealed in the Scriptures, in consequence of the false translation of many passages of Holy Writ. My mind is entirely delivered from the superstitious reverence which is attached to the English version of the Bible. King James's translators certainly were not inspired. I therefore claim the original as my standard, *believing that to have been inspired*, and I also claim to judge for myself what is the meaning of the inspired writers, because I believe it to be the solemn duty of every individual to search the Scriptures for themselves, with the aid of the Holy Spirit, and not to be governed by the views of any man, or set of men. . . .

The New Testament has been referred to, and I am willing to abide by its decisions, but must enter my protest against the false translation of some passages by the MEN who did that work and against the perverted interpretation by the MEN who undertook to write commentaries thereon. I am inclined to think, when we are admitted to the honor of studying Greek and Hebrew, we shall produce some various readings of the Bible a little different from those we have now. . . .

Men and women were CREATED EQUAL; and they are both moral and accountable beings, and whatever is *right* for man to do, is *right* for woman.

But the influence of woman, says the Association, is to be private and unobtrusive; her light is not to shine before man like that of her brethren; but she is passively to let the lords of the creation, as they call themselves, put the bushel over it, lest peradventure it appear that the world has been benefitted by the rays of *her* candle. . . . How monstrous, how anti-Christian, is the doctrine that woman is to be dependent on man! Where, in all the sacred Scriptures, is this taught? Alas! she has too well learned the lesson which MAN has labored to teach her. . . . "Rule by obedience and by submission sway," in other words, study to be a hypocrite, pretend to submit, but gain your point, has been the code of household morality which woman has been taught. . . . This doctrine of dependence upon man is utterly at variance with the doctrine of the Bible. . . .

But woman may be permitted to lead religious inquirers to the PASTORS for instruction. Now this is assuming that all pastors are better qualified to give instruction than woman. This I utterly deny. I have suffered too keenly from the teaching of man, to lead any one to him for instruction. The Lord Jesus says, — "Come unto me and learn of me." He points his followers to no man; and when woman is made the favored instrument of rousing a sinner to his lost and helpless condition, she has no right to substitute any teacher for Christ; all she has to do is, to turn the contrite inquirer to the "Lamb of God which taketh away the sins of the world." More souls have probably been lost by going down to Egypt for help, and by trusting in man in the early stages of religious experience, than by any other error. . . . That woman can have but a poor conception of the privilege of being taught of God, what he alone can teach, who would turn the "religious inquirer aside" from the fountain of living waters, where he might slake his thirst for spiritual instruction, to those broken cisterns which can hold no water, and therefore cannot satisfy the panting spirit. The business of men and women, who are ORDAINED OF GOD to preach the "unsearchable riches of Christ" to a lost and perishing world, is to lead souls to Christ, and not to Pastors for instruction. . . .

Anticipating the strategy of Harriet Beecher Stowe's *Uncle Tom's Cabin,* which, in depicting slavery as the degradation of motherhood, aroused the antislavery sympathies of women readers, Angelina Grimké tried to forge an abolitionist solidarity among northern women based on a common spiritual identity transcending boundaries of region, class, and race.

From Angelina Grimké's *An Appeal to the Women of the Nominally Free States* (1838)

[In] a country where women are degraded and brutalized, and where their exposed persons bleed under the lash—where they are sold in the shambles of "negro brokers"—robbed of their hard earnings—torn from their husbands, and forcibly plundered of their virtue and their offspring, surely in *such* a country, it is very natural that *women* should wish to know "the reason *why*"—especially when these outrages of blood and nameless horror are practiced in violation of the principles of our national Bill of Rights and the preamble of our Constitution. We do not, then, and cannot concede the position, that because this is a *political subject* women ought to fold their hands in idleness, and close their eyes and ears to the "horrible things" that are practiced in our land. The denial of our duty to act is a bold denial of our right to act; and if we have no right to act, then may *we* well be termed "the white slaves of the North"—for, like our brethren in bonds, we must seal our lips in silence and despair. . . .

Out of the millions of slaves who have been stolen from Africa, a very great number must have been women who were torn from the arms of their fathers and husbands, brothers and children, and subjected to all the horrors of the middle passage and the still greater sufferings of slavery in a foreign land. Multitudes of these were cast upon our inhospitable shores; some of them now toil out a life of bondage, "one hour of which is fraught with more misery than ages of that" which our fathers rose in rebellion to oppose. But the great mass of female slaves in the southern States are the descendants of these hapless strangers; 1,000,000 of them now wear the iron yoke of slavery in this land of boasted liberty and law. They are our country women—*they are our sisters*; and to us, as women, they have a right to look for sympathy with their sorrows, and effort and prayer for their rescue. Upon those of us especially who have named the name of Christ, they have peculiar claims, and claims which *we must answer, or we shall incur a heavy load of guilt.* . . .

[Another] reason we would urge for the interference of northern women with the system of slavery is, that in consequence of the odium which the degradation of slavery has attached to *color* even in the free States, our *colored sisters* are dreadfully oppressed here. Our seminaries of learning are closed to them, they are almost entirely banished from our lecture rooms, and even in the house of God they are separated from their white brethren and sisters as though we were afraid to come in contact with a colored skin. . . .

Here, then, are some of the bitter fruits of that inveterate prejudice which the vast proportion of northern women are cherishing towards their colored sisters; and let us remember that every one of us who denies the sinfulness of this prejudice, . . . is awfully guilty in the sight of Him who is no respecter of persons. . . .

But our colored sisters are oppressed in other ways. As they walk the streets of our cities, they are continually liable to be insulted with the vulgar epithet of "nigger"; no matter how respectable or wealthy, they cannot visit the Zoological Institute of New York except in the capacity of nurses or servants—no matter how worthy, they cannot gain admittance into or receive assistance from any of the charities of this city. In Philadelphia, they are cast out of our widow's Asylum, and their children are refused admittance to the House of Refuge, the Orphan's House and the Infant School connected with the Alms-House, though into these are gathered the very offscouring of our population. These are only specimens of that soul-crushing influence from which the colored women of the north are daily suffering. Then, again, some of them have been robbed of their husbands and children by the heartless kidnapper, and others have themselves been dragged into slavery. If they attempt to travel, they are exposed to great indignities and great inconveniences. Instances have been known of their actually dying in consequence of the exposure to which they were subjected on board of our steamboats. No money could purchase the use of a berth for a delicate female because she had a colored skin. Prejudice, then, degrades and fetters the minds, persecutes and murders the bodies of our free colored sisters. Shall *we* be silent at such a time as this? . . .

Multitudes of instances will continually occur in which you will have the opportunity of *identifying yourselves with this injured class* of our fellow-beings: embrace these opportunities at all times and in all places, in the true nobility of our great Exemplar, who was ever found among the *poor and despised*, elevating and blessing them with his counsels and presence. In this way, and this alone, will you be enabled to subdue that deep-rooted prejudice which is doing the work of oppression in the free States to a most dreadful extent.

When this demon has been cast out of your own hearts, when *you* can recognize the colored women as a WOMAN—*then* will you be prepared to send out an appeal to our Southern sisters, entreating them to "go and do likewise."

REBECCA COX JACKSON
(1795–1891)

Antebellum evangelical preacher Rebecca Jackson belongs to a nineteenth-century activist tradition of African American women based on their commitment to a self-empowering religious faith and a universal social justice. A few of these women are well known: Phillis Wheatley, Sojourner Truth (see page 125), Harriet Tubman. But the autobiographical voices of many others have been retrieved only recently by feminist scholars. Belonging to this tradition of faith-inspired activists whose spirituality is preserved in conversion narratives and public speeches are Jarena Lee, Amanda Berry Smith, Maria Stewart, Zilpha Elaw, Julia Foote, Frances Harper, and Rebecca Jackson. The latter's account of a vision of the Mother nature of God, excerpted here, suggests the deepening of imagination such an angle of belief opens to the visionary. Founder of the first black Shaker community in Philadelphia in 1851, Jackson recorded her many visions in diaries that span the years between 1830 and 1864. Jean McMahon Humez edited the previously unpublished journals of Rebecca Cox Jackson, entitled *Gifts of Power: The Writings of Rebecca Cox Jackson, Black Visionary, Shaker Eldress* (1981).

From the Diaries

At night we went to meeting and while they were worshiping God, I saw the head and wings of their blessed Mother in the center of the ceiling over their heads. She appeared in a glorious color. Her face was round like a full moon, with the glory of the sun reflecting from her head, formed itself into a round circle with a glorious crown. And her face in the midst. And she was beautiful to look upon. Her wings were gold. She being in the center, she extended her golden wings across the room over the children, with her face toward me and said, "These are all mine," though she spoke not a word. And what a Mother's look she gave me. And at that look, my soul was filled with love and a motion was in my body, like one moving in the waves of the sea. I was happy. And I felt to embrace all her children in the arms of my soul. I understood by one of the discerners that there was sixteen angels in the room that night. I only saw our Blessed Mother, and that was as much as I was able to bear. . . .

Oh, how I love thee, my Mother! I did not know that I had a Mother. She was with me, though I knew it not, but now I know Her and She said I should do a work in this city, which is to make known the Mother of the New Creation of God. Because Thou art the Mother of all the children of Eve that ever can be saved, as Christ is the Father of all the regenerated children of Adam. And none can come to God in the new birth but through Christ the Father, and through Christ the Mother. . . . And I then understood the Mother I saw in the Deity, in 1834 or 1835, when the ministers shut their church doors against me and gave orders to their members not to suffer me to come in their doors, if they did they should be turned out of church, and the drunken man opened his house and said, "I don't belong to church. Let the woman come and hold her meeting in my house." And then it was that I had the first light on a Mother in the Deity. And then I could also see how often I had been led, comforted, and counseled in time of trial by a tender Mother and knowed it not.

SOJOURNER TRUTH
(*c. 1797–1883*)

bell hooks (see page 289) situates the legendary Sojourner Truth in her proper context of religious experience. She was a runaway slave, a mother who saw two of her four surviving children sold into slavery and an evangelical preacher and mystic. Her "emancipatory politics," in hooks's words, "emerged from her religious faith. People need to remember that the name Isabel Humphrey took, Sojourner Truth, was rooted in her religious faith, that the truth she saw herself seeking was the truth of Oneness with God and her sense that, by choosing God, she was choosing to serve in the emancipation struggle of Black people. She was also the first Black woman to publicly link the struggle against racism with gender liberation." In 1843, in response to her mystical voices and visions, she became a sojourner throughout the United States who told the truth, as she saw it, about a loving and kind God who willed the freedom, not the enslavement, of all his children. Her speeches, part of a partially preserved oral tradition, were written down by others. The following account of her conversion, taken from the *Narrative of Sojourner Truth, Northern Slave,* written by Olive Gilbert in 1850, expresses one of her favorite themes, the emotional freedom and joy that await the soul open to the spiritual dimension of experience.

From *Narrative of Sojourner Truth*

. . . She says that God revealed himself to her, with all the suddenness of a flash of lightning, showing her, "in the twinkling of an eye, that he was *all over*"—that he pervaded the universe—"and that there was no place where God was not." She became instantly conscious of her great sin in forgetting her almighty Friend and "ever-present help in time of trouble." All her unfulfilled promises arose before her, like a vexed sea whose waves run mountains high; and her soul, which seemed but one mass of lies, shrunk back aghast from the "awful look" of Him whom she had formerly talked to, as if he had been a being like herself; and she would now fain have hid herself in the bowels of the earth, to have escaped his dread presence. But she plainly saw there was no place, not even in hell, where he was not: and where could she flee? Another such "a look," as she expressed it, and she felt that she must be extinguished forever, even as one, with the breath of his mouth, "blows out a lamp," so that no spark remains.

. . . [She said,] "Oh, God, I did not know you were so big," walked into the house, and made an effort to resume her work. But the workings of the inward man were too absorbing to admit of much attention to her avocations. She desired to talk to God, but her vileness utterly forbade it, and she was not able to prefer a petition. "What!" said she, "shall I lie again to God? I have told him nothing but lies; and shall I speak again, and tell another lie to God?" She could not; and now she began to wish for someone to speak to God for her. Then a space seemed opening between her and God, and she felt that if some one, who was worthy in the sight of heaven, would but plead *for* her in their own name, and not let God know it came from *her*, who was so unworthy, God might grant it. At length a friend appeared to stand between herself and an insulted Deity; and she felt as sensibly refreshed as when, on a hot day, an umbrella had been interposed between her scorching head and a burning sun. But who was this friend? became the next inquiry. Was it Deencia, who had so often befriended her? She looked at her with her new power of sight—and, lo! she, too, seemed all "bruises and putrefying sores," like herself. No, it was some one very different from Deencia.

"Who *are* you?" she exclaimed, as the vision brightened into a form distinct, beaming with the beauty of holiness, and radiant with love. She then said, audibly addressing the mysterious visitant—"I *know* you, and I *don't* know you." Meaning, "You seem perfectly familiar; I feel that you not only love me, but that you *always* have loved me—yet I know you not—I cannot call you by name." When she said, "I know you," the subject of the vision remained distinct and quiet. When she said, "I don't know you," it moved restlessly about, like agitated waters. So while she repeated without intermission, "I know you, I know you," that the vision might remain— "Who are you?" was the cry of her heart, and her whole soul was in one deep prayer that this heavenly personage might be revealed to her, and remain with her. At length, after bending both soul and body with the intensity of this desire, till breath and strength seemed failing, and she could maintain her position no longer, an answer came to her, saying distinctly, "It is Jesus." "Yes," she responded, "it is *Jesus.*"

Previous to these exercises of mind, she heard Jesus mentioned in reading or speaking, but had received from what she heard no impression that he was any other than an eminent man, like a Washington or a Lafayette. Now he appeared to her delighted mental vision as so mild, so good, and so every way lovely, and he loved her so much! And, how strange that he had always loved her, and she had never known it! And how great a blessing he conferred, in that he should stand between her and God! And God was no longer a terror and a dread to her.

ELIZABETH BARRETT BROWNING
(1806–1861)

Elizabeth Barrett Browning's sense of self and politics had their foundation in a spiritual consciousness that defined her posture as a radical humanist toward many of the most controversial issues of the nineteenth century. She supported the cause of abolition in the United States, child welfare in Britain, and unification in Italy out of a belief in democracy as an expression of the equality and dignity every human being deserves as a child of God. Her feminism, expressed in the verse novel *Aurora Leigh*, attacked a cultural system that imposed such limits on the experience of women as to deny their identity as human beings with equal entitlements to the full range of human possibilities. As the *Sonnets from the Portuguese* suggest, she imagined her passionate love for Robert Browning as implicating a larger mystical identity than simply the romantic love of one person for another. With the meditative and ardent cadences of prayer, the following sonnets define love as *the* inspiriting force: It brings the spirit back to life; it gives the lovers eternal significance.

From *Sonnets from the Portuguese*

X X

Beloved, my Belovèd, when I think
That thou wast in the world a year ago,
What time I sat alone here in the snow
And saw no footprint, heard the silence
    sink
No moment at thy voice, but, link by link,
Went counting all my chains as if that so
They never could fall off at any blow
Struck by thy possible hand,—why, thus
    I drink
Of life's great cup of wonder! Wonder
    ful,
Never to feel thee thrill the day or night
With personal act or speech,—nor ever
    cull
Some prescience of thee with the blossoms
    white
Thou sawest growing! Atheists are as
    dull,
Who cannot guess God's presence out of
    sight.

XXI

Say over again, and yet once over again,
That thou dost love me. Though the
     word repeated
Should seem "a cuckoo-song," as thou dost
     treat it,
Remember, never to the hill or plain,
Valley and wood, without her cuckoo-
     strain
Comes the fresh Spring in all her green
     completed.
Belovèd, I, amid the darkness greeted
By a doubtful spirit-voice, in that doubt's
     pain
Cry, "Speak once more—thou lovest!"
     Who can fear
Too many stars, though each in heaven
     shall roll,
Too many flowers, though each shall
     crown the year?
Say thou dost love me, love me, love me—
     toll
The silver iterance!—only minding,
     Dear,
To love me also in silence with thy soul.

XXII

When our two souls stand up erect and
       strong,
Face to face, silent, drawing nigh and
       nigher,
Until the lengthening wings break into fire
At either curvèd point,—what bitter
       wrong
Can the earth do to us, that we should not
       long
Be here contented? Think. In mounting
       higher,
The angels would press on us and aspire
To drop some golden orb of perfect song
Into our deep, dear silence. Let us stay
Rather on earth, Belovèd,—where the
       unfit
Contrarious moods of men recoil away
And isolate pure spirits, and permit
A place to stand and love in for a day,
With darkness and the death-hour
       rounding it.

XXVI

I lived with visions for my company
Instead of men and women, years ago,
And found them gentle mates, nor thought
     to know
A sweeter music than they played to me.
But soon their trailing purple was not free
Of this world's dust, their lutes did silent
     grow,
And I myself grew faint and blind below
Their vanishing eyes. Then THOU didst
come—to be,
Belovèd, what they seemed. Their shining
     fronts,
Their songs, their splendors (better, yet
     the same,
As river-water hallowed into fonts),
Met in thee, and from out thee overcame
My soul with satisfaction of all wants:
Because God's gifts put man's best dreams
     to shame.

XXVII

My own Belovèd, who has lifted me
From this drear flat of earth where I was
    thrown,
And, in betwixt the languid ringlets, blown
A life-breath, till the forehead hopefully
Shines out again, as all the angels see,
Before thy saving kiss! My own, my
    own,
Who camest to me when the world was
    gone,
And I who looked for only God, found
    thee!
I find thee; I am safe, and strong, and
    glad.
As one who stands in dewless asphodel
Looks backward on the tedious time he
    had
In the upper life,—so I, with bosom-
    swell,
Make witness, here, between the good and
    bad,
That Love, as strong as Death, retrieves as
    well.

QURRAT AL-'AYN
(?–1852)

Babi teacher and poet and a saint of Islam, Qurrat al-'Ayn, after a long ministry of evading the orthodox authorities, who resented her role as a religious leader, was martyred in 1852. Islamic scholar Margaret Smith explains that Sufis regard Babism as "a systematized Sufism," similar in doctrine with Sufi pantheism: "[I]ts fundamental teaching is the divine spark latent in man, by the cultivation of which he can attain to . . . Annihilation in God." For her powerful preaching and public theological arguments with many doctors and sages, Qurrat al-'Ayn was recognized as an important spiritual guide to the way of Babism.

Because of her great beauty, she had to sit behind a curtain when she preached and lectured to her disciples at Kerbela. Though she was almost arrested by government authorities in Baghdad many times because of complaints about a woman preaching publicly to men, she continued to preach and make converts among orthodox Muslims and was given a high position in the Babi church. At the time of the Mazandaran insurrection in 1849, she was arrested and sent to Teheran, where she was imprisoned for three years before she was executed. Islamic scholars describe her religious poems as among the favorite and best-known songs of the people. The following ghazel resounds with the mystical spirit and theme similar to the prayers of Rabi'a: The poet desires the complete surrender of the lover-soul to the will of the holy Beloved.

Ghazel

The thralls of yearning love constrain in the bands
    of pain and calamity
These broken-hearted lovers of Thine to yield their
    lives in their zeal for Thee.
Though with sword in hand my Darling stand with
    intent to slay, though I sinless be,
If it pleases Him, this tyrant's whim, I am well content
    with His tyranny.
As in sleep I lay at the dawn of day that cruel Charmer
    came to me,
And in the grace of His form and face the dawn of the
    morn I seemed to see.
The musk of Cathay might perfume gain from the
    scent those fragrant tresses rain,
While his eyes demolish a faith in vain attacked by the
    pagans of Tartary.
With you, who contemn both love and wine for the
    hermit's cell and the zealot's shrine,
What can I do? For our faith divine you hold as a thing
    of infamy.
The tangled curls of thy darling's hair, and thy saddle
    and steed are thine only care;
In thy heart the Infinite hath no share, nor the thought
    of the poor man's poverty.

> Sikandar's pomp and display be thine, the Kalendar's
>   habit and way be mine;
> That, if it please thee, I resign, while this, though bad,
>   is enough for me.
> The country of "I" and "We" forsake; thy home in
>   Annihilation make,
> Since fearing not this step to take, thou shalt gain the
>   highest felicity.

ELIZABETH CADY STANTON
(1815–1902)

With her friend Lucretia Mott, abolitionist Elizabeth Cady Stanton, mother of seven children, organized the women's rights convention at Seneca Falls, New York, in 1848. Throughout her life she worked to overturn what she saw as the most basic obstacle to women's equality: the prohibition of their right to vote. Though she grew up a Presbyterian, as an adult she rejected organized religion as the root of women's oppression. Addressing the World Parliament of Religions in Chicago in 1893, she declared that the only way to salvation is to help the poor. Because she believed the Bible had been misinterpreted to justify women's subordination to men—a sin against the God-given humanity of women—she edited an alternative Scripture, *The Woman's Bible* (1895–1898). Her introduction follows.

From *The Woman's Bible*

INTRODUCTION

From the inauguration of the movement for woman's emancipation the Bible has been used to hold her in the "divinely ordained sphere," prescribed in the Old and New Testaments.

The canon and civil law; church and state; priests and legislators; all political parties and religious denominations have alike taught that woman was made after man, of man, and for man, an inferior being, subject to man. Creeds, codes, Scriptures and statutes, are all based on this idea. The fashions, forms, ceremonies and customs of society, church ordinances and discipline all grow out of this idea.

Of the old English common law, responsible for woman's civil and political status, Lord Brougham said, "it is a disgrace to the civilization and Christianity of the Nineteenth Century." Of the canon law, which is responsible for woman's status in the church, Charles Kingsley said, "this will never be a good world for women until the last remnant of the canon law is swept from the face of the earth."

The Bible teaches that woman brought sin and death into the world, that she precipitated the fall of the race, that she was arraigned before the judgment seat of Heaven, tried, condemned and sentenced. Marriage for her was to be a condition of bondage, maternity a period of suffering and anguish, and in silence and subjection, she was to play the role of a dependent on man's bounty for all her material wants, and for all the information she might desire on the vital questions of the hour, she was commanded to ask her husband at home. Here is the Bible position of woman briefly summed up.

Those who have the divine insight to translate, transpose and transfigure this mournful object of pity into an exalted, dignified personage, worthy our worship as the mother of the race, are to be congratulated as having a share of the occult mystic power of the eastern Mahatmas.

The plain English to the ordinary mind admits of no such liberal interpretation. The unvarnished texts speak for themselves. The canon law, church ordinances and Scriptures, are homogeneous, and all reflect the same spirit and sentiments.

These familiar texts are quoted by clergymen in their pulpits, by statesmen in the halls of legislation, by lawyers in the courts, and are echoed by the press of all civilized nations, and accepted by woman herself as "The Word of God." So perverted is the religious element in her nature, that with faith and works she is the chief support of the church and clergy; the very powers that make her emancipation impossible. When, in the early part of the Nineteenth Century, women began to protest against their civil and political degradation, they were referred to the Bible for an answer. When they protested against their unequal position in the church, they were referred to the Bible for an answer.

This led to a general and critical study of the Scriptures. Some, having made a fetish of these books and believing them to be the veritable "Word of God," with liberal translations, interpretations, allegories and symbols, glossed over the most objectionable features of the various books and clung to them as divinely inspired. Others, seeing the family resemblance between the Mosaic code, the canon law, and the old English common law, came to the conclusion that all alike emanated from the same source; wholly human in their origin and inspired by the natural love of domination in the historians. Others, bewildered with their doubts and fears, came to no conclusion. While their clergymen told them on the one hand, that they owed all the blessings and freedom they enjoyed to the Bible, on the other, they said it clearly marked out their circumscribed sphere of action: that the demands for political and civil rights were irreligious, dangerous to the stability of the home, the state and the church. Clerical appeals were circulated from time to time conjuring members of their churches to take no part in the anti-slavery or woman suffrage movements, as they were infidel in their tendencies, undermining the very foundations of society. No wonder the majority of women stood still, and with bowed heads, accepted the situation.

Listening to the varied opinions of women, I have long thought it would be interesting and profitable to get them clearly stated in book form. To this end six years ago I proposed to a committee of women to issue a Woman's Bible, that we might have women's commentaries on women's position in the Old and New Testaments. It was agreed on by several leading women in England and America and the work was begun, but from various causes it has been delayed, until now the idea is received with renewed enthusiasm, and a large committee has been formed, and we hope to complete the work within a year.

Those who have undertaken the labor are desirous to have some Hebrew and Greek scholars, versed in Biblical criticism, to gild our pages with their learning. Several distinguished women have been urged to do so, but they are afraid that their high reputation and scholarly attainments might be compromised by taking part in an enterprise that for a time may prove very unpopular. Hence we may not be able to get help from that class.

Others fear that they might compromise their evangelical faith by affiliating with those of more liberal views, who do not regard the Bible as the "Word of God," but like any other book, to be judged by its merits. If the Bible teaches the equality of Woman, why does the church refuse to ordain women to preach the gospel, to fill the offices of deacons and elders, and to administer the Sacraments, or to admit them as delegates to the Synods, General Assemblies and Conferences of the different denominations? They have never yet invited a woman to join one of their Revising Committees, nor tried to mitigate the sentence pronounced on her by changing one count in the indictment served on her in Paradise.

The large number of letters received, highly appreciative of the undertaking, is very encouraging to those who have inaugurated the movement, and indicate a growing self-respect and self-assertion in the women of this generation. But we have the usual array of objectors to meet and answer. One correspondent conjures us to suspend the work, as it is "ridiculous" for "women to attempt the revision of the Scriptures." I wonder if any man wrote to the late revising committee of Divines to stop their work on the ground that it was ridiculous for men to revise the Bible. Why is it more ridiculous for women to protest against her present status in the Old and New Testament, in the ordinances and discipline of the church, than in the statutes and constitution of the state? Why is it more ridiculous to arraign ecclesiastics for their false teaching and acts of injustice to women, than members of Congress and the House of Commons? Why is it more audacious to review Moses than Blackstone, the Jewish code of laws, than the English system of jurisprudence? Women have compelled their legislators in every state in this Union to so modify their statutes for women that the old common law is now almost a dead letter. Why not compel Bishops and Revising Committees to modify their creeds and dogmas? Forty years ago it seemed as ridiculous to timid, time-serving and retrograde folk for women to demand an expurgated edition of the laws, as it now does to demand an expurgated edition of the Liturgies and the Scriptures. Come, come, my conservative friend, wipe the dew off your spectacles, and see that the world is moving. Whatever your views may be as to the importance of the proposed work, your political and social degradation are but an outgrowth of your status in the Bible. When you express your aversion, based on a blind feeling of reverence in which reason has no control, to the revision of the Scriptures, you do but echo Cowper, who, when asked to read Paine's "Rights of Man," exclaimed, "No man shall convince me that I am improperly governed while I *feel* the contrary."

Others say it is not *politic* to rouse religious opposition. This much-lauded policy is but another word for *cowardice.* How can woman's position be changed from that of a subordinate to an equal, without opposition, without the broadest discussion of all the questions involved in her present degradation? For so far-reaching and momentous a reform as her complete independence, an entire revolution in all existing institutions is inevitable.

Let us remember that all reforms are interdependent, and that whatever is done to establish one principle on a solid basis, strengthens all. Reformers who are always compromising, have not yet grasped the idea that truth is the only safe ground to stand upon. The object of an individual life is not to carry one fragmentary measure in human progress, but to utter the highest truth clearly seen in all directions, and thus to round out and perfect a well balanced character. Was not the sum of influence exerted by John Stuart Mill on political, religious and social questions far greater than that of any statesman or reformer who has sedulously limited his sympathies and activities to carrying one specific measure? We have many women abundantly endowed with capabilities to understand and revise what men have thus far written. But they are all suffering from inherited ideas of their inferiority; they do not perceive it, yet such is the true explanation of their solicitude, lest they should seem to be too self-asserting.

Again there are some who write us that our work is a useless expenditure of force over a book that has lost its hold on the human mind. Most intelligent women, they say, regard it simply as the history of a rude people in a barbarous age, and have no more reverence for the Scriptures than any other work. So long as tens of thousands of Bibles are printed every year, and circulated over the whole habitable globe, and the masses in all English-speaking nations revere it as the word of God, it is vain to belittle its influence. The sentimental feelings we all have for those things we were educated to believe sacred, do not readily yield to pure reason. I distinctly remember the shudder that passed over me on seeing a mother take out a family Bible to make a high seat for her child at table. It seemed such a desecration. I was tempted to protest against its use for such a purpose, and this, too, long after my reason had repudiated its divine authority.

To women still believing in the plenary inspiration of the Scriptures, we say give us by all means your exegesis in the light of the higher criticism learned men are now making, and illumine the Woman's Bible, with your inspiration.

Bible historians claim special inspiration for the Old and New Testaments containing most contradictory records of the same events, of miracles opposed to all known laws, of customs that degrade the female sex of all human and animal life, stated in most questionable language that could not be read in a promiscuous assembly, and call all this "The Word of God."

The only points in which I differ from all ecclesiastical teaching is that I do not believe that any man ever saw or talked with God, I do not believe that God inspired the Mosaic code, or told the historians what they say he did about woman, for all the religions on the face of the earth degrade her, and so long as woman accepts the position that they assign her, her emancipation is impossible. Whatever the Bible may be made to do in Hebrew or Greek, in plain English it does not exalt and dignify woman. My standpoint for criticism is the revised edition of 1888. I will so far honor the revising committee of nine men who have given us the best exegesis they can according to their ability, although Disraeli said the last one before he died, contained 150,000 blunders in the Hebrew, and 7,000 in the Greek.

But the verbal criticism in regard to woman's position amounts to little. The spirit is the same in all periods and languages, hostile to her as an equal.

There are some general principles in the holy books of all religions that teach love, charity, liberty, justice and equality for all the human family, there are many grand and beautiful passages, the golden rule has been echoed and re-echoed around the world. There are lofty examples of good and true men and women, all worthy of our acceptance and example whose lustre cannot be dimmed by the false sentiments and vicious characters bound up in the same volume. The Bible cannot be accepted or rejected as a whole, its teachings are varied and its lessons differ widely from each other. In criticising the peccadilloes of Sarah, Rebecca and Rachel, we would not shadow the virtues of Deborah, Huldah and Vashti. In criticising the Mosaic code we would not question the wisdom of the golden rule and the fifth Commandment. Again the church claims special consecration for its cathedrals and priesthood, parts of these aristocratic churches are too holy for women to enter, boys were early introduced into the choirs for this reason, woman singing in an obscure corner closely veiled. A few of the more democratic denominations accord women some privileges, but invidious discriminations of sex are found in all religious organizations, and the most bitter outspoken enemies of woman are found among clergymen and bishops of the Protestant religion.

The canon law, the Scriptures, the creeds and codes and church discipline of the leading religions bear the impress of fallible man, and not of our ideal great first cause, "the Spirit of all Good," that set the universe of matter and mind in motion, and by immutable law holds the land, the sea, the planets, revolving round the great centre of light and heat, each in its own elliptic, with millions of stars in harmony all singing together, the glory of creation forever and ever.

GEORGE ELIOT
(1819–1880)

Dorothea Brooke, the main character of Eliot's *Middlemarch*, is an intensely religious, practical, and independent-minded woman, a nineteenth-century version of Teresa of Avila (see page 92). But she has no context for the realization of her ideals and reforms. The Catholic Counter Reformation has long passed, and traditional Protestant Christianity is no longer a compelling moral force; Eliot herself renounced it as a young woman. So Dorothea is literally "a foundress of nothing," perhaps the novel's first post-Christian heroine. Without an institutional structure to support her utopian and countercultural vision amid the materialism and philistinism of early Victorian England, she wastes her youth on a first marriage to a fake scholar whose only product is the alienation of both partners. Her second marriage, though contested by critics for what it reveals about Eliot's view of women's possibilities, allows Dorothea the freedom of love. For its insight into the spiritual fruits of suffering and loss, the novel—of which Emily Dickinson said, "What do I think of *Middlemarch?* What do I think of glory?"—qualifies as Wisdom literature. Empathy is the liberating truth that Eliot shows her lonely heroine. The "Prelude" and a portion of the "Finale" follow.

From *Middlemarch*

PRELUDE

Who that cares much to know the history of man, and how the mysterious mixture behaves under the varying experiments of Time, has not dwelt, at least briefly, on the life of Saint Theresa, has not smiled with some gentleness at the thought of the little girl walking forth one morning hand-in-hand with her still smaller brother, to go and seek martyrdom in the country of the Moors? Out they toddled from rugged Avila, wide-eyed and help-less-looking as two fawns, but with human hearts, already beating to a national idea; until domestic reality met them in the shape of uncles, and turned them back from their great resolve. That child-pilgrimage was a fit beginning. Theresa's passionate, ideal nature demanded an epic life: what were many-volumed romances of chivalry and the social conquests of a brilliant girl to her? Her flame quickly burned up that light fuel; and, fed from within, soared after some illimitable satisfaction, some object which would never justify weariness, which would reconcile self-despair with the rapturous consciousness of life beyond self. She found her epos in the reform of a religious order.

That Spanish woman who lived three hundred years ago, was certainly not the last of her kind. Many Theresas have been born who found for themselves no epic life wherein there was a constant unfolding of far-resonant action; perhaps only a life of mistakes, the offspring of a certain spiritual grandeur ill-matched with the meanness of opportunity; perhaps a tragic failure which found no sacred poet and sank unwept into oblivion. With dim lights and tangled circumstance they tried to shape their thought and deed in noble agreement; but after all, to common eyes their struggles seemed mere inconsistency and formlessness; for these later-born Theresas were helped by no coherent social faith and order which could perform the function of knowledge for the ardently willing soul. Their ardour alternated between a vague ideal and the common yearning of wom-

anhood; so that the one was disapproved as extravagance, and the other condemned as a lapse.

Some have felt that these blundering lives are due to the inconvenient
indefiniteness with which the Supreme Power has fashioned the natures
of women: if there were one level of feminine incompetence as strict as
the ability to count three and no more, the social lot of women might be
treated with scientific certitude. Meanwhile the indefiniteness remains,
and the limits of variation are really much wider than any one would imagine from the sameness of women's coiffure and the favourite love-stories
in prose and verse. Here and there a cygnet is reared uneasily among the
ducklings in the brown pond, and never finds the living stream in fellowship with its own oary-footed kind. Here and there is born a Saint Theresa,
foundress of nothing, whose loving heart-beats and sobs after an unat-
tained goodness tremble off and are dispersed among hindrances, instead
of centering in some long-recognizable deed.

*   *   *

[Dorothea's final wisdom is the fruit of what she sees beyond herself, outside her window—all the others, their "palpitating life."]

It had taken long for her to come to that question, and there was light
piercing into the room. She opened her curtains, and looked out towards
the bit of road that lay in view, with fields beyond, outside the entrance-
gates. On the road there was a man with a bundle on his back and a
woman carrying her baby; in the field she could see figures moving—perhaps the shepherd with his dog. Far off in the bending sky was the pearly
light; and she felt the largeness of the world and the manifold wakings of
men to labour and endurance. She was a part of that involuntary, palpitating life, and could neither look out on it from her luxurious shelter as
a mere spectator, nor hide her eyes in selfish complaining. . . .

FINALE

Every limit is a beginning as well as an ending. Who can quit young lives
after being long in company with them, and not desire to know what be-
fell them in their after-years? For the fragment of a life, however typical,
is not the sample of an even web: promises may not be kept, and an ardent
outset may be followed by declension; latent powers may find their long-
waited opportunity; a past error may urge a grand retrieval.

Marriage, which has been the bourne of so many narratives, is still a great beginning, as it was to Adam and Eve, who kept their honeymoon in Eden, but had their first little one among the thorns and thistles of the wilderness. It is still the beginning of the home epic—the gradual conquest or irremediable loss of that complete union which makes the advancing years a climax, and age the harvest of sweet memories in common.

Some set out, like Crusaders of old, with a glorious equipment of hope and enthusiasm, and get broken by the way, wanting patience with each other and the world. . . .

Sir James never ceased to regard Dorothea's second marriage as a mistake; and indeed this remained the tradition concerning it in Middlemarch, where she was spoken of to a younger generation as a fine girl who married a sickly clergyman, old enough to be her father, and in little more than a year after his death gave up her estate to marry his cousin—young enough to have been his son, with no property, and not well-born. Those who had not seen anything of Dorothea usually observed that she could not have been "a nice woman," else she would not have married either the one or the other.

Certainly those determining acts of her life were not ideally beautiful. They were the mixed result of a young and noble impulse struggling amidst the conditions of an imperfect social state, in which great feelings will often take the aspect of error, and great faith the aspect of illusion. For there is no creature whose inward being is so strong that it is not greatly determined by what lies outside it. A new Theresa will hardly have the opportunity of reforming a conventual life, any more than a new Antigone will spend her heroic piety in daring all for the sake of a brother's burial: the medium in which their ardent deeds took shape is for ever gone. But we insignificant people with our daily words and acts are preparing the lives of many Dorotheas, some of which may present a far sadder sacrifice than that of the Dorothea whose story we know.

Her finely-touched spirit had still its fine issues, though they were not widely visible. Her full nature, like that river of which Cyrus broke the strength, spent itself in channels which had no great name on the earth. But the effect of her being on those around her was incalculably diffusive: for the growing good of the world is partly dependent on unhistoric acts; and that things are not so ill with you and me as they might have been, is half owing to the number who lived faithfully a hidden life, and rest in unvisited tombs.

FLORENCE NIGHTINGALE
(1820–1910)

"On February 7, 1837, God spoke to me and called me to His service." Thus believed Florence Nightingale, a daughter of the landed gentry disenchanted with the vocational prospects allowed by her class: marriage, dinner parties, idleness. Like Joan of Arc, Florence Nightingale was convinced that God had called her, but unlike the peasant girl of Domrémy, she did not know her specific mission. Her family was horrified when, defying its code of class and gender roles, she devoted her life to caring for the sick. Her bravery on the Crimean War front is legendary. The religious sources of her commitment and her resistance to the British Army's indifference to the suffering of the infantry are not. (The duke of Wellington had referred to the infantry as "the scum of the earth.") The letters excerpted from *Florence Nightingale at Rome* (1847) show her early responsiveness to a world larger than and different from the self (as a practicing Anglican she was open to the spirit of Roman Catholicism embodied in its holy city); the piece from *Cassandra,* an important text of British feminism, interprets the waste of women's talents within a spiritual frame; the waste signifies a rejection of women's God-given identity and responsibility.

From *Florence Nightingale at Rome*

LETTER VI

Rome. November 11, 1847

Yes, my dears, here we are, I can hardly believe it. On Tuesday, the 9th of November, 1847, we came here from Civita Vecchia. The last 3 hours were in the dark, and I felt as if we were passing through the Valley of the Shadow of Death, on our way to the Celestial City. I looked out every five minutes to see the lights of the city on the hill, but in vain—the earth was sending forth her fragrance of night like an incense to heaven, for the Campagna is covered with thyme—the stars were all out—there was a solemn silence, not a trace of habitation, all desert solitude, and we were feverish and very tired, which increased the likeness of the Valley of the Shadow.

At last, without the least preparation, not a house, not a suburb, we knocked at a little gate — "Chi ē la?" "Carrozza." "Venga," was all that passed — the door opened quietly — not a word at the guard house — we took up the Doganiere on the carriage — just a little stop during which, I heard the sound of the fountains of St. Peter's, softly plashing in the stillness of night, and in a moment we were passing the colonnades slowly au petit pas. I saw the Obelisk, the Dome, the Vatican, dimly glooming in the twilight, then the Angel of the Last Judgment. We crossed Ponte Sant'Angelo. Oh Tiber, father Tiber, to whom the Romans pray, a Roman's life, a Roman's arms, take thou in charge this day. Though it was hardly 9 o'clock, not a carriage, scarcely a living being, as we drove slowly up Via di Ripetta, (all was solemn and still like a city of times gone by) to Piazza del Popolo, where we silently and stilly went to bed.

I could not sleep for knowing myself in the Eternal City and towards dawn I got up, scoured myself, and cleaned myself from the dust of many days, and as soon as it was daylight, (forgive an ancient fool who found herself for the first time in her old age in the land of Rome) I went out, and I almost ran till I came to St. Peter's. I would not look to the right or left, (I know I passed through Piazza Navona,) till I came to the Colonnades, and there was the first ray of the rising sun just touching the top of the fountain. The Civic Guard was already exercising in the Piazza. The dome was much smaller than I expected. But that enormous Atrio. I stopped under it, for my mind was out of breath, to recover its strength before I went in. No event in my life, except my death can ever be greater than that first entrance into St. Peter's, the concentrated spirit of the Christianity of so many years, the great image of our Faith which is the worship of grief. I went in. I could not have gone there for the first time except alone, no, not in the company of St. Peter himself, and walked up to the Dome. There was hardly a creature there but I. There I knelt down. You know I have no art, and it was not an artistic effect it made on me — it was the effect of the presence of God.

From *Cassandra*

WOMEN'S TIME

> "Yet I would spare no pang,
> Would wish no torture less,
> The more that anguish racks,
> The earlier it will bless."

Give us back our suffering, we cry to Heaven in our hearts—suffering rather than indifferentism; for out of nothing comes nothing. But out of suffering may come the cure. Better have pain than paralysis! A hundred struggle and drown in the breakers. One discovers the new world. But rather, ten times rather, die in the surf, heralding the way to that new world, than stand idly on the shore!

Passion, intellect, moral activity—these three have never been satisfied in a woman. In this cold and oppressive conventional atmosphere, they cannot be satisfied. To say more on this subject would be to enter into the whole history of society, of the present state of civilisation. . . .

Look at the poor lives we lead. It is a wonder that we are so good as we are, not that we are so bad. In looking round we are struck with the power of the organisations we see, not with their want of power. Now and then, it is true, we are conscious that *there* is an inferior organisation, but, in general, just the contrary. Mrs. A. has the imagination, the poetry of a Murillo, and has sufficient power of execution to show that she might have had a great deal more. Why is she not a Murillo? From a material difficulty, not a mental one. If she has a knife and fork in her hands for three hours of the day, she cannot have a pencil or brush. Dinner is the great sacred ceremony of this day, the great sacrament. To be absent from dinner is equivalent to being ill. Nothing else will excuse us from it. Bodily incapacity is the only apology valid. If she has a pen and ink in her hands during other three hours, writing answers for the penny post, again, she cannot have her pencil, and *so ad infinitum* through life. People have no type before them in their lives, neither fathers nor mothers, nor the children themselves. They look at things in detail. They say, "It is very desirable that A., my daughter, should go to such a party, should know such a lady, should sit by such a person." It is true. But what standard have they before them of the nature and destination of man? The very words are rejected as pedantic. But might they not, at least, have a type in their minds that such an one might be a discoverer through her intellect, such another through her art, a third through her moral power?

*   *   *

THE SAVIOUR OF HER RACE

Women dream till they have no longer the strength to dream; those dreams against which they so struggle, so honestly, vigorously, and conscientiously, and so in vain, yet which are their life, without which they could not have lived; those dreams go at last. All their plans and visions seem vanished, and they know not where; gone, and they cannot recall them. They do not even remember them. And they are left without the food of reality or of hope.

Later in life, they neither desire nor dream, neither of activity, nor of love, nor of intellect. The last often survives the longest. They wish, if their experiences would benefit anybody, to give them to someone. But they never find an hour free in which to collect their thoughts, and so discouragement becomes ever deeper and deeper, and they less and less capable of undertaking anything.

It seems as if the female spirit of the world were mourning everlasting over blessings, not *lost*, but which she has never had, and which, in her discouragement she feels that she never will have, they are so far off.

The more complete a woman's organisation, the more she will feel it, till at last there shall arise a woman, who will resume, in her own soul, all the sufferings of her race, and that woman will be the Saviour of her race.

Jesus Christ raised women above the condition of mere slaves, mere ministers to the passions of the man, raised them by His sympathy, to be Ministers of God. He gave them moral activity. But the Age, the World, Humanity, must give them the means to exercise this moral activity, must give them intellectual cultivation, spheres of action.

There is perhaps no century where the woman shows so meanly as in this. Because her education seems entirely to have parted company with her vocation; there is no longer unity between the woman as inwardly developed, and as outwardly manifested.

In the last century it was not so. In the succeeding one let us hope that it will no longer be so.

But now she is like the Archangel Michael as he stands upon Saint Angelo at Rome. She has an immense provision of wings, which seem as if they would bear her over earth and heaven; but when she tries to use them, she is petrified into stone, her feet are grown into the earth, chained to the bronze pedestal.

Nothing can well be imagined more painful than the present position of woman, unless, on the one hand, she renounces all outward activity and keeps herself within the magic sphere, the bubble of her dreams; or, on the other, surrendering all aspiration, she gives herself to her real life, soul and body. For those to whom it is possible, the latter is best; for out of activity may come thought, out of mere aspiration can come nothing.

*　　*　　*

We live in the world, it is said, and must walk in its ways.

Was Christ called a complainer against the world? Yet all these great teachers and preachers must have had a most deep and ingrained sense, a continual feeling of the miseries and wrongs of the world. Otherwise they would not have been impelled to devote life and death to redress them. Christ, Socrates, Howard, they must have had no ear for the joys, compared to that which they had for the sorrows of the world.

They acted, however, and we complain. The great reformers of the world turn into the great misanthropists, if circumstances or organisation do not permit them to act. Christ, if He had been a woman, might have been nothing but a great complainer. Peace be with the misanthropists! They have made a step in progress; the next will make them great philanthropists; they are divided but by a line.

The next Christ will perhaps be a female Christ. But do we see one woman who looks like a female Christ? or even like "the messenger before" her "face," to go before her and prepare the hearts and minds for her?

To this will be answered that half the inmates of Bedlam begin in this way, by fancying that they are "the Christ."

People talk about imitating Christ, and imitate Him in the little trifling formal things, such as washing the feet, saying His prayer, and so on; but if anyone attempts the real imitation of Him, there are no bounds to the outcry with which the presumption of that person is condemned.

For instance, Christ was saying something to the people one day, which interested Him very much, and interested them very much; and Mary and His brothers came in the middle of it, and wanted to interrupt Him, and take Him home to dinner, very likely—(how natural that story is! does it not speak more home than any historic evidences of the Gospel's reality?), and He, instead of being angry with their interruption of Him in such an important work for some trifling thing, answers, "Who is my mother? and who are my brethren? Whosoever shall do the will of my Father which is in heaven, the same is my brother and sister and mother." But if *we* were to say that, we should be accused of "destroying the family tie, of diminishing the obligation of the home duties."

He might well say, "Heaven and earth shall pass away, but my words shall not pass away." His words will never pass away. If He had said, "Tell them that I am engaged at this moment in something very important; that the instruction of the multitude ought to go before any personal ties; that I will remember to come when I have done," no one would have been impressed by His words; but how striking is that, "Behold my mother and my brethren!"

EMILY DICKINSON
(1830–1886)

"The final direction of her poetry," writes the critic Charles Anderson, "can only be described as religious." Dickinson biographer Richard Sewall interprets the religious dimension of her work as "that of the ever-questing mind, not so much (in her case) rejecting the orthodoxies as pressing them for an assurance that continually eluded her. Although perhaps the most religious person in town, she had stopped going to church by the time she was thirty." Critic Wendy Martin in *An American Triptych* shows the connections between the responses of poets Anne Bradstreet, Emily Dickinson, and Adrienne Rich to the Puritan tradition, emphasizing Dickinson's rebelliousness and independence. An enigmatic, reclusive, and mystical poet, Dickinson conceived of her writing as a sacred calling, a countercultural liturgy of language in a theophanous universe, an invitation to the hidden realms of wisdom.

From *The Poems*

3 0 3

The Soul selects her own Society—
Then—shuts the Door—
To her divine Majority—
Present no more—

Unmoved—she notes the Chariots—pausing—
At her low Gate—
Unmoved—an Emperor be kneeling
Upon her Mat—

I've known her—from an ample nation—
Choose One—
Then—close the Valves of her attention—
Like Stone—

3 2 4

Some keep the Sabbath going to Church—
I keep it, staying at Home—
With a Bobolink for a Chorister—
And an Orchard, for a Dome—

Some keep the Sabbath in Surplice—
I just wear my Wings—
And instead of tolling the Bell, for Church,
Our little Sexton—sings.

God preaches, a noted Clergyman—
And the sermon is never long,
So instead of getting to Heaven, at last—
I'm going, all along.

c. 1860

7 9 0

Nature—the Gentlest Mother is,
Impatient of no Child—
The feeblest—or the waywardest—
Her Admonition mild—

In Forest—and the Hill—
By Traveller—be heard—
Restraining Rampant Squirrel—
Or too impetuous Bird—

How fair Her Conversation—
A Summer Afternoon—
Her Household—Her Assembly—
And when the Sun go down—

Her Voice among the Aisles
Incite the timid prayer
Of the minutest Cricket—
The most unworthy Flower—

When all the Children sleep—
She turns as long away
As will suffice to light Her lamps—
Then bending from the Sky—

With infinite Affection—
And infiniter Care—
Her Golden finger on Her lip—
Wills Silence—Everywhere—

c. 1863

4 3 5

Much Madness is divinest Sense—
To a discerning Eye—
Much Sense—the starkest Madness—
'Tis the Majority
In this, as All, prevail—
Assent—and you are sane—
Demur—you're straightway dangerous—
And handled with a Chain—

6 5 7

I dwell in Possibility—
A fairer House than Prose—
More numerous of Windows—
Superior—for Doors—
Of Chambers as the Cedars—
Impregnable of Eye—
And for an Everlasting Roof
The Gambrels of the Sky—
Of Visiters—the fairest—
For Occupation—This—
The spreading wide my narrow Hands
To gather Paradise—

CHRISTINA ROSSETTI
(1830–1894)

Christina Rossetti, described as "a sort of nun of art," did in fact live at
the end of her sad High Anglican life as a nun in All Saints Home,
Margaret Street, London. This event enacts the theme of some of her
strongest poems, especially "The Convent Threshold": the renunciation
of passion for the sake of a future spiritual paradise. The yearning for a
safe heaven beyond the world of desire and tormented love shapes many
of her extensive devotional essays and poems, one of which follows here.
Her losses of human love are the biographical context of this emphasis, as
is her growing up the youngest child of Gabriele Rossetti, an embittered
Italian exile-poet-librettist-professor given to paranoia and despair, and
the sibling rival of a flamboyant painter-poet brother, Dante Gabriel
Rossetti. Her volunteer work with prostitutes at Highgate Penitentiary
inspired the extraordinary poem "Goblin Market," an acclaimed work
that manifests her feminist sympathy and the erotic imagination that in
most of her poetry remains unexpressed.

Poems

A SOUL

She stands as pale as Parian statues* stand;
Like Cleopatra when she turned at bay,
And felt her strength above the Roman sway,
And felt the aspic writhing in her hand.
Her face is steadfast toward the shadowy land,
For dim beyond it looms the land of day:
Her feet are steadfast, all the arduous way
That foot-track doth not waver on the sand.
She stands there like a beacon through the night,
A pale clear beacon where the storm-drift is—
She stands alone, a wonder deathly-white:
She stands there patient nerved with inner might,
Indomitable in her feebleness,
Her face and will athirst against the light.

*Statues made with marble from the Greek island of Paros.

I LOOK FOR THE LORD

Our wealth has wasted all away,
    Our pleasures have found wings;
The night is long until the day;
    Lord, give us better things—
A ray of light in thirsty night
    And secret water-springs.

Our love is dead, or sleeps, or else
    Is hidden from our eyes:
Our silent love, while no man tells
    Or if it lives or dies.
Oh give us love, O Lord, above
    In changeless Paradise.

Our house is left us desolate,
    Even as Thy word hath said.
Before our face the way is great;
    Around us are the dead.
Oh guide us, save us from the grave,
    As Thou Thy saints hast led.

Lead us where pleasures evermore
    And wealth indeed are placed,
And home on an eternal shore,
    And love that cannot waste:
Where joy Thou art unto the heart,
    And sweetness to the taste.

ANNIE BESANT
(1847–1933)

By the time Annie Wood Besant discovered Madame Blavatsky's
Theosophical Society in 1889 and became one of its leading advocates,
she had run a zigzag course through the causes of agnosticism, theism,
atheism, socialism, women's and workers' rights, and environmentalism.
George Bernard Shaw, who shared her Irish blood and socialism, hailed
her as the greatest orator of the day. The potato famine had forced her

family to leave Galway for London in 1845, but the emotional bond remained, explaining in part her fierce energy, rebelliousness, and deep mystical impulse. "Three-quarters of my blood and all my heart was Irish," she writes in her *Autobiography* (1893). Her take on the spiritual life—"all work done in the world is God's work"—has the ring of the pantheism of the medieval Irish philosopher John Scotus Erigena: He saw all reality as a continuum, admitting no distinction between God and His creation. Besant's love of India, and her role in Krishnamurti's becoming an important voice in a deinstitutionalized modern spirituality (see the selection by Diana Eck, page 341), reflect her sense of wisdom as a timeless tradition that flows out of a universal compassion for the sufferings of humankind.

From *The Spiritual Life in the World*

A complaint which we hear continually from thoughtful and earnest-minded people, a complaint against the circumstances of their lives, is perhaps one of the most fatal: "If my circumstances were different from what they are, how much more I could do; if only I were not so surrounded by business, so tied by anxieties and cares, so occupied with the work of the world, then I would be able to live a more spiritual life."

Now that is not true. No circumstances can ever make or mar the unfolding of the spiritual life. Spirituality does not depend upon the environment; it depends upon one's attitude towards life.

I want to point out to you the way in which the world may be turned to the service of the spirit instead of submerging it, as it often does. If people do not understand the relation of the material and the spiritual; if they separate the one from the other as incompatible and hostile; if on the one side they put the life of the world, and on the other the life of the spirit as rivals, as antagonists, as enemies, then the pressing nature of worldly occupations, the powerful shocks of the material environment, the constant lure of physical temptation, and the occupying of the brain by physical cares— these things are apt to make the life of the spirit unreal. They seem to be the only reality, and we have to find some alchemy, some magic, by which the life of the world shall be seen to be the unreal, and the life of the spirit the only reality. If we can do that, then the reality will express itself through the life of the world, and that life will become its means of expression, and not a bandage round its eyes, a gag which stops the breath.

Now, you know how often in the past this question of whether a person can lead a spiritual life in the world has been answered in the negative. In every land, in every religion, in every age of the world's history, when the question has been asked, the answer has been no, the man or woman of the world cannot lead a spiritual life. That answer comes from the deserts of Egypt, the jungles of India, the monastery and the nunnery in Roman Catholic countries, in every land and place where people have sought to find God by shrinking from the company of others. If for the knowledge of God and the leading of the spiritual life it is necessary to fly from human haunts, then that life for most of us is impossible. For we are bound by circumstance that we cannot break to live the life of the world and to accommodate ourselves to its conditions separating the sacred from the profane.

I submit to you that this idea is based on a fundamental error that is largely fostered in our modern life, not by thinking of secluded life in jungle or desert, in cave or monastery, but rather by thinking that the religious and the secular must be kept apart. That tendency is because of the modern way of separating the so-called sacred from that which is called profane. People speak of Sunday as the Lord's Day, as though every day were not equally for serving him. To call one day the Lord's Day is to deny that same lordship to every other day in the week and to make six parts of life outside the spiritual, while only one remains recognized as dedicated to the Spirit. And so common talk of sacred history and profane history, religious education and secular education, all these phrases that are so commonly used, hypnotize the public mind into a false view of the Spirit and the world. The right way is to say that the Spirit is the life, the world the form, and the form must be the expression of the life; otherwise you have a corpse devoid of life, an unembodied life separated from all means of effective action.

I want to put broadly and strongly the very foundation of what I believe to be right and sane thinking in this matter. The world is the thought of God, the expression of the Divine Mind. All useful activities are forms of Divine Activity. The wheels of the world are turned by God, and we are only his hands, which touch the rim of the wheel. All work done in the world is God's work, or none is his at all. Everything that serves humanity and helps in the activities of the world is rightly seen as a divine activity, and wrongly seen when called secular or profane. The clerk behind his counter and the doctor in the hospital are quite as much engaged in a divine activity as any preacher in his church. Until that is realized the world is vulgarized, and until we can see one life everywhere and all things rooted in that life, it is we who are hopelessly profane in attitude, we who are blind to the beatific vision which is the sight of the one life in everything, and all things as expressions of that life.

DIVINITY EVERYWHERE

An ancient Indian scripture says, "I established this universe with one fragment of Myself, and I remain." Now, if there is only one life in which you and I are partakers, one creative thought by which the worlds were formed and maintained, then, however mighty may be the unexpressed Divine Existence—however true that Divinity transcends manifestation, nonetheless the manifestation is still divine. By understanding this we touch the feet of God. If it is true that he is everywhere and in everything, then he is as much in the marketplace as in the desert, as much in the office as in the jungle, as easily found in the street of the crowded city as in the solitude of the mountain peak.

I do not mean that it is not easier for you and for me to realize the divine greatness in the splendor of snow-clad mountains, the beauty of some pine forest, the depth of some marvelous secret valley where Nature speaks in a voice that may be heard. I mean that although we hear more clearly there, it is because we are deaf, and not because the Divine Voice does not speak.

It is our weakness that the rush and the bustle of life in the city make us deaf to the Voice that is ever speaking. If we were stronger, if our ears were keener, if we were more spiritual, then we could find the Divine Life as readily in the rush of Holborn Viaduct as in the fairest scene that Nature has ever painted in the solitude of the mountain or the magic of the midnight sky. That is the first thing to realize—that we do not find because our eyes are blinded.

WORLDLY ATTRACTIONS

Now let us see what are the conditions by which the man or woman of the world may lead the spiritual life, for there are conditions. Have you ever asked yourself why objects that attract you, things you want to possess are found on every side? Your desires answer to the outer beauty, the attractiveness of the endless objects that are scattered over the world. If they were not meant to attract, they would not be there; if they were really hindrances, why should they have been put in our path? For the same reasons that a mother, wanting to coax her child into the exertion that will induce it to walk, dangles before its eyes a little out of reach some dazzling toy, some tinsel attraction. The child's eyes turn to the brilliant object, and the child wants to grasp it. He tries to get on his feet, falls, and rises again, endeavors to walk, struggles to reach it. The value of the attraction is not in the tinsel that presently the child grasps, crushes, and throws away, wanting something more, but in the stimulus to the life within, which makes him endeavor to move in order to gain the glittering prize, which he despises when he has won it.

The great mother-heart by which we are trained is ever dangling in front of us some attractive object, some prize for the child-spirit, turning outwards the powers that live within. In order to induce exertion, in order to make the effort by which alone those inward-turned powers will turn outwards into manifestation, we are bribed and coaxed and induced to make efforts by the endless toys of life scattered on every side. We struggle, we endeavor to grasp. At last we do grasp and hold. After a short time the brilliant apple turns to ashes, as in Milton's fable, and the prize that seemed so valuable loses all its attractiveness, becomes worthless, and something else is desired. In that way we grow. The result is in ourselves; some power has been brought out, some faculty has been developed, some inner strength has become a manifested power, some hidden capacity has become faculty in action. That is the object of the Divine Teacher. The toy is thrown aside when the result of the exertion to gain it has been achieved.

So we pass from one point to another, from one stage of evolution to the next. Although until you believe in the great fact of continual rebirth and ever-continuing experience, you will not realize to the full the beauty and the splendor of the Divine Plan, still, even in one brief life you know you gain by your struggle and not by your accomplishment, and the reward of the struggle is in the power that you possess. In the words of Edward Carpenter, nineteenth-century English author, limited in scope if you do not believe in reincarnation, "Every pain that I suffered in one body was a power that I wielded in the next." Even in one brief span from the cradle to the grave you can trace the working of the law. You grow, not by what you gain of outer fruit, but by the inner unfolding necessary for your success in the struggle.

THE TWENTIETH CENTURY

---

*I. Voices of Faith,
Imagination, and Protest*

T HE WRITERS IN our century who have articulated their experience
of a spiritual dimension of life—a larger world to live in—have grounded
their insights variously. Some visions are theistic; others are not. Some demand political activism; others generate a more complex and liberating understanding. But no matter what the range or limits of a particular
experience, the general news from the writers' sense of the reality of spirit
comes across as a harmony of themes. The following selections of Part I
blend the love of freedom, the search for meaning, and the related desire
for universal justice; many writers dismiss the notion of the autonomous
self as the supreme fiction, a common theme of all spiritual traditions. They
know and write a self that is inspirited.

The most dominant chord, joining the voices of poets, storytellers, theorists, and activists, is the affirmation, in different keys, of ordinary life.

The search for sources to restore or enlarge the significance of the ordinary, the locus of most women's lives, covers diverse territories of meaning, as the theoretical and autobiographical selections in Part II, the final
section of the book, reflect. The written evidence from scholars, teachers,
shamans, witches, and theologians shows that the search for and the recovery of meanings in this genocidal and nihilistic century are insistent,
passionate, and indifferent to artificial boundaries of place and time. At the
end of our century Eastern and Western spiritual traditions enrich each
other, and the relational wisdom expressed especially by writers who have
found in nature the organic pattern of material and spiritual connectedness and complementarity—reality as a continuum—echoes the visionary

wisdom of the ancient testimonies and the medieval mystics represented in the first half of this book.

The prophetic and practical wisdom of women—that the gift of life comes with the responsibility to love and protect it wherever we find it, regardless of our particular identifications within borders of race, religion, gender, and class—has never waned. Vision and conscience are its continuing signs; hope and anger its dissonant emotional tones. The anger is induced by the vast evidence of the waste of the lives of many and the feast of life reserved for the privileged few.

Written testimonies like the diverse ones that follow here can move us to contemplate, if we choose, the idea of the sacred grounding of our lives and the practical consequences of such contemplation. Spiritual freedom can be a matter of whom you read and whether she is wise.

WILLA CATHER
(1873–1947)

In a richly insightful essay, "American Beauty: The Triumph of Willa Cather," writer and critic Vivian Gornick calls Cather a "wise" woman, designating her third novel, *The Song of the Lark* (1915), the "manifesto" of her wisdom. In it Cather renders the interaction of landscape and character and shows the transformative effect of mystical experience grounded in nature on a woman's soul and conscience. After her solitary retreat to Panther Canyon in the Native American Southwest, the heroine, the musician Thea Kronborg, achieves a sense of self and vocation. Cather knew the two cannot be separated. In Gornick's words, Cather knew that "to be oneself was not a given, that it was, in fact, a monumental problem. . . . In all human beings, she felt, there is what she called a soul, an essential spirit, an expressive, inviolable self. She knew it was the task of every life to fashion an existence that would feed the expressive self." In the excerpt from the novel that follows here, contemplation of the ancient earth and remembrance of the layers of history and meaning it holds are a source of such wisdom.

From *The Song of the Lark*

I

The San Francisco Mountain lies in Northern Arizona, above Flagstaff, and its blue slopes and snowy summit entice the eye for a hundred miles across the desert. About its base lie the pine forests of the Navajos, where the great red-trunked trees live out their peaceful centuries in that sparkling air. The *piñons* and scrub begin only where the forest ends, where the country breaks into open, stony clearings and the surface of the earth cracks into deep canyons. The great pines stand at a considerable distance from each other. Each tree grows alone, murmurs alone, thinks alone. They do not intrude upon each other. The Navajos are not much in the habit of giving or of asking help. Their language is not a communicative one, and they never attempt an interchange of personality in speech. Over their forests there is the same inexorable reserve. Each tree has its exalted power to bear.

That was the first thing Thea Kronborg felt about the forest, as she drove through it one May morning in Henry Biltmer's democrat wagon—and it was the first great forest she had ever seen. She had got off the train at Flagstaff that morning, rolled off into the high, chill air when all the pines on the mountain were fired by sunrise, so that she seemed to fall from sleep directly into the forest.

Old Biltmer followed a faint wagon trail which ran southeast, and which, as they traveled, continually dipped lower, falling away from the high plateau on the slope of which Flagstaff sits. The white peak of the mountain, the snow gorges above the timber, now disappeared from time to time as the road dropped and dropped, and the forest closed behind the wagon. More than the mountain disappeared as the forest closed thus. Thea seemed to be taking very little through the wood with her. The personality of which she was so tired seemed to let go of her. The high, sparkling air drank it up like blotting-paper. It was lost in the thrilling blue of the new sky and the song of the thin wind in the *piñons*. The old, fretted lines which marked one off, which defined her,—made her Thea Kronborg, Bowers's accompanist, a soprano with a faulty middle voice,—were all erased.

So far she had failed. Her two years in Chicago had not resulted in anything. She had failed with Harsanyi, and she had made no great progress with her voice. She had come to believe that whatever Bowers had taught her was of secondary importance, and that in the essential things she had made no advance. Her student life closed behind her, like the forest, and she doubted whether she could go back to it if she tried. Probably she would teach music in little country towns all her life. Failure was not so tragic as she would have supposed; she was tired enough not to care.

She was getting back to the earliest sources of gladness that she could remember. She had loved the sun, and the brilliant solitudes of sand and sun, long before these other things had come along to fasten themselves upon her and torment her. That night, when she clambered into her big German feather bed, she felt completely released from the enslaving desire to get on in the world. Darkness had once again the sweet wonder that it had in childhood.

I I

Thea's life at the Ottenburg ranch was simple and full of light, like the days themselves. She awoke every morning when the first fierce shafts of sunlight darted through the curtainless windows of her room at the ranch house. After breakfast she took her lunch-basket and went down to the canyon. Usually she did not return until sunset.

Panther Canyon was like a thousand others—one of those abrupt fissures with which the earth in the Southwest is riddled; so abrupt that you might walk over the edge of any one of them on a dark night and never know what had happened to you. This canyon headed on the Ottenburg ranch, about a mile from the ranch house, and it was accessible only at its head. The canyon walls, for the first two hundred feet below the surface, were perpendicular cliffs, striped with even-running strata of rock. From there on to the bottom the sides were less abrupt, were shelving, and lightly fringed with *piñons* and dwarf cedars. The effect was that of a gentler canyon within a wilder one. The dead city lay at the point where the perpendicular outer wall ceased and the V-shaped inner gorge began. There a stratum of rock, softer than those above, had been hollowed out by the action of time until it was like a deep groove running along the sides of the canyon. In this hollow (like a great fold in the rock) the Ancient People had built their houses of yellowish stone and mortar. The overhanging cliff above made a roof two hundred feet thick. The hard stratum below was an everlasting floor. The houses stood along in a row, like the buildings in a city block, or like a barracks.

In both walls of the canyon the same streak of soft rock had been washed out, and the long horizontal groove had been built up with houses. The dead city had thus two streets, one set in either cliff, facing each other across the ravine, with a river of blue air between them.

The canyon twisted and wound like a snake, and these two streets went on for four miles or more, interrupted by the abrupt turnings of the gorge, but beginning again within each turn. The canyon had a dozen of these false endings near its head. Beyond, the windings were larger and less perceptible, and it went on for a hundred miles, too narrow, precipitous, and terrible for man to follow it. The Cliff Dwellers liked wide canyons, where the great cliffs caught the sun. Panther Canyon had been deserted for hundreds of years when the first Spanish missionaries came into Arizona, but the masonry of the houses was still wonderfully firm; had crumbled only where a landslide or a rolling boulder had torn it.

All the houses in the canyon were clean with the cleanness of sun-baked, wind-swept places, and they all smelled of the tough little cedars that twisted themselves into the very doorways. One of these rock-rooms Thea took for her own. Fred had told her how to make it comfortable. The day after she came old Henry brought over on one of the pack-ponies a roll of Navajo blankets that belonged to Fred, and Thea lined her cave with them. The room was not more than eight by ten feet, and she could touch the stone roof with her fingertips. This was her old idea: a nest in a high cliff, full of sun. All morning long the sun beat upon her cliff, while the ruins on the opposite side of the canyon were in shadow. In the afternoon, when she had the shade of two hundred feet of rock wall, the ruins on the other side of the gulf stood out in the blazing sunlight. Before her door ran the narrow, winding path that had been the street of the Ancient People. The yucca and niggerhead cactus grew everywhere. From her doorstep she looked out on the ocher-colored slope that ran down several hundred feet to the stream, and this hot rock was sparsely grown with dwarf trees. Their colors were so pale that the shadows of the little trees on the rock stood out sharper than the trees themselves. When Thea first came, the chokecherry bushes were in blossom, and the scent of them was almost sickeningly sweet after a shower. At the very bottom of the canyon, along the stream, there was a thread of bright, flickering, golden-green—cottonwood seedlings. They made a living, chattering screen behind which she took her bath every morning.

Thea went down to the stream by the Indian water trail. She had found a bathing-pool with a sand bottom, where the creek was dammed by fallen trees. The climb back was long and steep, and when she reached her little house in the cliff she always felt fresh delight in its comfort and inaccessibility. By the time she got there, the woolly red-and-gray blankets were saturated with sunlight, and she sometimes fell asleep as soon as she stretched her body on their warm surfaces. She used to wonder at her own inactivity. She could lie there hour after hour in the sun and listen to the strident whir of the big locusts, and to the light, ironical laughter of the quaking asps. All her life she had been hurrying and sputtering, as if she had been born behind time and had been trying to catch up. Now, she reflected, as she drew herself out long upon the rugs, it was as if she were waiting for something to catch up with her. She had got to a place where she was out of the stream of meaningless activity and undirected effort.

Here she could lie for half a day undistracted, holding pleasant and incomplete conceptions in her mind—almost in her hands. They were scarcely clear enough to be called ideas. They had something to do with fragrance and color and sound, but almost nothing to do with words. She was singing very little now, but a song would go through her head all morning, as a spring keeps welling up, and it was like a pleasant sensation indefinitely prolonged. It was much more like a sensation than like an idea, or an act of remembering. Music had never come to her in that sensuous form before. It had always been a thing to be struggled with, had always brought anxiety and exaltation and chagrin—never content and indolence. Thea began to wonder whether people could not utterly lose the power to work, as they can lose their voice or their memory. She had always been a little drudge, hurrying from one task to another—as if it mattered! And now her power to think seemed converted into a power of sustained sensation. She could become a mere receptacle for heat, or become a color, like the bright lizards that darted about on the hot stones outside her door; or she could become a continuous repetition of sound, like the cicadas.

I I I

The faculty of observation was never highly developed in Thea Kronborg. A great deal escaped her eye as she passed through the world. But the things which were for her, she saw; she experienced them physically and remembered them as if they had once been a part of herself. The roses she used to see in the florists' shops in Chicago were merely roses. But when she thought of the moonflowers that grew over Mrs. Tellamantez's door, it was as if she had been that vine and had opened up in white flowers every night. There were memories of light on the sand hills, of masses of prickly-pear blossoms she had found in the desert in early childhood, of the late afternoon sun pouring through the grape leaves and the mint bed in Mrs. Kohler's garden, which she would never lose. These recollections were a part of her mind and personality. In Chicago she had got almost nothing that went into her subconscious self and took root there. But here, in Panther Canyon, there were again things which seemed destined for her.

Panther Canyon was the home of innumerable swallows. They built nests in the wall far above the hollow groove in which Thea's own rock chamber lay. They seldom ventured above the rim of the canyon, to the flat, wind-swept tableland. Their world was the blue air-river between the canyon walls. In that blue gulf the arrow-shaped birds swam all day long, with only an occasional movement of the wings. The only sad thing about them was their timidity; the way in which they lived their lives between the echoing cliffs and never dared to rise out of the shadow of the canyon walls. As they swam past her door, Thea often felt how easy it would be to dream one's life out in some cleft in the world.

From the ancient dwelling there came always a dignified, unobtrusive sadness; now stronger, now fainter,—like the aromatic smell which the dwarf cedars gave out in the sun,—but always present, a part of the air one breathed. At night, when Thea dreamed about the canyon,—or in the early morning when she hurried toward it, anticipating it,—her conception of it was of yellow rocks baking in sunlight, the swallows, the cedar smell, and that peculiar sadness—a voice out of the past, not very loud, that went on saying a few simple things to the solitude eternally.

Standing up in her lodge, Thea could with her thumb nail dislodge flakes of carbon from the rock roof—the cooking-smoke of the Ancient People. They were that near! A timid, nest-building folk, like the swallows. How often Thea remembered Ray Kennedy's moralizing about the cliff cities. He used to say that he never felt the hardness of the human struggle or the sadness of history as he felt it among those ruins. He used to say, too, that it made one feel an obligation to do one's best. On the first day that Thea climbed the water trail she began to have intuitions about the women who had worn the path, and who had spent so great a part of their lives going up and down it. She found herself trying to walk as they must have walked, with a feeling in her feet and knees and loins which she had never known before,—which must have come up to her out of the accustomed dust of that rocky trail. She could feel the weight of an Indian baby hanging to her back as she climbed.

The empty houses, among which she wandered in the afternoon, the blanketed one in which she lay all morning, were haunted by certain fears and desires; feelings about warmth and cold and water and physical strength. It seemed to Thea that a certain understanding of those old people came up to her out of the rock shelf on which she lay; that certain feelings were transmitted to her, suggestions that were simple, insistent, and monotonous, like the beating of Indian drums. They were not expressible in words, but seemed rather to translate themselves into attitudes of body, into degrees of muscular tension or relaxation; the naked strength of youth, sharp as the sun-shafts; the crouching timorousness of age, the sullenness of women who waited for their captors. At the first turning of the canyon there was a half-ruined tower of yellow masonry, a watch-tower upon which the young men used to entice eagles and snare them with nets. Sometimes for a whole morning Thea could see the coppery breast and shoulders of an Indian youth there against the sky; see him throw the net, and watch the struggle with the eagle.

Old Henry Biltmer, at the ranch, had been a great deal among the Pueblo Indians who are the descendants of the Cliff-Dwellers. After supper he used to sit and smoke his pipe by the kitchen stove and talk to Thea about them. He had never found any one before who was interested in his ruins. Every Sunday the old man prowled about in the canyon, and he had come to know a good deal more about it than he could account for. He had gathered up a whole chestful of Cliff-Dweller relics which he meant to take back to Germany with him some day. He taught Thea how to find things among the ruins: grinding-stones, and drills and needles made of turkey-bones. There were fragments of pottery everywhere. Old Henry explained to her that the Ancient People had developed masonry and pottery far beyond any other crafts. After they had made houses for themselves, the next thing was to house the precious water. He explained to her how all their customs and ceremonies and their religion went back to water. The men provided the food, but water was the care of the women. The stupid women carried water for most of their lives; the cleverer ones made the vessels to hold it. Their pottery was their most direct appeal to water, the envelope and sheath of the precious element itself. The strongest Indian need was expressed in those graceful jars, fashioned slowly by hand, without the aid of a wheel.

When Thea took her bath at the bottom of the canyon, in the sunny pool behind the screen of cottonwoods, she sometimes felt as if the water must have sovereign qualities, from having been the object of so much service and desire. That stream was the only living thing left of the drama that had been played out in the canyon centuries ago. In the rapid, restless heart of it, flowing swifter than the rest, there was a continuity of life that reached back into the old time. The glittering thread of current had a kind of lightly worn, loosely knit personality, graceful and laughing. Thea's bath came to have a ceremonial gravity. The atmosphere of the canyon was ritualistic.

One morning, as she was standing upright in the pool, splashing water between her shoulder-blades with a big sponge, something flashed through her mind that made her draw herself up and stand still until the water had quite dried upon her flushed skin. The stream and the broken pottery: what was any art but an effort to make a sheath, a mould in which to imprison for a moment the shining, elusive element which is life itself,—life hurrying past us and running away, too strong to stop, too sweet to lose? The Indian women had held it in their jars. In the sculpture she had seen in the Art Institute, it had been caught in a flash of arrested motion. In singing, one made a vessel of one's throat and nostrils and held it on one's breath, caught the stream in a scale of natural intervals.

I V

Thea had a superstitious feeling about the potsherds, and liked better to leave them in the dwellings where she found them. If she took a few bits back to her own lodge and hid them under the blankets, she did it guiltily, as if she were being watched. She was a guest in these houses, and ought to behave as such. Nearly every afternoon she went to the chambers which contained the most interesting fragments of pottery, sat and looked at them for a while. Some of them were beautifully decorated. This care, expended upon vessels that could not hold food or water any better for the additional labor put upon them, made her heart go out to those ancient potters. They had not only expressed their desire, but they had expressed it as beautifully as they could. Food, fire, water, and something else—even here, in this crack in the world, so far back in the night of the past! Down here at the beginning that painful thing was already stirring; the seed of sorrow, and of so much delight.

There were jars done in a delicate overlay, like pine cones; and there were many patterns in a low relief, like basket-work. Some of the pottery was decorated in color, red and brown, black and white, in graceful geometrical patterns. One day, on a fragment of a shallow bowl, she found a crested serpent's head, painted in red on terra-cotta. Again she found half a bowl with a broad band of white cliff-houses painted on a black ground. They were scarcely conventionalized at all; there they were in the black border, just as they stood in the rock before her. It brought her centuries nearer to these people to find that they saw their houses exactly as she saw them.

Yes, Ray Kennedy was right. All these things made one feel that one ought to do one's best, and help to fulfill some desire of the dust that slept there. A dream had been dreamed there long ago, in the night of ages, and the wind had whispered some promise to the sadness of the savage. In their own way, those people had felt the beginnings of what was to come. These potsherds were like fetters that bound one to a long chain of human endeavor.

Not only did the world seem older and richer to Thea now, but she herself seemed older. She had never been alone for so long before, or thought so much. Nothing had ever engrossed her so deeply as the daily contemplation of that line of pale-yellow houses tucked into the wrinkle of the cliff. Moonstone and Chicago had become vague. Here everything was simple and definite, as things had been in childhood. Her mind was like a ragbag into which she had been frantically thrusting whatever she could grab. And here she must throw this lumber away. The things that were really hers separated themselves from the rest. Her ideas were simplified, became sharper and clearer. She felt united and strong.

FLORIDA SCOTT-MAXWELL
(1883–1979)

Written when she was eighty-five, Florida Scott-Maxwell's memoir reproduces her notebook meditations on ultimate questions of meaning, of the mystery of suffering and historical evil, of the inevitable losses that mark a long life, of the value of silence. Rather than give into despair and bitterness, the more acutely Scott-Maxwell probes the sorrows of time, the more profound her sympathy with "human-kind," as she puts it, becomes. Without ignoring the horrors of the twentieth century and the pain of mortality, she writes an old woman's luminous wisdom. Anne Morrow Lindbergh called *The Measure of My Days* "pure gold, essential writing, profound and compassionate."

From *The Measure of My Days*

In some central part of us mankind must always be trying to understand God. In that poignant core where we call out our questions, and cry for an answer. It is in each of us, even if question and answer are both despair. We are always talking to God even while we argue him out of existence. It is not easy to commune with that great force. Can we do less than speak as creator to creator since that seems the role given us, and in our seeking we honour the honour done us.

I suppose this is what religion is about, and always has been ever since man began to suffer and to care why he suffered. I've taken a long time to feel it as very truth. The last years may matter most.

What frightens me is modern man's preference for the arid. He claims to understand, yet knows himself so little that he dares dispel mystery, deny the depths of the human psyche, and prefers to bypass the soul. It is inevitable that he arrives in a desert without values. Life is being sterilized, crime increases, and even children become murderers. It is as though God said, "You think to create order? Here is the appropriate disorder, since they are one."

In the midst of these contradictions something is stirring, something that feels like the beginning of a new pact. Man seems to be saying to the god within us, "Let us come closer. We know what we have been in your name, and we begin to see what we may be without you. We have begun to fear ourselves. We ask for recognition of a new thing in us. We are trying to extend our human understanding, to take on further responsibility for what we are. Help us to make a new image. If we have lost our fear of you, do not doubt our terror of ourselves. It is real."

*　　*　　*

I don't like to write this down, yet it is much in the minds of the old. We wonder how much older we have to become, and what degree of decay we may have to endure. We keep whispering to ourselves, "Is this age yet? How far must I go?" For age can be dreaded more than death. "How many years of vacuity? To what degree of deterioration must I advance?" Some want death now, as release from old age, some say they will accept death willingly, but in a few years. I feel the solemnity of death, and the possibility of some form of continuity. Death feels a friend because it will release us from the deterioration of which we cannot see the end. It is waiting for death that wears us down, and the distaste for what we may become.

These thoughts are with us always, and in our hearts we know ignominy as well as dignity. We are people to whom something important is about to happen. But before then, these endless years before the end, can we summon enough merit to warrant a place for ourselves? We go into the future not knowing the answer to our question.

But we also find that as we age we are more alive than seems likely, convenient, or even bearable. Too often our problem is the fervour of life within us. My dear fellow octogenarians, how are we to carry so much life, and what are we to do with it?

Let no one say it is "unlived life" with any of the simpler psychological certitudes. No one lives all the life of which he was capable. The unlived life in each of us must be the future of humanity. When truly old, too frail to use the vigour that pulses in us, and weary, sometimes even scornful of what can seem the pointless activity of mankind, we may sink down to some deeper level and find a new supply of life that amazes us.

All is uncharted and uncertain, we seem to lead the way into the unknown. It can feel as though all our lives we have been caught in absurdly small personalities and circumstances and beliefs. Our accustomed shell cracks here, cracks there, and that tiresomely rigid person we supposed to be ourselves stretches, expands, and with all inhibitions gone we realize that age is not failure, nor disgrace; though mortifying we did not invent it. Age forces us to deal with idleness, emptiness, not being needed, not able to do, helplessness just ahead perhaps. All this is true, but one has had one's life, one could be full to the brim. Yet it is the end of our procession through time, and our steps are uncertain.

Here we come to a new place of which I knew nothing. We come to where age is boring, one's interest in it by-passed; further on, go further on, one finds that one has arrived at a larger place still, the place of release. There one says, "Age can seem a debacle, a rout of all one most needs, but that is not the whole truth. What of the part of us, the nameless, boundless part who experienced the rout, the witness who saw so much go, who remains undaunted and knows with clear conviction that there is more to us than age? Part of that which is outside age has been created by age, so there is gain as well as loss. If we have suffered defeat we are somewhere, somehow beyond the battle."

Now that I am sure this freedom is the right garnering of age I am so busy being old that I dread interruptions. This sense of vigour and spaciousness may cease, and I must enjoy it while it is here. It makes me feel, "I serve life, certain that it is the human soul that discerns the spirit, and that we are creators." But victims too. Life happens to us. Plan and try as we will, think, believe, it is still that inscrutable mood of the time that casts the die. We suffer as we change, that life may change in us. We also destroy, and the pain that for me is inherent in life is that we do not know when we create and when we destroy. That is our incurable blindness, but perhaps we are less dangerous if we know we do not see.

A *long life* makes me feel nearer truth, yet it won't go into words, so how can I convey it? I can't, and I want to. I want to tell people approaching and perhaps fearing age that it is a time of discovery. If they say—"Of what?" I can only answer, "We must each find out for ourselves, otherwise it won't be discovery." I want to say—"If at the end of your life you have only yourself, it is much. Look, you will find."

I would like to be as outspoken as old people feel, but honesty gives pain. Few enjoy honesty for it arouses feeling, and to avoid the pain of feeling many prefer to live behind steel doors. It is not being able to say conflicting things with one breath that is the sad division between human beings. As some dislike the paradoxical we forego the fun of admitting what we know, and so miss the entertainment of being mutually implicated in truth.

One cannot be honest even at the end of one's life, for no one is wholly alone. We are bound to those we love, or to those who love us, and to those who need us to be brave, or content, or even happy enough to allow them not to worry about us. So we must refrain from giving pain, as our last gift to our fellows. For love of humanity consume as much of your travail as you can. Not all, never that terrible muteness that drains away human warmth. But when we are almost free of life we must retain guile that those still caught in life may not suffer more. The old must often try to be silent, if it is within their power, since silence may be like space, the intensely alive something that contains all. The clear echo of what we refrained from saying, everything, from the first pause of understanding, to the quiet of comprehension.

ELEANOR ROOSEVELT
(1884–1962)

The conscience of the New Deal, Eleanor Roosevelt was denounced by the fascist press in Germany and Italy as a "bad influence" on her husband and ridiculed by the right-wing American press as "the great gab." When Francis Cardinal Spellman accused her of anti-Catholicism for her opposition to federal aid to parochial schools, calling her "an unworthy American mother," she responded with a wise self-possession: "The final judge, my dear Cardinal Spellman, of the worthiness of all human beings is in the hands of God." Political philosopher Jean Bethke Elshtain in *Power Trips and Other Journeys* (1990) discusses the seldom mentioned religious sources of Roosevelt's commitment to social justice and progressive politics. The spirituality of Roosevelt's indefatigable witness defines the point of her short book *The Moral Basis of Democracy* (1940), excerpted here.

From *The Moral Basis of Democracy*

At a time when the whole world is in a turmoil and thousands of people are homeless and hungry, it behooves all of us to reconsider our political and religious beliefs in an effort to clarify in our minds the standards by which we live.

What does Democracy mean to any of us? What do we know of its history? Are there any religious beliefs which are essential to the Democratic way of life?

Our Democracy in this country had its roots in religious belief, and we had to acknowledge soon after its birth that differences in religious belief are inherent in the spirit of true Democracy. Just because so many beliefs flourished side by side, we were forced to accept the fact that "a belief" was important, but "what belief" was important only to the individual concerned. Later it was accepted that an individual in this land of ours had the right to any religion, or to no religion. The principle, however, of the responsibility of the individual for the well-being of his neighbors which is akin to: "Love thy neighbor as thyself," in the New Testament, seems always to have been a part of the development of the Democratic ideal which has differentiated it from all other forms of government. . . . The motivating force of the theory of a Democratic way of life is still a belief that as individuals we live co-operatively, and, to the best of our ability, serve the community in which we live, and that our own success, to be real, must contribute to the success of others.

*   *   *

[W]ithin our nation there are many who do not understand the values of Democracy, and we have been unable to spread these values throughout the world, because as a people we have been led by the gods of Mammon from the spiritual concepts and from the practical carrying-out of those concepts conceived for our nation as a truly free and democratic people.

*   *   *

It is often said that we are free, and then sneeringly it is added: "free to starve if we wish." In some parts of our country that is no idle jest. Moreover, no one can honestly claim that either the Indians or the Negroes of this country are free. These are obvious examples of conditions which are not compatible with the theory of Democracy. We have poverty which enslaves, and racial prejudice which does the same. There are other racial and religious groups among us who labor under certain discriminations, not quite so difficult as those we impose on the Negroes and the Indians, but still sufficient to show we do not completely practice the Democratic way of life.

It is quite obvious that we do not practice a Christ-like way of living in our relationship to submerged people, and here again we see that a kind of religion which gives us a sense of obligation about living with a deeper interest in the welfare of our neighbors is an essential to the success of Democracy.

✳   ✳   ✳

The citizens of a Democracy must model themselves on the best and most unselfish life we have known in history. They may not all believe in Christ's divinity, though many will; but His life is important simply because it becomes a shining beacon of what success means. If we once establish this human standard as a measure of success, the future of Democracy is secure.

✳   ✳   ✳

People say that the churches have lost their hold and that therein is found one of our greatest difficulties. Perhaps they have, but if that is true, it is because the churches have thought about the churches and not about religion as a need for men to live by. Each man may have his own religion; the church is merely the outward and visible symbol of the longing of the human soul for something to which he can aspire and which he desires beyond his own strength to achieve.

If human beings can be trained for cruelty and greed and a belief in power which comes through hate and fear and force, certainly we can train equally well for gentleness and mercy and the power of love which comes because of the strength of the good qualities to be found in the soul of every individual human being.

   While force is abroad in the world we may have to use that weapon of force, but if we develop the fundamental beliefs and desires which make us considerate of the weak and truly anxious to see a Christ-like spirit on earth, we will have educated ourselves for Democracy in much the same way that others have gone about educating people for other purposes. We will have established something permanent because it has as its foundation a desire to sacrifice for the good of others, a trait which has survived in some human beings in one form or another since the world began.

We live under a Democracy, under a form of government which above all other forms should make us conscious of the need we all have for this spiritual, moral awakening. It is not something which must necessarily come through any one religious belief, or through people who go regularly to church and proclaim themselves as members of this or that denomination. We may belong to any denomination, we may be strict observers of certain church customs or we may be neglectful of forms, but the fundamental thing which we must all have is the spiritual force which the life of Christ exemplifies. We might well find it in the life of Buddha, but as long as it translates itself into something tangible in aspirations for ourselves and love for our neighbors, we should be content; for then we know that human nature is struggling toward an ideal.

Real Democracy cannot be stable and it cannot go forward to its fullest development and growth if this type of individual responsibility does not exist, not only in the leaders but in the people as a whole.

DOROTHY SAYERS
(1890–1957)

The creator of the beloved detective Lord Peter Wimsey and the marvelous Harriet Vane (without Sayers, it is said, Ruth Rendell and P. D. James could not have existed), Dorothy Sayers was also in the great tradition of English writers of Christian theology, which included G. K. Chesterton, C. S. Lewis, J. R. R. Tolkien, and Charles Williams. The only child of an Oxford don, whom she called "Tootles," she was conjugating Latin verbs at the age of six. Sayers's incarnational vision saw the immortal in the mortal, the eternal in the temporal, the holy in the flesh of the world. Chronically incorrect politically, she did not believe that women were a class by themselves. "The more clamor we make about 'the women's point of view,' " she wrote in a letter in 1936, "the more we ram into people that the women's point of view is different, and frankly I do not think it is." The following piece is taken from *Unpopular Opinions: Twenty-one Essays*.

From *Unpopular Opinions: Twenty-one Essays*

Women are not human. They lie when they say they have human needs: warm and decent clothing; comfort in the bus; interests directed immediately to God and His universe, not intermediately through any child of man. They are far above man to inspire him, far beneath him to corrupt him; they have feminine minds and feminine natures, but their mind is not one with their nature like the minds of men; they have no human mind and no human nature. "Blessed be God," says the Jew, "that hath not made me a woman."

God, of course, may have His own opinion, but the Church is reluctant to endorse it. I think I have never heard a sermon preached on the story of Martha and Mary that did not attempt, somehow, somewhere, to explain away its text. Mary's, of course, was the better part—the Lord said so, and we must not precisely contradict Him. But we will be careful not to despise Martha. No doubt, He approved of her too. We could not get on without her, and indeed (having paid lip-service to God's opinion) we must admit that we greatly prefer her. For Martha was doing a really feminine job, whereas Mary was just behaving like any other disciple, male or female; and that is a hard pill to swallow.

Perhaps it is no wonder that the women were first at the Cradle and last at the Cross. They had never known a man like this Man—there never has been such another. A prophet and teacher who never nagged at them, never flattered or coaxed or patronised; who never made arch jokes about them, never treated them either as "The women, God help us!" or "The ladies, God bless them!"; who rebuked without querulousness and praised without condescension; who took their questions and arguments seriously; who never mapped out their sphere for them, never urged them to be feminine or jeered at them for being female; who had no axe to grind and no uneasy male dignity to defend; who took them as he found them and was completely unself-conscious. There is no act, no sermon, no parable in the whole Gospel that borrows its pungency from female perversity; nobody could possibly guess from the words and deeds of Jesus that there was anything "funny" about woman's nature.

But we might easily deduce it from His contemporaries, and from His prophets before Him, and from His Church to this day. . . .

DOROTHY DAY
(1897–1980)

The following pieces are taken from Dorothy Day's *Selected Writings*, in which editor Robert Ellsberg introduces the thought of the cofounder of the Catholic Worker movement. A journalist and novelist before her conversion to Catholicism, Day, in her long solidarity with the poor and nonviolent, lived a version of Catholic Christianity that her followers found more attuned to the original Gospel message than the brick-and-mortar Catholicism formed by the accretions of history. Day's witness to social justice, civil rights, and disarmament took her to jail, to the barricades, to the communal soup kitchens of the Worker's houses of hospitality, which still serve the hungry in urban slums. Her commitment to the works of mercy roused the Federal Bureau of

Investigation to compile a five-hundred-page file in which J. Edgar Hoover denounced her as "a very erratic and irresponsible person . . . [with] a hostile and belligerent attitude towards the Bureau."

From *Selected Writings*

WE SCARCELY KNOW OURSELVES

The following piece served as an introduction to Dorothy Day's first autobiographical work, *From Union Square to Rome* (1938).

It is difficult for me to dip back into the past, yet it is a job that must be done, and it hangs over my head like a cloud. St. Peter said that we must give a reason for the faith that is in us, and I am trying to give you those reasons. . . .

While it is often true that horror for one's sins turns one to God, what I want to bring out in this book is a succession of events that led me to His feet, glimpses of Him that I received through many years which made me feel the vital need of Him. I will try to trace for you the steps by which I came to accept the faith that I believe was always in my heart. . . .

Though I felt the strong, irresistible attraction to good, yet there was also, at times, a deliberate choosing of evil. How far I was led to choose it, it is hard to say. How far professors, companions, and reading influenced my way of life does not matter now. The fact remains that there was much of deliberate choice in it. Most of the time it was "following the devices and desires of my own heart." Sometimes it was perhaps the Baudelairean idea of choosing "the downward path which leads to salvation." Sometimes it was of choice, of free will, though perhaps at the time I would have denied free will. And so, since it was deliberate, with recognition of its seriousness, it was grievous mortal sin and may the Lord forgive me. It was the arrogance and suffering of youth. It was pathetic, little, and mean in its very excuse for itself.

Was this desire to be with the poor and the mean and the abandoned not unmixed with a distorted desire to be with the dissipated? Mauriac tells of this subtle pride and hypocrisy: "There is a kind of hypocrisy which is worse than that of the Pharisees; it is to hide behind Christ's example in order to follow one's own lustful desires and to seek out the company of the dissolute."

I write these things now because sometimes when I am writing I am seized with fright at my presumption. I am afraid, too, of not telling the truth or of distorting the truth. I cannot guarantee that I do not, for I am writing of the past. But my whole perspective has changed and when I look for causes for my conversion sometimes it is one thing and sometimes it is another that stands out in my mind.

Much as we want to, we do not really know ourselves. Do we really want to see ourselves as God sees us, or even as our fellow human beings see us? Could we bear it, weak as we are? . . . We do not want to be given that clear inward vision which discloses to us our most secret faults. In the Psalms there is that prayer "Deliver me from my secret sins." We do not really know how much pride and self-love we have until someone whom we respect or love suddenly turns against us. Then some sudden affront, some sudden offense we take, reveals to us in all its glaring distinctness our self-love, and we are ashamed.

I write in the very beginning of finding the Bible and the impression it made on me. I must have read it a good deal, for many passages remained with me through my earlier years to return to haunt me. Do you know the Psalms? They were what I read most when I was in jail in Occoquan. I read with a sense of coming back to something that I had lost. There was an echoing in my heart. And how can anyone who has known human sorrow and human joy fail to respond to these words?

> Out of the depths I have cried to thee, O Lord:
> Lord, hear my voice. Let thy ears be attentive to the voice
>   of my supplication.
> If thou, O Lord, wilt mark iniquities:
> Lord, who shall stand it.
> For with thee there is merciful forgiveness: and by reason
>   of thy law, I have waited for thee,
> O Lord. My soul hath relied on his word: my soul hath
>   hoped in the Lord.
> From the morning watch even until night, let Israel hope
>   in the Lord.
> Because with the Lord there is mercy; and with him plentiful
>   redemption.
> And he shall redeem Israel from all his iniquities . . .

All through those weary first days in jail when I was in solitary confinement, the only thoughts that brought comfort to my soul were those lines in the Psalms that expressed the terror and misery of man suddenly stricken and abandoned. Solitude and hunger and weariness of spirit—these sharpened my perceptions so that I suffered not only my own sorrow but the sorrows of those about me. I was no longer myself. I was mankind. I was no longer a young girl, part of a radical movement seeking justice for those oppressed; I was the oppressed. I was that drug addict, screaming and tossing in her cell, beating her head against the wall. I was that shoplifter who, for rebellion, was sentenced to solitary. I was that woman who had killed her children, who had murdered her lover.

The blackness of hell was all about me. The sorrows of the world encompassed me. I was like one gone down into the pit. Hope had forsaken me. . . .

And yet if it were not the Holy Spirit that comforted me, how could I have been comforted, how could I have endured, how could I have lived in hope?

The *Imitation of Christ* is a book that followed me through my days. Again and again I came across copies of it and the reading of it brought me comfort. I felt in the background of my life a waiting force that would lift me up eventually.

I later became acquainted with the poem of Francis Thompson, "The Hound of Heaven," and was moved by its power. Eugene O'Neill first recited it to me in the back room of a saloon on Sixth Avenue where the Provincetown players and playwrights used to gather after the performances.

> I fled Him, down the nights and down the days;
> I fled Him, down the arches of the years;
> I fled Him, down the labyrinthine ways
> Of my own mind; and in the mist of tears
> I hid from Him . . .

Through all my daily life, in those I came in contact with, in the things I read and heard, I felt that sense of being followed, of being desired; a sense of hope and expectation.

        *   *   *

But always the glimpses of God came most when I was alone. Objectors cannot say that it was fear of loneliness and solitude and pain that made me turn to Him. It was in those few years when I was alone and most happy that I found Him. I found Him at last through joy and thanksgiving, not through sorrow.

Yet how can I say that either? Better let it be said that I found Him through His poor, and in a moment of joy I turned to Him. I have said, sometimes flippantly, that the mass of bourgeois smug Christians who denied Christ in His poor made me turn to Communism, and that it was the Communists and working with them that made me turn to God. . . .

OF JUSTICE AND BREADLINES

Why do we give so much attention in *The Catholic Worker* to such matters as the condition of workers, unions, boycotts? This month I have had several letters, written undoubtedly by sincere and pious people who want to think only of contributing to breadlines and the immediate needs of the poor. "Please spend this money for bread," they will write, "not on propaganda."

Let me say here that the sight of a line of men, waiting for food, ragged, dirty, obviously "sleeping out" in empty buildings, is something that I never will get used to. It is a deep hurt and suffering that this is often all we have to give. Our houses will not hold any more men and women, nor do we have workers to care for them. Nor are there enough alternatives or services to take care of them. They are the wounded in the class struggle, men who have built the railroads, worked in mines, on ships, and in steel mills. They are men from prison, from mental hospitals. And women, too. They are simply the unemployed.

We will never stop having "lines" at Catholic Worker houses. As long as men keep coming to the door, we will keep on preparing each day the food they need. There were six hundred on Thanksgiving day in Los Angeles. I helped serve there.

Even now as I write I can see the Berlin-line wall, the high riot fencing topped with rolls of barbed wire, which separates the barrios of Tijuana from the lush fields of southern California. As far as the eye can see there are those shacks made of cartons and old bits of tarpaper and carpeting, wall to wall, the wall of one a wall for the next, acres and acres of destitution. Most horrible of all, there is caught in that barbed wire topping the high fences, bits of clothing, a sleeve of a coat, a sock, a ragged shirt, caught there and torn from the scratched and bleeding body of some desperate person trying to get over the fence.

There are so many empty buildings belonging to the Church, so many Sisters and Brothers who want to serve the poor, surely there should be more guest houses, hostels, than there are.

But I repeat: Breadlines are not enough, hospices are not enough. I know we will always have men on the road. But we need communities of work, land for the landless, true farming communes, cooperatives and credit unions. There is much that is wild, prophetic, and holy about our work — it is that which attracts the young who come to help us. But the heart hungers for that new social order wherein justice dwelleth.

January 1972

A BRIEF SOJOURN IN JAIL

Though the Catholic Worker had originally been conceived, at least in part, as a voice for the workers, Dorothy had gradually become disillusioned with the limited vision of the trade union movement. Too often, she felt, the unions settled for improvements in wages and hours, rather than working to build a new social order. After World War II, the paper devoted relatively little space to labor news. The major exception to this was Dorothy's consistent support, over fifteen years, for the United Farm Workers' Union, led by Cesar Chavez. The U.F.W., she believed, was a social and religious movement, building community, fighting for justice and the dignity of the most victimized of all workers, while educating the public as to the power and meaning of nonviolent action.

In a tribute written after Dorothy's death, Chavez referred to the experience recounted in this article:

> It makes us very proud that Dorothy's last trip to jail took place in Fresno, California, with the farm workers. The summer of 1973 was probably the most painful period we have gone through—the union's future existence was being decided in the strike and later in the boycott. Thousands of farm workers went to jail that summer rather than obey unconstitutional injunctions against picketing, hundreds were injured, dozens were shot and two were killed. And Dorothy came to be with us in Fresno, along with nearly a hundred priests and nuns and lay people. The picture that was taken of her that day, sitting amongst the strikers and the police, is a classic portrayal of her internal peace and strength in the midst of turmoil and conflict. Dorothy Day has gone to be with God. We in the farm workers' movement give thanks for her life and for the gifts she has given us. We know she is at peace and we know we shall never forget her.

July 30. We left Kennedy Airport at noon for San Francisco, Eileen Egan and I. She was attending, as I, too, was supposed to, the 50th Anniversary of the War Resisters League. Joan Baez had invited me to be at her Institute for the Study of Nonviolence for the week with some members of Cesar Chavez's United Farm Workers' Union. When we arrived, the plans had changed because of the mass arrests of farm workers for defying an injunction against mass picketing in Kern County. There was now a strike in the vineyards, as well as the lettuce fields, because the growers would not renew their contracts with the farm workers and were instead making new contracts with the Teamsters.

The strike was widespread and mass arrests were continuing. My path was clear: the U.F.W. has everything that belongs to a new social order.

Since I had come to picket where an injunction was prohibiting picketing, it appeared that I would spend my weeks in California in jail, not at
conferences.

July 31. A very hot drive down the valley to Delano, arriving as the strike
meeting ended. Today many Jesuits were arrested. Also Sisters who had
been attending a conference in San Francisco. Mass in the evening at Bak-
ersfield ended a tremendous demonstration, flag-carrying Mexicans,
singing, chanting, marching. When the Mass began there were so many
people that it was impossible to kneel, but there was utter silence.

August 1. Up at 2 a.m., picketed all day, covering many vineyards. Im-
pressive lines of police, all armed—clubs and guns. We talked to them,
pleaded with them to lay down their weapons. One was black. His mouth
twitched as he indicated that, no, he did not enjoy being there. Two other
police came and walked away with him. I told the other police I would
come back the next day and read the Sermon on the Mount to them. I was
glad I had my folding chair-cane so I could rest occasionally during picketing, and sit there before the police to talk to them. I had seen a man that
morning sitting at the entrance to workers' shacks with a rifle across his
knees.

August 2. Slept at Sanger with nurses from one of the farm workers' clin-
ics. Up at 4 a.m., was at the park before dawn. Cesar came and spoke to
us about the injunction and arrests (wonder when he sleeps?) and we set
out in cars to picket the area where big and small growers had united to
get the injunction. Three white police buses arrived some time later and
we were warned that we were to disperse. When we refused we were ush-
ered into the buses and brought to this "industrial farm" (which they do
not like us to call a jail or prison, though we are under lock and key and
our barracks surrounded by barbed wire). Here we are, ninety-nine women
and fifty men, including thirty Sisters and two priests.

August 3. Maria Hernandez got ill in the night. Taken to Fresno Hospital,
cardiograph taken, and she was put in the Fresno jail. (She was returned
to us still ill August 7. She worries about her children.) Another Mexican
mother in our barracks has ten children and there certainly was a crowd
visiting her. Such happy, beautiful families—it reminded me of the tribute paid to the early Christians when they were imprisoned and the hordes
of their fellow Christians visited them, and made a great impression on their
guards.

I must copy down the charges made against me (we were listed in groups
of ten): "The said defendants, on or about August 2, were persons remaining present at the place of a riot, rout and unlawful assembly, who

did willfully and unlawfully fail, refuse and neglect after the same had been lawfully warned to disperse."

Some of the other women listed in the criminal complaint in my group of ten were Demetria Landavazo de Leon, Maria de Jesus Ochoa, Efigenia Garcia de Rojas, Esperanza Alanis de Perales. How I wish I could list them all.

During crucial meetings between Cesar Chavez and the Teamsters the Sisters all signed up for a night of prayer, taking two-hour shifts all through the night, while the Mexican woman all knelt along the tables in the center and prayed the rosary together. Barracks A, B, and D were alive with prayer.

Tonight a young Mexican legal assistant of the union was brutally and contemptuously ordered out when he attempted to talk to us. There were only three incidents I could have complained of: another case of rudeness, and the attempt to search the bodies of the prisoners for food smuggled in.

Today I had interesting conversations with Jo von Gottfried, a teacher of rhetoric in Berkeley, a great lover of St. Thomas and St. Augustine. I tried to understand what "rhetoric" really means and she explained, but I cannot remember now.

August 8. Today Joan Baez, her mother, and Daniel Ellsberg visited us. Joan sang to us and the other prisoners in the yard. There was a most poignant prison song. It tore at your heart. She was singing when other prisoners were being brought to the dining room and she turned her back to us and sang to all of them directly, as they stopped their line to listen.

Daniel Ellsberg said Cesar Chavez, the thought of him, had given him courage during his two-year ordeal in the courts.

August 9. I'm all mixed up in my dates. Dr. Evan Thomas came today, ninety-one and tall, lean, strong-looking. God bless him. And Father Don Hessler, whom we've known since he was a seminarian at Maryknoll. He suffered years of imprisonment under the Japanese in World War II.

August 11. Good talks with Sister Felicia and Sister Timothy of Barracks B, who are good spokeswomen for our group. Two writers from *Newsweek* called. They were interested in "the religious slant" of the strike.

August 12. Union lawyers visiting us say we'll be free tomorrow. A peaceful Sunday. Mass in the evening. Today the Mexican girls were singing and clapping and teaching the Sisters some Mexican dancing. They reminded me of St. Teresa of Avila playing her castanets at recreation.

August 13. We packed our bags last night and a first busload, including me, left our farm labor camp this morning, reached the jail, and were turned back! We then spent hours in the "rec" hall, where a team of "public defenders," whom we were supposed to have seen Sunday, sat around (perhaps I saw *one* working), while Sister Felicia interviewed all the women in our barracks for the rest of the day and filled out the forms which the judge required.

In the evening we were all finally loaded in vans and brought to Fresno, where, with a great crowd in the park in front of the courthouse, we celebrated Mass.

There is still no contract signed by grape growers with the union. Instead, there have been two deaths, that of Naji Daifullah, an Arab striker from Yemen, and Juan de la Cruz of Delano. We attended the funeral service of Naji at Forty Acres. A mile-long parade of marchers walked the four miles in a broiling sun from Delano with black flags, black armbands, and ribbons, and stood through the long service while psalms from the Office of the Dead were heard clearly over loudspeakers and the words from the Book of Wisdom: "In the sight of the unwise they seemed to die but they are at peace." There were Moslem chants as well. Five hundred Arabs recently came here from Yemen—to this land of opportunity—and one has met with death, his skull fractured by a deputy wielding a heavy flashlight.

Juan de la Cruz was shot in the chest. His funeral Mass was offered by Bishop Arzube of Los Angeles. Two men have shed their blood. Cesar Chavez has requested a three-day fast and a renewed zeal in boycotting lettuce and grapes. There is no money left in the treasury of the union, especially after death benefits have been paid to the families of the dead strikers. One of the Mexican girls in jail told me proudly that their $3.50 dues paid benefits for lives born and lives lost. And there were all the clinics operating at Calexico, Delano, Sanger, and other places. The Farm Workers' Union is a community to be proud of, and would that all our unions might become a "community of communities."

I must mention a prayer I wrote in the front of my New Testament, and hope our readers, while they read, say this for the strikers:

Dear Pope John—please, yourself a *campesino*, watch over the United Farm Workers. Raise up more and more leader-servants throughout the country to stand with Cesar Chavez in this nonviolent struggle with Mammon, in all the rural districts of North and South, in the cotton fields, beet fields, potato fields, in our orchards and vineyards, our orange groves— wherever men, women, and children work on the land. Help make a new order wherein justice flourishes, and, as Peter Maurin, himself a peasant, said so simply, "where it is easier to be good."

September 1973

IRIS ORIGO
(1902–1988)

The details of the life of the marchesa Origo appear in her autobiography, *Images and Shadows* (1970), the conclusion of which follows here. Born of an American father who was a student of Santayana's at Harvard (Santayana's letter appears in the conclusion of her book) and an Anglo-Irish mother, she grew up in family homes on Long Island, New York, in Ireland, and in Florence. After her marriage to an Italian she and her husband bought a farm in Tuscany, La Foce, in the Val d'Orcia, which they restored and farmed while they raised their children. During World War II, at considerable risk, Origo turned La Foce into a safe haven–school–health clinic for homeless orphans, refugees, and Allied soldiers who had escaped from prison camps. The war years of 1943 and 1944 are the subject of her elegantly simple chronicle of daily life, *War in Val d'Orcia: An Italian War Diary, 1943–1944*, recently published in English. The wisdom of Origo's insights in *Images and Shadows*, infusing her prose style with a serene confidence, also marks her studies of Byron, of the Italian writer Ignazio Silone, of St. Bernardino of Siena, and the fascinating merchant of the fourteenth century, Francesco Datini.

From *Images and Shadows*

And now we are back where we started. If life is indeed 'a perpetual allegory', if what we seek in it is awareness, understanding, then the small stream of events I have set down here has only been a means—a means to what? I seem to have been diverted a long way from my original inquiry, but perhaps it has not really been so very far, since it has only been through my affections that I have been able to perceive, however imperfectly, some faint 'intimations of immortality', a foretaste, perhaps, granted to the short-sighted of another, transcendental love.

Looking back at the first thirty years of my life, two events have an outstanding significance: my father's death, when I was seven and a half, and Gianni's,* when he was the same age that I was then. And both of these events are significant for the same reason—that neither of them was an end-

---

*The author's son, who died in childhood.

ing. I do not mean of course that there was not the pain of parting—but that separation did not prevent my father's personality from pervading my childhood, as Gianni's has pervaded the rest of my life. Since then, a few years ago, there has been the death of Elsa, the closest companion of my middle age, and the same has been true about her. I am not speaking now about an orthodox belief in "another life"—nor am I entering upon the complex question of the survival of personality. All that I can affirm is what I know of my own experience: that though I have never ceased to miss my father, child and friend, I have also never lost them. They have been to me, at all times, as real as the people I see every day, and it is this, I think, that has conditioned my whole attitude both to death and to human affections.

It is very easy, on this subject, to become sentimental or woolly, or to say more than one really means. I think I am only trying to say something very simple: that my own personal experience has given me a very vivid sense of the continuity of love, even after death, and that it has also left me believing in the truth of Burke's remark that society—or I should prefer to say, life itself—is 'a partnership not only between those who are living, but between those who are living, those who are dead, and those who are to be born'. Not only are we not alone, but we are not living only in a bare and chilly now. We are irrevocably bound to the past—and no less irrevocably, though the picture is less clear to us, to the future. It is this feeling that has made death seem to me not less painful, never that—for there is no greater grief than that of parting—but not, perhaps, so very important, and has caused affection, in its various forms, to be the guiding thread of my life.

At the time of Gianni's death, I received a letter from George Santayana (who in his later years to some extent returned, at least in feeling, to his Spanish, Catholic origins) which expresses, far better than I ever could, my feelings upon this subject.

. . . We have no claim to any of our possessions. We have no claim to exist; and, as we have to die in the end, so we must resign ourselves to die piecemeal, which really happens when we lose somebody or something that was closely intertwined with our existence. It is like a physical wound; we may survive, but maimed and broken in that direction; dead there.

Not that we can, or ever do at heart, renounce our affections. Never that. We cannot exercise our full nature all at once in every direction; but the parts that are relatively in abeyance, their centre lying perhaps in the past or the future, belong to us inalienably. We should not be ourselves if we cancelled them. I don't know how literally you may believe in another world, or whether the idea means very much to you. As you know, I am not myself a believer in the ordinary sense, yet my *feeling* on this subject is like that of believers, and not at all like that of my fellow-materialists. The reason is that I disagree utterly with that modern philosophy which regards *experience* as fundamental. Experience is a mere whiff or rumble, produced by enormously complex and ill-deciphered causes of experience; and in the other direction, experience is a mere peephole through which glimpses come down to us of eternal things. These are the only things that, in so far as we are spiritual beings, we can find or can love at all. All our affections, when clear and pure and not claims to possession, transport us to another world; and the loss of contact, here or there, with those eternal beings is merely like closing a book which we keep at hand for another occasion.*

About more orthodox beliefs, I am very hesitant to write, for fear of saying a little more or less than I mean or than is true. I have spent a good deal of my life in various forms of wishful thinking—trying to persuade myself, in one way or another, that things were a little better than they really were: my feelings or convictions deeper, and situations pleasanter or clearer, than was in fact the case—and I think it is time to stop. For this is what Plato called "the true lie," the lie in the soul, "hated by gods and men," of which the lie in words is 'only a kind of imitation and shadowy image."

Yet it is also true that all my life (though not steadily, but rather in fitful waves) I have been seeking a meaning, a framework, a goal—I should say, more simply, God. *"Tu ne me chercherais pas si tu ne m'avais trouvé,"* was Pascal's reply—but is this not too easy a way out for a fitful purpose and a vacillating mind? I remember a passage in Julian Green's *Journal:* *"Je lis les mystiques comme on lit les récits des voyageurs qui reviennent de pays lointains ou l'on sait bien que l'on n'ira jamais. On voudrait visiter la Chine, mais quel voyage! Et pourtant je crois que jusqu'à la fin de mes jours je conserverai ce déraisonnable espoir."*

That "unreasonable hope" is always latent: one should perhaps open the door to it more often. Someone to whom I once spoke about these matters suggested that instead of nourishing a sense of guilt for what one cannot comprehend or fully accept, it would be better to start by dwelling upon what one honestly can believe. I think the advice is good, and have tried to ask myself that question.

I have seen and believe in goodness: the indefinable quality which is immediately and unhesitatingly recognised by the most different kinds of men: the simple goodness of an old nurse or the mother of a large family; the more complex and costly goodness of a priest, a doctor or a teacher. When such people are also believers, their beliefs are apt to be *catching*—

*Published in *The Letters of George Santayana*, ed. Daniel Cory, London: Constable & Co.; New York: Charles Scribner's Sons.

or so I myself, at least, have found. It is the Eastern principle of the *guru* and his disciples: goodness and faith conveyed (or perhaps evil and disbelief dispelled) by an actual, living presence.

The outstanding instance in our lifetime has been that of Pope John XXIII. I do not think that anyone—believer or agnostic—who was present in St. Peter's Square during the Mass said for him as he lay dying could fail to have a sense of what was meant by "the communion of the faithful," or to receive a dim apprehension of his own vision of "one flock and one shepherd," of the love of mankind as a whole. And if, since then, the realisation of this dream has been full of complexities, and many minds have been disturbed and confused by conflicts, upheavals and innovations, the vision still endures.

I believe in the dependence of people upon each other. I believe in the light and warmth of human affection, and in the disinterested acts of kindness and compassion of complete strangers. I agree with Simone Weil that 'charity and faith, though distinct, are inseparable'—and I share her conviction "whoever is capable of a movement of pure compassion (which incidentally is very rare) towards an unhappy man, possesses, implicitly but truly, faith and the love of God."

I believe, not theoretically, but from direct personal experience, that very few of the things that happen to us are purposeless or accidental (and this includes suffering and grief—even that of others), and that sometimes one catches a glimpse of the link between these happenings. I believe—even when I am myself being blind and deaf, or even indifferent—in the existence of a mystery.

Beyond this, I still do not know—nor do I feel inclined to examine here—how far I can go. Yet I derive comfort, at times, from a passage in one of Dom John Chapman's letters. "There is worry and anxiety and trouble and bewilderment, and there is also an unfelt, yet real acquiescence in being anxious, troubled and bewildered, and a consciousness that the *real* self is at peace, while the anxiety and worry are unreal. It is like a peaceful lake, whose surface reflects all sorts of changes, because it is calm."

A still lake, ruffled only upon the surface: a world of clouds, through which it is possible to break to the light—are these indeed metaphors more true than I can yet fully perceive?

> Man is one world, and hath
> Another to attend him.

HANNAH ARENDT
(1906–1975)

Hannah Arendt fled Nazi Germany in the thirties, worked in France relocating dispossessed Jewish refugee children, and came to the United States to become an important voice in the New York intellectual community of the forties. She achieved prominence with the publication of the multivolume *The Origins of Totalitarianism* and controversy over her coverage of the Adolf Eichmann trial in Jerusalem, originally published in installments in *The New Yorker. The Human Condition*, excerpted here, originally a series of lectures delivered at the University of Chicago, is considered her masterpiece by many of her peers: "history on a great scale, deep, powerful, compassionate," in the words of one critic. Elisabeth Young-Bruehl's biography *Hannah Arendt: For Love of the World* (1982) provides an illuminating portrayal of Arendt and the centuries of intellectual and spiritual culture her thought and writing address.

From *The Human Condition*

IRREVERSIBILITY AND THE POWER TO FORGIVE

We have seen that the *animal laborans* could be redeemed from its predicament of imprisonment in the ever-recurring cycle of the life process, of being forever subject to the necessity of labor and consumption, only through the mobilization of another human capacity, the capacity for making, fabricating, and producing of *homo faber*, who as a toolmaker not only eases the pain and trouble of laboring but also erects a world of durability. The redemption of life, which is sustained by labor, is worldliness, which is sustained by fabrication. We saw furthermore that *homo faber* could be redeemed from his predicament of meaninglessness, the "devaluation of all values," and the impossibility of finding valid standards in a world determined by the category of means and ends, only through the interrelated faculties of action and speech, which produce meaningful stories as naturally as fabrication produces use objects. If it were not outside the scope of these considerations, one could add the predicament of thought to these instances; for thought, too, is unable to "think itself" out of the predicaments which the very activity of thinking engenders. What in each of these instances saves man—man *qua animal laborans, qua homo faber, qua* thinker—is something altogether different; it comes from the outside—not, to be sure, outside of man, but outside of each of the respective activities. From the viewpoint of the *animal laborans,* it is like a miracle that it is also a being which knows of and inhabits a world; from the viewpoint of *homo faber,* it is like a miracle, like the revelation of divinity, that meaning should have a place in this world.

The case of action and action's predicaments is altogether different. Here, the remedy against the irreversibility and unpredictability of the process started by acting does not arise out of another and possibly higher faculty, but is one of the potentialities of action itself. The possible redemption from the predicament of irreversibility—of being unable to undo what one has done though one did not, and could not, have known what he was doing—is the faculty of forgiving. The remedy for unpredictability, for the chaotic uncertainty of the future, is contained in the faculty to make and keep promises. The two faculties belong together in so far as one of them, forgiving, serves to undo the deeds of the past, whose "sins" hang like Damocles' sword over every new generation; and the other, binding oneself through promises, serves to set up in the ocean of uncertainty, which the future is by definition, islands of security without which not even continuity, let alone durability of any kind, would be possible in the relationships between men.

Without being forgiven, released from the consequences of what we have done, our capacity to act would, as it were, be confined to one single deed from which we could never recover; we would remain the victims of its consequences forever, not unlike the sorcerer's apprentice who lacked the magic formula to break the spell. Without being bound to the fulfilment of promises, we would never be able to keep our identities; we would be condemned to wander helplessly and without direction in the darkness of each man's lonely heart, caught in its contradictions and equivocalities—a darkness which only the light shed over the public realm through the presence of others, who confirm the identity between the one who promises and the one who fulfils, can dispel. Both faculties, therefore, depend on plurality, on the presence and acting of others, for no one can forgive himself and no one can feel bound by a promise made only to himself; forgiving and promising enacted in solitude or isolation remain without reality and can signify no more than a role played before one's self.

*   *   *

The discoverer of the role of forgiveness in the realm of human affairs was Jesus of Nazareth. The fact that he made this discovery in a religious context and articulated it in religious language is no reason to take it any less seriously in a strictly secular sense. It has been in the nature of our tradition of political thought (and for reasons we cannot explore here) to be highly selective and to exclude from articulate conceptualization a great variety of authentic political experiences, among which we need not be surprised to find some of an even elementary nature. Certain aspects of the teaching of Jesus of Nazareth which are not primarily related to the Christian religious message but sprang from experiences in the small and closely knit community of his followers, bent on challenging the public authorities in Israel, certainly belong among them, even though they have been neglected because of their allegedly exclusively religious nature. The only rudimentary sign of an awareness that forgiveness may be the necessary corrective for the inevitable damages resulting from action may be seen in the Roman principle to spare the vanquished (*parcere subiectis*) — a wisdom entirely unknown to the Greeks — or in the right to commute the death sentence, probably also of Roman origin, which is the prerogative of nearly all Western heads of state.

It is decisive in our context that Jesus maintains against the "scribes and pharisees" first that it is not true that only God has the power to forgive,[1] and second that this power does not derive from God — as though God, not men, would forgive through the medium of human beings — but on the contrary must be mobilized by men toward each other before they can hope to be forgiven by God also. Jesus' formulation is even more radical. Man in the gospel is not supposed to forgive because God forgives and he must do "likewise," but "if ye from your hearts forgive," God shall do "likewise."[2] The reason for the insistence on a duty to forgive is clearly "for they know not what they do" and it does not apply to the extremity of crime and willed evil, for then it would not have been necessary to teach: "And if he trespass against thee seven times a day, and seven times in a day turn again to thee, saying, I repent; thou shalt forgive him."[3] Crime and willed evil

1. This is stated emphatically in Luke 5:21–24 (cf. Matt. 9:4–6 or Mark 12:7–10), where Jesus performs a miracle to prove that "the Son of man hath power upon earth to forgive sins," the emphasis being on "upon earth." It is his insistence on the "power to forgive," even more than his performance of miracles, that shocks the people, so that "they that sat at meat with him began to say within themselves, Who is this that forgives sins also?" (Luke 7:49).
2. Matt. 18:35; cf. Mark 11:25; "And when ye stand praying, forgive, . . . that your Father also which is in heaven may forgive you your trespasses." Or: "If ye forgive men their trespasses, your heavenly Father will also forgive you: But if ye forgive not men their trespasses, neither will your Father forgive your trespasses" (Matt. 6:14–15). In all these instances, the power to forgive is primarily a human power: God forgives "us our debts, as we forgive our debtors."
3. Luke 17:3–4. It is important to keep in mind that the three key words of the text — *aphienai, metanoein,* and *hamartanein* — carry certain connotations even in New Testament Greek which the translations fail to render fully. The original meaning of *aphienai* is "dismiss" and "release" rather than

are rare, even rarer perhaps than good deeds; according to Jesus, they will be taken care of by God in the Last Judgment, which plays no role whatsoever in life on earth, and the Last Judgment is not characterized by forgiveness but by just retribution *(apodounai)*.[4] But trespassing is an everyday occurrence which is in the very nature of action's constant establishment of new relationships within a web of relations, and it needs forgiving, dismissing, in order to make it possible for life to go on by constantly releasing men from what they have done unknowingly.[5] Only through this constant mutual release from what they do can men remain free agents, only by constant willingness to change their minds and start again can they be trusted with so great a power as that to begin something new.

In this respect, forgiveness is the exact opposite of vengeance, which acts in the form of re-acting against an original trespassing, whereby far from putting an end to the consequences of the first misdeed, everybody remains bound to the process, permitting the chain reaction contained in every action to take its unhindered course. In contrast to revenge, which is the natural, automatic reaction to transgression and which because of the irreversibility of the action process can be expected and even calculated, the act of forgiving can never be predicted; it is the only reaction that acts in an unexpected way and thus retains, though being a reaction, something of the original character of action. Forgiving, in other words, is the only reaction which does not merely re-act but acts anew and unexpectedly, unconditioned by the act which provoked it and therefore freeing from its consequences both the one who forgives and the one who is forgiven. The freedom contained in Jesus' teachings of forgiveness is the freedom from vengeance, which incloses both doer and sufferer in the relentless automatism of the action process, which by itself need never come to an end.

"forgive"; *metanoein* means "change of mind" and—since it serves also to render the Hebrew *shuv*— "return," "trace back one's steps," rather than "repentance" with its psychological emotional overtones; what is required is: change your mind and "sin no more," which is almost the opposite of doing penance. *Hamartanein*, finally, is indeed very well rendered by "trespassing" in so far as it means rather "to miss," "fail and go astray," than "to sin" (see Heinrich Ebeling, *Griechisch-deutsches Wörterbuch zum Neuen Testamente* [1923]). The verse which I quote in the standard translation could also be rendered as follows: "And if he trespass against thee . . . and . . . turn again to thee, saying, I *changed my mind*; thou shalt *release* him."

4. Matt. 16:27.

5. This interpretation seems justified by the context (Luke 17:1–5): Jesus introduces his words by pointing to the inevitability of "offenses" *(skandala)* which are unforgivable, at least on earth; for "woe unto him, through whom they come! It were better for him that a millstone were hanged about his neck, and he cast into the sea"; and then continues by teaching forgiveness for "trespassing" *(hamartanein)*.

MOTHER TERESA OF CALCUTTA
(1910–   )

Since Mother Teresa founded her order, the Society of the Missionaries of Charity, in Calcutta's slums in 1948, she has worked to bring help and dignity to the poor and dying both in her adopted country, India, and in more than twenty-five other countries. *Life in the Spirit,* excerpted here, a collection of her reflections, meditations, and prayers, reflects her ministry of love, which has won her the admiration of people worldwide and recognition as Nobel Peace Prize laureate.

From *Life in the Spirit*

> *Inasmuch as ye have done it unto one of the least of these my brethren, ye have done it unto me.*

> MATT. 25–40

> *For I was an hungred, and ye gave me no meat:*
> *I was thirsty, and ye gave me no drink:*
> *I was a stranger, and ye took me not in:*
> *naked, and ye clothed me not:*
> *sick, and in prison, and ye visited me not.*

> MATT. 25.42–3

God has identified himself with the hungry, the sick, the naked, the homeless; hunger not only for bread, but for love, for care, to be somebody to someone; nakedness, not of clothing only, but nakedness of that compassion that very few people give to the unknown; homelessness, not only just for a shelter made of stone but that homelessness that comes from having no one to call your own.

Let each of us, as we have resolved to become a true child of God, a carrier of God's love, let us love others as God has loved each one of us, for Jesus has said love one another as I have loved you.

The spiritual poverty of the western world is much greater than the physical poverty of our people. You in the West have millions of people who suffer such terrible loneliness and emptiness. They feel unloved and unwanted.

These people are not hungry in the physical sense but they are in another way. They know they need something more than money, yet they don't know what it is. What they are missing really is a living relationship with God.

Today, the poor are hungry for bread and rice—and for love and the living word of God.

The poor are thirsty—for water and for peace, truth and justice.

The poor are homeless—for a shelter made of bricks, and for a joyful heart that understands, covers, loves.

The poor are naked—for clothes, for human dignity and compassion for the naked sinner.

They are sick—for medical care, and for that gentle touch and a warm smile.

The "shut-in," the unwanted, the unloved, the alcoholics, the dying destitutes, the abandoned and the lonely, the outcasts and the untouchables, the leprosy sufferers—all those who are a burden to human society—who have lost all hope and faith in life—who have forgotten how to smile—who have lost the sensibility of the warm hand-touch of love and friendship—they look to us for comfort. If we turn our back on them, we turn it on Christ, and at the hour of our death we shall be judged if we have recognized Christ in them, and on what we have done for and to them. There will only be two ways, "come" or "go."

Therefore, I appeal to every one of you—poor and rich, young and old—to give your own hands to serve Christ in his poor and your hearts to love him in them. They may be far or near, materially poor or spiritually poor, hungry for love and friendship, ignorant of the riches of the love of God for them, homeless for want of a home made of love in your heart; and since love begins at home maybe Christ is hungry, naked, sick or homeless in your own heart, in your family, in your neighbours, in the country you live in, in the world.

WHO ARE THE POOR?

The poor are the materially and the spiritually destitute
The poor are the hungry and the thirsty
The poor are those who need clothing
The poor are the homeless and the harbourless
The poor are the sick
The poor are the physically and mentally handicapped
The poor are the aged
The poor are those imprisoned
The poor are the lonely
The poor are the ignorant and the doubtful
The poor are the sorrowful
The poor are the comfortless
The poor are the helpless
The poor are the persecuted
The poor are those who suffer injustice
The poor are the ill-mannered
The poor are the bad-tempered
The poor are the sinners and the scoffers
The poor are those who do us wrong
The poor are the unwanted, the outcasts of society
The poor are somehow or other—we ourselves

TILLIE OLSEN
(1913–   )

Author of *Tell Me a Riddle, Yonnondio: From the Thirties*, and *Silences*, Tillie Olsen led the feminist retrieval of the writing of women from oblivion. Restoring *Life in the Iron Mills* by Rebecca Harding Davis to the canon of American literature, she inspired the Feminist Press to reprint such neglected writers as Agnes Smedley, Charlotte Perkins Gilman, Mary Wilkins Freeman, Meridel Le Sueur, Kate Chopin, Zora Neale Hurston, and Dorothy West. Olsen believes that women writers' renderings of ordinary and difficult lives produce a down-to-earth redemption. As she puts it in the following account of her mother's dying wisdom, the essential legacy is the understanding of "song, food, warmth, expressions of human love"; these are the experiential foundation of moral conscience and action. They are the roots of our "courage, hope, resistance, belief."

From *Mother to Daughter Daughter to Mother*

DREAM-VISION

In the winter of 1955, in her last weeks of life, my mother—so much of whose waking life had been a nightmare, that common everyday nightmare of hardship, limitation, longing; of baffling struggle to raise six children in a world hostile to human unfolding—my mother, dying of cancer, had beautiful dream-visions—in color.

Already beyond calendar time, she could not have known that the last dream she had breath to tell came to her on Christmas Eve. Nor, conscious, would she have named it so. As a girl in long ago Czarist Russia, she had sternly broken with all observances of organized religion, associating it with pogroms and wars; "mind forg'd manacles"; a repressive state. We did not observe religious holidays in her house.

Perhaps, in her last consciousness, she *did* know that the year was drawing towards that solstice time of the shortest light, the longest dark, the cruellest cold, when—as she had explained to us as children—poorly sheltered ancient peoples in northern climes had summoned their resources to make out of song, light, food, expressions of human love—festivals of courage, hope, warmth, belief.

It seemed to her that there was a knocking at her door. Even as she rose to open it, she guessed who would be there, for she heard the neighing of camels. (I did not say to her: "Ma, camels don't neigh.") Against the frosty lights of a far city she had never seen, "a city holy to three faiths," she said, the three wise men stood: magnificent in jewelled robes of crimson, of gold, of royal blue.

"Have you lost your way?" she asked, "Else, why do you come to me? I am not religious, I am not a believer."

"To talk with *you*, we came," the wise man whose skin was black and robe crimson, assured her, "to talk of whys, of wisdom."

"Come in then, come in and be warm—and welcome. I have starved for such talk."

But as they began to talk, she saw that they were not men, but women:
That they were not dressed in jewelled robes, but in the coarse everyday

shifts and shawls of the old country women of her childhood, their feet wrapped round and round with rags for lack of boots; snow now sifting into the room;

That their speech was not highflown, but homilies; their bodies not lordly in bearing, magnificent, but stunted, misshapen—used all their lives as a beast of burden is used;

That the camels were not camels, but farm beasts, such as were kept in the house all winter, their white cow breaths steaming into the cold.

And now it was many women, a babble.

One old woman, seamed and bent, began to sing. Swaying, the others joined her, their faces and voices transfiguring as they sang; my mother, through cracked lips, singing too—a lullaby.

For in the shining cloud of their breaths, a baby lay, breathing the universal sounds every human baby makes, sounds out of which are made all the separate languages of the world.

Singing, one by one the women cradled and sheltered the baby.

"The joy, the reason to believe," my mother said, "the hope for the world, the baby, holy with possibility, that is all of us at birth." And she began to cry, out of the dream and its telling now.

"Still I feel the baby in my arms, the human baby," crying now so I could scarcely make out the words, "the human baby, before we are misshapen; crucified into a sex, a color, a walk of life, a nationality . . . and the world yet warrings and winter."

I had seen my mother but three times in my adult life, separated as we were by the continent between, by lack of means, by jobs I had to keep and by the needs of my four children. She could scarcely write English—her only education in this country a few months of night school. When at last I flew to her, it was in the last days she had language at all. Too late to talk with her of what was in our hearts; or of harms and crucifying and strengths as she had known and experienced them; or of whys and knowledge, of wisdom. She died a few weeks later.

She, who had no worldly goods to leave, yet left to me an inexhaustible legacy. Inherent in it, this heritage of summoning resources to make—out of song, food, warmth, expressions of human love—courage, hope, resistance, belief; this vision of universality, before the lessenings, harms, divisions of the world are visited upon it.

She sheltered and carried that belief, that wisdom—as she sheltered and carried us, and others—throughout a lifetime lived in a world whose season was, as still it is, a time of winter.

ETTY HILLESUM
(1914–1943)

Born into a family of privileged Dutch Jews, Etty Hillesum lived in
Amsterdam and kept her journals from 1941 to 1943, the years of Nazi
occupation. Educated, sophisticated, independent, she writes as a
contemporary twenty-seven-year-old woman about her life, her love of
literature, of music, of an older man, of her friends. The diaries come
across as an adult version of Anne Frank's *Diary of a Young Girl.* As the
Nazi menace and the Holocaust became increasingly present amid the
transactions of daily life, the writer's voice changes from that of a
worldly, pleasure-loving young woman into a person confronting tragedy
and despair with a mystical intensity and compassion. The diary breaks
off in September 1943, on Hillesum's deportation to Auschwitz, where
she was murdered. D. M. Thomas described her diaries as "a testimony
of faith, hope, and love, written in hell itself."

From *An Interrupted Life: The Diaries of Etty Hillesum*

WEDNESDAY MORNING. I'm afraid I did not pray hard enough last night.
When I read S.'s note this morning something broke inside me and overwhelmed me. I was busy laying the breakfast table and suddenly I had to
stop in the middle of the room and fold my hands and bow my head, and
the tears that had been locked up inside me for so long welled up from my
heart.

It must sound odd, but these few faint, untidy pencil scrawls are the first
real love letter I have ever received. I have suitcases full of others, of the
so-called love letters men have written me in the past. Passionate and tender, pleading and demanding, so many words with which they tried to
warm themselves and me and so often it was all a flash in the pan.

But these words of his, yesterday, "Oh you, my heart is so heavy," and
this morning, "Dear one, I so want to go on praying." They are the most
precious presents ever laid before my spoilt heart.

EVENING. No, I don't think I shall perish. This afternoon a brief spell of so
much despair and sadness, not for everything that is happening but simply for myself. And the thought that I will have to leave S., not even grief
about the longing I shall feel for him but grief about the longing he will

feel for me. A few days ago I thought that nothing more could happen to me, that I had suffered everything in anticipation, but today I suddenly realised that things can indeed weigh more heavily on me than ever I thought possible. And they were very, very heavy. "I was unfaithful to You, God, but not entirely." It is good to have such moments of despair and of temporary extinction; continuous calm would be superhuman. But now I know again that I shall always get the better of despair. This afternoon I should not have thought it possible that, by this evening, I would be so calm again and so hard at work at my desk. But now my head is clearer than ever before. Tomorrow I must speak to S. at length about our fate and our attitude. I must!

The Rilke letters have come, those covering the years 1907–1914 and 1914–1921, I hope I shall be allowed to finish them. And the Schubert, too. Jopie brought them. . . .

When I pray, I never pray for myself, always for others, or else I hold a silly, naive or deadly serious dialogue with what is deepest inside me, which for the sake of convenience I call God. Praying to God for something for yourself strikes me as being too childish for words. Tomorrow I must ask S. if he ever prays for himself. To pray for another's wellbeing is something I find childish as well; one should only pray that another should have enough strength to shoulder his burden. If you do that, you lend him some of your own strength.

*   *   *

12.10.42. My impressions are scattered like glittering stars on the dark velvet of my memory.

The soul has a different age from that recorded in the register of births and deaths. At your birth, the soul already has an age that never changes. One can be born with a 12-year-old soul. One can also be born with a thousand-year-old soul . . . I believe the soul is that part of man that he is least aware of, particularly the West European, for I think that Orientals "live" their souls much more fully. We Westerners do not really know what to do with them; indeed we are ashamed of our souls as if they were something immoral. "Soul" is quite different from what we call "heart." There are plenty of people who have a lot of "heart" but very little soul.

Yesterday I asked Maria about somebody, "Is she intelligent?" "Yes," said Maria, "but only as far as her brains are concerned." S. always said of Tide, "She has an 'intelligent soul.' " Whenever S. and I spoke about the great difference in our ages he always said, "Who can tell whether your soul is not much older than mine?"

Sometimes it bursts into full flame within me, as it has just done again: all the friendship and all the people I have known this past year rise up in over-whelming number and fill me with gratitude. And though I am sick and anaemic and more or less bedridden, every minute seems so full and so precious—what will it be like when I am healthy once more? 'I rejoice and exult time and again, oh God: I am grateful to You for having given me this life.'

A soul is forged out of fire and rock crystal. Something rigorous, hard in an Old Testament sense, but also as gentle as the gesture with which his tender fingertips sometimes stroked my eyelashes.

*   *   *

Westerbork,* 18 August [1943]

Darling Tide,

I thought at first I would give my writing a miss today because I'm so ter-ribly tired and also because I thought I had nothing to say just now. But of course I have a great deal to write about. I shall allow my thoughts free rein; you are bound to pick them up anyway. This afternoon I was resting on my bunk and suddenly I just had to write these few words in my diary, and I now send them to you:

"You have made me so rich, oh God, please let me share out Your beauty with open hands. My life has become an uninterrupted dialogue with You, oh God, one great dialogue. Sometimes when I stand in some corner of the camp, my feet planted on Your earth, my eyes raised towards Your Heaven, tears sometimes run down my face, tears of deep emotion and gratitude. At night, too, when I lie in my bed and rest in You, oh God, tears of gratitude run down my face, and that is my prayer. I have been ter-ribly tired for several days, but that, too, will pass; things come and go in a deeper rhythm and people much be taught to listen to it, it is the most important thing we have to learn in this life. I am not challenging You, oh God, my life is one great dialogue with You. I may never become the great artist I would really like to be, but I am already secure in You, God. Some-times I try my hand at turning out small profundities and uncertain short stories, but I always end up with just one single word: God. And that says everything and there is no need for anything more. And all my creative pow-ers are translated into inner dialogues with You; the beat of my heart has grown deeper, more active and yet more peaceful, and it is as if I were all the time storing up inner riches."

Inexplicably, Jul has been floating above this heath of late. He teaches me something new every day. There are many miracles in a human life,

---

*A transit camp in the eastern Netherlands, the last stop before Auschwitz.

my own is one long sequence of inner miracles, and it's good to be able to say so again to somebody. Your photograph is in Rilke's *Book of Hours*, next to Jul's photograph, they lie under my pillow together with my small Bible. Your letter with the quotations has also arrived. Keep writing, please, and fare you well, my dear.

Etty

NATALIA GINZBURG
(1916–1991)

The child of socialist parents, Natalia Ginzburg and her first husband lived in forced residence under Fascist rule in the Abruzzi during World War II. Her husband, an anti-Fascist activist, was murdered in 1944 after being tortured in a Nazi prison. Ginzburg became Italy's most important postwar woman writer, compared in stature with Alberto Moravia and the late Italo Calvino. Her books include *Family Sayings*, *The Road to the City*, and *All Our Yesterdays*. She was also a member of the Italian Parliament and a translator of Proust and Flaubert. To all the essays in *The Little Virtues*, but especially the title one, which follows here, she brings the wisdom of a courageous conviction and the authoritative simplicity of a great literary intelligence.

The Little Virtues

As far as the education of children is concerned I think they should be taught not the little virtues but the great ones. Not thrift but generosity and an indifference to money; not caution but courage and a contempt for danger; not shrewdness but frankness and a love of truth; not tact but love for one's neighbour and self-denial; not a desire for success but a desire to be and to know.

Usually we do just the opposite; we rush to teach them a respect for the little virtues, on which we build our whole system of education. In doing this we are choosing the easiest way, because the little virtues do not involve any actual dangers, indeed they provide shelter from Fortune's blows. We do not bother to teach the great virtues, though we love them and want our children to have them; but we nourish the hope that they will spontaneously appear in their consciousness some day in the future, we think of them as being part of our instinctive nature, while the others, the little virtues, seem to be the result of reflection and calculation and so we think that they absolutely must be taught.

In reality the difference is only an apparent one. The little virtues also arise from our deepest instincts, from a defensive instinct; but in them reason speaks, holds forth, displays its arguments as the brilliant advocate of self-preservation. The great virtues well up from an instinct in which reason does not speak, an instinct that seems to be difficult to name. And the best of us is in that silent instinct, and not in our defensive instinct which harangues, holds forth and displays its arguments with reason's voice.

Education is only a certain relationship which we establish between ourselves and our children, a certain climate in which feelings, instincts and thoughts can flourish. Now I believe that a climate which is completely pervaded by a respect for the little virtues will, insensibly, lead to cynicism or to a fear of life. In themselves the little virtues have nothing to do with cynicism or a fear of life, but taken together, and without the great virtues, they produce an atmosphere that leads to these consequences. Not that the little virtues are in themselves contemptible; but their value is of a complementary and not of a substantial kind; they cannot stand by themselves without the others, and by themselves and without the others they provide but meagre fare for human nature. By looking around himself a man can find out how to use the little virtues—moderately and when they are necessary—he can drink them in from the air, because the little virtues are of a kind that is common among men. But one cannot breathe in the great virtues from the surrounding air, and they should be the basis of our relationship with our children, the first foundation of their education. Besides, the great can also contain the little, but by the laws of nature there is no way that the little can contain the great.

In our relationships with our children it is no use our trying to remember and imitate the way our parents acted with us. The time of our youth and childhood was not one of little virtues; it was a time of strong and sonorous words that little by little lost all their substance. The present is a time of cold, submissive words beneath which a desire for reassertion is perhaps coming to the surface. But it is a timid desire that is afraid of ridicule. And so we hide behind caution and shrewdness. Our parents knew neither caution nor shrewdness and they didn't know the fear of ridicule either: they were illogical and incoherent but they never realized this; they constantly contradicted themselves but they never allowed anyone to contradict them. They were authoritarian towards us in a way that we are quite incapable of being. Strong in their principles, which they believed to be indestructible, they reigned over us with absolute power. They deafened us with their thunderous words: a dialogue was impossible because as soon as they suspected that they were wrong they ordered us to be quiet: they beat their fists on the table and made the room shake. We remember that gesture but we cannot copy it. We can fly into a rage and howl like wolves, but deep in our wolf's howl there lies a hysterical sob, the hoarse bleating of a lamb.

And so we have no authority; we have no weapons. Authority in us would be a hypocrisy and a sham. We are too aware of our own weakness, too melancholy and insecure, too conscious of our illogicality and incoherence, too conscious of our faults; we have looked within ourselves for too long and seen too many things there. And so as we don't have authority we must invent another kind of relationship.

In these days, when a dialogue between parents and their children has become possible — possible though always difficult, always complicated by mutual prejudices, bashfulness, inhibitions — it is necessary that in this dialogue we show ourselves for what we are, imperfect, in the hope that our children will not resemble us but be stronger and better than us.

As we are all moved in one way or another by the problem of money, the first little virtue that it enters our heads to teach our children is thrift. We give them a moneybox and explain to them what a fine thing it is to save money instead of spending it, so that after a few months there will be lots of money, a nice little hoard of it; and how good it is not to give in to the wish to spend money so that in the end we can buy something really special. We remember that when we were children we were given a similar moneybox; but we forget that money, and a liking for saving it, were much less horrible and disgusting things when we were children than they are today; because the more time passes the more disgusting money becomes. And so the moneybox is our first mistake. We have installed a little virtue into our system of education.

That innocent-looking moneybox made of earthenware, in the shape of a pear or an apple, stays month after month in our children's room and they become used to its presence; they become used to the money saved inside it, money which in the dark and in secret grows like a seed in the womb of the earth; they like the money, at first innocently, as we like anything — plants and little animals for example — that grows because we take care of it; and all the time they long for that expensive something they saw in a shop window and which they will be able to buy, as we have explained to them, with the money they have saved up. When at last the moneybox is smashed and the money is spent, the children feel lonely and disappointed; there is no longer any money in their room, saved in the belly of the apple, and there isn't even the rosy apple any more; instead there is something longed for from a shop window, something whose importance and price we have made a great fuss about, but which, now that it is in their room, seems dull and plain and ordinary after so much waiting and so much money. The children do not blame money for this disappointment, but the object they have bought; because the money they have lost keeps all its alluring promise in their memories. The children ask for a new moneybox and for more money to save, and they give their thoughts and attention to money in a way that is harmful to them. They prefer money to things. It is not bad that they have suffered a disappointment; it is bad that they feel lonely without the company of money.

We should not teach them to save, we should accustom them to spending money. We should often give children a little money, small sums of no importance, and encourage them to spend it immediately and as they wish, to follow some momentary whim; the children will buy some small rubbishy toy which they will immediately forget as they will immediately forget money spent so quickly and thoughtlessly, and for which they have no liking. When they find the little rubbishy toy—which will soon break—in their hands they will be a bit disappointed but they will quickly forget the disappointment, the rubbishy toy and the money; in fact they will associate money with something momentary and silly, and they will think that money is silly, as it is right that they should think whilst they are children.

It is right that in the first years of their life children should live in ignorance of what money is. Sometimes this is impossible, if we are very poor; and sometimes it is difficult because we are very rich. All the same when we are very poor and money is strictly a matter of daily survival, a question of life or death, then it turns itself before the baby's eyes into food, coal or blankets so quickly that it is unable to harm his spirit. But if we are so-so, neither rich nor poor, it is not difficult to let a child live during its infancy unaware of what money is and unconcerned about it. And yet it is necessary, not too soon and not too late, to shatter this ignorance; and if we have economic difficulties it is necessary that our children, not too soon and not too late, become aware of this, just as it is right that they will at a certain point share our worries with us, the reasons for our happiness, our plans and everything that concerns the family's life together. And we should get them used to considering the family's money as something that belongs to us and to them equally, and not to us rather than to them; or on the other hand we can encourage them to be moderate and careful with the money they spend, and in this way the encouragement to be thrifty is no longer respect for a little virtue, it is not an abstract encouragement to respect something which is in itself not worth our respect, like money, rather it is a way of reminding the children that there isn't a lot of money in the house; it encourages them to think of themselves as adult and responsible for something that involves us as much as them, not something particularly beautiful or pleasant but serious, because it is connected with our daily needs.

But not too soon and not too late; the secret of education lies in choosing the right time to do things.

Being moderate with oneself and generous with others; this is what is meant by having a just relationship with money, by being free as far as money is concerned. And there is no doubt that it is less difficult to educate a child so that he has such a sense of proportion, such a freedom, in a family in which money is earned and immediately spent, in which it flows like clear spring water and practically does not exist as money. Things become complicated where money exists and exists heavily, where it is a leaden stagnant pool that stinks and gives off vapours. The children are soon aware of the presence of this money in the family, this hidden power which no one ever mentions openly but to which the parents refer by means of complicated and mysterious names when they are talking among themselves with a leaden stillness in their eyes and a bitter curl to their lips; money which is not simply kept in a desk drawer but which accumulates who knows where and which can at any moment be sucked back into the earth, disappearing for ever and swallowing up both house and family. In families like this the children are constantly told to spend money grudgingly, every day the mother tells them to be careful and thrifty as she gives them a few coins for their tram fare; in their mother's gaze there is that leaden preoccupation and on her forehead there is that deep wrinkle which appears whenever money is discussed; there is the obscure fear that all the money will dissolve into nothing and that even those few coins might signify the first dust of a mortal and sudden collapse. The children in families like this often go to school in threadbare clothes and worn-out shoes and they have to pine for a long time, and sometimes in vain, for a bicycle or a camera, things which some of their friends who are certainly poorer than they are have had for quite a while. And then when they are given the bicycle they want the present is accompanied by severe orders not to damage it, not to lend such a magnificent object—which has cost a great deal of money—to anyone. In such a house admonitions to save money are constant and insistent—school books are usually bought second-hand, and exercise books at a cheap supermarket. This happens partly because the rich are often mean, and because they think they are poor, but above all because mothers in rich families are—more or less subconsciously—afraid of the consequences of money and try to protect their children by surrounding them with the lie of simple habits, even making them grow accustomed to little instances of privation. But there is no worse error than to make a child live in such a contradiction; everywhere in the house money talks its unmistakeable language; it is there in the china, in the furniture, in the heavy silverware, it is there in the comfortable journeys, in the luxurious summer holidays, in the doorman's greeting, in the servants' rituals; it is there in his parents' conversation, it is the wrinkle on his father's forehead, the leaden perplexity in his mother's gaze; money is everywhere, untouchable perhaps because it is so fragile, it is something he is not allowed to joke about, a sombre god to whom he can only turn in a whisper, and to honour this god, so as not to disturb its mournful immobility, he has to wear last year's overcoat that has got too small, learn his lessons from books that are in tatters and falling to pieces, and amuse himself with a country bumpkin's bicycle.

If we are rich and want to educate our children so that they have simple habits it must in that case be made very clear that all the money saved by following such simple habits is to be spent, without any hint of meanness, on other people. Such habits mean only that they are not greed or fear but a simplicity that has—in the midst of wealth—been freely chosen. A child from a rich family will not learn moderation because they have made him wear old clothes, or because they have made him eat a green apple for tea, or because they deny him a bicycle he has wanted for a long time; such moderation in the midst of wealth is pure fiction, and fictions always lead to bad habits. In this way he will only learn to be greedy and afraid of money. If we deny him a bicycle which he wants and which we could buy him we only prevent him from having something that it is reasonable a boy should have, we only make his childhood less happy in the name of an abstract principle and without any real justification. And we are tacitly saying to him that money is better than a bicycle; on the contrary he should learn that a bicycle is always better than money.

The true defence against wealth is not a fear of wealth—of its fragility and of the vicious consequences that it can bring—the true defence against wealth is an indifference to money. There is no better way to teach a child this indifference than to give him money to spend when there is money—because then he will learn to part with it without worrying about it or regretting it. But, it will be said, then the child will be used to having money and will not be able to do without it; if tomorrow he is not rich, what is he to do? But it is easier not to have money once we have learnt to spend it, once we have learnt how quickly it runs through our hands; and it is easier to learn to do without money when we are thoroughly familiar with it than when we have paid it the homage of our reverence and fear throughout our childhood, than when we have sensed its presence all around us and not been allowed to raise our eyes and look it in the face.

As soon as our children begin to go to school we promise them money as a reward if they do well in their lessons. This is a mistake. In this way we mix money—which is an ignoble thing—with learning and the pleasures of knowledge, which are admirable and worthy things. The money we give our children should be given for no reason; it should be given indifferently so that they will learn to receive it indifferently; but it should be given not so that they learn to love it, but so that they learn not to love it, so that they realize its true nature and its inability to satisfy our truest desires, which are those of the spirit. When we elevate money into a prize, a goal, an object to be striven for, we give it a position, an importance, a nobility, which it should not have in our children's eyes. We implicitly affirm the principle—a false one—that money is the crowning reward for work, its ultimate objective. Money should be thought of as a wage for work, not its ultimate objective but its wage—that is, its legitimate recognition; and it is clear that the scholastic work of children cannot have a wage. It is a small mistake—but a mistake—to offer our children money in return for domestic services, for doing little chores. It is a mistake because we are not our children's employers; the family's money is as much theirs as it is ours; those little services and chores should be done without reward, as a voluntary sharing in the family's life. And in general I think we should be very cautious about promising and providing rewards and punishments. Because life rarely has its rewards and punishments; usually sacrifices have no reward, and often evil deeds go unpunished, at times they are even richly rewarded with success and money. Therefore it is best that our children should know from infancy that good is not rewarded and that evil goes unpunished; yet they must love good and hate evil, and it is not possible to give any logical explanation for this.

We usually give a quite unwarranted importance to our children's scholastic performance. And this is nothing but a respect for the little virtue "success." It should be enough for us that they do not lag too far behind the others, that they do not fail their exams; but we are not content with this; we want success from them, we want them to satisfy our pride. If they do badly at school or simply not as well as we would wish, we immediately raise a barrier of nagging dissatisfaction between us and them; when we speak to them we assume the sulky, whining tone of someone complaining about an insult. And then our children become bored and distance themselves from us. Or we support them in their complaints that the teachers have not understood them and we pose as victims with them. And every day we correct their homework, and study their lessons with them. In fact school should be from the beginning the first battle which a child fights for himself, without us; from the beginning it should be clear that this is his battlefield and that we can give him only very slight and occasional help there. And if he suffers from injustice there or is misunderstood it is necessary to let him see that there is nothing strange about this, because in life we have to expect to be constantly misunderstood and misinterpreted, and to be victims of injustice; and the only thing that matters is that we do not commit injustices ourselves. We share the successes and failures of our children because we love them, but just as much and in the same way that they, little by little as they grow up, share our successes and failures, our joys and anxieties. It is not true that they have a duty to do well at school for our sake and to give the best of their skills to studying. Once we have started them in their lessons, their duty is simply to go forward. If they wish to spend the best of their skills on things outside school—collecting Coleoptera or learning Turkish—that is their business and we have no right to reproach them, or to show that our pride has been hurt or that we feel dissatisfied with them. If at the moment the best of their skills do not seem to be applied to anything, then we do not have the right to shout at them very much in that case either; who knows, perhaps what seems laziness to us is really a kind of daydreaming and thoughtfulness that will bear fruit tomorrow. If it seems they are wasting the best of their energies and skills lying on the sofa reading ridiculous novels or charging around a football pitch, then again we cannot know whether this is really a waste of energy and skill or whether tomorrow this too will bear fruit in some way that we have not yet suspected. Because there are an infinite number of possibilities open to the spirit. But we, the parents, must not let ourselves be seized by a terror of failure. Our remonstrances must be like a squall of wind or a sudden storm—violent, but quickly forgotten—and not anything that could upset the nature of our relationship with our children, that could muddy its clarity and peace. We are there to console our children if they are hurt by failure; we are there to give them courage if they are humiliated by failure. We are also there to bring them down a peg or two when success has made them too pleased with themselves. We are there to reduce school to its narrow, humble limits; it is not something that can mortgage their future, it is simply a display of offered tools, from which it is perhaps possible to choose one which will be useful tomorrow.

What we must remember above all in the education of our children is that their love of life should never weaken. This love can take different forms, and sometimes a listless, solitary, bashful child is not lacking in a love of life, he is not overwhelmed by a fear of life, he is simply in a state of expectancy, intent on preparing himself for his vocation. And what is a human being's vocation but the highest expression of his love of life? And so we must wait, next to him, while his vocation awakens and takes shape. His behaviour can be like that of a mole, or of a lizard that holds itself still and pretends to be dead but in reality it has detected the insect that is its prey and is watching its movements, and then suddenly springs forward. Next to him, but in silence and a little aloof from him, we must wait for this leap of his spirit. We should not demand anything; we should not ask or hope that he is a genius or an artist or a hero or a saint; and yet we must be ready for everything; our waiting and our patience must compass both the possibility of the highest and the most ordinary of fates.

A vocation, an ardent and exclusive passion for something in which there is no prospect of money, the consciousness of being able to do something better than others, and being able to love this thing more than anything else—this is the only, the unique way in which a rich child can completely escape being conditioned by money, so that he is free of its claims; so that he feels neither the pride nor the shame of wealth when he is with others. He will not even be conscious of what clothes he is wearing, or of the clothes around him, and tomorrow he will be equal to any privation because the one hunger and thirst within him will be his own passion which will have devoured everything futile and provisional and divested him of every habit learnt in childhood, and which alone will rule his spirit. A vocation is man's one true wealth and salvation.

What chance do we have of awakening and stimulating in our children the birth and development of a vocation? We do not have much; however there is one way open to us. The birth and development of a vocation needs space, space and silence, the free silence of space. Our relationship with our children should be a living exchange of thoughts and feelings, but it should also include deep areas of silence: it should be an intimate relationship but it must not violently intrude on their privacy; it should be a just balance between silence and words. We must be important to our children and yet not too important; they must like us a little, and yet not like us too much—so that it does not enter their heads to become identical to us, to copy us and the vocation we follow, to seek our likeness in the friends they choose throughout their lives. We must have a friendly relationship with them, and yet we must not be too friendly with them otherwise it will be difficult for them to have real friends with whom they can discuss things they do not mention to us. It is necessary that their search for friends, their love-life, their religious life, their search for a vocation, be surrounded by silence and shadows, so that they can develop separately from us. But then, it will be said, our intimacy with our children has been reduced to very little. But in our relationships with them all these things—their religious life, their intellectual life, their emotional life, their judgement of other human beings—should be included as it were in summary form; for them we should be a simple point of departure, we should offer them the springboard from which they make their leap. And we must be there to help them, if help should be necessary; they must realize that they do not belong to us, but that we belong to them, that we are always available, present in the next room, ready to answer every possible question and demand as far as we know how to.

And if we ourselves have a vocation, if we have not betrayed it, if over the years we have continued to love it, to serve it passionately, we are able to keep all sense of ownership out of our love for our children. But if on the other hand we do not have a vocation, or if we have abandoned it or betrayed it out of cynicism or a fear of life, or because of mistaken parental love, or because of some little virtue that exists within us, then we cling to our children as a shipwrecked mariner clings to a tree trunk; we eagerly demand that they give us back everything we have given them, that they be absolutely and inescapably what we wish them to be, that they get out of life everything we have missed; we end up asking them for all the things which can only be given to us by our own vocation; we want them to be entirely our creation, as if having once created them we could continue to create them throughout their whole lives. We want them to be entirely our creation, as if we were not dealing with human beings but with products of the spirit. But if we have a vocation, if we have not denied or betrayed it, then we can let them develop quietly and away from us, surrounded by the shadows and space that the development of a vocation, the development of an existence, needs. This is perhaps the one real chance we have of giving them some kind of help in their search, for a vocation—to have a vocation ourselves, to know it, to love it and serve it passionately; because love of life begets a love of life.

MADELEINE L'ENGLE
(1918–   )

Author of the classic of children's literature *A Wrinkle in Time* (1962), Madeleine L'Engle displays the spiritual foundations of her prolific imagination in the autobiographical trilogy entitled *The Crosswicks Journal: A Circle of Quiet* (1972), *The Summer of the Great-Grandmother* (1974), and *The Irrational Season* (1977). The title of the first volume, from which the following passage is taken, refers to her favorite brookside place of retreat and meditation on the property of Crosswicks, her Connecticut country home. There she confides to her journal the poetry of the ordinary as she contemplates the epiphanies of her everyday life as writer, mother, friend, wife, neighbor.

From A *Circle of Quiet*

A self is not something static, tied up in a pretty parcel and handed to the child, finished and complete. A self is always becoming. *Being* does mean becoming, but we run so fast that it is only when we seem to stop—as sitting on the rock at the brook—that we are aware of our own *isness*, of being.

But certainly this is not static, for this awareness of being is always a way of moving from the selfish self—the self-image—and towards the real.

Who am I, then? Who are you?

*   *   *

We hadn't spent more than one winter at Crosswicks when I found myself the choir director in the village church. I had no qualifications as choir director beyond a passionate love of music, and I knew nothing about church music; in fact, since the crisis in faith (more jargon) that so often comes during college, I had seldom darkened the doors of a church when a service was going on. Neither had my husband.

But when our children were born, two things happened simultaneously. We cleaned up our language; we had been careless about four-letter words—I'd been rather proud of those I'd picked up from stage hands; we no longer used them indiscriminately. And we discovered that we did not want our children to grow up in a world which was centered on man to the exclusion of God. We did know that bedtime prayers were not enough and that it made no sense whatsoever to send the children to Sunday School unless we went to church ourselves. The inconsistency of parents who use the church as a free baby-sitting service on Sunday mornings, while they stay home and read the Sunday papers, did not have to be pointed out to us. I found myself earnestly explaining to the young minister that I did not believe in God, "but I've discovered that I can't live as though I didn't believe in him. As long as I don't need to say any more than that I try to live as though I believe in God, I would very much like to come to church—if you'll let me."

So I became the choir director. Grandma was the organist and she had been the organist since she started playing for Sunday School when she was eleven years old, and she was, when we first knew her, up in her eighties. She had had a large family, and in all those years had missed only two Sundays. Hugh and I visualized Grandma rushing through the last hymn just in time to go have her baby so she could be back in church the following Sunday.

Grandma and I loved each other. She had been distressed because the church had been for so long without a choir, and would bring in occasional soloists. But the standard of music was low, what I called "Blood of the lamb-y." When I was asked to get together a group of people in the village who might like to sing on a few Sundays during the year, I replied, "No, but I'll start a choir, if you like. And we'll sing every Sunday. Summer, too. God doesn't take the summer off, and if we have a choir, neither will we." I might not believe in God, but I knew that much about him.

The choir was completely volunteer, and completely ecumenical. Before ecumenism was "in," we had Episcopalian, Lutheran, Presbyterian, Dutch Reform, Methodist, and Southern Baptist choristers, and all in the Congregational Church. Musically, I was certainly Episcopalian. It was the church into which I was born, and my father loved good church music. In New York as a child I was taken to church much as I was taken to the opera.

I wanted the choir to be good. I wanted us to sing good music, and to be a success. Some of the volunteer singers had beautiful voices; one had a great one. Some of them couldn't stay in tune and pulled the whole group down into a flat, sodden mass. One woman stayed in key, all right, but at full volume at all times, and with an unpleasant, nasal whine. If the choir was to be a success, the obvious first thing to do was to ease out some of the problem voices.

I couldn't do it. I don't know why, but something told me that every single person in that choir was more important than the music. "But the music is going to be terrible," I wailed to this invisible voice. "That doesn't matter. That's not the reason for this choir." I didn't ask what was, but struggled along. The extraordinary, lovely thing was that the music got to be pretty good, far better, I am now convinced, than it would have been if I'd put the music first and the people second. I suppose, long before I'd heard the word, I was being ontological.

I did have subversive means of getting my own way about what music we sang. I'd bring out something I loved, Palestrina, for instance, and everybody would groan, so I'd put it away. A couple of weeks later I'd bring it out again, and someone would remark, "That's kind of nice." "I'm afraid it's too difficult for us," I'd say, and put it away again. Two more weeks, and out it would come, and someone would exclaim, "That's beautiful! Can we learn that?" And we did, and everybody loved it. I, in my turn, learned to love some of the music I had felt "above."

As the choir developed, choice of music became limited by only one factor: Grandma, growing older, could no longer play in sharps. I felt great sympathy with her in this. Flats are lots easier than sharps for me, too. At first she could play in three sharps, then two, and finally none. Quinn, our young minister, would select hymns which fitted well with his sermon, and I'd have to say, "Sorry, Quinn, you can't have that; it's in four sharps."

And Grandma preferred major to minor. But, because we loved each other, that was no problem. I'd put my arm about her tiny, bowed little back (her legs could barely stretch to reach the organ pedals) and say, "Grandma, will you let us sing this, please? I know it's minor, but we've done major anthems for three weeks, and I love this one." "All right, Madeleine. For you." I don't think Grandma ever liked the minor anthems, but she played them most graciously.

Grandma and the choir taught me something about persons, how to be a self myself, and how to honor the self in others.

*   *   *

One evening I went to choir rehearsal; in the morning's mail had been a rejection slip. The choir was singing well, and I went to the back of the church to listen to the anthem and see if the voices were balanced, and caught myself thinking bitterly, "Is this all I'm good for? to direct a second-rate choir in a village church?"

I was in that area of despair where one is incapable of being ontological. In my definition of the word, this is sin.

IRIS MURDOCH
(1919–   )

Philosopher and novelist Iris Murdoch, Dublin-born, grew up in England, the only child of Irish Protestants. She cites Plato as the major influence on her thought. "Plato is king," she told BBC interviewer Rosemary Hartill. "He set up the first great philosophical picture of the human soul." Often her novels (twenty-three as of 1989) explore Christian themes infused with Platonism: the search for goodness in a fallen world; selfishness versus unselfishness; human life as a pilgrimage through a world of false images to the discovery of a higher spiritual truth. Literature thus conceived she considers religious. Dramatizing the purification and enlargement of the soul, it affirms the sense of another dimension. The following excerpt from *The Sovereignty of Good* (1970) elaborates on her belief that religion is about the death of the ego, about the stripping away of illusions to reveal truth, a perspective she considers consistent with Buddhism. Though she describes herself as a Christian, Murdoch is interested in the "demythologisation" of theology and in religion that has to do with "a reverence for what is holy and good."

From *The Sovereignty of Good*

What is a good man like? How can we make ourselves morally better? *Can* we make ourselves morally better? These are questions the philosopher should try to answer. We realize on reflection that we know little about good men. There are men in history who are traditionally thought of as having been good (Christ, Socrates, certain saints), but if we try to contemplate these men we find that the information about them is scanty and vague, and that, their great moments apart, it is the simplicity and directness of their diction which chiefly colours our conception of them as good. And if we consider contemporary candidates for goodness, if we know of any, we are likely to find them obscure, or else on closer inspection full of frailty. Goodness appears to be both rare and hard to picture. It is perhaps most convincingly met with in simple people—inarticulate, unselfish mothers of large families—but these cases are also the least illuminating.

*   *   *

If, still led by the clue of art, we ask further questions about the faculty which is supposed to relate us to what is real and thus bring us to what is good, the idea of compassion or love will be naturally suggested. It is not simply that suppression of self is required before accurate vision can be obtained. The great artist sees his objects (and this is true whether they are sad, absurd, repulsive or even evil) in a light of justice and mercy. The direction of attention is, contrary to nature, outward, away from self which reduces all to a false unity, towards the great surprising variety of the world, and the ability so to direct attention is love.

One might at this point pause and consider the picture of human personality, or the soul, which has been emerging. It is in the capacity to love, that is to *see*, that the liberation of the soul from fantasy consists. The freedom which is a proper human goal is the freedom from fantasy, that is the realism of compassion. What I have called fantasy, the proliferation of blinding self-centred aims and images, is itself a powerful system of energy, and most of what is often called "will" or "willing" belongs to this system. What counteracts the system is attention to reality inspired by, consisting of, love. In the case of art and nature such attention is immediately rewarded by the enjoyment of beauty. In the case of morality, although there are sometimes rewards, the idea of a reward is out of place. Freedom is not strictly the exercise of the will, but rather the experience of accurate vision which, when this becomes appropriate, occasions action. It is what lies behind and in between actions and prompts them that is important, and it is this area which should be purified. By the time the moment of choice has arrived the quality of attention has probably determined the nature of the act. This fact produces that curious separation between consciously rehearsed motives and action which is sometimes wrongly taken as an experience of freedom. . . .

A genuine mysteriousness attaches to the idea of goodness and the Good. This is a mystery with several aspects. The indefinability of Good is connected with the unsystematic and inexhaustible variety of the world and the pointlessness of virtue. In this respect there is a special link between the concept of Good and the ideas of Death and Chance. (One might say that Chance is really a subdivision of Death. It is certainly our most effective *memento mori*.) A genuine sense of mortality enables us to see virtue as the only thing of worth; and it is impossible to limit and foresee the ways in which it will be required of us. That we cannot dominate the world may be put in a more positive way. Good is mysterious because of human frailty, because of the immense distance which is involved. If there were angels they might be able to define good but we would not understand the definition. We are largely mechanical creatures, the slaves of relentlessly strong selfish forces the nature of which we scarcely comprehend. At best, as decent persons, we are usually very specialized. We behave well in areas where this can be done fairly easily and let other areas of possible virtue remain undeveloped. There are perhaps in the case of every human being insuperable psychological barriers to goodness. The self is a divided thing and the whole of it cannot be redeemed any more than it can be known. And if we look outside the self what we see are scattered intimations of Good. There are few places where virtue plainly shines: great art, humble people who serve others. And can we, without improving ourselves, really see these things clearly? It is in the context of such limitations that we should picture our freedom. Freedom is, I think, a mixed concept. The true half of it is simply a name of an aspect of virtue concerned especially with the clarification of vision and the domination of selfish impulse. The false and more popular half is a name for the self-assertive movements of deluded selfish will which because of our ignorance we take to be something autonomous.

We cannot then sum up human excellence for these reasons: the world is aimless, chancy, and huge, and we are blinded by self. There is a third consideration which is a relation of the other two. It is *difficult* to look at the sun: it is not like looking at other things. We somehow retain the idea, and art both expresses and symbolizes it, that the lines really do converge. There is a magnetic centre. But it is easier to look at the converging edges than to look at the centre itself. We do not and probably cannot know, conceptualize, what it is like in the centre. It may be said that since we cannot see anything there why try to look? And is there not a danger of damaging our ability to focus on the sides? I think there is a sense in trying to look, though the occupation is perilous for reasons connected with masochism and other obscure devices of the psyche. The impulse to worship is deep and ambiguous and old. There are false suns, easier to gaze upon and far more comforting than the true one.

Plato has given us the image of this deluded worship in his great allegory. The prisoners in the cave at first face the back wall. Behind them a fire is burning in the light of which they see upon the wall the shadows of puppets which are carried between them and the fire and they take these shadows to be the whole of reality. When they turn round they can see the fire, which they have to pass in order to get out of the cave. The fire, I take it, represents the self, the old unregenerate psyche, that great source of energy and warmth. The prisoners in the second stage of enlightenment have gained the kind of self-awareness which is nowadays a matter of so much interest to us. They can see in themselves the sources of what was formerly blind selfish instinct. They see the flames which threw the shadows which they used to think were real, and they can see the puppets, imitations of things in the real world, whose shadows they used to recognize. They do not yet dream that there is anything else to see. What is more likely than that they should settle down beside the fire, which though its form is flickering and unclear is quite easy to look at and cosy to sit by?

I think Kant was afraid of this when he went to such lengths to draw our attention away from the empirical psyche. This powerful thing is indeed an object of fascination, and those who study its power to cast shadows are studying something which is real. A recognition of its power may be a step towards escape from the cave; but it may equally be taken as an end-point. The fire may be mistaken for the sun, and self-scrutiny taken for goodness. (Of course not everyone who escapes from the cave need have spent much time by the fire. Perhaps the virtuous peasant has got out of the cave without even noticing the fire.) Any religion or ideology can be degraded by the substitution of self, usually in some disguise, for the true object of veneration. However, in spite of what Kant was so much afraid of I think there is a place both inside and outside religion for a sort of contemplation of the Good, not just by dedicated experts but by ordinary people: an attention which is not just the planning of particular good actions but an attempt to look right away from self towards a distant transcendent perfection, a source of uncontaminated energy, a source of *new* and quite undreamt-of virtue. This attempt, which is a turning of attention away from the particular, may be the thing that helps most when difficulties seem insoluble, and especially when feelings of guilt keep attracting the gaze back towards the self. This is the true mysticism which is morality, a kind of undogmatic prayer which is real and important, though perhaps also difficult and easily corrupted.

I have been speaking of the indefinability of the Good; but is there really nothing else that we can say about it? Even if we cannot find it another name, even if it must be thought of as above and alone, are there not other concepts, or another concept, with which it has some quite special relation? Philosophers have often tried to discern such a relationship: Freedom, Reason, Happiness, Courage, History have recently been tried in the role. I do not find any of these candidates convincing. They seem to represent in each case the philosopher's admiration for some specialized aspect of human conduct which is much less than the whole of excellence and sometimes dubious in itself. I have already mentioned a concept with a certain claim and I will return to that in conclusion. I want now to speak of what is perhaps the most obvious as well as the most ancient and traditional claimant, though one which is rarely mentioned by our contemporary philosophers, and that is Love. Of course Good is sovereign over Love, as it is sovereign over other concepts, because Love can name something bad. But is there not nevertheless something about the conception of a refined love which is practically identical with goodness? Will not "Act lovingly" translate "Act perfectly," whereas "Act rationally" will not? It is tempting to say so.

However I think that Good and Love should not be identified, and not only because human love is usually self-assertive. The concepts, even when the idea of love is purified, still play different roles. We are dealing here with very difficult metaphors. Good is the magnetic centre towards which love naturally moves. False love moves to false good. False love embraces false death. When true good is loved, even impurely or by accident, the quality of the love is automatically refined, and when the soul is turned towards Good the highest part of the soul is enlivened. Love is the tension between the imperfect soul and the magnetic perfection which is conceived of as lying beyond it. (In the *Symposium* Plato pictures Love as being poor and needy.) And when we try perfectly to love what is imperfect our love goes to its object *via* the Good to be thus purified and made unselfish and just. The mother loving the retarded child or loving the tiresome elderly relation. Love is the general name of the quality of attachment and it is capable of infinite degradation and is the source of our greatest errors; but when it is even partially refined it is the energy and passion of the soul in its search for Good, the force that joins us to Good and joins us to the world through Good. Its existence is the unmistakable sign that we are spiritual creatures, attracted by excellence and made for the Good. It is a reflection of the warmth and light of the sun.

Perhaps the finding of other names for Good or the establishing of special relationships cannot be more than a sort of personal game. However I want in conclusion to make just one more move. Goodness is connected with the acceptance of real death and real chance and real transience and only against the background of this acceptance, which is psychologically so difficult, can we understand the full extent of what virtue is like. The acceptance of death is an acceptance of our own nothingness which is an automatic spur to our concern with what is not ourselves. The good man is humble; he is very unlike the big neo-Kantian Lucifer. He is much more like Kierkegaard's tax collector. Humility is a rare virtue and an unfashionable one and one which is often hard to discern. Only rarely does one meet somebody in whom it positively shines, in whom one apprehends with amazement the absence of the anxious avaricious tentacles of the self. In fact any other name for Good must be a partial name; but names of virtues suggest directions of thought, and this direction seems to me a better one than that suggested by more popular concepts such as freedom and courage. The humble man, because he sees himself as nothing, can see other things as they are. He sees the pointlessness of virtue and its unique value and the endless extent of its demand. Simone Weil tells us that the exposure of the soul to God condemns the selfish part of it not to suffering but to death. The humble man perceives the distance between suffering and death. And although he is not by definition the good man perhaps he is the kind of man who is most likely of all to become good.

AMY CLAMPITT
(1920–   )

Since the appearance of *The Kingfisher* in 1983, Amy Clampitt has been recognized as a classic American poet. She has written that "as a poet I'm trying to sort out values . . . to discriminate between the authentic and the phony—to preserve what is worth preserving." Reviewing her latest volume of poetry, *A Silence Opens* (1994)—the title poem follows here—poet and memoirist Patricia Hampl (see page 264) wrote: "Poetry has always laid claim to the spirit. And it probably should be no surprise that a secular society like ours conceals plenty of religious ache. Yet the assumption of a secular consciousness in American cultural life is so strong that when contemporary American poets not only address God directly but make it clear that the search for God lies at the core of their enterprise, it can come as a jolt." Clampitt is a religious poet, "not simply of sensibility," Hampl continues, but "of history and politics." She believes that it is in silence that even the religious fakes discover "the infinite/love of God. And silence is "an entrance to poetry, not its absence."

From *A Silence Opens*

A Silence

past parentage or gender
beyond sung vocables
the slipped-between
the so infinitesimal
fault line
a limitless
interiority

beyond the woven
unicorn   the maiden
(man-carved   worm-eaten)
God at her hip
incipient
the untransfigured
cottontail
bluebell and primrose
growing wild   a strawberry
chagrin   night terrors
past the earthlit
unearthly masquerade

(we shall be changed)

a silence opens
itself its own
raw stuffs'
hooked silk-hung
relinquishment

behind the mask
the milkfat   shivering
sinew   isinglass
uncrumpling   transient
greed to reinvest

names have been
given   (revelation
kif   nirvana

syncope)   for
whatever gift
unasked
gives birth to

torrents
fixities
reincarnations of
the angels
Joseph Smith
enduring
martyrdom

a cavernous
compunction driving
founder-charlatans
who saw in it
the infinite

love of God
and had
(George Fox
was one)
great openings

CATHERINE DE VINCK
(1923–   )

Catherine de Vinck grew up in Belgium and came to the United States
in 1948 speaking French and not knowing English. Since then she has
published ten volumes of poetry, received numerous honorary
doctorates of letters, and raised six children. She says her writing is
"soaked in a theology of hope, that is, in the knowledge that death has
no dominion, that light overcomes darkness, and that love is a divine
power of transformation and renewal." Denise Levertov (see page 222)
has said that de Vinck's poetry conveys "an ecstatic celebration of
living." Thomas Merton praised her "wonderful Blake-like response to
the sacred world." Poet Michele Murray wrote that as a religious poet
"de Vinck belongs next to George Herbert and the Traherne of
Centuries of Meditations."

"VENUS — AGHIA SOPHIA"

Above the waves
the lady stands in the pink shell,
innocent and sexual, flowing
in the lover's mind:
white opalescence, mother of all images,
discovered, denied.
Her voice low, she speaks
of ancient things, diagrams
of inner measures that shape
the world into a single unit,
a house of good proportion
built for the living.
Wisteria, iris, daffodil,
her language opens the garden gate.
Did you know in the past
the innumerable ways of seeds
and roots, the design of branches
spreading a filigree of newspun leaves
into an enameled sky?
Did you know the concordance
that links not only heaven and earth
but the most antique fragment of baked clay
to the very blood that pumps your heart
full of desire and dream?

In the center of your eye,
the lady is naked but modestly covered
by hair and hand; she is not to be taken
lightly; she brings a taste for excellence,
for recovery, more than healing:
strength; not the power to slay passion
but to orient the blinding risk
of love.
Is happiness controlled, pulled
by strings held
in some enormous hidden will?
Or is it born of water and flame,
of unbetrayed trust, of pain
that grinds flesh and bone
into a fine powder that the wind lifts?

The lady made of moon-foam, stepped
down from her sea-chariot
to warm the night, to nurse
the man-child with a tender urgency
lightyears removed from pleasure,
from play. "Be gentle," she says,
"learn that your inexhaustible yearning
cannot take final rest in me.
If you take suck
it is not only at my breast
but from the rose-beginning of the day,
from the open bud of creation,
from the dancing tip of life.
I am an icon of the master work,
and if you, enthralled, reach out
for the body of the poem, I will lead
you beyond the walled room
of the shell, unbinding your sight,
cutting the knots of raging hunger,
waking you
beyond the limit of my own meaning
to the universal heart of the fire."

The Womanly Song of God

I am the woman dancing the world
    alive:
birds on my wrists
    sun-feathers in my hair
I leap through hoops of atoms;
    under my steps
plants burst into bloom
    birches tremble in their silver.
Can you not see the roundness of me:
    curve of the earth
maternal arms of the sea
    encircling you wetly as you swim?
I am the birthing woman
    kneeling by the river
heaving, pushing forth a sacred body
    not mud, not stone: flesh and blood.

Round, round the wind
  spinning itself wild
drawing great circles of music
  across the sky.
Round the gourd full of seeds
  round the moon in its ripeness
round the door through which I come
  stooping into your house.
I am a God of a thousand names:
  why cannot one of them be
Woman Singing?

DENISE LEVERTOV
(1923–   )

Recognized as one of the most important and respected poets of the
second half of this century, Denise Levertov, both before and since she
came to the United States from her native England in the 1940s, reveals
in her writing and political activism a long commitment to, in her
words, "the obligation of social conscience." Many of her poems express
her mystical sense of the oneness that joins all the forms of creation,
requiring a response of solidarity. Along with other voices in this book
(Margaret Fell, the Grimkés, Eleanor Roosevelt, Dorothy Day, Judith
Plaskow, Starhawk), Levertov admits no separation between authentic
spirituality and the works of social justice. Concrete, sensate, mysterious
life grounds the compassionate faith expressed in the following examples
of her poetry and prose. As she puts it in her poem "Variation and
Reflection on a Theme by Rilke," "We must breathe time as fishes
breathe water. / God's flight circles us."

"O TASTE AND SEE"

The world is
not with us enough.
O Taste and See

the subway Bible poster said,
meaning The Lord, meaning
if anything all that lives
to the imagination's tongue,

grief, mercy, language,
tangerine, weather, to
breathe them, bite,
savor, chew, swallow, transform

into our flesh our
deaths, crossing the street, plum, quince,
living in the orchard and being

hungry, and plucking
the fruit.

Work That Enfaiths
(1990)

What a fraud I feel, sitting down to write about faith that works! What a
fraud I shall feel when I am actually giving this paper to a gathering of people who, I know in advance, will each of them have a degree of faith not
only far beyond my own but perhaps beyond anything I shall ever attain,
or possess, or—since those verbs both seem ill-chosen—shall ever be
blessed with! I know such faith only at second or third hand: that's to say,
I have just enough faith to believe it exists. To imagine it. And to feel a
kind of pity for people who can't imagine it at all, who *don't* believe it exists, who diminish its possibility in their minds by calling it self-delusion
or superstition. Belief is something else. I can say the creed without per-
jury. But faith. . . . When my mother tried a few times to tell me about the
faith she did indeed possess, she sought the right words in vain, although
she was an articulate woman; and if she conveyed something of her experience to me so convincingly, it was more by her tone of voice than by the
words she found. A singer (she was Welsh), she loved Handel's *Messiah*
aria, "I know that my Redeemer liveth," and despised any performance of
it which, though technically excellent, failed to give the emphasis of conviction to that word, "know": "I *know* that my Redeemer liveth." Such passionate knowledge, recurrent, intermittent, or in some cases even sustained,
is what I know I don't have. "Flickering Mind"* confesses the fact:

> Lord, not you,
> it is I who am absent.
> At first
> belief was a joy I kept in secret,

A Door in the Hive, 1989.

stealing alone
into sacred places:
a quick glance, and away—and back,
circling.
I have long since uttered your name
but now
I elude your presence.
I stop
to think about you, and my mind
at once
like a minnow darts away,
darts
into the shadows, into gleams that fret
unceasing over
the river's purling and passing.
Not for one second
will my self hold still, but wanders
anywhere,
everywhere it can turn. Not you,
it is I am absent.
You are the stream, the fish, the light,
the pulsing shadow,
you the unchanging presence, in whom all
moves and changes.
How can I focus my flickering, perceive
at the fountain's heart
the sapphire I know is there?

But if I feel fraudulent, why have I agreed to participate in this event? To talk about "faith that works"?

Well, because I'm a poet, and I do have faith in what Keats called the *truth of the imagination*; and because, when I'm following the road of imagination (*following a leading,* as the Quakers say), both in the decisions of a day and in the word-by-word, line-by-line decisions of a poem in the making, I've come to see certain analogies, and also some interaction, between the journey of art and the journey of faith.

The analogies are recognizable if one thinks of the necessary combination in any artist of discipline and inspiration, work and luck, technique and talent, or craft and genius. Every work of art is an "act of faith" in the vernacular sense of being a venture into the unknown. The artist must dive into waters whose depths are unplumbed, and trust that he or she will neither be swallowed up nor come crashing against a cement surface four foot down, but will rise and be buoyed upon them. Every work of art, even if long premeditated, enters a stage of improvisation as soon as the artist moves from thinking about it to beginning to form its concrete reality. That step, from entertaining a project for a poem or other work of art, to actually painting, composing, dancing, writing it, resembles moving from intellectual assent to opening the acts of daily life to permeation by religious faith. I know the first from experience; I know the second only from a distance, but my experience enables me to imagine it, and to see that such permeation is "faith that works."

The *interaction* I perceive between the journey of art and the journey of faith necessitates my speaking rather personally. As I became, a few years ago, more and more occupied with questions of belief, I began to embark on what I'll call "do-it-yourself theology." Sometimes I was merely trying to clarify my mind and note down my conclusions-in-process by means of the totally undistinguished prose of journal entries. Sometimes, however, it was in poems that the process took place, and most notably in the first such poem I wrote, a longish piece called *Mass for the Day of St. Thomas Didymus* ("doubting Thomas"). The poem began as an experiment in structure. I had attended a choral recital for which the choir director had put together parts of Masses from many periods—medieval, renaissance, baroque, classical, and modern, not in chronological order. The program had a striking unity, nevertheless. It was obviously the traditional liturgical framework that not only enabled such a variety of styles to avoid clashing, but provided a cohesive overall effect, so that the concert was itself a work, a composed entity. And I thought to myself that it might be possible to adapt this framework, which had served such a diversity of musicians, to the creation of a poem. At the time—and even when, a couple of years later, I actually undertook this experiment—I still considered myself an agnostic. I thought of the poem as "an agnostic Mass" (using the word Mass merely as a formal description, as one might in saying of a Baroque composer, "He wrote over thirty Masses"), basing each part on what seemed its primal character: the Kyrie a cry for mercy, the Gloria a praise-song, the Credo an individual assertion, and so on: each a personal, secular meditation. But a few months later, when I had arrived at the Agnus Dei, I discovered myself to be in a different relationship to the material and to the liturgical form from that in which I had begun. The experience of writing the poem—that long swim through waters of unknown depth—had been also a conversion process, if you will.

Another instance of the interaction of artistic labor and incipient faith—shall I say, of the workings of the Holy Spirit, or is that too presumptuous?—concerns the way in which, writing a libretto about El Salvador for a composer who'd been commissioned to write an oratorio, I dwelt longer on the work and words of Archbishop Oscar Romero than I might have done otherwise, with my tendency to rush ahead too swiftly from one experience to another. Since I intended to quote directly from Romero, the thought of him remained constantly present to me and became a factor in my growing ability to stop making such a *fuss*, inside my mind, about various points of doubt. (If a Romero—or a Dorothy Day, an Anthony Bloom, a Raymond Hunthausen, a Jean Sulivan, or a Thomas Merton—or a Pascal, for that matter!—could believe, who was I to squirm and fret, as if I required more refined mental nourishment than theirs?)

As to my more substantial stumbling block, the suffering of the innocent and the consequent question of God's nonintervention, which troubled me less in relation to individual instances than in regard to the global panorama of oppression and violence, it was through poetry—through images given me by creative imagination while pondering this matter—that I worked through to a theological explanation which satisfied me. God's nature, as Love, demands a freely given requital from that part of the creation which particularly embodies Consciousness: the Human. God therefore gives to human beings the power to utter yes or no—to perceive the whole range of dualities without which there could be no freedom. An *imposed* requital of love would be a contradiction in terms. Invisible wings are given to us too, by which, if we would dare to acknowledge and use them, we might transcend the dualities of time and matter—might be upheld to walk on water. Instead, we humans persistently say no, and persistently experience our wings only as a dragging weight on our backs. And so God remains nailed to the Cross—for the very nature of God as Love would be violated by taking back the gift of choice which is *our* very nature. It's an idea, or theory, undoubtedly familiar to many of you through works of religious philosophy; but *for me* it was original, not only because I hadn't come across such expositions of it but also because the concrete images which emerged in the process of writing convinced me at a more intimate level of understanding than abstract argument would have done. The poem I called "Standoff"* articulates this idea.

> Assail God's hearing with gull-screech knifeblades.
>
> Cozen the saints to plead our cause, claiming
> grace abounding.
>
> God crucified on the resolve not to displume
> our unused wings

Breathing the Water, 1987.

hears: nailed palms
cannot beat off the flames of insistent sound,

strident or plaintive,
nor reach to annul freedom—

nor would God renege.

Our shoulders ache. The abyss
gapes at us.

When shall we
dare to fly?

In a somewhat earlier, related poem called "The Task"* I had pictured
God as a weaver sitting at his loom in a vast wilderness, solitary as a bear in
the Alaskan tundra, listening to the cries of anguish far off, audible above the
clack of the loom because all else is so quiet—and hastening his task; for the
cloth must be woven before the "terrible beseeching" can cease. A friend's
description of the heavenly but awesome quiet of the wilderness near Mount
Denali was one source for this poem. Another source was what Julian of Norwich tells us she learned in one of her "showings": that there is a divine plan,
both temporal and transcendent, which will account for the unchecked miseries of the world, a plan which our finite minds are incapable of grasping.
God informs her, you remember, to trust this, and tells her that "All shall be
well, and all manner of thing shall be well." The time is not yet ripe for us
to comprehend this mystery, she is told. But meanwhile all manner of thing
is *not* well, and "The Task" images the toil of a lonely God.

As if God were an old man
always upstairs, sitting about
in sleeveless undershirt, asleep,
arms folded, stomach rumbling,
his breath from open mouth
strident, presaging death . . .

No, God's in the wilderness next door
—that huge tundra room, no walls and a sky roof—
busy at the loom. Among the berry bushes,
rain or shine, that loud clacking and whirring,

Oblique Prayers, 1984.

irregular but continuous;
God is absorbed in work, and hears
the spacious hum of bees, not the din,
and hears far-off
our screams. Perhaps
listens for prayers in that wild solitude.
And hurries on with the weaving:
till it's done, the great garment woven,
our voices, clear under the familiar
    blocked-out clamor of the task,
can't stop their

        terrible beseeching. God
imagines it sifting through, at last, to music
in the astounded quietness, the loom idle,
the weaver at rest.

In other poems I have explored passages of Julian of Norwich and passages of the Gospel—for example, the parables of the mustard seed, which have always seemed to me, for the simplest botanical reason, to be misinterpreted (it is not a simple assertion along the lines of "great oaks from little acorns grow!"). Or again, the sheer *daring* of the Virgin Mary in the Annunciation narrative, contrasted with her so often-alleged meekness; or what I imagined as the state of mind of St. Thomas before and after his meeting with the risen Christ. Before, I imagine Thomas as one "whose entire being had knotted itself / into the one tightdrawn question"—the question raised dramatically by such an encounter as that of Jesus with the possessed child in Mark 9, which I assume he witnessed.

        Why,
why has this child lost his childhood in suffering,
        why is this child who will soon be a man
tormented, torn, twisted?
        Why is he cruelly punished
who has done nothing except be born?

Thomas identifies with the father's cry of "Lord, I believe, help thou my unbelief"; but his harrowing doubt remains with him despite all the miracles he witnesses, for they do not address the profoundly disturbing matter of the suffering of the innocent. Even his meeting with the risen Christ does not suffice to give him certitude as long as it is visual alone; it is the concreteness of touch, of flesh and blood, which frees him at last. He is

moved from tenuous belief to an illuminated conviction in which he can
rest, like Lady Julian, from the nagging need for explanation, recognizing
that (as Robert McAfee Brown has said) "puzzles are to be solved, but mysteries are to be experienced."

But when my hand
               led by His hand's firm clasp
entered the unhealed wound,
                     my fingers encountering
rib-bone and pulsing heat,
              what I felt was not
scalding pain, shame for my
                 obstinate need,
but light, light streaming
             into me, over me, filling the room
as if I had lived till then
            in a cold cave, and now
coming forth for the first time,
              the knot that bound me unravelling,
I witnessed
       all things quicken to color, to form,
my question
       not answered but given
               its part
in a vast unfolding design lit
       by a risen sun.*

The writing of each of these poems has brought me a little bit closer to
faith as distinct from mere shaky belief. Thus for me the subject is really
reversed: not "faith that works" but "work that enfaiths."

I was encouraged to be "as personal as you wish"—but what has all this
personal history to do with the other issue we were commissioned to address? Has it any relevance to "the world of higher education and learning" and to "the problems of our wider world"?

My partial response has to do with the fate of poems after they leave the
writer's desk. In writing, I was of course following personal imperatives, as
any artist must. But it could not fail to occur to me that, once these poems
of religious quest were published, I was likely to lose some of my readers.
This proved not to be true. In fact, the positive response I've had to them
from people I'd have expected to be hostile or disappointed has amazed
me. Of course, there have been some who have said they just "couldn't get

*"St. Thomas Didymus," *A Door in the Hive,* 1989.

into" poems of Christian content and terminology; but the reverse has more often been the case. My Jewish readers, for instance—while not subscribing, of course, to whatever is specifically Christian in the poems—responded to them without hostility, and with solidarity in the basic interfaith assumption of belief in God. We often hear it said that there is much spiritual hunger in our society—but I have been surprised by how much quiet, unadvertised religious *commitment* there is among people one can loosely characterize as intellectuals—the people who constitute the audience for contemporary poetry in twentieth-century America.

This being so, one becomes aware that in so secular a society little in contemporary literature articulates the beliefs or yearnings which such people hold almost secretly. Just as I was shy about frankly uttering my beliefs in print, and did so with a resigned anticipation of negative response, yet was relieved and indeed exhilarated at the consequences, so, I think, do many crypto-Christians experience relief and pleasure when a poet whose work they already know, and with whose politics they are familiar and sympathetic, turns out to be one of themselves.

In recent years, the impulse to search for or return to cultural roots has been a factor in making religious practices less "uncool" for Jewish intellectuals than for their Christian counterparts. For Gentile intellectuals with Christian roots or leanings, a great deterrent is the disgusting vulgarity of "born-again" hucksters and their poisonous alliance with militarism and repression. Catholic intellectuals have an easier time, because despite many conflicts, within the Church and about it, regarding a number of very important issues, many non-Catholics as well as Catholics find inspiration in the heroes and martyrs of Latin America and elsewhere and in the church's leadership in peace and justice concerns in many places. Moreover, the Catholic Church has modern traditions of high intellectual discourse and major artistic contributions. One thinks of Messiaen in music, David Jones in poetry, Rouault in painting, Flannery O'Connor in fiction—to name a few off the top of my head. These are artists whom even avowed atheists respect and admire (often with a certain wistful envy), without fear of being considered naive and stupid by their peers.

Yet there is not a whole lot of contemporary poetry—in English, anyway—which articulates a faith-life (or quest) parallel to that of the many readers who appear to welcome such poetry when they do find it. The appeal of Wendell Berry's work is partly due, surely, to the way in which his land ethic has more and more seemed to draw on underlying Christian themes. (The converse is probably also true: readers drawn first to his ecological concerns are led through those concerns to an assimilation of his spirituality.)

Of course, attempting to supply a demand would be fatal to artistic integrity. But supply sometimes happens, by surprise, to meet demand; and in my own case I think the fact that my poems have been addressing doubts and hopes rather than proclaiming certainties has turned out to make them accessible to some readers, letting them into the process as I have engaged in building my own belief structure step by step. They are poems written on the road to an imagined destination of faith. That imagination of faith acts as yeast in my life as a writer: in that sense I do experience "faith that *works*" as well as "work that enfaiths." If the results sometimes attain their own autonomous life in the world, as every artist hopes will happen, it is possible that they may contribute to the life of other people. If they do, it must be first and foremost as works of art, on the same basis as any others, regardless of content. But since content evolves its forms and permeates them, each work that satisfies formally will bring with it the character of its content.

Finally, a poet speaking from within the Christian tradition and using traditional terms (though not necessarily upholding every orthodoxy) may have more resonance for our intellectual life than is supposed. The Incarnation, the Passion, the Resurrection—these words have some emotive power even for the most secular minds. Perhaps a contemporary poetry that incorporates old terms and old stories can help readers to reappropriate significant parts of their own linguistic, emotional, cultural heritage, whether or not they share doctrinal adherences.

FLANNERY O'CONNOR
(1925–1964)

When asked the major influences on her life, Flannery O'Connor answered, "Probably being a Catholic, and a Southerner, and a writer." "The Catholic sacramental view of life," she said, "is one that maintains and supports at every turn the vision that the storyteller must have if he is going to write fiction of any depth." O'Connor's letters, collected under the title *The Habit of Being*, have been praised as "correspondence that gleams with consciousness," comparable to the great letters of Byron, Keats, Lawrence, Wilde, and Joyce. Intelligent, ornery, and without cant, they reflect the spirit of a brave woman— O'Connor suffered from incurable lupus—possessed of an acerbic humor and unapologetic religious conviction.

From *The Habit of Being*

TO ALFRED CORN

Milledgeville
30 May 62

Dear Mr. Corn,

I think that this experience you are having of losing your faith, or as you think, of having lost it, is an experience that in the long run belongs to faith; or at least it can belong to faith if faith is still valuable to you, and it must be or you would not have written me about this.

I don't know how the kind of faith required of a Christian living in the 20th century can be at all if it is not grounded on this experience that you are having right now of unbelief. This may be the case always and not just in the 20th century. Peter said, "Lord, I believe. Help my unbelief." It is the most natural and most human and most agonizing prayer in the gospels, and I think it is the foundation prayer of faith.

As a freshman in college you are bombarded with new ideas, or rather pieces of ideas, new frames of reference, an activation of the intellectual life which is only beginning, but which is already running ahead of your lived experience. After a year of this, you think you cannot believe. You are just beginning to realize how difficult it is to have faith and the measure of a commitment to it, but you are too young to decide you don't have faith just because you feel you can't believe. About the only way we know whether we believe or not is by what we do, and I think from your letter that you will not take the path of least resistance in this matter and simply decide that you have lost your faith and that there is nothing you can do about it.

One result of the stimulation of your intellectual life that takes place in college is usually a shrinking of the imaginative life. This sounds like a paradox, but I have often found it to be true. Students get so bound up with difficulties such as reconciling the clashing of so many different faiths such as Buddhism, Mohamedanism, etc., that they cease to look for God in other ways. Bridges once wrote Gerard Manley Hopkins and asked him to tell him how he, Bridges, could believe. Bridges was an agnostic. He must have expected from Hopkins a long philosophical answer. Hopkins wrote back, "Give alms." He was trying to say to Bridges that God is to be experienced in Charity (in the sense of love for the divine image in human beings). Don't get so entangled with intellectual difficulties that you fail to look for God in this way.

The intellectual difficulties have to be met, however, and you will be meeting them for the rest of your life. When you get a reasonable hold on one, another will come to take its place. At one time, the clash of the different world religions was a difficulty for me. Where you have absolute solutions, however, you have no need of faith. Faith is what you have in the absence of knowledge. The reason this clash doesn't bother me any longer is because I have got, over the years, a sense of the immense sweep of creation, of the evolutionary process in everything, of how incomprehensible God must necessarily be to be the God of heaven and earth. You can't fit the Almighty into your intellectual categories. I might suggest that you look into some of the works of Pierre Teilhard de Chardin (*The Phenomenon of Man* et al.). He was a paleontologist—helped to discover Pekin man—and also a man of God. I don't suggest you go to him for answers but for different questions, for that stretching of the imagination that you need to make you a sceptic in the face of much that you are learning, much of which is new and shocking but which when boiled down becomes less so and takes its place in the general scheme of things. What kept me a sceptic in college was precisely my Christian faith. It always said: wait, don't bite on this, get a wider picture, continue to read.

If you want your faith, you have to work for it. It is a gift, but for very few is it a gift given without any demand for equal time devoted to its cultivation. For every book you read that is anti-Christian, make it your business to read one that presents the other side of the picture; if one isn't satisfactory read others. Don't think that you have to abandon reason to be a Christian. A book that might help you is *The Unity of Philosophical Experience* by Etienne Gilson. Another is Newman's *The Grammar of Assent*. To find out about faith, you have to go to the people who have it and you have to go to the most intelligent ones if you are going to stand up intellectually to agnostics and the general run of pagans that you are going to find in the majority of people around you. Much of the criticism of belief that you find today comes from people who are judging it from the standpoint of another and narrower discipline. The Biblical criticism of the 19th century, for instance, was the product of historical disciplines. It has been entirely revamped in the 20th century by applying broader criteria to it, and those people who lost their faith in the 19th century because of it, could better have hung on in blind trust.

Even in the life of a Christian, faith rises and falls like the tides of an invisible sea. It's there, even when he can't see it or feel it, if he wants it to be there. You realize, I think, that it is more valuable, more mysterious, altogether more immense than anything you can learn or decide upon in college. Learn what you can, but cultivate Christian scepticism. It will keep you free—not free to do anything you please, but free to be formed by something larger than your own intellect or the intellects of those around you.

I don't know if this is the kind of answer that can help you, but any time you care to write me, I can try to do better.

Yours,

TO ALFRED CORN

Milledgeville
Georgia
16 June 62

Dear Mr. Corn,

I certainly don't think that the death required that "ye be born again," is the death of reason. If what the Church teaches is not true, then the security and emotional release and sense of purpose it gives you are of no value and you are right to reject it. One of the effects of modern liberal Protestantism has been gradually to turn religion into poetry and therapy, to make truth vaguer and vaguer and more and more relative, to banish intellectual distinctions, to depend on feeling instead of thought, and gradually to come to believe that God has no power, that he cannot communicate with us, cannot reveal himself to us, indeed has not done so, and that religion is our own sweet invention. This seems to be about where you find yourself now.

Of course, I am a Catholic and I believe the opposite of all this. I believe what the Church teaches—that God has given us reason to use and that it can lead us toward a knowledge of him, through analogy; that he has revealed himself in history and continues to do so through the Church, and that he is present (not just symbolically) in the Eucharist on our altars. To believe all this I don't take any leap into the absurd. I find it reasonable to believe, even though these beliefs are beyond reason.

If you are interested, the enclosed book will give you one general line of reasoning about why I do. I'm not equipped to talk philosophically; this man is. I want it back sometime, but I am in no hurry for it. It shouldn't be read rapidly.

Satisfy your demand for reason always but remember that charity is beyond reason, and that God can be known through charity.

Regards,

TO SALLY AND ROBERT FITZGERALD

Milledgeville
15 March 63

Dear S&R,

I should have given you Caroline's address. It is 436 University Avenue, Davis, Calif.

I have just got back from the Symposium on Religion & Art at Sweet Briar and boy do I have a stomach full of liberal religion! The devil had his day there. It began with Boaz talking about Art & Magic. I don't know what he meant to say but he left the impression that religion was good because it was art and magic. Nothing behind it but it's good for you. Then they had the Dean of Theological School at Drew. He was a Methodist-Universalist. I gather this means you don't drink but about theology you are as vague as possible and talk a lot about how the symbology has played out in Christianity and how it's up to artists to make up a new symbology. At these things you are considered great in direct proportion to how often you can repeat the word symbology. They wedged me and James Johnson Sweeney in there somewhere. He was above the fray as he confined himself to Art, but I waded in and gave them a nasty dose of orthodoxy, which I am sure they thought was pretty quaint. It ended with John Chiardi who told them why religion was no good—or so I hear, I didn't go to his lecture.

James Johnson Sweeney asked most especially for you when he found out I knew you. I didn't get a chance to say much to him as everywhere they sat me I was next to the Methodist-Universalist. He left in the middle of my talk. I don't think it was a protest gesture, I just think he thought he could live a useful life without it. I told them that when Emerson decided in 1832 that he could no longer celebrate the Lord's supper unless the bread and wine were removed that an important step in the vaporization of religion in America had taken place. It was somewhere after that I think that he left.

Let us know your plans when the madwoman sends them. Could this be Alma Savage? If you can, stop by here and take yourself a rest between labors.

I haven't seen it in print but somebody told me he thought you got the Bollingen Prize. I congratulate you. You should have got it if you didn't. I guess you saw that Powers got the National Book Award. I was much cheered at that. I got the O. Henry this year. Walker Percy got the N'tl Book Award last year. Katherine Anne will probably get the Pulitzer prize. I think you ought to judge the prize by the book but even so these hold up and all these people are Catlicks so this should be some kind of answer to the people who are saying we don't contribute to the arts.

Cheers to you all,

P.S. Have you read about the lady who is having a chapel built in the shape of John Glen's capsule?

KABITA SINHA
(1931–   )

Bengali poet Kabita Sinha was born in Calcutta and grew up free to use the large library in her mother's family palatial house in Andul. With her parents' encouragement, she began writing as a child, studied botany at university in Calcutta, and married a writer. She has published many novels, including *For Angry Young Women* (1956), *The Story of a Bad Woman* (1958), and *Heroine, Anti-Heroine* (1960), but she is best known for her poetry. "Ishwarke Eve," the poem that follows here, is taken from her highly acclaimed volume *Poetry Is the Supreme Being* (1976). Her writing has received numerous awards and been translated into many languages. A selection of her poems is available in the Feminist's Press' excellent two-volume anthology *Women Writing in India* (1993).

Ishwarke Eve
(Eve Speaks to God)

I was first
to realize
that which rises
must fall
inevitably.
Like light
like dark
like you
I was first
to know.

Obeying you
or disobeying
means the same.
I was first
to know.

I was first
to touch
the tree of knowledge
first
to bite
the red apple.
I was first,
first—
first to distinguish
between modesty
and immodesty—
by raising a wall
with a fig leaf
I changed things
totally.

I was first.
I was first
pleasure,
my body
consoled
the first sorrow.
I was first
to see
your face
of a child.
Amidst grief and joy
I was first.
I first
knew
sorrow and pleasure,
good and evil,
made life
so uncommon.
I was first
to break

the golden shackles
of luxurious
pleasure.
I was never
a puppet
to dance
to your tune
like
meek Adam.

I was
rebellion
first
on your earth.

Listen, love,
yes, my slave,
I was the first
rebel—
banished from paradise,
exiled.
I learned
that human life
was greater
than paradise.
I was first
to know.

Translated by Pritish Nandy

AUDRE LORDE
(1934–1992)

When black feminist lesbian poet Audre Lorde died of cancer in 1992, she had published seventeen volumes of poetry, essays, and autobiography. *A Burst of Light,* a collection of essays, won an American Book Award in 1989. In "My Words Will Be There" she named erotic experience as the source of women's wisdom. "The love expressed between women," she wrote, "is particular and powerful, because we have had to love in order to live; love has been our survival." As the founding mother of the spirituality of eroticism, she lived to see her ideas achieve wide currency in contemporary feminist theology, as some of the theoretical selections in the last section of this book indicate. She puts what might be the core truth of her influential vision this way: "We as women tend to reject our capacity for feeling . . . because it has been devalued. But it is within this that lies so much of our power."

Uses of the Erotic: The Erotic as Power

THERE ARE MANY kinds of power, used and unused, acknowledged or otherwise. The erotic is a resource within each of us that lies in a deeply female and spiritual plane, firmly rooted in the power of our unexpressed or unrecognized feeling. In order to perpetuate itself, every oppression must corrupt or distort those various sources of power within the culture of the oppressed that can provide energy for change. For women, this has meant a suppression of the erotic as a considered source of power and information within our lives.

We have been taught to suspect this resource, vilified, abused, and devalued within western society. On the one hand, the superficially erotic has been encouraged as a sign of female inferiority; on the other hand, women have been made to suffer and to feel both contemptible and suspect by virtue of its existence.

It is a short step from there to the false belief that only by the suppression of the erotic within our lives and consciousness can women be truly strong. But that strength is illusory, for it is fashioned within the context of male models of power.

As women, we have come to distrust that power which rises from our deepest and nonrational knowledge. We have been warned against it all our lives by the male world, which values this depth of feeling enough to keep women around in order to exercise it in the service of men, but which fears this same depth too much to examine the possibilities of it within themselves. So women are maintained at a distant/inferior position to be psychically milked, much the same way ants maintain colonies of aphids to provide a life-giving substance for their masters.

But the erotic offers a well of replenishing and provocative force to the woman who does not fear its revelation, nor succumb to the belief that sensation is enough.

The erotic has often been misnamed by men and used against women. It has been made into the confused, the trivial, the psychotic, the plasticized sensation. For this reason, we have often turned away from the exploration and consideration of the erotic as a source of power and information, confusing it with its opposite, the pornographic. But pornography is a direct denial of the power of the erotic, for it represents the suppression of true feeling. Pornography emphasizes sensation without feeling.

The erotic is a measure between the beginnings of our sense of self and the chaos of our strongest feelings. It is an internal sense of satisfaction to which, once we have experienced it, we know we can aspire. For having experienced the fullness of this depth of feeling and recognizing its power, in honor and self-respect we can require no less of ourselves.

It is never easy to demand the most from ourselves, from our lives, from our work. To encourage excellence is to go beyond the encouraged mediocrity of our society. But giving in to the fear of feeling and working to capacity is a luxury only the unintentional can afford, and the unintentional are those who do not wish to guide their own destinies.

This internal requirement toward excellence which we learn from the erotic must not be misconstrued as demanding the impossible from ourselves nor from others. Such a demand incapacitates everyone in the process. For the erotic is not a question only of what we do; it is a question of how acutely and fully we can feel in the doing. Once we know the extent to which we are capable of feeling that sense of satisfaction and completion, we can then observe which of our various life endeavors bring us closest to that fullness.

The aim of each thing which we do is to make our lives and the lives of our children richer and more possible. Within the celebration of the erotic in all our endeavors, my work becomes a conscious decision—a longed-for bed which I enter gratefully and from which I rise up empowered.

Of course, women so empowered are dangerous. So we are taught to separate the erotic demand from most vital areas of our lives other than sex. And the lack of concern for the erotic root and satisfactions of our work is felt in our disaffection from so much of what we do. For instance, how often do we truly love our work even at its most difficult?

The principal horror of any system which defines the good in terms of profit rather than in terms of human need, or which defines human need to the exclusion of the psychic and emotional components of that need— the principal horror of such a system is that it robs our work of its erotic value, its erotic power and life appeal and fulfillment. Such a system reduces work to a travesty of necessities, a duty by which we earn bread or oblivion for ourselves and those we love. But this is tantamount to blinding a painter and then telling her to improve her work, and to enjoy the act of painting. It is not only next to impossible, it is also profoundly cruel.

As women, we need to examine the ways in which our world can be truly different. I am speaking here of the necessity for reassessing the quality of all the aspects of our lives and of our work, and of how we move toward and through them.

The very word *erotic* comes from the Greek word *eros*, the personification of love in all its aspects—born of Chaos, and personifying creative power and harmony. When I speak of the erotic, then, I speak of it as an assertion of the lifeforce of women; of that creative energy empowered, the knowledge and use of which we are now reclaiming in our language, our history, our dancing, our loving, our work, our lives.

There are frequent attempts to equate pornography and eroticism, two diametrically opposed uses of the sexual. Because of these attempts, it has become fashionable to separate the spiritual (psychic and emotional) from the political, to see them as contradictory or antithetical. "What do you mean, a poetic revolutionary, a meditating gunrunner?" In the same way, we have attempted to separate the spiritual and the erotic, thereby reducing the spiritual to a world of flattened affect, a world of the ascetic who aspires to feel nothing. But nothing is farther from the truth. For the ascetic position is one of the highest fear, the gravest immobility. The severe abstinence of the ascetic becomes the ruling obsession. And it is one not of self-discipline but of self-abnegation.

The dichotomy between the spiritual and the political is also false, resulting from an incomplete attention to our erotic knowledge. For the bridge which connects them is formed by the erotic—the sensual—those physical, emotional, and psychic expressions of what is deepest and strongest and richest within each of us, being shared: the passions of love, in its deepest meanings.

Beyond the superficial, the considered phrase, "It feels right to me," acknowledges the strength of the erotic into a true knowledge, for what that means is the first and most powerful guiding light toward any understanding. And understanding is a handmaiden which can only wait upon, or clarify, that knowledge, deeply born. The erotic is the nurturer or nursemaid of all our deepest knowledge.

The erotic functions for me in several ways, and the first is in providing the power which comes from sharing deeply any pursuit with another person. The sharing of joy, whether physical, emotional, psychic, or intellectual, forms a bridge between the sharers which can be the basis for understanding much of what is not shared between them, and lessens the threat of their difference.

Another important way in which the erotic connection functions is the open and fearless underlining of my capacity for joy. In the way my body stretches to music and opens into response, hearkening to its deepest rhythms, so every level upon which I sense also opens to the erotically satisfying experience, whether it is dancing, building a bookcase, writing a poem, examining an idea.

That self-connection shared is a measure of the joy which I know myself to be capable of feeling, a reminder of my capacity for feeling. And that deep and irreplaceable knowledge of my capacity for joy comes to demand from all of my life that it be lived within the knowledge that such satisfaction is possible, and does not have to be called *marriage*, nor *god*, nor *an afterlife*.

This is one reason why the erotic is so feared, and so often relegated to the bedroom alone, when it is recognized at all. For once we begin to feel deeply all the aspects of our lives, we begin to demand from ourselves and from our life-pursuits that they feel in accordance with that joy which we know ourselves to be capable of. Our erotic knowledge empowers us, becomes a lens through which we scrutinize all aspects of our existence, forcing us to evaluate those aspects honestly in terms of their relative meaning within our lives. And this is a grave responsibility, projected from within each of us, not to settle for the convenient, the shoddy, the conventionally expected, nor the merely safe.

During World War II, we bought sealed plastic packets of white, uncolored margarine, with a tiny, intense pellet of yellow coloring perched like a topaz just inside the clear skin of the bag. We would leave the margarine out for a while to soften, and then we would pinch the little pellet to break it inside the bag, releasing the rich yellowness into the soft pale mass of margarine. Then taking it carefully between our fingers, we would knead it gently back and forth, over and over, until the color had spread throughout the whole pound bag of margarine, thoroughly coloring it.

I find the erotic such a kernel within myself. When released from its intense and constrained pellet, it flows through and colors my life with a kind of energy that heightens and sensitizes and strengthens all my experience.

We have been raised to fear the *yes* within ourselves, our deepest cravings. But, once recognized, those which do not enhance our future lose their power and can be altered. The fear of our desires keeps them suspect and indiscriminately powerful, for to suppress any truth is to give it strength beyond endurance. The fear that we cannot grow beyond whatever distortions we may find within ourselves keeps us docile and loyal and obedient, externally defined, and leads us to accept many facets of our oppression as women.

When we live outside ourselves, and by that I mean on external directives only rather than from our internal knowledge and needs, when we live away from those erotic guides from within ourselves, then our lives are limited by external and alien forms, and we conform to the needs of a structure that is not based on human need, let alone an individual's. But when we begin to live from within outward, in touch with the power of the erotic within ourselves, and allowing that power to inform and illuminate our actions upon the world around us, then we begin to be responsible to ourselves in the deepest sense. For as we begin to recognize our deepest feelings, we begin to give up, of necessity, being satisfied with suffering and self-negation, and with the numbness which so often seems like their only alternative in our society. Our acts against oppression become integral with self, motivated and empowered from within.

In touch with the erotic, I become less willing to accept powerlessness, or those other supplied states of being which are not native to me, such as resignation, despair, self-effacement, depression, self-denial.

And yes, there is a hierarchy. There is a difference between painting a back fence and writing a poem, but only one of quantity. And there is, for me, no difference between writing a good poem and moving into sunlight against the body of a woman I love.

This brings me to the last consideration of the erotic. To share the power of each other's feelings is different from using another's feelings as we would use a kleenex. When we look the other way from our experience, erotic or otherwise, we use rather than share the feelings of those others who participate in the experience with us. And use without consent of the used is abuse.

In order to be utilized, our erotic feelings must be recognized. The need for sharing deep feeling is a human need. But within the european-american tradition, this need is satisfied by certain proscribed erotic comings-together. These occasions are almost always characterized by a simultaneous looking away, a pretense of calling them something else, whether a religion, a fit, mob violence, or even playing doctor. And this misnaming of the need and the deed give rise to that distortion which results in pornography and obscenity—the abuse of feeling.

When we look away from the importance of the erotic in the development and sustenance of our power, or when we look away from ourselves as we satisfy our erotic needs in concert with others, we use each other as objects of satisfaction rather than share our joy in the satisfying, rather than make connection with our similarities and our differences. To refuse to be conscious of what we are feeling at any time, however comfortable that might seem, is to deny a large part of the experience, and to allow ourselves to be reduced to the pornographic, the abused, and the absurd.

The erotic cannot be felt secondhand. As a Black lesbian feminist, I have a particular feeling, knowledge, and understanding for those sisters with whom I have danced hard, played, or even fought. This deep participation has often been the forerunner for joint concerted actions not possible before.

But this erotic charge is not easily shared by women who continue to operate under an exclusively european-american male tradition. I know it was not available to me when I was trying to adapt my consciousness to this mode of living and sensation.

Only now, I find more and more women-identified women brave enough to risk sharing the erotic's electrical charge without having to look away, and without distorting the enormously powerful and creative nature of that exchange. Recognizing the power of the erotic within our lives can give us the energy to pursue genuine change within our world, rather than merely settling for a shift of characters in the same weary drama.

For not only do we touch our most profoundly creative source, but we do that which is female and self-affirming in the face of a racist, patriarchal, and anti-erotic society.

LUCILLE CLIFTON
(1936–   )

Of Lucille Clifton's *The Book of Light*, from which the following poems are taken, poet Sharon Olds has written: "These are poems of fierce joy, made as if under the pressure of passionate witness. They are faithful to the intimate, the private, the inner heart, and they are heroic, speaking truths not spoken before about the moral life of our species. They have the exactness and authority of laws of nature—they are principles of life." The author of numerous volumes of highly respected poetry, Clifton describes herself in her autobiographical memoir *Generations* (1976) as coming from a family that "tends to be a spiritual and even perhaps mystical one." That experience has convinced her that "things don't fall apart. Things hold. Lines connect in ways that last and last and lives become generations made out of pictures and words just kept."

From *The Book of Light*

> *love the human*
>
> —Gary Snyder

the rough weight of it
scarring its own back
the dirt under the fingernails
the bloody cock   love
the thin line secting the belly
the small gatherings
gathered in sorrow or joy
love the silences
love the terrible noise
love the stink of it
love it all   love
even the improbable foot   even
the surprised and ungrateful eye

THEL

was my first landscape,
red brown as the clay
of her georgia.
sweet attic of a woman,
repository of old songs.
there was such music in her;
she would sit, shy as a wren
humming alone and lonely
amid broken promises,
amid the sweet broken bodies
of birds.

SONG AT MIDNIGHT

> *. . . do not*
> *send me out*
> *among strangers*
>
> —Sonia Sanchez

brothers,
this big woman
carries much sweetness
in the folds of her flesh.
her hair
is white with wonderful.
she is
rounder than the moon
and far more faithful.
brothers,
who will hold her,
who will find her beautiful
if you do not?

won't you celebrate with me
what i have shaped into
a kind of life? i had no model.
born in babylon
both nonwhite and woman
what did i see to be except myself?
i made it up
here on this bridge between
starshine and clay,
my one hand holding tight
my other hand; come celebrate
with me that everyday
something has tried to kill me
and has failed.

JUNE JORDAN
(1936–   )

A self-described "dissident poet and writer," as well as activist and professor of African American studies and women's studies at the University of California at Berkeley, Brooklyn-born June Jordan has published twenty-two books to date. Most recently she has written and coproduced the Broadway *Earthquake/Romance*, a story in songs entitled "I Was Looking at the Ceiling and Then I Saw the Sky." In an interview she said, "The core of . . . my work is to advance the cause of justice and, therefore, peace. I'm very much dedicated to intelligent love, and trying to develop connections among us so that we can move to a good place, here and throughout the world." In the following essay, expounding on the biblical story of Ruth and Naomi (see page 13) as the Ur text of the saving power of friendship in the lives of women, Jordan joins a new stage in women's relations to the Bible, the rereading of ancient stories to find a biblical female tradition of lived wisdom that has meaning in contemporary contexts.

Ruth and Naomi, David and Jonathan: One Love

"Entreat me not to leave you or to return from following you; for where you go I will go, and where you lodge I will lodge; your people shall be my people, and your God my God where you die I will die, and there will I be buried. May the Lord do so to me and more also if even death parts me from you" (Ruth 1:16–17). From earliest childhood, I remember one or another version of these passionate words. As far as I knew, they were the only memorable, and even startling, thoughts attributed to any woman in the Bible. And, as a little girl, I appropriated the fierce loyalty, and the all-out loving commitment embodied by this passage, as an ideal towards which I could and should eagerly aspire. But the story around those unparalleled declarations remained rather wan, and confused, and confusing, in my mind, until this past summer.

Yes, I knew it was a woman named Ruth who had so declared herself to Naomi. But I did not understand why. And, as a child, it was not necessary for me to clearly get the context for their relationship, or even for me to clearly fathom their reasons for knowing each other. What mattered to me was that, finally, somewhere, in that big Holy Book, there were words uttered by somebody female to another somebody female. And, what was most important was that her words matched up to the heroic qualities of the other biblical figures I came to memorize and assimilate inside the pantheon of my young heart.

I distinctly remember, for example, my time at an all-girls' camp, Robin Hood, in upstate New York. Whenever any of us decided there was need to ceremoniously remark our friendship, we would invent a secret name for ourselves, such as The Dare Devils, and we would mix blood from the inside of our wrists, thereby becoming "blood brothers." Blood sisters simply would not fly; what would that connote? Where was the precedent for "blood sisters" in any literature, or film, or theater piece? Ruth and Naomi, maybe. But did they ever do anything like stealing into the night in order to set loose all of the rowboats, or taking an increasingly perilous walk through the woods—a walk punctuated by bigger and bigger crevasses over which it was necessary to jump—or else retire, humiliated, as a coward?

And were they sisters? I was never sure. But I was certain about David and Jonathan. I knew that Jonathan had been the son of King Saul. And King Saul frequently rushed into battle against the Philistines. And one of the Philistines was Goliath, that huge freak of a warrior on the wrong side. And young David, as just a slender boy, came and slew the giant Goliath with his slingshot. And the King was much impressed. As were all the rest of the Israelites. But none was more moved by the gallantry and intelligence of David than Jonathan. "Jonathan loved him as his own soul" (1 Sam. 18:1).

And after that victory, King Saul insisted that David come and live in the royal palace. But the women of Israel sang, "Saul has slain his thousands, and David his ten thousands" (1 Sam. 21:11), and the King heard this popular outcry of comparison and he became truly jealous. And from that day forward, he eyed David with malice aforethought and, in every way possible, tried to devise David's death. Again and again the King sent young David into battle, hoping that he would be killed. And, even beyond that, the King schemed for David's execution. But, again, and again, the King's son, Jonathan, raced from the palace to warn his friend David and, thereby, saved his life. And after many battles, and much fight and much flight, finally it was obvious that the Lord was with David and that David was, therefore, invincible. And David prevailed. And when David learned of the eventual war deaths of King Saul and of Jonathan, who loved David "as his own soul," David tore his clothes and raised a lamentation that concludes,

"How are the mighty fallen
in the midst of the battle!

Jonathan lies slain upon thy high places.
I am distressed for you, my brother Jonathan;
    very pleasant have you been to me;
    your love to me was wonderful,
    passing the love of women."

(2 Sam. 1:25–26)

So Jonathan had defied his father for the sake of David. And repeatedly he had rescued David from the nefarious intent of his father, the King, thereby jeopardizing his own, otherwise natural, succession to the throne of Israel. And when the King died, David did not rejoice because the King had been "the Lord's anointed." And when Jonathan died, David did not rejoice because to him, Jonathan's love "was wonderful / passing the love of women." Theirs was great reciprocal love. The dimensions of the interaction between the two men approached the mythical in scale. And the content of their intersecting histories is the very stuff of spectacular movie suspense, climax, and triumph.

This summer I became one of the too many thousands of women who must fight breast cancer. From the surgery to determine whether or not there was a malignancy through the surgery for removal of the malignant tissue (a partial radical mastectomy) and the removal of lymph nodes to determine whether or not the cancer had spread, I suddenly became wholly dependent upon the kindnesses of my friends. I had to depend on my friends for my personal care, for the walking of my dog, for the securement of groceries, for the cooking and serving of food, for the cleaning up of the kitchen and of the house, for transportation to and from the doctors, for the handling of correspondence and for diplomatic dealing with innumerable phone calls: for my life.

At different points, you would find an elaborate schedule for every day of every week, sometimes broken into hourly segments. Slotted into each segment of each day you would find the name of one or another or yet another friend—a woman friend. And I felt overwhelmed by the exhaustive, seamlessly graceful, and indispensable caretaking organized by these women. How could I possibly have survived any of the ordeal of this fight, and how could I possibly hope to heal, and defeat this cancer, without the unstinting love given to me?

It was Angela, for example, who read everything published on breast cancer and who drove me to the doctor on the morning when the doctor told me that the cancer had spread to the lymph nodes and that, consequently, he was revising his prognosis from 90 percent likely to survive to 40 percent. It was Angela who drove me away from that terrible news to a neighborhood hairdresser whom she begged to "do something" and who in fact, created a small fire on the top of my head: an electric orange stripe that she bleached into my hair.

It was Adrienne who washed my back and cleansed the wound and told me there was nothing horrible about that horrible procedure, while she changed the sterile dressing. And it was Adrienne who slept through the nights in a chair next to my hospital bed.

It was Lauren who brought bananas just perfectly not quite ripe. And Stephanie who organized my friends into a computer wizardry of a failproof network.

And it was the other Adrienne who traveled all the way from Santa Cruz to bring lunch and laughter and new anthologies of poetry. And Martha who came from New York.

And it was Camille who came at midnight with medicine when the pain was quite unbearable. And Pratibha who came from London.

And it was Sara who talked me through yet another nightmare of giving blood so that the hospital could run necessary, pre-op tests. And Phyllis who watered the garden several times a week, on her way to work.

And on and on for several months. And I thought, "This is the love of women. This is the mighty love that is saving my life. And where were the public instances of praise and celebration of this love?"

And I found my Bible and, when I could read again, I looked up the story of Ruth to see if I could make better sense of it now.

And I could. And I did.

"In the days when the judges ruled there was a famine in the land," (Ruth 1:1) and for this reason Naomi and her husband and their two sons left Bethlehem and went to a more promising country, the country of Moab. While they stayed there, Naomi's husband died. Her two sons took to themselves two Moabite wives, Orpah and Ruth. And then Naomi's sons died. And Naomi decided she would return to Bethlehem, since the famine had now ended. And so she arranged to bid her widowed daughters-in-law farewell. And one of them, Orpah, wept, and kissed Naomi, and accepted her counsel: She would stay in Moab. But the other daughter-in law, Ruth, refused to separate from Naomi, and she said, "Entreat me not to leave you or to return from following you." And when Naomi saw that Ruth could not be dissuaded, she allowed her daughter-in-law to return with her, to Bethlehem.

Now when the two women returned there, they could not provide for themselves; neither of them was married; neither of them had a husband to protect and feed and honor her. And it was very hard. But Naomi was not about to give up and perish. Nor was she about to permit Ruth to become prey to wanton depredations, or hunger. Therefore, Naomi conceived of a plan whereby Ruth would become appealing to a wealthy farmer and kinsman. Ruth obeyed Naomi and she succeeded in pleasing the kinsman so that he made her his wife. And then Ruth bore the kinsman, whose name was Boaz, a son. And that son became the joy of Naomi's old age. "Then Naomi took the child and laid him in her bosom, and became his nurse," (Ruth 4:16) And Naomi was no longer without family and shelter. And the son of Ruth and Boaz was Obed. And Obed was the father of Jesse. And Jesse was the father of David. Here ended the Book of Ruth.

At first, I was dismayed. The evident dependency of both Naomi and Ruth upon their menfolk struck me as extreme. It was not as though they had set up house together and/or started up a small subsistence farm that then became an amazing commune for other stranded women. And, really, Ruth had to literally put herself at the very feet of Boaz in order to gain the favors of his attention. And suppose Ruth had not found Boaz attractive, or kind, or fun?

And then I realized I was being obtuse. Ruth and Naomi had made brave choices in a circumstance that allowed them no freedom. And they had chosen to do whatever would allow them to stay together, without undue penury, or censure by the townspeople of Bethlehem, And, yes, they could not ride horses into battle and slay the sources for their grief or slay the enemies of their joy. And, yes, they were neither princes nor kings, but, rather, slaves to a social environment that would not permit them any liberty, any respect, any safety, any assurance, even, of work with the reward of food—unless at last one of them became somebody's wife.

But is it not marvelously true that Ruth's love for Naomi was the equal of Jonathan's great love for David? And is it not wonderfully true that Ruth's love for Naomi surpassed her love of men even as David's love of Jonathan surpassed his love of women?

And is it not fitting that the child of Ruth and Naomi should become the father of the father of David? From Ruth and Naomi through David and Jonathan we possess the fabulous history of one love. And, yes, differences of gender have made for huge differences in the documented public display of their differing but always passionate and virtuous attachments. But it is one love. It is love that supersedes given boundaries of birthright or birthplace or conventions of romance or traditions of loyalty. It is one love that yields to no boundary. It is one love that takes you to its bosom and that saves your life.

And we would be foolish to neglect the cultivation and the celebration of such love within our own heroic and our own quite ordinary passage here, on earth.

MARGE PIERCY
(1936–   )

The author of twelve volumes of poetry, including *Stone, Paper, Knife* (1983) from which the following poem is taken, and six novels, feminist writer Marge Piercy has long confessed to a faith in ecology rather than postscarcity. Themes of women's spirituality, especially a reverence for the body of mother earth, are prominent in *Woman on the Edge of Time* and in much of her poetry, especially *The Moon Is Always Female*. The poetry editor of *Tikkun* magazine, she lives in Massachusetts.

From *Stone, Paper, Knife*

THE COMMON LIVING DIRT

The small ears prick on the bushes,
furry buds, shoots tender and pale.
The swamp maples blow scarlet.
Color teases the corner of the eye,
delicate gold, chartreuse, crimson,
mauve speckled, just dashed on.

The soil stretches naked. All winter
hidden under the down comforter of snow,
delicious now, rich in the hand
as chocolate cake: the fragrant busy
soil the worm passes through her gut
and the beetle swims in like a lake.

As I kneel to put the seeds in
careful as stitching, I am in love.
You are the bed we all sleep on.
You are the food we eat, the food
we ate, the food we will become.
We are walking trees rooted in you.

You can live thousands of years
undressing in the spring your black
body, your red body, your brown body
penetrated by the rain. Here
is the goddess unveiled,
the earth opening her strong thighs.

Yet you grow exhausted with bearing
too much, too soon, too often, just
as a woman wears through like an old rug.
We have contempt for what we spring
from. Dirt, we say, you're dirt
as if we were not all your children.

We have lost the simplest gratitude.
We lack the knowledge we showed ten
thousand years past, that you live
a goddess but mortal, that what we take
must be returned; that the poison we drop
in you will stunt our children's growth.

Tending a plot of your flesh binds
me as nothing ever could, to the seasons,
to the will of the plants, clamorous
in their green tenderness. What
calls louder than the cry of a field
of corn ready, or trees of ripe peaches?

I worship on my knees, laying
the seeds in you, that worship rooted
in need, in hunger, in kinship,
flesh of the planet with my own flesh,
a ritual of compost, a litany of manure.
My garden's a chapel, but a meadow

gone wild in grass and flower
is a cathedral. How you seethe
with little quick ones, vole, field
mouse, shrew and mole in their thousands,
rabbit and woodchuck. In you rest
the jewels of the genes wrapped in seed.

Power warps because it involves joy
in domination; also because it means
forgetting how we too starve, break
like a corn stalk in the wind, how we
die like the spinach of drought,
how what slays the vole slays us.

Because you can die of overwork, because
you can die of the fire that melts
rock, because you can die of the poison
that kills the beetle and the slug,
we must come again to worship you
on our knees, the common living dirt.

ROSEMARY RADFORD RUETHER
(1937–   )

Feminist theologian Rosemary Radford Ruether is the prolific author and editor of numerous works that have been of great importance to the growth of an ecumenical feminist spirituality. Among her titles are *Gaia and God: An Ecofeminist Theology of Earth Healing, Womanguides: Readings toward a Feminist Theology*, and, with Rosemary Skinner Keller, *In Our Own Voices: Four Centuries of American Women's Religious Writing* and the three-volume *Women and Religion in America*. Professor of applied theology on the joint Ph.D. faculty of Northwestern University and Garrett-Evangelical Theological Seminary in Evanston, Illinois, Ruether shows in the following profile of her first "wise woman" the experiential source of her being able to think of God as female, "very much like that Wisdom of God described in scripture." (Examples are represented in the first section of *Wise Women.*)

A Wise Woman

I can name several intellectual and academic mentors, but in the nurturing of my faith and spiritual life I can think of only one important person: Rebecca Cresap Ord Radford, my mother. Rebecca was born in 1895 in Monterey, Mexico, a member of an English Catholic family who were pioneers in California in the 1840s. Her family lived in Mexico until Rebecca was nine, and my mother enjoyed speaking and reading Spanish all her life. Her favorite book was an ancient leather-bound tome of Cervantes.

My mother's Catholicism was a lucid balance of serious spirituality and intellectual freedom. I have no idea how she achieved this balance, but I assume it had something to do with her mother. It seemed to be typical of her sister, Lucy, as well. I grew up taking for granted that the two capacities coincided and that anyone who didn't understand that union wasn't well educated or spiritually developed. My mentor in that assumption was my mother, who taught by way of the example of her own life rather than by preaching to us.

My mother saw to it that we went to mass weekly and attended Catholic schools in primary and most of secondary school, although she made no special effort to send us to Catholic colleges (she herself received her B.A. from Elmira College in 1916). In retrospect I realized that she always steered us carefully toward that kind of Catholicism which she regarded as intellectually respectable and authentic, and away from what she regarded implicitly as "vulgar Catholicism."

Vulgar Catholicism meant dogmatic, narrow-minded pastors who made you feel like you were on the road to hell if you ate hamburger on Friday and nuns who were shocked because, as an art student, I was drawing nudes at the age of 13. Authentic Catholicism was intellectually sophisticated and united with deep sacramental and contemplative spirituality and corporal works of mercy. My mother pursued that kind of Catholicism all her life, but as her own personal option. She didn't push it on anyone else.

Ecumenism was taken for granted in my family. My mother's English (with a touch of Austro-Hungarian) Catholicism assumed a respectful relation with Anglicans, and both my father's and her brother's families were Anglican. My favorite uncle was a Jew, and my great-aunt had married a Russian diplomat (before the revolution) and leaned toward Russian Orthodoxy. In her old age most of my mother's formerly Anglican friends attended the La Jolla, California, Quaker meeting. I sometimes went to Christ Church, Georgetown, in Washington, D.C., with my father on the two times of the year he attended (Christmas and Easter), and in La Jolla I occasionally attended the Quaker meeting.

For as long as I knew her my mother spent time in personal prayer each morning and night and also went to daily mass. When I was growing up, being a daily communicant was the highest goal of lay Catholic life in the minds of nuns and priests. But this kind of brownie-point mentality about going to mass was banally offensive as a description of my mother's spirituality. My mother went to mass every day because that was the way she wanted to start her day.

My mother also cultivated relationships with Catholic communities that she thought were really serving others. One of these was a convent of Carmelite nuns around the corner from our family home in Georgetown. These Carmelites, who had a joyful spirit and created a welcoming atmosphere, took care of the aged. My mother served on their board and went to their chapel each morning for mass.

She also pursued lectures and readings by those Catholic theologians she regarded as "good." These were usually French, Dutch or Belgian, teachers at Louvain or the Institut Catholique in Paris. In her 70s, after moving back to her childhood home in La Jolla, she and her friends would gather weekly for spiritual reading—usually reading mystics, such as Meister Eckhart. What she was saying to me, implicitly, was that Catholicism should be judged by this kind of intellectual and spiritual depth. Pronouncements that fell below that standard could be set aside.

Her standard was not primarily one of intellectual sophistication, however, but of spiritual authenticity. My mother also found that kind of authenticity in simple people: the Carmelite nuns, their elderly charges and the Mexican women she befriended in La Jolla, usually by helping them with immigration problems. It meant that your heart was in the right place, in tune with God and generous to others. What it did not mean was making people feel guilty about religious trivia.

My mother had what I would describe as a true leisure culture, in the sense that Joseph Pieper uses the term in his 1948 book, *Leisure, the Basis of Culture*. Indeed, when I read this book in college it made a great impression on me because it named what I saw in my mother. Pieper describes the split between work and leisure that has deformed both. My mother had a paying job before she married at age 33, and again after my father died when she was in her 50s and 60s. She also raised three daughters. But I never felt that the core of my mother's identity was given over to either of these roles. The center of her being was cultured leisure, in the sense of the cultivation of the mind, heart and soul through prayer, intellectual thought and service. This was more a state of being than of particular activities. I have seldom found that quality among others who claim to be Christian teachers, with the exception of one or two luminous Benedictine monks. I would call it wisdom.

My mother pushed me neither toward marriage nor a career. Rather I went to college to cultivate my mind, and it was the purest accident that this turned out also to be preparation for employment. In college I found myself arguing about religion with both Catholic and Protestant teachers. The Protestant teachers were anti-Catholic and thought that I needed to become a Protestant in order to be free to think. I found this assumption insulting, both personally and to my tradition.

The Catholic teachers alternated between being worried that I was becoming too educated, trying to enforce a docile acceptance of church teaching, and confessing to me their own problems with church authority. The first stance I found insulting; the second, disappointing. In several cases when I pursued intellectual conversation with Catholic priests (including an 18-month correspondence with Thomas Merton between August 1966 and December 1967) I ended up feeling that I was mentoring them, rather than the reverse.

It was a long time before I met any Catholic theologians who I felt had really worked out the kind of unified intellectual and spiritual authenticity I sought. I realized that I would have to work it out for myself. So I became a theologian. My mother read and enjoyed all my books, and I dedicated the 1974 volume I edited, *Religion and Sexism: Images of Women in the Jewish and Christian Traditions*, to her. The inscription reads: "To my mother, Rebecca Cresap Ord Radford, a wise woman."

It seems very appropriate to me to think of God as female, indeed very much like that Wisdom of God described in scripture:

> In Wisdom there is a spirit intelligent and holy, unique in its kind, yet made up of many parts, subtle, free-moving, lucid, clear, invulnerable, loving what is good, eager, unhindered, beneficent, kindly towards humans, steadfast, . . . age after age she enters into holy souls and makes them God's friends and prophets [Wisdom of Solomon 7:22, 27].

I was fortunate to have been mothered by one who was touched by that spirit of Wisdom.

PAULA GUNN ALLEN
(1939–   )

Born of Laguna Pueblo–Scots-Irish–Lebanese-American ancestry, Paula Gunn Allen grew up in New Mexico, studied at the University of New Mexico, and is now professor of Native American studies and ethnic studies at UCLA. Her many books of poetry, fiction, and nonfiction include the influential *The Sacred Hoop: Recovering the Feminine in American Indian Tradition* (1984). She has identified "the sense of the

connectedness of all things, of the spiritness of all things, of the
intelligent consciousness of all things" as the fundamental characteristic
of American Indian tribal poetry, a theme that calls to mind other
spiritualities—ecological, Buddhist—represented in this book. The
following selection is taken from *Skins and Bones: Poems 1979–87*.

Kopis'taya (A Gathering of Spirits)

Because we live in the browning season
the heavy air blocking our breath,
and in this time when living
is only survival, we doubt the voices
that come shadowed on the air,
that weave within our brains
certain thoughts, a motion that is soft,
imperceptible, a twilight rain,
      soft feather's fall, a small body
dropping into its nest, rustling, murmuring,
settling in for the night.

Because we live in the hardedged season,
where plastic brittle and gleaming shines
and in this space that is cornered and angled,
we do not notice wet, moist, the significant
drops falling in perfect spheres
that are the certain measures of our minds;
almost invisible, those tears,
soft as dew, fragile, that cling to leaves,
petals, roots, gentle and sure,
every morning.

We are the women of daylight; of clocks and steel
foundries, of drugstores and streetlights,
of superhighways that slice our days in two.
Wrapped around in glass and steel we ride
our lives; behind dark glasses we hide our eyes,
our thoughts, shaded, seem obscure, smoke
fills our minds, whisky husks our songs,
polyester cuts our bodies from our breath,
our feet from the welcoming stones of earth.
Our dreams are pale memories of themselves,
and nagging doubt is the false measure of our days.

Even so, the spirit voices are singing,
their thoughts are dancing in the dirty air.
Their feet touch the cement, the asphalt
delighting, still they weave dreams upon our
shadowed skulls, if we could listen.
If we could hear.
Let's go then. Let's find them. Let's
listen for the water, the careful gleaming drops
that glisten on the leaves, the flowers. Let's
ride the midnight, the early dawn. Feel the wind
striding through our hair. Let's dance
the dance of feathers, the dance of birds.

MARIAN WRIGHT EDELMAN
(1939–   )

Civil rights lawyer Marian Wright Edelman (named for Marian
Anderson) founded the Children's Defense Fund in "the cauldron of
Mississippi's summer project of 1964 and in the Head Start battles of
1965." The mother of three sons, she identifies parenting, as well as
growing up in a South Carolina family of Baptist ministers, as the
inspiration for her best-selling book *The Measure of Our Success: A
Letter to My Children and Yours*, excerpted here. Defining the legacies
that have shaped her commitment to the work of protecting children,
she emphasizes that they were "not material" but rather "a living faith
reflected in daily service, the discipline of hard work . . . and a capacity
to struggle in the face of adversity. Giving up and 'burnout' were not
part of the language of my elders. . . . They had grit." The
spirituality/politics of taking care of children—and the larger politics it
implies—join her thought to the ethical feminism of Sara Ruddick's
Maternal Thinking, political philosopher Jean Bethke Elshtain, and
theologian Judith Plaskow (see page 321).

From *The Measure of Our Success: A Letter to My Children and Yours*

It is not easy for anybody to grow up, to craft a purposeful role in the world,
to develop a positive passion for life, and to discover God's will. If you are
of mixed racial and religious heritage, as you are, some small and insecure

people whose self-esteem seems to rest on looking down on others whom they perceive as "different" may make growing up and life more challenging. But I hope you will always recognize your rich dual heritage as the special gift and blessing that it is; know deep within yourself who you are; and draw strength and pride from the legacies you have inherited from two peoples—Blacks and Jews—who have survived the worst persecution the world can offer. That in recent history these two peoples were slaves and not enslavers, were segregated and discriminated against and were not segregators and discriminators, is an achievement to be proud rather than ashamed of if you take seriously, as I do, the first principle of every great religion: to treat others as you'd like to be treated. It is the only ethical standard in life you need.

It is utterly exhausting being Black in America—physically, mentally, and emotionally. While many minority groups and women feel similar stress, there is no respite or escape from your badge of color. The daily stress of nonstop racial mindfulness and dealings with too many self-centered people who expect you to be cultural and racial translators and yet feel neither the need nor responsibility to reciprocate—to see or hear you as a human being rather than just as a Black or a woman or a Jew—is wearing. It can be exhausting to be a Black student on a "white" college campus or a Black employee in a "white" institution where some assume you are not as smart as comparable whites. The constant burden to "prove" that you are as smart, as honest, as interesting, as wide-gauging and motivated as any other individual tires you out—as does the need to decide repeatedly whether you'll prove to anybody what they have no right to assume or demand.

I understand the resentment of some young Blacks who have decided "who needs it?" and are opting for Black colleges where their "personness" is not under constant assault and testing. They are freed (for a short while) from having to decide whether to ignore, think about, or challenge the constant daily insensitivities of some whites who expect every Black to be a general expert on everything Black at breakfast, lunch, and dinner when you'd rather discuss art, gossip, or simply listen, or who assume you are less competent than they are because of "affirmative action." Black colleges have done an extraordinary job in preparing many of our young to swim in mainstream society. But there really is no hiding place out there or escape from negative racial attitudes in this era of racial backlash fueled by clever and cynical political and media manipulation. So you have to be ready to meet those attitudes and change them.

Affirmative action does not and shuld not mean that unqualified people get an advantage. Everybody has to be able to do the work in school or on the job to succeed. Nobody should use affirmative action as a favor, a crutch, or as an excuse not to be prepared or not to do a first-rate job—or to stigmatize.

White Anglo-Saxon males never have felt inferior as a result of their centuries of "affirmative action" and quotas (which are *not* the same) in jobs from which Jews, racial minorities, and women were excluded and too often still are. So while you and your brothers must and can make it on the basis of your individual ability, motivation, and disciplined hard work, do not feel defensive about the judgments of some that affirmative action somehow taints a whole race or you as individuals. Just work as hard as you can to perform up to your ability. You are the person you must compare yourself to. Have your own high standards for performance and conduct, not mine or your Dad's or your employers' or your peers'.

There are no easy answers to the continuing dilemmas of race in America. You must grapple with them like those who have gone before you: DuBois in *The Souls of Black Folk* and James Weldon Johnson and Countee Cullen and Paul Laurence Dunbar and Ralph Ellison and Maya Angelou and James Baldwin and Toni Morrison and Alice Walker and countless Black bards and writers who speak to this extra Black burden. The bottom line, however, is to believe in yourself and not let anybody—of any color—limit or define you solely by race or undermine your acceptance and love inside yourself for who you are. Race and gender are givens of God, which neither you nor anyone else chose or earned at birth. Your race is a fact. Being racist and sexist are a state of mind and a choice.

Dr. King, James Baldwin, and Malcolm X all reminded us that "whiteness is a state of mind" and that the struggle for racial justice is a struggle of conscience and not of race. As such, it is not just a minority responsibility. (And who created the problem?) Nor can minorities be justified in fueling racial divisions any more than those who mistreated them, however understandable the temptation may be. George Washington Carver once warned against letting any man drag you so low as to make you hate him.

Gandhi advised: "Let our first act every morning be the following resolve: 'I shall not fear anyone on earth. I shall fear only god. I shall bear ill-will towards no one. I shall not submit to injustice from anyone.'" No one, Eleanor Roosevelt said, can make you feel inferior without your consent. *Never* give it. Respect other people only on the basis of their individual character and personal efforts, struggles, and achievements. Never defer to another on the basis of his or her race, religion, gender, class, fame, wealth, or position. Whites did not create Blacks. Men did not create women nor Christians Jews. What then gives any human being the presumption to judge, diminish, or exclude another or expect deference solely on such bases? It does not take character, intellect, or talent to inherit a million dollars or to be born white or male. Why should more admiration be given to those who started life with far more advantages and supports than those with none or few? No person has the right to rain on your dreams. No person has a right to define you on the basis of what you have or what you look like.

Affirm who you are inside regardless of the world's judgments: God's and my very precious children who are loved unconditionally, not for what you do, look like, or own, but simply because you are a gift of a loving God.

NANCY MAIRS
(1943–   )

Despite years of suffering—worsening multiple sclerosis, acute agoraphobia, and chronic "unipolar" depression—Nancy Mairs's books of essays (Plaintext, Remembering the Bone House, Carnal Acts, Voice Lessons: On Becoming a (Woman) Writer) map the territory of a survivor, a prophet, and a wit. The following excerpt is taken from Ordinary Time: Cycles in Marriage, Faith, and Renewal (1993), the story of her conversion from New England Protestantism to post–Vatican II Catholicism in the context of heartbreaking family crisis. Barbara Kingsolver called it "a book of friendly, compassionate wisdom."

From Ordinary Time

GOD'S WILL

The Human City beings with me and my neighbour.
The Universal City begins with me and my neighbour.

—Philip Allott, *Eunomia*

A couple of years ago, I had an experience that struck me, in spite of its familiar setting and maybe even, in some people's lives, its predictability, as odd. I was at the Newman Center Mass I often attend on Saturday afternoons. Still walking in those days, I had just received communion and returned to my pew, where I knelt and, after one coherent little prayer, began the interior jumble that forms my post-communion meditation.

This was even more of a mess than usual because I felt panic-stricken: my multiple sclerosis was getting worse, almost by the day, and my resolve to cope bravely, in a manner befitting my stern Yankee heritage, was weakening even faster than my muscles were. I just wanted to get rid of the damned disease. "God, God, God," I prayed, "please, heal me!" And then, for the first and only time in my life, I got a response. I'd never heard voices, and I didn't hear one now. Three monosyllables simply materialized in my consciousness: "But I am."

I'm no mystic, although when I was much younger, especially while I was reading Dame Julian of Norwich and St. John of the Cross, I wished that I were one. In later years I've come to think it's just as well that I'm not. If I had a mystical experience—saw Jesus, say, or felt his hand in mine—I'd behave badly, I suspect: screech, the way I do when a spider surprises me, or faint away. And yet, that once, those words formed, and I accepted them. I took them into my life. I didn't understand, and still don't, what they mean: how an relentless degeneration of my central nervous system can function to "heal" me. But I had no trouble recognizing the message, or believing it. Why not? I wondered then. I still do.

I'd asked for the wrong thing, of course. What I wanted, plainly and simply, was to be cured of MS: to arise from my pew on two strong legs and stride firmly out into the world, where I would once again go dancing, ride a bicycle, maybe even learn to ski, resume needlework and calligraphy, and then join the Peace Corps for the grand adventure of my life. Since "cure" and "heal" can be used interchangeably, I didn't reflect before making my choice. Their meanings are subtly different, however. What I had asked for was not to be freed from my limp or my nasty habits, which might be effected instantaneously, but to be made whole, which might entail collecting scattered fragments and painstakingly fitting and gluing them into place. The one occurrence is not necessarily more miraculous than the other, but the drama of it—the paralytic rising to his feet and trudging with his pallet past the outraged scribes, Lazarus staggering from the cave's mouth in his stinking graveclothes—distracts and delights as healing's tedium cannot do.

I believe in those spectacular curative miracles. I also believe that Emma Woodhouse married Mr. Knightley at last and Emma Bovary gulped handfuls of arsenic and died in writhing agony, events that have no claim on historicity at all, and so my belief may reveal more about the habits of a student of literature than about religious faith. We students are not, when you come right down to it, models of rationality. Otherwise, I would probably try to explain the miracles away—the blind man was merely hysterical, his eyesight restored by the power of suggestion; spooked by an unseen wolf, the swine pell-melled like lemmings into the sea—anything to avoid looking a gullible fool. But fretting over whether these miracles "really" occurred misses the point: a very long time ago, a person came into the world whose actions and utterances so amazed the people around him by their divine implications that they never forgot them. In view of the frailty of human memory, something extraordinary happened and has gone on happening to this day: Emmanu-el: God With Us. What better grammar than miracles for communicating such an astounding state of affairs?

And so I willingly believe in signifying miracles of this sort. But I also believe that they are very, very rare. I do not expect one to happen to me. Some would say that through skepticism I disqualify myself, that if only I had faith as a grain of mustard seed I could be cured, but I don't have faith as a grain of mustard seed, I don't have faith as a paramecium or even a quark, so I'll just have to go on as I am. (There are, I'm willing to bet, worse ways to be, though you wouldn't know from the amount of complaining I do that I thought so.) God is no White Knight who charges into the world to pluck us like distressed damsels from the jaws of dragons, or diseases. God chooses to become present to and through us. It is up to us to rescue one another.

"I love how ordinary some of the miracles are," George tells me. "Feeding multitudes with a few loaves and a couple of fishes. Any of us could do it." He knows whereof he speaks. Our friend Kansas has just called to report he's retrieved a bounty of bags of potato chips from the dumpster behind Fry's Supermarket, and can George drive them down to Casa María for Friday's lunches? Those potato chips were there not by the will of God, I'm sure, but by the will of the store manager who noticed the expiration date; and the hand of Kansas, not the hand of God, gleaned them. There is nothing supernatural at work here. *That's* the miracle: not that some unseen almighty force showers potato chips down upon our heads but that a man goes dumpster-diving and rescues the potato chips while most of them are probably still edible. Since this man does not want the potato chips for himself—he couldn't possibly consume them all—from a personal perspective his act is wholly gratuitous. It signifies love. Through performing this miracle over and over and over again, we are made whole.

PATRICIA HAMPL
(1946–   )

Her first memoir, A *Romantic Education* (1981), praised as "marvelous" and "rare," shows Hampl's genius for, as one critic puts it, "joining poetic perception with history and political awareness." Her second book, *Virgin Time* (1992), excerpted here, joins travel writing with the writer's search for meaning and a recovery of a sense of the presence of God. Themes of interior and outward pilgrimage converge to produce an extraordinarily affecting story, told without pretense. Exploring the mysterious depths of the self in relation to the world, Hampl makes faith feel like an authentic destination and, in her case, an emotional necessity. The beginning of her spiritual journey—up in the air—and its ending—at a Cistercian retreat in northern California—are the settings of the following pages.

From *Virgin Time*

FAITH

1

There is nothing to be afraid of. But the plane lifts, and here I go again, crashing down fathoms of dread. God (whom I usually have no trouble cutting out of the picture) doesn't want us to fly. I know this.

To fly: such presumption. Didn't the nuns tell us *human pride* was the one sin that couldn't be forgiven, the worst of the Seven Deadly, inviting the vengeance of the Most High? Phrases like this slither up, smiting from their Old Testament ambush. Wrinkles of terror run along the soles of my feet. My toes curl toward Earth. Then the baleful *thunk thunk* of the landing wheels retracting.

"I've never been on an airplane before," the boy next to me says, startling me out of a deal I'm trying to cut with the Almighty. A fresh haircut has laid bare his skull. It's hard to tell if he's handsome; he looks skinned. And happy, wildly happy.

"I'm from Eveleth," he says, naming one of the hard-luck towns on the Minnesota Iron Range. "I'm on my way to West Point." The jubilant voice of travel—of escape—is unmistakable. "We get two days in New York City first. Never been to New York City. That's a lot of firsts for this kid. This time tomorrow I'll be on top of the Empire State Building."

"The World Trade Towers are taller," I say, roused from terror by this stray fact, but it's a pedant's mean-spirited remark.

It barely grazes him. "Yeah," he says, grinning, "I'll be there, too."

We both look out his window ("I said, give me the window seat, I don't care smoking or no smoking, but I've got to have a window seat"). St. Paul, sweet bluffy town of every age of my life, tilts away. Below us, the Minnesota River knots itself onto the Mississippi's muddy ribbon. There's the green dome of the cathedral where my mother (she *likes* to fly) and my father (he just wants to go fishing up north at Leech Lake) were married a million years ago in 1940.

The world isn't just disappearing; it's becoming anonymous. The dome's oxydized copper looks like a patch of lichen spreading on an outcrop of gray rock. We all die. Why not me, right here, like this. Later, an anchorwoman will say, "Luckily, the plane was only half full."

No one else seems to be facing death, all these strangers reading *USA Today*, entranced as children deep in comic books. The stewardess recites the oxygen mask demo and makes her appalling suggestion about using the orange seat cushion "as a flotation device in the unlikely event of . . ."

It's always like this. Barely controlled terror. Not so bad I can't fly; I wish it were that decisive. I read with admiration about celebrities, sportscasters—some of them big tough guys—who refuse to fly. They take trains or hire a whole bus to get them around. I'm not quite scared enough. I go ahead. Get the non-refundable ticket, chatter about my trip with both feet planted on the ground, my heart ticking like a set bomb. Lucky me, going here, going there. Going, this time, to Italy.

In my pocket, my damp hand closes on the gold airplane brooch my husband gave me as a lucky charm. He has also given me a magazine article outlining the extreme statistical unlikelihood of an airplane crash. But what about terrorists? Those bombs soft as chewed gum lurking in cassette recorders? What about evil? Numbers are cold comfort to someone fed from girlhood on the corrupting Catholic sweets of being *special*, chosen, outside the proletariat of statistics. Not for me the consolations of probability. I stuff the magazine article in the pocket of the seat back in front of me, and go for the totem.

The brooch is a cunningly exact replica of a DC-3. The tiny propellers can be twirled, and the landing wheels, tinier still, spin in their mountings. Windows are etched on the slanting flank of the plane's body. The entire spirit of the thing is brave and buoyant.

The pin once belonged to my husband's Aunt Leah, who was a flapper, went to Paris, had an affair with a French (or Romanian?) prince, then married a rich American (for love). Later, she lived in Las Vegas, a hard-drinking divorcée (love never lasts), and hobnobbed with Names. She played golf with Betty Grable. Somewhere along the line she was given this solid gold airplane by Howard Hughes as a souvenir—of what? A memento from the launching of one of his fleet? Or (love never ends) a trophy of romance? The facts, if there ever were any, are lost.

I rub Howard Hughes's plane in a rhythm of safety known only to my terror. I repeat silently, in a brainless mantra, *Played golf with Grable, golf with Grable, golf with Grable*. The green dome of the toy cathedral is gone.

The river is a flick of light, and we are just piercing the cloud cover, entering our climb.

"We may be experiencing a little turbulence, ladies and gentlemen," the captain is saying in that commander-of-the-ship drawl they all seem to have. He advises us to keep our seatbelts secured, as he does. "We'll get above this stuff, and find us a nice smooth ride on out to the New York area." Smooth, smooth, the drawl of doom. St. Paul is gone, all my life in its streets, and we are experiencing turbulence. The West Point cadet has his face up against the window. I rub the DC-3 and repeat my mantra silently, *Golf, golf, golf.*

I must be praying. Proving once again, without meaning to, that there's no stopping the mind's grab for salvation, o ye of little faith, o all of us on the go who hardly know what we believe in anymore. Most of the time I'm so removed from belief I confuse it with having an opinion. As if God were a candidate who may or may not get the vote of my focus group. Then this other thing lunges from its corner, not fear, but the stunning acuity born of fear. How keen the terrified mind is. Its cry is prayer. Planes are my foxhole, I'm always on my knees in them.

But just yesterday I was sitting in the cool, shadowy parlor of San Damiano Monastery outside Minneapolis, visiting Donnie (Sister Mary Madonna, but we're beyond that after my months—years now—of weekly visits). I was trying to explain to her why I was going on this trip. Looking for something, couldn't explain.

"You're going on a pilgrimage," she said, meaning to be helpful.

"No," I said, bristling, "I'm just going." Something about the word set my teeth on edge. *Pilgrimage.* I wince at the eau-de-cologne language of spirituality, but the whole world as I first understood it comes rushing back on the merest scent. I still want to embrace it—so, of course, when it dares to draw close, I slap it clean across the mouth. Love and loathing, those old partners.

Mine was a Catholic girlhood spent gorging on metaphor—Mystical Body, transubstantiation, dark night of the soul, the little martyrdom of everyday life. And remember, girls, life is a journey. Your own life is a pilgrimage. Maybe we had too much meaning too early. It was like having too much money. The quirkiness of life was betrayed, given inflated significance by our rich symbology. We powered around our ordinary lives in the Cadillac language of Catholic spirituality, looking on with pity as the Protestants pedaled their stripped-down bicycles.

Even the spring flowers of that Catholic past—window-box tulips, hyacinths the dog rooted up and pissed on, the alleys of lilac cloaking the garbage cans—were not just our improbable spring after the savage Minnesota winter. They belonged to Mary, our Mother. The public-school children carried nosegays for their teachers' desks, but in May we walked down Summit Avenue to St. Luke's grade school, lugging bouquets almost as big as ourselves to their true owner, the Queen of the May.

Nothing was just itself, nothing was left alone. We were clasped, suffocating and yet happy, to the great bosom of Meaning. Which doesn't let me off the hook for snapping at Donnie. She carries it all lightly, as in a day pack, while I can barely lift my trunkful of Catholic memorabilia. "I don't know why I'm going," I told her finally.

"Yes," she said, in that interested way of hers. "Not knowing—that's the spiritual part."

Donnie is over fifty, looks younger (except for the eyes). Her hair is shaped in what used to be called a pixie cut, a sort of monastic tonsure without the bald spot. It suits her. There is an elfin quality to her—tough elf. She's been a contemplative nun since she was seventeen. Not a woman easily rattled. No doubt she sees my grouchiness as "the spiritual part." I can't figure her. Yet I keep going back to visit her, to sort out what I thought was the past, my dead Catholic past, only to find it isn't dead at all.

"It's called 'spiritual direction,' what we're doing," she said one day. "Do you mind?" She's sympathetic to my language foibles. What could I say? Whatever we were doing, I found I required it, though I frown at the terms—spiritual direction, pilgrimage.

The plane heaves and climbs. It's struggling, doesn't anyone else sense this? I'm being asked what I want to drink. I'm taking the foil packet of peanuts. I'm the only one dying. Beads of water sweat across the window. I can't see a thing. *Golf, golf. God, God.*

"Don't worry," Donnie said yesterday. "I'll be in the chapel, praying for you. I'll hold you up there all the way across the ocean." She laughed, a nutty Druid laugh, Irish and ironic. The laugh made me almost believe her. Maybe that's faith: the smart little laugh that holds the world up.

The plane lurches and seethes. I'm a goner, and Donnie is safe on the ground, praying into the sky.

"Look!" The skinhead cadet has turned his moon-face to me, and now he points out the window. We're still tipped slightly upward, still laboring through the wads of wet gray cotton. The plane, surging and unsettled, penetrates the cloud-batten in awful lurches. And there, just crowning, the blue arc of the sky emerges, brittle with the sun's gold. The cadet is gleaming, too, blind with wonder, as we hurtle into heaven.

I got on the plane, against the better judgment of my terror, because I'd come to the conviction that I had to see the old world of Catholicism. More than see—had to touch it. Was it still breathing? Making its low murmur over the votive flames in the dark?

But I also knew that the "old world of Catholicism" was right at home. In me. I was born there, under the wide eye of postwar American Catholicism. Forget Vatican II: ours was the Church triumphant, not the Church reforming and defensive. Going to that world was just a matter of remembering. That's what I thought at first. I would roll out the memories, wrapping them up like a wedding dress bundled in tissue and put absolutely away. Remembering was the only roaming I needed to do. I could do even better. I'm a writer: I would write it up. I would write it away.

But reminiscence is a nag deep in its nosebag of memory. The grass of remembrance is never quite green, having been trod so often. And how many more rages and dumb jokes about the nuns, poor penguins, does the Catholic memory need to tramp to dust? The past is no destination anyway, though it seems so utterly a *place*. The trouble is, there are no humans there. All the figures have turned to wax—nuns in their Renaissance garments, the oracular voices of immigrant priests poised above us in bronze pulpits, the clairvoyant bridal froth of First Communion dresses, the Saturday-night confession buzz of all the wrong sins. You can only get so much story out of these statues.

As a result, people like me, fused by fascination to their past, find themselves taking planes to distant places, boarding with an urgency that suggests a family emergency is calling us home. Looking for our roots, we say. But roots are buried: they're supposed to be. And the past isn't alive. Only our urgency is. Maybe this urgency *is* the past, the only juice still spurting from the source that made us. It must be this urgency, a peculiar form of desire, that makes us zoom around, looking for what time has put back in its breast pocket.

The cadet touches my arm with his moth finger. " 'Scuse me, ma'am." My eyes are shut, reverent with fear. "I was just wondering if you were going to use those peanuts."

I hand him the packet.

"Thanks. This is great." He has three cans of Coke lined up on his tray table.

I look at his profile, the military tonsure, the happiness. It suddenly hits me: *he's* not going to crash. The plane is still thudding around, searching for a smooth lane of air, but he's all right. He glows with future. I smile at him. Safety courses through me, all sea breezes. I go limp with reassurance, and the little gold plane drops to the bottom of my pocket.

He's off to his future. Never mind if it's somebody's war, or the floating crap game called peace. He'll fly with it.

And I'm off to the past, is that it? Donnie is down there on the ground, keeping us aloft. She got the last word on what I'm up to, after all. As I left the monastery yesterday, she said, "Well, it was good enough for Chaucer."

"What was?"

"Your trip," Donnie said. "It's springtime. Remember?

> *"Whan that Aprille with hise shoures sote*
> *The droghte of March hath percèd to the rote . . .*
> *Thanne longen folk to goon on pilgrimages." . . .*

[Following her European pilgrimage, Hampl returns to a retreat house in northern California.]

Silence

THURSDAY

I waited, I waited for the Lord
and He stooped down to me;
He heard my cry.

He drew me from the deadly pit,
from the miry clay.
He set my feet upon the rock
and made my footsteps firm.

He put a new song into my mouth,
praise of our God.
Many shall see and fear
and shall trust in the Lord.

You do not ask for sacrifice and offerings,
but an open ear.
You do not ask for holocaust and victim.
Instead, here am I.

Copied from the Psalter. The ancient words, but I write them as if they're off the wire and I'm a journalist taking down the latest, my ballpoint moving fast over the page. News I need.

At breakfast, the apple jelly and the honey are so good I eat spoonfuls, like soup. Cecile smiles.

The white thumbs of radishes: a bucketful, two hours.

Lunch. The retreatants eat separately from the community, except for the serene, silent breakfast. We have an airy room with sliding doors that feels like a porch, and the Sisters bring us our meals there. A portrait of a beautiful woman, framed in severe black, takes up a central position on the wall we face. Who is she, we keep asking each other, but we forget to ask the Sister who brings the food. We forget because it's hard to break the habit of silence, though we've been told we're free to talk at lunch and dinner if we wish.

The woman in the portrait looks a little like the *Casablanca* Ingrid Bergman: that lyric beauty, that ineffable suffering bred of kindness and strength. The image of the Virgin Mary I carry forward from girlhood: not the perfect Catholic wife-and-mother, but the woman who "ponders all these things in her heart." The contemplative face. No one knows who she is, but as the days go by, people give her a story: she's probably the foundress of the community, Bob says. Maybe she's some early twentieth-century saint, someone else suggests. The photograph, greatly enlarged, does seem somehow from an earlier era. Who's a twentieth-century saint? the psychology professor asks. Nobody can think of a twentieth-century saint. "St. Maria Goretti?" Sister Jane suggests. But we all agree she's too old; Maria Goretti was a teenager. This woman is mature; her beauty partakes of wisdom.

Though there's no rule against talking, people fall silent anyway, and conversation starts up slowly, almost regretfully, at each meal. Today at our table the talk, once started, ran almost entirely to animals or flowers people had observed. Human activities have dimmed. We keep meaning to find out who this presiding beauty on the wall is, but the enterprises of other life forms have become significant, worth reporting. The human recedes.

For a moment there at lunch, we were a table of squirrels gathered around our bowls of nuts, telling the day's news. Everyone had something to say, interrupting one another to describe a bird, a cloud, the blue paper of an iris unfurling.

Mass late in the afternoon, just before dinner. At the time given over to personal intercessions, the nuns all praying for the big things: world hunger, El Salvador, the Middle East, the long list that is the contemplative lot. Then Thomas, who never speaks: "I pray for everyone I ever met," he says, head down, "especially those I never think about." One of those sappy remarks that aren't sappy, that capture the evanescence of relationship.

To pray for those we never think about. Especially those. They're all *there*, that crowd of former intimacies, or the potential ones, all the meet-

ings of eyes, the brief lifts of the drapery of indifference. The choral murmur in each life, composed not only of the divas of the family with their
grand arias, or the lost loves, the broken friendships with their stuttered refrains. These others are here, too, the people on trains, on airplanes, sitting in restaurants, waiting at the dentist. The pilgrims and strangers, the
lost and the luckily forgotten. All the cameos in a life. For them, yes, for
those whose names are never spoken. They are not loved: love them.

And Thomas himself, whom I will never see again and will not think of:
for him. His clear voice, surprisingly deep for that small, bent body. And
the slightly hesitant, searching tone of the voice as he tries to articulate his
impulse. He wants to get it right.

> *You have put into my heart a greater joy*
> *than they have from abundance of corn and new wine.*
>
> *I will lie down in peace and sleep comes at once,*
> *for you alone, Lord, make me dwell in safety.*

FRIDAY

What is prayer?
   I make a list:

> *Praise*
> *Gratitude*
> *Begging/pleading/cutting deals*
> *Fruitless whining and puling*
> *Focus*

There the list breaks off; I had found my word. Prayer only looks like an
act of language; fundamentally it is a position, a placement of oneself.
Focus. Get there, and all that's left to say is the words. They come: from
ancient times (here, the round of Psalms, wheeling through the seasons
endlessly in the Office), from the surprisingly eloquent heart (taciturn
Thomas last night with his intercession, precise as a poet), from the gush
and chatter of the day's detail longing to be rendered.

So what is silence?

Silence speaks, the contemplatives say. But really, I think, silence sorts.
An ordering instinct sends people into the hush where the voice can be
heard. This is the sorting intelligence of poetry, marked by the unbroken
certainty of rhythm, perfect pitch, the placing of things in right order as in

metrical form. Not rigid categories, but the recognition of a shape always there but ordinarily obscured by—what? By noise, which is ourselves trying to do the sorting in an order that may be a heroic effort but is bound to be a fantasy.

Silence, that inspired dealer, takes the day's deck, the life, all in a crazy heap, lays it out, and plays its flawless hand of solitaire, every card in place. Scoops them up, and does it all over again.

And the dark night of the soul?

Is the joker constantly turning up? It's in every hand.

Woke stiff as a chair, every muscle creaking. Yesterday I pulled the radishes. Today they're pulling me.

"Working in the garden," I said to Thomas, "really focuses the mind."

"Yes," he said, as if this were a new observation, "it frees the mind."

Focus. Freedom. The same thing to him.

And Cecile the other night saying, "Dogma. Always a thorn. Dogma is only the expression of the deeper symbol. If it's treated as the thing that counts, it kills symbol. Just kills it *dead*." The assumption that symbol is alive, not a unit of fantasy. The only absolutely real thing, but frighteningly vulnerable, ever a potential murder victim. A life requiring protection, as any creature does.

And Donnie one time, trying yet again to explain to me: "It's when the Church tries to tame the metaphors that we get in trouble. You can't control the images. That's not what they're for. You have to get *in* there with them."

So that's what this monastic life is, after all, and its core element, prayer, both so devoted to symbol. They aren't "poetic." They are poetry itself. Not in a decorative sense, not even having to do with an aesthetic experience. Rather, like poetry, monastic life seizes upon daily life and renders it as symbol, attuned to season, to hour, to the cycle on which our lives depend.

The praying monastery as life within poetry. Or say it this way: to become the lines and white space of a poem. That's what the Divine Office is, after all: time reckoned as poetry, hours made into verses, with the white space of silence, work (another kind of silence), and community in between the stanzas.

"They knew what they were doing," Thomas said, looking around the garden, "when they got into agriculture."

Like the Franciscans in Assisi, like Donnie, he speaks of his medieval forebears as of near neighbors. He meant Benedict and the early monastic founders, the ones who took silence out of the desert (a mistake? well, an inevitability) and put it to work in the great monastery hives of what, strangely, we call the Dark Ages. More truly, the Silent Ages. We like to think nothing happened then. Just waiting around in the dark for the Renaissance to screw in the light bulb. Time stopped. Nothing went forward. It went inward. And what was found there, we choose not to know. We leave it buried. It is a poem, and we do not read poetry anymore.

Just like Thaddeus and Francine and all the Franciscans in Assisi, Thomas speaks of that medieval history as *here*, immediate, still warm. Not only because his life here mimics the way of life laid down then, but because he knows, from the literature and *secundum traditionem*, the very people who created or developed the model he lives. He knows them well: there is no person as real as a fictive one, someone made not by the writer finally but the Benedict, the Francis, the Clare created by the humble reader, Thomas, willing to give his full attention. That is, his life, as Donnie was saying.

> So teach us to number our days,
> that we may get us a heart of wisdom.

Noon prayer, Psalm 90. The contemplative point of view: time turned into poetry. The day is a verse, the season a stanza. Number the days: know you will die. Wisdom belongs to the heart, go there.

LINDA HOGAN
(1947–   )

Award-winning poet, essayist, and novelist (her novel *Mean Spirit* was a finalist for the Pulitzer Prize in 1991), Linda Hogan is a member of the Chickasaw people, whom she identifies as the source of her spirituality: "My writing comes from and goes back to the community, both the human and the global community. I am interested in the deepest questions, those of spirit, of shelter, of growth and movement toward peace and liberation, inner and outer." The following pages are taken from her essay "Department of the Interior," in which she examines the modern divorce between the self and the land: "[O]ur lack of connection is destroying our capacity for deep love." Without a sense of the "sacred dimensions" of humanity's inner space and the exterior space of the world, our culture, she warns, can only die of violence and disease.

From "Department of the Interior"

REANIMATION OF THE WORLD

Culture evolves out of the experience of living with a land. For traditional Indian people, this habitation with land has developed over centuries, in some cases longer than 10,000 years. Deep knowledge of the land has meant survival, in terms of both sustenance and healing. Native people recognize that disease of the body is often caused by imbalance, sometimes originating within the human body and spirit, sometimes in the outside world. Either way, relationship with all the rest of creation is central to healing. Cure begins, and ends, with relationship. The purpose of ceremony is to restore the individual to their place within all the rest. If medicinal herbs are used, the effectiveness of the cure depends on an intimate knowing of the plant, the land around it, the mineral content of the soil, whether there has been lightning in the region, rainfall, and even which animals have passed through the territory of the plant. The healing capacity of plants is strengthened inside human knowledge; the stories of the plant, both mythic and historical, are essential, adding the human dimension to the world of nonhuman nature. It's an intricate science, reconnecting and restoring the human body with earth, cosmos.

There has been a growing understanding among non-Indians of the need for such relationship and connectedness. In the young science of ecology, it is known that every piece of the puzzle of life is necessary. This is a time of what I call the reanimation of the natural world by white men, as they are newly discovering an old understanding, that everything on earth is alive and that the relationship between all these lives makes for the whole living planet. While native people have been ridiculed for these views, James Lovelock has been hailed as a genius for his return to old Indian ways of thinking and knowing, for originating what he has called the Gaia hypothesis.

This is not an entirely new concept to Western culture; Paracelsus, like traditional Indian people, knew that harmony with the land and universe was the goal of healing, that body and land, such as in the tribal ceremonial sense, are intricately connected.

But by and large, the Western way of knowing has lost track of this understanding of the world, and the body is still associated with a kind of wilderness; there are dangers inside us, it is believed. And the body truly speaks its own tongue. When we go inside ourselves, there is fear, sometimes, and sorrow, a language of pain and need that we wish to avoid. What dancer Martha Graham meant when she spoke of the house of pelvic truth is that the body is a landscape of truth-telling. Our animal selves are more than nails and teeth that remain from before evolution, and that have torn their way through the world. The experience of the wild is inside us, beyond our mental control, and it lies alongside the deep memory of wilderness, and it has rules and laws that do not obey our human will.

More than symbol, more than the bread and wine of Christ, the body is a knowing connection, it is the telling thing, the medium of experience, expression, being, and knowing. Just as the earth is one of the bodies of the universe, we are the bodies of earth, accidental atoms given this form. An ancient and undivided world lies curled inside us with an ancestral memory that remembers our lives in the wilderness. What the body knows and where it takes us is navigated from an inner map not always carried in daily consciousness.

*   *   *

We are in need of an integrity of being that recognizes [the] disregarded inner world. I mean integrity in the true sense of this word, the sense that addresses a human wholeness and completeness, an entirety of living, with body, land, and the human self in relationship with all the rest, and with a love that remembers itself.

There are sacred dimensions to such love and they allow for viewing the world in all its beauty with gratitude, depth, and the thread of connection. For as we breathe, we are air. We are water. We are earth. We are what is missing from the equation of wholeness.

The body, made of earth's mud and breathed into, is the temple, and we need to learn to worship it as such, to move slowly within it, respecting it, loving it, treating ourselves and all our loved ones with tenderness. And the love for the body and for the earth are the same love.

Crazy Horse, one of the brilliant and compassionate leaders of the Sioux nation who witnessed the death of the animals and loved ones, wore a stone beneath his arm that was given him by an old medicine man named Chips. The stone was his ally. For Indian people, even now, the earth and its inhabitants all have spirit, matter is alive, and the world is an ally. This is necessary to remember as we go about a relearning of the sacred flesh, that we are energized by the stars, by the very fire of life burning within all the containers and kinds of skin, even the skin of water, of stone.

ALL MY RELATIONS

It is a sunny, clear day outside, almost hot, and a slight breeze comes through the room from the front door. We sit at the table and talk. As is usual in an Indian household, food preparation began as soon as we arrived and now there is the snap of potatoes frying in the black skillet, the sweet smell of white bread overwhelming even the grease, and the welcome black coffee. A ringer washer stands against the wall of the kitchen, and the counter space is taken up with dishes, pans, and boxes of food.

I am asked if I still read books and I admit that I do. Reading is not "traditional" and education has long been suspect in communities that were broken, in part, by that system, but we laugh at my confession because a television set plays in the next room.

In the living room there are two single beds. People from reservations, travelers needing help, are frequent guests here. The man who will put together the ceremony I have come to request sits on one, dozing. A girl takes him a plate of food. He eats. He is a man I have respected for many years, for his commitment to the people, for his intelligence, for his spiritual and political involvement in concerns vital to Indian people and nations. Next to him sits a girl eating potato chips, and from this room we hear the sounds of the freeway.

After eating and sitting, it is time for me to talk to him, to tell him why we have come here. I have brought him tobacco and he nods and listens as I tell him about the help we need.

I know this telling is the first part of the ceremony, my part in it. It is a story, really, that finds its way into language, and story is at the very crux of healing, at the heart of every ceremony and ritual in the older America.

The ceremony itself includes not just our own prayers and stories of what brought us to it, but includes the unspoken records of history, the mythic past, and all the other lives connected to ours, our family, nations, and all other creatures.

I am sent home to prepare. I tie fifty tobacco ties, green. This I do with Bull Durham tobacco, squares of cotton that are tied with twine and left strung together. These are called prayer ties. I spend the time preparing in silence and alone. Each tie has a prayer in it. I will also need wood for the fire, meat and bread for food.

On the day of the ceremony, we meet in the next town and leave my car in public parking. My daughters and I climb into the backseat of my friend's car. The man who will help us is drumming and singing in front of us. His wife drives and chats. He doesn't speak. He is moving between the worlds, beginning already to step over the boundaries of what we think, in daily and ordinary terms, is real and present. He is already feeling, hearing, knowing what else is there, that which is around us daily but too often unacknowledged, a larger life than our own small ones. We pass billboards and little towns and gas stations. An eagle flies overhead. It is "a good sign," we all agree. We stop to watch it.

We stop again, later, at a convenience store to fill the gas tank and to buy soda. The leader still drums and is silent. He is going into the drum, going into the center, even here as we drive west on the highway, even with our conversations about other people, family.

It is a hot balmy day, and by the time we reach the site where the ceremony is to take place, we are slow and sleepy with the brightness and warmth of the sun. In some tribes, men and women participate in separate sweat lodge ceremonies, but here, men, women, and children all come together to sweat. The children are cooling off in the creek. A woman stirs the fire that lives inside a circle of black rocks, pots beside her, a jar of oil, a kettle, a can of coffee. The leaves of the trees are thick and green.

In the background, the sweat lodge structure stands. Birds are on it. It is still skeletal. A woman and man are beginning to place old rugs and blankets over the bent cottonwood frame. A great fire is already burning and the lava stones that will be the source of heat for the sweat are being fired in it.

A few people sit outside on lawn chairs and cast-off couches that have the stuffing coming out. We sip coffee and talk about the food, about recent events. A man tells us that a friend gave him money for a new car. The creek sounds restful. Another man falls asleep. My young daughter splashes in the water. Heat waves rise up behind us from the fire that is preparing the stones. My tobacco ties are placed inside, on the framework of the lodge.

By late afternoon we are ready, one at a time, to enter the enclosure. The hot lava stones are placed inside. They remind us of earth's red and fiery core, and of the spark inside all life. After the flap, which serves as a door, is closed, water is poured over the stones and the hot steam rises around us. In a sweat lodge ceremony, the entire world is brought inside the enclosure. The soft odor of smoking cedar accompanies this arrival of everything. It is all called in. The animals come from the warm and sunny distances. Water from dark lakes is there. Wind. Young, lithe willow branches bent overhead remember their lives rooted in ground, the sun their leaves took in. They remember that minerals and water rose up their trunks, and that birds nested in their leaves, and that planets turned above their brief, slender lives. The thunder clouds travel in from far regions of earth. Wind arrives from the four directions. It has moved through caves and breathed through our bodies. It is the same air elk have inhaled, air that passed through the lungs of a grizzly bear. The sky is there, with all the stars whose lights we see long after the stars themselves have gone back to nothing. It is a place grown intense and holy. It is a place of immense community and of humbled solitude; we sit together in our aloneness and speak, one at a time, our deepest language of need, hope, loss, and survival. We remember that all things are connected.

Remembering this is the purpose of the ceremony. It is part of a healing and restoration. It is the mending of a broken connection between us and the rest. The participants in a ceremony say the words "All my relations" before and after we pray; those words create a relationship with other people, with animals, with the land. To have health it is necessary to keep all these relations in mind.

The intention of a ceremony is to put a person back together by restructuring the human mind. This reorganization is accomplished by a kind of inner map, a geography of the human spirit and the rest of the world. We make whole our broken-off pieces of self and world. Within ourselves, we bring together the fragments of our lives in a sacred act of renewal, and we reestablish our connections with others. The ceremony is a point of return. It takes us toward the place of balance, our place in the community of all things. It is an event that sets us back upright. But it is not a finished thing. The real ceremony begins where the formal one ends, when we take up a new way, our minds and hearts filled with the vision of earth that holds us within it, in compassionate relationship to and with our world.

We speak. We sing. We swallow water and breathe smoke. By the end of the ceremony, it is as if skin contains land and birds. The places within us have become filled. As inside the enclosure of the lodge, the animals and ancestors move into the human body, into skin and blood. The land merges with us. The stones come to dwell inside the person. Gold rolling hills take up residence, their tall grasses blowing. The red light of canyons is there. The black skies of night that wheel above our heads come to live inside the skull. We who easily grow apart from the world are returned to the great store of life all around us and there is the deepest sense of being at home here in this intimate kinship. There is no real aloneness. There is solitude and the nurturing silence that is relationship with ourselves, but even then we are part of something larger.

After a sweat lodge ceremony, the enclosure is abandoned. Quieter now, we prepare to drive home. We pack up the kettles, the coffeepot. The prayer ties are placed in nearby trees. Some of the other people prepare to go to work, go home, or cook a dinner. We drive home. Everything returns to ordinary use. A spider weaves a web from one of the cottonwood poles to another. Crows sit inside the framework. It's evening. The crickets are singing. All my relations.

KATHLEEN NORRIS
(1947–   )

Traveling on the East Coast, away from her South Dakota home, Kathleen Norris watches a crowd of commuters in Penn Station: "I was happy to be one among many, and a powerful calm came over me. I began to see each of us as a treasure-bearer, carrying our souls like a great blessing through the world." Her book about life on the Great Plains, *Dakota: A Spiritual Geography*, excerpted here, has a similar eye for epiphany in the context of the ordinary. An autobiographical portrait of the harsh, desolate, yet sublime landscape of America's vast midsection and its spiritual effects—both fundamentalism and tolerance are powerful forces—*Dakota* has been called "a deeply spiritual book," "a book of prayer," "a gift of hope." An associate or oblate of a community of Benedictine monks, Norris describes herself as a married woman, "thoroughly Protestant, who often has more doubt than anything resembling faith." *The Cloister Walk* (1995), a national best-seller, continues the theme of place and spirit.

Ghosts: A History

In this place of which you say, "It is a waste" . . . there
shall be heard again the voice of mirth and the voice of
gladness, the voice of the bridegroom and the voice
*   of the bride, the voices of those who sing.*

—Isaiah 33:10–11

The church was music to me when I was little, an enthusiastic member of the cherub choir in the large Methodist church in Arlington, Virginia, where my dad was choir director. We wore pale blue robes with voluminous sleeves, stiff white collars, and floppy black bow ties, which I thought made me look like one of the angels in my picture hymnal.

I sang from that book every day at home. One of my strongest memories of early childhood is of sitting on my mother's lap at our old, battered Steinway upright as she played the hymns and I sang. By the time I was three, long before I knew how to read, I'd turn the pages and on seeing the illustration would begin singing the right song in the right pitch.

But music was no longer enough once I discovered the rosary owned by a Catholic friend in first grade. I decided I should have one too, and when my parents said I couldn't, I took an old necklace my mom had given me and said my own grace with it at the table, after family prayers. I had to mumble, because I had no idea what I was supposed to be saying.

This was too much for my father's Methodist blood. His grandfather had been a circuit rider in West Virginia and a chaplain in the Confederate Army. His father, my grandfather, had been a stonemason, lumberjack, and jug band banjo picker who got saved one night at a tent revival, worked his way through West Virginia Wesleyan, and spent the rest of his life preaching the Word. My dad said, ominously, that I could become a Catholic if I wanted to, but he also told me they had a list of books and movies I'd be forbidden to see. For the first time in my life I had come up against the idea that when something seems too good to be true, it probably is.

And this is who I am: a complete Protestant with a decidedly ecumenical bent. I never got that rosary when I was seven, but a friend gave me one when I'd been a Benedictine oblate for nearly five years. I still value music and story over systematic theology—an understatement, given the fact that I was so dreamy as a child that I learned not from Sunday school but from a movie on television that Jesus dies. Either my Sunday school teachers had been too nice to tell me (this was the 1950s), or, as usual, I wasn't paying attention. I am just now beginning to recognize the truth of my original vision: we go to church in order to sing, and theology is secondary.

I remember very little about my confirmation class in a Congregational church in Waukegan, Illinois, except that it was easy because I was good at memorizing, and the minister was a kindly man. I was still singing in my dad's choir, and music still seemed like the real reason for church. In high school in Hawaii, my Methodist Youth Fellowship played volleyball with the Young Buddhist League.

My interest in religion deepened in adolescence, when my family joined a politically active United Church of Christ congregation, where adult classes were taught by professors of religion, one of them a German who had studied with Bultmann at Heidelberg. He was a good Lutheran, too; once, in his student days, he had a theological argument with his brother that got so bad the police had to be called.

I had a crush on him, and took a number of his classes, still totally innocent of both romance and theology; it's only with hindsight that I see I was on a disaster course. I was not yet a poet, but was destined to become one. I needed a teacher who would not have scorned Evelyn Underhill's *Mysticism*, a book I had found on my own, looking for some useful definition of religious experience. I needed liturgy and a solid grounding in the practice of prayer, not a demythologizing that left me feeling starved, thinking: If this is religion, I don't belong. Growing up and discovering who I was meant not going near a church again for nearly twenty years.

During that time I became a writer. I used to think that writing had substituted for religion in my life, but I've come to see that it has acted as a spiritual discipline, giving me the tools I needed to rediscover my religious heritage. It is my Christian inheritance that largely defines me, but for years I didn't know that.

In the early 1970s, when I was just out of college, working in New York City and hovering on the fringe of the Andy Warhol scene, a question crept into my consciousness one day, seemingly out of the blue: "What is sin?" I thought I should know, but my mind was blank. I felt like the little boy in *The Snow Queen* who, as he's being carried off in the Queen's carriage, tries desperately to remember the Lord's Prayer but can think of nothing but the multiplication tables.

"What is sin?" It never occurred to me to go to a church for the answer. If the church hadn't taught me in my first twenty years what sin was, it probably never would. I now realize that the question was raised by the pious Protestant grandmother at my core. I had no idea she was there, and didn't know how to listen to her. I didn't realize it at the time, but my move in 1974 from New York to South Dakota was an attempt to hear her voice more clearly. It was a search for inheritance, for place. It was also a religious pilgrimage; on the ground of my grandmother's faith I would find both the means and the end of my search.

All of my grandparents lived out their faith on the Plains. My paternal grandparents, the Reverend John Luther Norris and his wife, Beatrice, served twelve Methodist churches in South Dakota and several more in Iowa. Prairie people have long memories, and they still tell stories about my grandfather's kindness. One man recalls that after his wife died, leaving him with several small children, he began drinking heavily. My grandfather came to his house one day to do the family's laundry, and though the man was drinking the whole time, my grandfather never preached about it; he just kept talking to him about his plans for the future, and, as he put it, "helped me straighten up my life." In his youth, my grandfather had been a black sheep in the Methodist fold, and he often exhibited more tolerance and flexibility than his wife, who clung to a rigid and often fierce fundamentalism.

My maternal grandfather, Frank Totten, was a doctor who practiced medicine in South Dakota for fifty-five years after moving from Kansas in 1909. He could be sentimental about religion but lacked faith; his wife, Charlotte, a former schoolteacher, was a quietly pious Presbyterian, renowned in her church for the excellent Bible studies she conducted for the women's group. She was just about the only adult who could make me mind when I was little, and it was to her house that I moved in 1974, shortly after her death. I'm convinced that her spirit visited me in her kitchen and taught me how to bake bread using her bowl, her old wooden spoon and bread board. And for a time I tried on her Presbyterian church, the way I wore her old jackets and used her furniture. I still enjoyed singing hymns, but found that church was an uneasy exercise in nostalgia, and soon stopped going.

When some ten years later I began going to church again because I felt I needed to, I wasn't prepared for the pain. The services felt like word bombardment—agony for a poet—and often exhausted me so much I'd have to sleep for three or more hours afterward. Doctrinal language slammed many a door in my face, and I became frustrated when I couldn't glimpse the Word behind the words. Ironically, it was the language about Jesus Christ, meant to be most inviting, that made me feel most left out. Sometimes I'd give up, deciding that I just wasn't religious. This elicited an interesting comment from a pastor friend who said, "I don't know too many people who are so serious about religion they can't even go to church."

Even as I exemplified the pain and anger of a feminist looking warily at a religion that has so often used a male savior to keep women in their place, I was drawn to the strong old women in the congregation. Their well-worn Bibles said to me, "there is more here than you know," and made me take more seriously the religion that had caused my grandmother Totten's Bible to be so well used that its spine broke. I also began, slowly, to make sense of our gathering together on Sunday morning, recognizing, however dimly, that church is to be participated in and not consumed. The point is not what one gets out of it, but the worship of God; the service takes place both because of and despite the needs, strengths, and frailties of the people present. How else could it be? Now, on the occasions when I am able to actually worship in church, I am deeply grateful.

But the question of inheritance still haunts me, and I sometimes have the radical notion that I'm a Christian the way a Jew is a Jew, by maternal lineage. Flannery O'Connor remarks in her letters that "most of us come to the church by a means the church does not allow," and I may have put on my grandmother Totten's religion until it became my own. But the currents of this female inheritance spring from deep waters. Mary is also my ancestor, as is Eve. As Emily Dickinson once said, "You know there is no account of her death in the Bible, and why am I not Eve?" Or, why not my two grandmothers, reflecting two very different strains of American Protestantism that exist in me as a continual tension between curse and blessing, pietism and piety, law and grace, the God of wrath and the God of love.

When I was very small my fundamentalist grandmother Norris, meaning well, told me about the personal experience I'd have with Jesus one day. She talked about Jesus coming and the world ending. It sounded a lot like a fairy tale when the prince comes, only scarier. Fundamentalism is about control more than grace, and in effect my grandmother implanted the seed of fundamentalism within me, a shadow in Jungian terms, that has been difficult to overcome. Among other things, it made of Christological language a stumbling block, and told me that as a feminist, as a thinking and questioning person, I had no business being in church. More insidiously, it imbedded in me an unconscious belief in a Monster God. For most of my life you could not have convinced me that, to quote a Quaker friend, "trust comes before belief and faith is a response to love more than an acceptance of dogma."

Trust is something abused children lack, and children raised with a Monster God inside them have a hard time regaining it. My uncle told me once about having his mother sit at the edge of his bed and tell him that Jesus might come as a thief in the night and tomorrow could be that great day when the world ends. "That sucks when you'd been planning a ball game and a rubber gun battle," he said. He would pull the covers over his head when she left, and try to shut out the sounds of Jesus sneaking around in the dark.

A few years ago when I was on retreat at a monastery a poem came boiling up out of me. Called "The Jesus They Made For Us," it is an exorcism of the Monster God:

> He was a boy who drank his mother's milk
> He was always kind to children
> He swallowed them like fish
> He drank up all his mother's milk
> He ate up stars like candy
> He swallowed the sea like a hungry whale

This last image came from a dream I'd had in which I lay on a beach unable to move as a giant whale swam toward me, meaning to rape and crush me. I suspected that this whale was my true image of God, a legacy of my childhood.

A few days later I happened to visit with a little girl who showed me her drawing journal. A recent entry was a big blue whale with three words printed underneath it in purple crayon: "God Is Love." Startled, I said, "That's a wonderful picture," and she replied dreamily, "I just love that whale." With no small sense of awe I realized that we had each partaken of a powerful image, and the difference in how we perceived it amounted to the difference between us. This taught me a new appreciation of what it means to approach the holy as a little child, and some of my trust was restored.

But trust in the religious sphere has been hard to come by. Like many Americans of my baby boom generation, I had thought that religion was a constraint that I had overcome by dint of reason, learning, artistic creativity, sexual liberation. Church was for little kids or grandmas, a small-town phenomenon that one grew out of or left behind. It was a shock to realize that, to paraphrase Paul Simon, all the crap I learned in Sunday school was still alive and kicking inside me. I was also astonished to discover how ignorant I was about my own religion. Apart from a few Bible stories and hymns remembered from childhood I had little with which to start to build a mature faith. I was still that child in *The Snow Queen*, asking "what is sin?" but not knowing how to find out. Fortunately a Benedictine friend provided one answer: "Sin, in the New Testament," he told me, "is the failure to do concrete acts of love." That is something I can live with, a guide in my conversion. It's also a much better definition of sin than I learned as a child: sin as breaking rules.

Comprehensible, sensible sin is one of the unexpected gifts I've found in the monastic tradition. The fourth-century monks began to answer a question for me that the human potential movement of the late twentieth century never seemed to address: if I'm O.K. and you're O.K., and our friends (nice people and, like us, markedly middle class, if a bit bohemian) are O.K., why is the world definitely not O.K.? Blaming others wouldn't do. Only when I began to see the world's ills mirrored in myself did I begin to find an answer; only as I began to address that uncomfortable word, sin, did I see that I was not being handed a load of needless guilt so much as a useful tool for confronting the negative side of human behavior.

The desert monks were not moralists concerned that others behave in a proper way so much as people acutely aware of their own weaknesses who tried to see their situation clearly without the distortions of pride, ambition, or anger. They saw sin (what they called bad thoughts) as any impulse that leads us away from paying full attention to who and what we are and what we're doing; any thought or act that interferes with our ability to love God and neighbor. Many desert stories speak of judgment as the worst obstacle for a monk. "Abba Joseph said to Abba Pastor: 'Tell me how I can become a monk.' The elder replied: 'If you want to have rest here in this life and also in the next, in every conflict with another say, "Who am I?" and judge no one.' "

One of my favorite monastic stories in this regard concerns a desert monk who is surprised to hear that a gardener in a nearby city has a way of life more pleasing to God than his own. Visiting the city he finds the man selling vegetables, and asks for shelter overnight. The gardener, overcome with joy to be of service, welcomes the monk into his home. While the monk admires the gardener's hospitality and life of prayer, he is disturbed to find that the vulgar songs of drunks can be heard coming from the street, and asks the gardener: "Tell me, what do you conceive in your heart when you hear these things?" The man replies, "That they are all going to the kingdom." The old monk marvels and says, "This is the practice which surpasses my labor of all these years. Forgive me, brother, I have not yet approached this standard." And without eating, he withdraws again into the desert.

The monk, as virtuous as he is, recognizes that he has room for improvement. Chances are he would agree with Gregory of Nyssa, a fourth-century theologian, that sin is the failure to grow. In our own century, Carl Jung has reminded us that to grow we must eventually stop running from our "shadow" and turn to face it. Around the time I joined my grandmother's church I dreamed that a fundamentalist minister and his flock had surrounded my house, threatening to bury me alive under a truckload of rocks and dirt. I sat inside, feeling helpless as they sang hymns and shouted curses. Finally, however, I went outside to face them. I ordered them to leave, and woke up feeling as if a great weight had been lifted from me.

I realized just how far I'd come later that year in a writing workshop. One student was a Pentecostal Christian who wrote testimonies, and early one morning I wept as I read one. It could have been my grandmother Norris speaking and it frightened me for that reason, but her work was also in need of editing and I had a terrific responsibility, as the woman had never before submitted any writing for criticism. Fortunately, she took to editing like a duck to water, but what moved me deeply was her thanking me for being open to the religious nature of her work.

Religion is in my blood, and in my ghosts. My maternal grandmother Totten had a livable faith and a tolerance that allowed her to be open to the world. My grandmother Norris lived with the burden of a harder faith. She had married my grandfather—a divorced man whose wife had abandoned him and their two small children—after his conversion at a revival meeting. The older sister she revered became a medical missionary, but my grandmother found her mission in marriage and in raising seven children as the wife of a Plains pastor who served in seventeen churches in thirty-two years. Their first child born on the Plains, Kathleen Dakota, was born with rickets. While my grandmother was still nursing she conceived again; her doctor found her too exhausted and malnourished to sustain another pregnancy and performed an abortion. Early in their marriage her husband had rejected her affection in such a way that it was still fresh in her memory sixty years later. Long after he was dead she could calmly say, "You know, of course, he never loved me."

Her last child was born when she was in her forties, soon after her stepson, the eldest, died of meningitis. She prayed for another boy and promised the Lord that she would rear him to become a minister if her prayers were answered—Grandma Norris was nothing if not biblical. She had a son who tried and failed to live out her plans for him; only years later did she affirm him in his chosen vocation of teaching, reasoning that Jesus was a teacher, too. For most of her life she would ask of anyone she met: "Are you saved?"

It's this hard religion, adding fuel to an all-American mix of incest, rape, madness, and suicide, that nearly destroyed an entire generation in my family. My father's status as oldest remaining son, his musical talent, a sense of humor, and a solid marriage helped save him. But my aunts suffered terribly, and one was lost. I never met her; she died the year I was born. She died of lots of things: sex and fundamentalist religion and schizophrenia and postpartum despair. She was a good girl who became pregnant out of wedlock and could make no room for the bad girl in herself. She jumped out of a window at a state mental hospital a few days after she had her baby.

Looking at an old family photograph when I was twelve, I saw a face I didn't recognize. Asking who this was, I first heard her story. Suicides have a way of haunting the next generation, and adolescence is when most of us begin to know who we will be. I believe I became a writer in order to tell her story and possibly redeem it. This goes much deeper than anything I understand but, in part, I also joined a church because of her. I needed to find that woman sacrificed to a savage god. I needed to make sure she was forgiven and at peace.

The first time I stayed at a monastery hermitage I surfaced one day for morning prayer with the community. My stomach was growling, anticipating breakfast, and I was restless. A monk read what I've since learned is a prayer they say every morning, that all their deceased confreres, oblates, relatives, benefactors, and friends may rest in the peace of the risen Christ. That morning, I knew it was done; I didn't have to worry about my aunt any more. They tell me this is Catholic theology, not Protestant; I couldn't care less. Her name was Mary, and she had good pitch. The church was music to her, and she sang all her life in church choirs.

RITA DOVE
(1952–   )

United States poet laureate and the youngest poet so named, Rita Dove grew up in Ohio, took an M.F.A. at the Iowa Writers' Workshop, and is now Commonwealth Professor of English at the University of Virginia. She has written of her background in the AME (African Methodist Episcopal) Zion Church, where she loved the hymn singing and "the choral outbursts." She defines grace as "a state of being, not an assault." The poem "Gospel," which follows here, is taken from her 1987 Pulitzer prizewinning *Thomas and Beulah,* an extraordinary verse cycle loosely based on her grandparents' lives.

Gospel

Swing low so I
can step inside—
a humming ship of voices
big with all

the wrongs done
done them.
No sound this generous
could fail:

ride joy until
it cracks like an egg,
make sorrow
seethe and whisper.

From a fortress
of animal misery
soars the chill voice
of the tenor, enraptured

with sacrifice.
What do I see,

he complains, notes
brightly rising

towards a sky
blank with promise.
Yet how healthy
the single contralto

settling deeper
into her watery furs!
Carry me home,
she cajoles, bearing

down. Candelabras
brim. But he slips
through God's net and swims
heavenward, warbling.

BELL HOOKS
(1952–   )

Author of such highly acclaimed and provocative books as *Ain't I a
Woman: Black Women and Feminism* (1981) and *Talking Back:
Thinking Feminist, Thinking Black* (1988), bell hooks grew up as Gloria
Watkins in Kentucky. She is currently professor of English at City
College in New York City and a cultural activist in the movement to
create a spiritual, progressive, feminist, and ultimately organic definition
of black intellectuality. In the dialogue that follows here, excerpted from
Breaking Bread: Insurgent Black Intellectual Life (1991), hooks and
Cornel West grapple with the dilemmas, the contradictions, and
especially the spiritual foundations of black culture.

From *Breaking Bread: Insurgent Black Intellectual Life*

CW. . . Let's return to your work. The degree to which you infuse a kind
of spirituality, through the integration of existential issues, issues of psychic
survival, the absurd, political engagement, and a deep sense of history.
Those levels are interwoven in so many ingenious ways in your work. Take

for instance the devaluation of Black women which has been overlooked by White establishment but which has also been overlooked by male-dominated Black nationalist politics. How can we as a people talk seriously about spirituality and political engagement in order to project a future, while simultaneously coming to terms with the past?

bh It's interesting to me that you should combine discussion of Black spirituality with the devaluation of Black women because one of the things I've tried to say throughout my work, when I've talked about religion, is that however we might fault the Black church, it has always been a place where Black women have had dignity and respect. Growing up with a sense of the value of Black womanhood came, in part, from the place I saw Black women hold in the church. I think it is very hard for many people to understand that, despite the sexism of the Black church, it was also a place where many Black women found they could drop the mask that was worn all day in Miss Anne's house; they could drop that need to serve others. Church was a place you could be and say, "Father I stretch my hands to thee," and you could let go. In a sense you could drop the layers of daily existence and get to the core of yourself.

The degradation Black women may have experienced in daily life would fall away in the church. It was noting this difference as a young woman that made me think about how the larger society devalues Black womanhood—a devaluation that is perpetuated in our own communities.

What gives me some measure of hope is seeing Shahrazad Ali on the Phil Donahue show with Haki Madhubuti and hearing him say that he did not sell *The Black Man's Guide to Understanding the Black Woman* in his bookstore because it advocated violence against Black women. A subversive and important moment which was undercut when Donahue rushed in and said, "That's censorship." It's telling that a White male "liberal" can make the issue of censorship more important than violence against Black women. We are still in a society where violence against Black womanhood is seen as unimportant, not worthy of concern. Pearl Cleage's short book of essays, *Mad at Miles,* addresses the way violence against Black women is often not taken seriously in our communities—particularly by men.

What I wanted so much to do in my first book was to say there is a history that has produced this circumstance of devaluation. It is not something inherent in Black women that we don't feel good about ourselves, that we are self-hating. Rather it is an experience which is socially circumscribed, brought into being by historical mechanisms. I have to acknowledge here, Cornel, that writing *Ain't I a Woman* was an expression of spiritual devotion to Black womanhood.

*   *   *

CW This is what strikes me as being unique about your work, that in your four volumes critiquing European imperialism, critiquing patriarchy, critiquing class exploitation, critiquing misogyny, critiquing homophobia, what I discern, as well, is a preoccupation with the dynamics of spiritual and personal change so that there is a politics of conversion shot through the political, economic, and social critiques.

*   *   *

bh I would start with the question of devotion and discipline because when I look at the evolution of my identity as a writer I see it intimately tied to my spiritual evolution. If we think of the slaves as bringing to new world Christianity a sense of personal relationship with God, evidenced most easily in Black spirituals like the one that says, "When I die tomorrow I will say to the Lord, Oh Lord you been my friend." This sense of immediate connection, we find again when we look at mystical religious experience globally—Sufism, Islamic mysticism. The idea that it is not our collective relationship to God that brings about enlightenment and transformation, rather our personal relationship to God. This is intimately linked to the discipline of being a writer. Which is also why it is important to understand the role of solitude and contemplation in Malcolm's life.

One of the things that is very different in my life from the life of my siblings is this ability to be alone, to be with my inner self. When we talk about becoming an intellectual, in the real life-enhancing sense of that word, we're really talking about what it is to sit with one's ideas, where one's mind becomes a workplace, where one really takes enormous amounts of time to contemplate and critically reflect on things. That experience of aloneness undergirds my intellectual practice and it is rooted in spiritual discipline where I have sought aloneness with God and listened to the inner voice of God as it speaks to me in the stillness of my life. I think a great deal about young Black folks engaged in intellectual/artistic production, and wonder if they understand the story of Christ going into the desert, if they know an inner place of absence in which they can be renewed and experience spiritual enlightenment.

CW How do you reconcile those crucial points about solitude with community and the emphasis Black people have on community?

bh I've certainly engaged fully with a number of religious traditions, but in all of them one holds up the notion that when you are truly able to be alone in that sense of Christ going into the garden of Gethsemane or going into the desert, or Buddha sitting under the Boti tree, it actually enables you to re-enter community more fully. This is something that I grapple with a great deal, the sense of collective communal experience. The great gift of enlightenment for whomever it comes to is the sense that only after we are able to experience ourselves within a context of autonomy, aloneness, independence, are we able to come into community with knowledge of our place, and feeling that what we have to give is for the good of the whole. Think, for example, of the question of what it means to save someone's life, which was raised in *Mo' Better Blues*. In order to intervene and save someone's life, one must know, first of all, how to take individual accountability for who we are, for life choices we make. I see how questions of accountability affect my own relationship to community precisely because as I develop intellectually and spiritually, I need greater periods of time alone. And it seems the greater my need to be alone, the greater my need to re-enter community as well.

CW . . . One question about your own life. I think continually, incessantly, and obsessively about the title of James Baldwin's book *The Price of the Ticket*. One of the fundamental things about Black intellectual life is the cost that one has to pay for prophetic vocation, and we know James Baldwin himself paid a very high cost for that. How would you begin to talk about the price of the ticket, the price one has to pay as a prophetic intellectual?

bh Well, I already answered that when I spoke earlier about discipline, solitude, and community. The Buddhist monk Thich Nhat Hanh says that when a person decides to truly be themselves, they are going to find themselves alone. I think often about Martin Luther King's decision to oppose the Vietnam War and how his speeches were tied to a certain sense of isolation. He says in his sermon that many preachers will not agree with him and he will find himself alone, at which point he quotes that famous passage from Romans, "Do not be conformed to this world but be ye transformed that you may know what the will of God is, that which is good and perfect . . ." I have grappled with an enormous sense of isolation. We've had many Black women academics but, to some extent, we are a new generation. We represent the first generation of Black women thinkers who don't have to have children, or manage a household, if we choose. Molly Haskell, a White woman film critic, says, "To claim one's strength as a woman is a fearful thing. Easier to idealize the man or denigrate him, worship at the feet of male authority than explore and exhibit one's own soul, luxuriate in one's own power and risk ending up alone. Once we take responsibility for our mental processes we take responsibility for our lives, that is what feminism has become for me, looking fiercely and accurately not passively and defensively at the pattern of our lives and acknowledging all the ways which we are not victims but are responsible for the way which we connect the past to the present." These words moved me deeply because I think one of the costs that we pay for uncompromised intellectual pursuit is certain forms of isolation, where, if one does not take care to find community, can be very disenabling and debilitating.

CW Which community does one re-enter with this kind of critical consciousness, this kind of prophetic vocation?

bh Part of the joy of having these kinds of conversations with you is that this is a form of re-entering community. One of the things I sometimes say teasingly to myself is, I take my community where I find it. I used to have very utopian, idealized notion of community, long for the perfect relationship—me and another bohemian Black male intellectual, within the perfect Black community of like-minded souls. Now I'm learning to be nourished from wherever that sense of community comes from, and this way of thinking has enlarged my community. For too long we have conceptualized the Black community in narrow terms. We conceptualized it as a neighborhood that is all Black, something as superficial as that. When, in fact, it seems to me that it is by extending my sense of community that I am able to find nourishment, that I am able to think of this time spent with you in conversation as a kind of communion.

I think back to why we considered calling our dialogues together *Breaking Bread*—the sense of taking one's nourishment in that space where you find it.

ANNE LAMOTT
(1954–   )

Anne Lamott's very funny *Operating Instructions: A Journal of My Son's First Year* (1993), excerpted here, is as much about faith and the miracle of love as the experience of single motherhood. The wisdom that grows from adversity, a theme of many of the lives and narratives represented in this book, comes through in Lamott's writing with a humor and originality that lift you up and set you free. A novelist, teacher, and recovered alcoholic, Lamott survives her various crises with the help of her friends and the people of St. Andrew Presbyterian Church, Marin City, California, where she lives. As she puts it, quoting an old *New Yorker* story, "we are not here to see through one another, but to see one another through." One review described her book as "gracious . . . with a deep, infectious religiosity throughout." When Dorothy Sayers (see page 174) read Dante's "Paradiso," she wrote: "This is what he thought reality was like, when you got to the *eterna fontana* at the center of it: this laughter, this inebriation, this riot of charity and hilarity." Anne Lamott is on the same wavelength.

From *Operating Instructions*

SEPTEMBER 17

Sam was an angel today, no fussing, no colic, sweet and pretty as a movie baby, all eyes and thick dark hair. We went to church and a blissed-out Alma got to hold him almost the entire time. She keeps shaking her fist and saying, "This is *our* baby, *our* baby." Alma is about eighty, very very black, about four-foot-two, and wears these amazing outfits and hats that are like polyester Coco Chanels. Our pastor Harrell showed a ten-minute movie that was one of the purest statements of faith I've ever seen. It was about a tall, sweet-looking, blind man running in the Dipsea race on the arm of his best friend, who could see. The Dipsea race goes over Mount Tamalpais and ends up in the Pacific Ocean at Stinson Beach; it is grueling beyond words, very steeply uphill and then equally steeply down, exquisitely beautiful to look at, all woods and redwoods and rich rich earth and millions of wild animals. The trail lies on rugged, rocky terrain; it is hard to *hike* up and down it, let alone run. I always end up feeling like Rose Kennedy after one of those hikes, incredibly old in the joints, especially in the knees, hobbling, panting, out of it. This movie tracks the two men amid the several thousand people who run the race every year, serious runners and *King of Hearts* types together, as they leave downtown Mill Valley and head up the steps that lead to the mountain path. The footage shows this landscape to be almost biblically beautiful and difficult, just like real life. I have come to believe more with every passing year that despite technological evidence to the contrary, it is still secretly an Old Testament world out there.

The seeing man called out every root, every rock, holding the hand of his blind friend. They ran together joyfully, the seeing man calling, "Step, step, step, step, step," as they went up and down eighty-degree steps and "Roots roots roots," as they navigated trails laced with huge tree roots. They ran bobbingly, like football players stepping quickly in and out of tires during practice. "Good good, uh-oh *rock*," the seeing man would say. They both tripped a bunch of times, and the blind guy fell once, but mostly they seemed connected and safe.

I know it is odd to a lot of people that I am religious—I mean, it's odd to *me* that I'm religious, I never meant to be. I don't quite know how it happened: I think that at some point, a long time ago, I made a decision to believe, and then every step of the way, even through the worst of it, the two years my dad was sick with brain cancer, the last few years of my drinking, I could feel the presence of something I could turn to, something that would keep me company, give me courage, be there with me, like the seeing man in this movie. The movie so exactly captured how I feel these days, that Jesus is there with us everyplace Sam and I go.

When people used to say shit like this to me, I'd look at them politely and think, Well, isn't that special. Did we take our meds this morning? It was no different for me than listening to Scientologists babble about engrams and the space opera and having gotten cleared that morning. So I don't quite know what to say. Still, when I feel like I'm coming apart like a two-dollar watch, it helps me beyond words to look at myself through the eyes of Mary, totally adoring and gentle, instead of through the critical eyes of the men at the Belvedere Tennis Club, which is how I've looked at myself nearly all my life.

I don't think the men at the Belvedere Tennis Club would look at this big exhausted weepy baggy mentally ill cellulite unit we call Annie Lamott and see a beautiful precious heroic child. But Mary does.

RIGOBERTA MENCHU
(1959–   )

Rigoberta Menchu, a Quiche Indian of Guatemala, told her life story to anthropologist Elisabeth Burgos-Debray, herself a Latin American woman, who edited and translated the tapes into English, producing the book excerpted here, *I, Rigoberta Menchu*. Famous in Guatemala as a human rights advocate and leader, Menchu began her work on behalf of the protection of Indian peasants as a catechist, inspired by a deep religious belief. In 1978 her brother, father, and mother all were murdered in separate incidents of savagery on the part of the army. Six of her nine brothers and sisters disappeared and are presumed dead. She fled to Mexico in 1981. When she won the Nobel Peace Prize in 1992, the brutal rightist military and President Jorge Serrano scorned her award, calling it a victory for Guatemalan guerrillas. In the pages that follow, Menchu describes studying the Bible as a freedom narrative, taking the Jewish freedom fighter Judith (see page 18) as a model of self-defense for women.

"The Bible and Self-Defense: The Examples of Judith, Moses and David"

". . . when the strangers who came from the East arrived, when they arrived; the ones who brought Christianity which ended the power in the East, and made the heavens cry and filled the maize bread of the Katún with sadness . . ."

—Chilam Balam

"Their chief was not defeated by young warriors, nor wounded by sons of Titans. It was Judith, the daughter of Marari, who disarmed him with the beauty of her face."

—The Bible ('Judith')

We began to study the Bible as our main text. Many relationships in the Bible are like those we have with our ancestors, our ancestors whose lives were very much like our own. The important thing for us is that we started to identify that reality with our own. That's how we began studying the Bible. It's not something you memorize, it's not just to be talked about and prayed about, and nothing more. It also helped to change the image we had, as Catholics and Christians: that God is up there and that God has a great kingdom for we the poor, yet never thinking of our own reality as a reality that we were actually living. But by studying the scriptures, we did. Take "Exodus" for example, that's one we studied and analysed. It talks a lot about the life of Moses who tried to lead his people from oppression, and did all he could to free his people. We compare the Moses of those days with ourselves, the "Moses" of today. "Exodus" is about the life of a man, the life of Moses.

We began looking for texts which represented each one of us. We tried to relate them to our Indian culture. We took the example of Moses for the men, and we have the example of Judith, who was a very famous woman in her time and appears in the Bible. She fought very hard for her people and made many attacks against the king they had then, until she finally had his head. She held her victory in her hand, the head of the King. This gave us a vision, a stronger idea of how we Christians must defend ourselves. It made us think that a people could not be victorious without a just war. We Indians do not dream of great riches, we want only enough to live on. There is also the story of David, a little shepherd boy who appears in the Bible, who was able to defeat the king of those days, King Goliath. This story is the example for the children. This is how we look for stories and psalms which teach us how to defend ourselves from our enemies. I remember taking examples from all the texts which helped the community to understand their situation better. It's not only now that there are great kings, powerful men, people who hold power in their hands. Our ancestors suffered under them too. This is how we identify with the lives of our ancestors who were conquered by a great desire for power—our ancestors were murdered and tortured because they were Indians. We began studying more deeply and, well, we came to a conclusion. That being a Christian means thinking of our brothers around us, and that every one of our Indian race has the right to eat. This reflects what God himself said, that on this earth we have a right to what we need. The Bible was our principal text for study as Christians and it showed us what the role of a Christian is. I became a catechist as a little girl and I studied the Bible, hymns, the scriptures, but only very superficially. One of the things Catholic Action put in our heads is that everything is sinful. But we came round to asking ourselves: "If everything is sinful, why is it that the landowner kills humble peasants who don't even harm the natural world? Why do they take our lives?" When I first became a catechist, I thought that there was a God and that we had to serve him. I thought God was up there and that he had a kingdom for the poor. But we realized that it is not God's will that we should live in suffering, that God did not give us that destiny, but that men on earth have imposed this suffering, poverty, misery and discrimination on us. We even got the idea of using our own everyday weapons, as the only solution left to us.

I am a Christian and I participate in this struggle as a Christian. For me, as a Christian, there is one important thing. That is the life of Christ. Throughout his life Christ was humble. History tells us he was born in a little hut. He was persecuted and had to form a band of men so that his seed would not disappear. They were his disciples, his apostles. In those days, there was no other way of defending himself or Christ would have used it against his oppressors, against his enemies. He even gave his life. But Christ did not die, because generations and generations have followed him. And that's exactly what we understood when our first catechists fell. They're dead but our people keep their memory alive through our struggle against the government, against an enemy who oppresses us. We don't need very much advice, or theories, or documents: life has been our teacher. For my part, the horrors I have suffered are enough for me. And I've also felt in the deepest part of me what discrimination is, what exploitation is. It is the story of my life. In my work I've often gone hungry. If I tried to recount the number of times I'd gone hungry in my life, it would take a very long time. When you understand this, when you see your own reality, a hatred grows inside you for those oppressors that make the people suffer so. As I said, and I say it again, it is not fate which makes us poor.

It's not because we don't work, as the rich say. They say: "Indians are poor because they don't work, because they're always asleep." But I know from experience that we're outside ready for work at three in the morning. It was this that made us decide to fight. This is what motivated me, and also motivated many others. Above all the mothers and fathers. They remember their children. They remember the ones they would like to have with them now but who died of malnutrition, or intoxication in the *fincas*, or had to be given away because they had no way of looking after them. It has a long history. And it's precisely when we look at the lives of Christians in the past that we see what our role as Christians should be today. I must say, however, that I think even religions are manipulated by the system, by those same governments you find everywhere. They use them through their ideas or through their methods. I mean, it's clear that a priest never works in the *fincas*, picking cotton or coffee. He wouldn't know what picking cotton was. Many priests don't even know what cotton is. But our reality teaches us that, as Christians, we must create a Church of the poor, that we don't need a Church imposed from outside which knows nothing of hunger. We recognize that the system has wanted to impose on us: to divide us and keep the poor dormant. So we take some things and not others. As far as sins go, it seems to me that the concept of the Catholic religion, or any other more conservative religion than Catholicism, is that God loves the poor and has a wonderful paradise in Heaven for the poor, so the poor must accept the life they have on Earth. But as Christians, we have understood that being a Christian means refusing to accept all the injustices which are committed against our people, refusing to accept the discrimination committed against a humble people who barely know what eating meat is but who are treated worse than horses. We've learned all this by watching what has happened in our lives. This awakening of the Indians didn't come, of course, from one day to the next, because Catholic Action and other religions and the system itself have all tried to keep us where we were. But I think that unless a religion springs from within the people themselves, it is a weapon of the system. So, naturally, it wasn't at all difficult for our community to understand all this and the reasons for us to defend ourselves, because this is the reality we live.

As I was saying, for us the Bible is our main weapon. It has shown us the way. Perhaps those who call themselves Christians but who are really only Christians in theory, won't understand why we give the Bible the meaning we do. But that's because they haven't lived as we have. And also perhaps because they can't analyse it. I can assure you that any one of my community, even though he's illiterate and has to have it read to him and translated into his language, can learn many lessons from it, because he has no difficulty understanding what reality is and what the difference is between the paradise up above, in Heaven, and the reality of our people here on Earth. We do this because we feel it is the duty of Christians to create the kingdom of God on Earth among our brothers. This kingdom will exist only when we all have enough to eat, when our children, brothers, parents don't have to die from hunger and malnutrition. That will be the "Glory," a Kingdom for we who have never known it. I'm only talking about the Catholic church in general terms because, in fact, many priests came to our region and were anti-communists, but nevertheless understood that the people weren't communists but hungry; not communists, but exploited by the system. And they joined our people's struggle too, they opted for the life we Indians live. Of course many priests call themselves Christians when they're only defending their own petty interests and they keep themselves apart from the people so as not to endanger these interests. All the better for us, because we know very well that we don't need a king in a palace but a brother who lives with us. We don't need a leader to show us where God is, to say whether he exists or not, because, through our own conception of God, we know there is a God and that, as the father of us all, he does not wish even one of his children to die, or be unhappy, or have no joy in life. We believe that, when we started using the Bible, when we began studying it in terms of our reality, it was because we found in it a document to guide us. It's not that the document itself brings about the change, it's more that each one of us learns to understand his reality and wants to devote himself to others. More than anything else, it was a form of learning for us. Perhaps if we'd had other means to learn, things would have been different. But we understood that any element in nature can change man when he is ready for change. We believe the Bible is a necessary weapon for our people. Today I can say that it is a struggle which cannot be stopped. Neither the governments nor imperialism can stop it because it is a struggle of hunger and poverty. Neither the government nor imperialism can say: "Don't be hungry," when we are all dying of hunger.

To learn about self-defence, as I was saying, we studied the Bible. We began fashioning our own weapons. We knew very well that the government, those cowardly soldiers . . . perhaps I shouldn't talk of them so harshly, but I can't find another word for them. Our weapons were very simple. And at the same time, they weren't so simple when we all started using them, when the whole village was armed. As I said before, the soldiers arrived one night. Our people were not in their homes. They'd left the village and gone to the camp. They made sure that we hadn't abandoned the village altogether but thought it would be better to occupy it in the daytime. So sometime later, when we weren't expecting them, about fifteen days later, our lookouts saw the army approaching. We were in the middle of building houses for our neighbours. We needed some more huts there. We had two lookouts. One was supposed to warn the community and the other had to delay or stop the soldiers entering. They were aware that they might have to give their lives for the community. At a time like this, if someone can't escape, he must be ready to accept death. The army arrived, and the first two to enter wore civilian clothes. But our children can easily recognize soldiers, by the way they walk, and dress, and everything about them, so the lookouts knew they were soldiers in disguise. They asked the names of certain *compañeros* in the community so they could take them away, kidnap them. One of the lookouts got away and came to warn the village that the enemy was nearby. We asked him if he was sure and he said: "Yes, they are soldiers, two of them. But as I was coming up here I saw others coming, further off, with olive green uniforms." The whole community left the village straight away and gathered in one place. We were very worried because the other lookout didn't appear. They were capable of having kidnapped him. But he did turn up in the end and told us how many soldiers there were, what each one was like, what sort of weapons they had, how many in the vanguard and the rearguard. This information helped us decide what to do, because it was daytime and we hadn't set our traps. We said: "What are we going to do with this army?" They came into the village and began beating our dogs and killing our animals. They went into the houses and looted them. They went crazy looking for us all over the place. Then we asked: "Who is willing to risk their lives now?" I, my brothers and some other neighbours immediately put up our hands. We planned to give the army a shock and to show them we were organised and weren't just waiting passively for them. We had less than half an hour to plan how we were going to capture some weapons. We chose some people — the ones who'd go first, second, third, fourth, to surprise the enemy. How would we do it? We couldn't capture all ninety soldiers who'd come to the village, but we could get the rearguard. My village is a long way from the town, up in the mountains. You have to go over the mountains to get to another village. We have a little path to the village just wide enough for horses . . . and there are big rivers nearby so that the path isn't straight. It bends a lot. So we said, "Let's wait for the army on one of those bends and when the soldiers pass, we'll ambush the last one." We knew we were risking our lives but we knew that this example would benefit the village very much because the army would stop coming and searching the village all the time. And that's what we did.

We chose a *compañera*, a very young girl, the prettiest in the village. She was risking her life, and she was risking being raped as well. Nevertheless, she said: "I know very well that if this is my part in the struggle, I have to do it. If this is how I contribute to the community, I'll do it." So this *compañera* goes ahead on another path to a place that the army has to pass on

their way to the village. That's where we prepared the ambush. We didn't
have firearms, we had only our people's weapons. We'd invented a sort of
Molotov cocktail by putting petrol in a lemonade bottle with a few iron fil-
ings, mixed with oil, and a wick to light it. So if the army got one of us, or
if we couldn't do anything else, we'd set fire to them. This cocktail could
burn two or three soldiers because it could land on them and burn their
clothes. We had catapults too, or rather, they were the ones we'd always
used to protect the maize fields from the birds which would come into the
fields and eat the cobs when they were growing. The catapults could shoot
stones a long way and if your aim is good it lands where you want it to. We
had machetes, stones, sticks, chile and salt—all the different people's
weapons. We had none of the weapons the army had. The community decided that the young girl who went on ahead would try to flirt with the last
soldier and try to make him stop and talk to her. We all had numbers: who
would be the first to jump, who would get him off balance, who would
frighten him and who would disarm him. Each of us had a special task in
capturing the soldier.

First came the ones without weapons—they were members of the secret
police, soldiers in disguise. Then came the others. The whole troop. They
were about two metres away when the last one came. Our *compañera*
came along the path. She paid no attention to the others. It was a miracle
they didn't rape her, because when soldiers come to our area they usually
catch girls and rape them—they don't care who they are or where they're
from. The *compañera* was ready to endure anything. When she came to
the last soldier, she asked him where they'd been. And the soldier began
telling her: "We went to that village. Do you know what's happened to the
people?" The *compañera* said: "No, I don't know." And he said: "We've
been twice and there's no-one, but we know they live there." Then one of
our neighbours jumped onto the path, another came up behind the soldier. My job was to jump onto the path as well. Between us we got the soldier off balance. One of us said: "Don't move, hands up." And the soldier
thought there was a gun pointing at his head or his back. Whatever he
thought, he did nothing. Another *compañero* said: "Drop your weapon."
And he dropped it. We took his belt off and checked his bag. We took his
grenades away, his rifle, everything. I thought it was really funny, it's something I'll never forget, because we didn't know how to use it. We took his
rifle, his big rifle, and a pistol, and we didn't even know how to use the pistol. I remember that I took the soldier's pistol away and stood in front as if
I knew how to use it but I didn't know anything. He could have taken it
off me because I couldn't use it. But, anyway, we led him away at gun point.
We made him go up through the mountains so that if the others came back
they wouldn't find the path. If they had it would have been a massacre.

Two *compañeras* of about forty-five and a fifty-year-old *compañero* had taken part in the ambush. The little *compañera* who'd attracted the soldier was about fourteen.

We took the disarmed soldier to my house, taking all the necessary precautions. We blindfolded him so that he wouldn't recognize the house he was going to. We got him lost. We took him a round-about way so that he'd lose his sense of direction. We finally arrived back. I found it really funny, I couldn't stop laughing because we didn't know how to use the gun. We were very happy, the whole community was happy. When we got near the camp, the whole community was waiting for us. We arrived with our captured soldier. We reached my house. He stayed there for a long time. We took his uniform off and gave him an old pair of trousers and an old shirt so that if his fellow soldiers came back—we tried to keep him tied up—they wouldn't know he was a soldier. We also thought that those clothes could help us confuse the other soldiers later on. Then came a very beautiful part when all the mothers in the village begged the soldier to take a message back to the army, telling all the soldiers there to think of our ancestors. The soldier was an Indian from another ethnic group. The women asked him how he could possibly have become a soldier, an enemy of his own race, his own people, the Indian race. Our ancestors never set bad examples like that. They begged him to be the light within his camp. They explained to him that bearing a son and bringing him up was a big effort, and to see him turn into a criminal as he was, was unbearable. All the mothers in the village came to see the soldier. Then the men came too and begged him to recount his experience when he got back to the army and to take on the role, as a soldier, of convincing the others not to be so evil, not to rape the women of our race's finest sons, the finest examples of our ancestors. They suggested many things to him. We told the soldier that our people were organised, and were prepared to give their last drop of blood to counter everything the army did to us. We made him see that it wasn't the soldiers who were guilty but the rich who don't risk their lives. They live in nice houses and sign papers. It's the soldier who goes around the villages, up and down the mountains, mistreating and murdering his own people.

The soldier went away very impressed, he took this important message with him. When we first caught him, we'd had a lot of ideas, because we wanted to use the gun but didn't know how. It wasn't that we wanted to kill the soldier because we knew very well that one life is worth as much as many lives. But we also knew that the soldier would tell what he'd seen, what he'd felt and what we'd done to him, and that for us it could mean a massacre—the deaths of children, women, and old people in the village. The whole community would die. So we said: "What we'll do with this man is execute him, kill him. Not here in the village but outside." But people kept coming up with other ideas of what to do, knowing full well the risk we were running. In the end, we decided that, even though it might cost us our lives, this soldier should go and do what we'd asked him, and really carry through the role he had to play. After about three hours we let him go, in his new disguise. His comrades, the troop of ninety soldiers, hadn't come back for him because they thought he'd been ambushed by guerrillas and they were cowards. They ran off as fast as they could back to town and didn't try to save the soldier left behind. We didn't kill the soldier. The army itself took care of that when he got back to camp. They said he must be an informer, otherwise how could he possibly have stayed and then returned. They said the law says that a soldier who abandons his rifle must be shot. So they killed him.

This was the village's first action and we were happy. We now had two guns, we had a grenade, and we had a cartridge belt, but we didn't know how to use them, nobody knew. We all wanted to find someone who could show us but we didn't know where or who, because whoever we went to, we'd be accused of being guerrillas using weapons. It made us sad to open the rifle and see what was inside, because we knew it killed others. We couldn't use it but it was the custom always to keep anything important. A machete that's not being used for instance, is always smeared with oil and wrapped in a plastic bag so it doesn't rust with the damp or the rain. That's what we had to do with the weapons because we didn't know how to use them. From then on the army was afraid to come up to our villages. They never came back to our village because to get there they would have to go through the mountains. Even if they came by plane they had to fly over the mountains. They were terrified of the mountains and of us. We were happy. It was the most wonderful thing that had happened to us. We were all united. Nobody went down to the *finca*, nobody went to market, nobody went down to any other place, because they would be kidnapped. What we did was to go over the mountains, go to other towns where they sell local salt, or rather some black stones which are really salt. I don't know if you only get this type of black stone in Guatemala, it's black and it's salt. It tastes very good, delicious. So we got very large stones and cooked with these so we didn't have to buy salt in the market. The *compañeros* got salt by other means. You find these stones in Sacapúlas, a town in El Quiché. It's rather strange there because it's up on the *Altiplano* where it's cold and yet when you go down a bit, it's warm. It's on a hillside which produces all the fruits you get on the South coast. You get mangoes, water melon, bananas. And that's where you get this salt stone. They sell it but it's very cheap because nobody wants to buy. In Guatemala it's called "Indian salt." We don't eat sugar, we're not used to drinking coffee. Our drink is *atol*, ground maize made into *atol*. We produce the maize in our own areas and we do it collectively to grow things better and make better use of the land. The landowners were frightened to come near our village because they thought they would be kidnapped now that our village was organised. So they didn't come near us. The landowners went away, and didn't threaten us like before. The soldiers didn't come any more. So we stayed there, the owners of our little bit of land. We began cultivating things so we wouldn't have to go down to town. It was a discipline we applied to ourselves in the village to save lives and only to put ourselves at risk when we had to. My village was organised from this moment on.

I couldn't stay in my village any longer because, now that it could carry on its struggle, organise itself and take decisions, my role was not important. There was no room for a leader, someone telling others what to do any more. So I decided to leave my village and go and teach another community the traps which we had invented and which our own neighbours had used so successfully. It's now that I move on to teach the people in another village.

THE
TWENTIETH
CENTURY

II. New Insights:
The Goods of the Spirit according to
Shamans, Scholars, Witches, and Theologians

STARHAWK
(1951–   )

Author of *The Spiral Dance: A Rebirth of the Ancient Religion of the Great Goddess* and *Dreaming the Dark: Magic, Sex, and Politics*—the introduction to this book is excerpted here—Starhawk (Miriam Simos), a licensed minister of the Covenant of the Goddess, has for twelve years been practicing and teaching Witchcraft at various places including the Institute of Creation Spirituality in Oakland, California, and leading demonstrations against the development of nuclear power and weaponry. Witchcraft, as she has explained in numerous essays, dates back to the Paleolithic Age and the beginning of the Goddess tradition, more than thirty thousand years ago. The mysticism and rituals of Goddess religion were preserved in small groups called covens; this practice came to be called Wicca or Wicce, Anglo-Saxon for "witch." During the witch-hunts of the Middle Ages hundreds of thousands of witches—some estimate millions—most of whom were the women midwives, healers, and mystics of many European communities, were executed.

From *Dreaming the Dark*

As I write, the cats play on my desk, grooming themselves, batting my papers to the floor, or curling up to sleep, secure in the familiar. Their minds do not encompass 500-mile-an-hour winds, or the possibility that what is familiar can be transformed in a flash to charred bone and flesh.

We cannot feel as secure. The newspapers describe what would happen if the city were hit by a nuclear bomb; they tell of pesticides in well water, of a nuclear alert triggered by computer error, of children damaged by chemical wastes.

It seems the sun is going down on everybody's world, that we are about to lose what can never be reclaimed. Our acts of power seem frail compared with the powers of destruction. There are too many enemies, too many burial sites for chemical wastes, too many weapons already in the stockpiles. There are too many jobless, too many hopeless, too many rapists at large. Too many of those who wield great powers are unconcerned. They do not feel that they are a part of this world.

> Circle Three—eight miles across: winds of 160 miles an hour, destruction
> of brick and wood frame houses; exposed people seriously burned.

Even the small acts that ordinarily bring us pleasure or comfort become tinged at moments with horror. There are times when I walk down the street, and smile at the man who sits on his front stoop playing the radio, and the kids laying pennies on the streetcar tracks, and the woman whose dog plays with my dogs, but in between the blinks of my eyes they are gone. I see the flash, and then nothing is left—of these charmingly painted Victorian houses, of these ordinary people, or the features of the earth beneath these streets. Nothing—but ashes and a scorched, black void.

I know that I am not alone in being overwhelmed at times by hopelessness and despair. I hear the same fears from my friends, my family, from the clients who come to me for counseling. Everybody's personal pain is touched by this greater uncertainty: we are no longer confident of leaving a better world—of leaving a *living* world, to our children.

Yet the children must be fed, the dogs must still be walked, the work must go on, so we raise the barriers that defend us from unbearable pain, and in a state of numbness and denial we go on. The work may seem flat, but we carefully avoid questioning its meaning and its usefulness, even though we sense that something deep and sweet is missing from our lives, our families, our friendships; some sense of purpose, of power, is gone. And still the children grow up around us, no less beautiful than any other generation of children, and still when we poke a seed into the earth it continues to push forth roots and unfurl stem, leaf, flower, fruit. There are still moments when we see the processes of life continue to unfold, when we cannot help believing that life is moved by a power deeper than the power of the gun and the bomb; a power that might still prevail if we knew how to call it forth.

This book* is about the calling forth of power, a power based on a principle very different from power-over, from domination. For power-over is, ultimately, the power of the gun and the bomb, the power of annihilation that backs up all the institutions of domination.

Yet the power we sense in a seed, in the growth of a child, the power we feel writing, weaving, working, creating, making choices, has nothing to do with threats of annihilation. It has more to do with the root meaning of the word power, from the (late popular) Latin, *podere* ("to be able"). It is the power that comes from within.

There are many names for power-from-within, none of them entirely satisfying. It can be called *spirit*—but that name implies that it is separate from matter, and that false split, as we shall see, is the foundation of the institutions of domination. It could be called *God*—but the God of patriarchal religions has been the ultimate source and repository of power-over. I have called it *immanence*, a term that is truthful but somewhat cold and intellectual. And I have called it *Goddess*, because the ancient images, symbols, and myths of the Goddess as birth-giver, weaver, earth and growing plant, wind and ocean, flame, web, moon and milk, all speak to me of the powers of connectedness, sustenance, healing, creating.

The word *Goddess* makes many people who would define themselves as "political" uneasy. It implies religion, secularism, and can be mistaken for the worship of an external being. "Goddess" also makes many people who would define themselves as "spiritual" or "religious" uneasy; it smacks of Paganism, of blood, darkness, and sexuality, of lower powers.

Yet power-from-within *is* the power of the low, the dark, the earth; the power that arises from our blood, and our lives, and our passionate desire for each other's living flesh. And the political issues of our time are also issues of spirit, conflicts between paradigms or underlying principles. If we are to survive the question becomes: how do we overthrow, not those presently in power, but the principle of power-over? How do we shape a society based on the principle of power-from-within?

A change in paradigms, in consciousness, always makes us uneasy. Whenever we feel the slightly fearful, slightly embarrassed sensation that words like *Goddess* produce, we can be sure that we are on the track of a deep change in the structure as well as the content of our thinking. To reshape

---

Dreaming the Dark.

the very principle of power upon which our culture is based, we must shake up all the old divisions. The comfortable separations no longer work. The questions are broader than the terms *religious* or *political* imply; they are questions of complex connections. For though we are told that such issues are separate: that rape is an issue separate from nuclear war, that a woman's struggle for equal pay is not related to a black teenager's struggle to find a job or to the struggle to prevent the export of a nuclear reactor to a site on a web of earthquake faults near active volcanoes in the Philippines, all these realities are shaped by the consciousness that shapes our power relationships. Those relationships in turn shape our economic and social systems; our technology; our science; our religions; our views of women and men; our views of races and cultures that differ from our own; our sexuality; our Gods and our wars. They are presently shaping the destruction of the world.

I call this consciousness *estrangement* because its essence is that we do not see ourselves as part of the world. We are strangers to nature, to other human beings, to parts of ourselves. We see the world as made up of separate, isolated, nonliving parts that have no inherent value. (They are not even dead — because death implies life.) Among things inherently separate and lifeless, the only power relationships possible are those of manipulation and domination.

Estrangement is the culmination of a long historical process. Its roots lie in the Bronze-Age shift from matrifocal, earth-centered cultures whose religions centered on the Goddess and Gods embodied in nature, to patriarchal urban cultures of conquest, whose Gods inspired and supported war. Yahweh of the Old Testament is a prime example, promising His Chosen People dominion over plant and animal life, and over other peoples whom they were encouraged to invade and conquer. Christianity deepened the split, establishing a duality between spirit and matter that identified flesh, nature, woman, and sexuality with the Devil and the forces of evil. God was envisioned as male — uncontaminated by the processes of birth, nurturing, growth, menstruation, and decay of the flesh. He was removed from this world to a transcendent realm of spirit somewhere else. Goodness and true value were removed from nature and the world as well. As Engels saw it, "Religion is essentially the emptying of man and nature of all content, the transferring of this content to the phantom of a distant God who then in his turn graciously allows something from his abundance to come to human beings and to nature."

The removal of content, of value, serves as the basis for the exploitation of nature. Historian Lynn White states that when "the spirits *in* natural objects, which formerly had protected nature from man, evaporated" under the influence of Christianity, "man's effective monopoly on spirit in this world was confirmed, and the old inhibitions to the exploitation of nature crumbled." No longer were the groves and forests sacred. The concept of a sacred grove, of a spirit embodied in nature, was considered idolatrous. But when nature is empty of spirit, forest and trees become merely timber, something to be measured in board feet, valued only for its profitability, not for its being, its beauty, or even its part in the larger ecosystem.

The removal of content from human beings allows the formation of power relationships in which human beings are exploited. Inherent value, humanness, is reserved for certain classes, races, for the male sex; their power-over others is thus legitimized. Male imagery of God authenticates men as the carriers of humanness and legitimizes male rule. The whiteness of God, the identification of good with light and evil with dark, identifies whiteness as the carrier of humanness, and legitimizes the rule of whites over those with dark skin. Even when we no longer believe literally in a male, white God, the institutions of society embody his image in their structures. Women and people of color are not present in the top levels of the hierarchies that wield power-over. Our history, our experience, our presence can be erased, ignored, trivialized. The content of culture is assumed to be the history and the experience of white, upper-class males. The pain of all of us who are seen as *the other*—the poor and the working classes; lesbians and gay men; those who have physical disabilities; those who have been labeled mentally ill; the rainbow of different races, religions, and ethnic heritages; all women, but especially those who do not fit into culturally defined roles—is not just the pain of direct discrimination, it is the pain of being negated again and again. It is the pain of knowing that our concerns will not be addressed unless we bring them up ourselves, and that even then they will be seen as peripheral, not central, to culture, to art, to policy.

*   *   *

Because we doubt our own content, we doubt the evidence of our senses and the lessons of our own experience. We see our own drives and desires as inherently chaotic and destructive, in need of repression and control, just as we see nature as a wild chaotic force, in need of order imposed by human beings.

In *The Death of Nature*, Carolyn Merchant documents the way the rise of modern science and the economic needs of preindustrial capitalism in the sixteenth and seventeenth centuries shifted the "normative image" of that world from that of a living organism to that of a dead machine. That shift, accompanied and helped by the Witch persecutions, supported exploitation of nature on a scale previously unknown. . . . The "machine image," the view of the world as composed of isolated, nonliving parts blindly moving on their own, grew out of a Christian context in which divinity and spirit had long been removed from matter. Modern science undermined belief in the last repository of spirit when it killed off God after he had sucked the life out of the world. Nothing is left now but the littered corpses, the hierarchical patterns of our institutions—the Church, the army, the government, the corporation—all embodying the principle of authoritarian power, all formed in the image of the patriarchal God with his subordinated troops of angels, engaged in perpetual war with the patriarchal Devil and his subordinate troops of demons.

No longer do we see ourselves as having even a dubious dignity as flawed images of God. Instead we imagine ourselves in the image of the machine as flawed computers with faulty childhood programming. We are left in the empty world described ad nauseam in twentieth-century art, literature, and music—from Sartre to the Sex Pistols.

In the empty world, we trust only what can be measured, counted, acquired. The organizing principle of society becomes what Marcuse termed *the performance principle*, the stratification of society according to the economic performance of its members. Content is removed from work itself, which is organized not according to its usefulness or true value, but according to its ability to create profits. Those who actually produce goods or offer services are less well rewarded than those engaged in managing and counting this output, or stimulating false need. We are told in the business section of the morning paper that oil company Vice Presidents, for example, deny that their corporations are in the business of providing Americans with fuel and energy—rather, they are in the business of providing their investors with profits.

Science and technology, based on principles of isolation and domination of nature, grow crops and lumber by using pesticides and herbicides that also cause birth defects, nerve damage, and cancer when they infiltrate our food and water supplies. Claiming a high order of rationality, technologists build nuclear reactors producing wastes that remain dangerous for a quarter of a million years—and consign these wastes to storage containers that last from thirty to fifty years.

Estrangement permeates our educational system, with its separate and isolated disciplines. Estrangement determines our understanding of the human mind and the capabilities of consciousness, our psychology. Freud viewed human drives and libido as essentially dangerous, chaotic forces at odds with the "reality principle" of the ego. The behaviorists assure us that we are only what can be measured—only behavior and patterns of stimulus and response. Jung replaced a transcendent God with a set of transcendent archetypes, a slight improvement, but one that still leaves us caught in rigid, sex-role stereotypes.

Sexuality, under the rule of the Father-God, is identified with his Opposition—with nature, woman, life, death, and decay—the forces that threaten God's pristine abstraction and so are considered evil. In the empty world of the machine, when religious strictures fall away, sex becomes another arena of performance, another commodity to be bought and sold. The erotic becomes the pornographic; women are seen as objects empty of value except when they can be used. The sexual arena becomes one of domination, charged with rage, fear, and violence.

And so we live our lives feeling powerless and inauthentic—feeling that the real people are somewhere else, that the characters on the daytime soap operas or the conversations on the late-night talk shows are more real than the people and the conversations in our lives; believing that the movie stars, the celebrities, the rock stars, the *People Magazine*-people live out the real truth and drama of our times, while we exist as shadows, and our unique lives, our losses, our passions, which cannot be counted out or measured, which were not approved, or graded, or sold to us at a discount, are not the true value of this world.

Estrangement permeates our society so strongly that to us it seems to *be* consciousness itself. Even the language for other possibilities has disappeared or been deliberately twisted. Yet another form of consciousness is possible. Indeed, it has existed from earliest times, underlies other cultures, and has survived even in the West in hidden streams. This is the consciousness I call *immanence*—the awareness of the world and everything in it as alive, dynamic, interdependent, interacting, and infused with moving energies: a living being, a weaving dance.

The Goddess can be seen as the symbol, the normative image of immanence. She represents the divine embodied in nature, in human beings, in the flesh. The Goddess is not one image but many—a constellation of forms and associations—earth, air, fire, water, moon and star, sun, flower and seed, willow and apple, black, red, white, Maiden, Mother, and Crone. She includes the male in her aspects: He becomes child and Consort, stag and bull, grain and reaper, light and dark. Yet the femaleness of the Goddess is primary not to denigrate the male, but because it represents bringing life into the world, valuing the world. The Goddess, The Mother as symbol of that value, tells us that the world itself is the content of the world, its true value, its heart, and its soul.

Historically, cultures centered on the Goddess and Gods embodied in nature underlie all the later patriarchal cultures. Images of the Goddess are the first known images of worship, and are found in paleolithic sites. The beginnings of agriculture, weaving, pottery, writing, building, and city-dwelling—all the arts and sciences upon which later civilizations developed—began in cultures of the Goddess.

When patriarchy became the ruling force in Western culture, remnants of the religions and culture based on immanence were preserved by pagans [from the Latin word, *paganus* "rustic or country dweller"] in folk customs, in esoteric tradition, and in covens of Witches. The cultures of Native Americans and tribal peoples in Africa, Asia, and Polynesia were also based on a world-view of immanence that saw spirit and transformative power embodied in the natural world.

Ironically, as estranged science and technology advance, they have begun to bring us back to a consciousness of immanence. Modern physics no longer speaks of separate, discrete atoms of dead matter, but of waves of energy, probabilities, patterns that change as they are observed; it recognizes what Shamans and Witches have always known: that matter and energy are not separate forces, but different forms of the same thing.

The image of the Goddess strikes at the roots of estrangement. True value is not found in some heaven, some abstract otherworld, but in female bodies and their offspring, female and male; in nature; and in the world. Nature is seen as having its own inherent order, of which human beings are a part. Human nature, needs, drives, and desires are not dangerous impulses in need of repression and control, but are themselves expressions of the order inherent in being. The evidence of our senses and our experience is evidence of the divine—the moving energy that unites all being.

For women, the symbol of the Goddess is profoundly liberating, restoring a sense of authority and power to the female body and all the life processes: birth, growth, lovemaking, aging, and death. In Western culture the association of women and nature has been used to devalue both. The imagery of the immanent Goddess imparts both to women and to nature the highest value. At the same time culture is no longer seen as something removed from and opposed to nature. Culture is an outgrowth of nature—a product of human beings who *are* part of the natural world. The Goddess of nature is also the muse, the inspiration of culture, and women are full participants in creating and furthering culture, art, literature, and science. The Goddess as mother embodies creativity as much as biological motherhood. She represents women's authority over our own life processes, our right to choose consciously how and when and what we will create.

The female image of divinity does not, however, provide a justification for the oppression of men. The female, who gives birth to the male, includes the male in a way that male divinities cannot include the female. The Goddess gives birth to a pantheon that is inclusive rather than exclusive. She is not a jealous God. She is often seen with a male aspect—child or consort. In Witchcraft, the male aspect is seen as the Horned God of animal life, feeling, and vital energy. Manifesting within human beings and nature, the Goddess and God restore content and value to human nature, drives, desires, and emotions.

* * *

To say something is sacred is to say that we respect, cherish, and value it for its own being. When the world is seen as being made up of living, dynamic, interconnected, inherently valuable beings, power can no longer be "seen as something people have—kings, czars, generals *hold* power as one holds a knife." Immanent power, power-from-within, is not something we *have* but something we can do. We can choose to cooperate or to withdraw cooperation from any system. The power relationships and institutions of immanence must support and further the ability of individuals to shape the choices and decisions that affect them. And those choices must also recognize the interconnectedness of individuals in a community of beings and resources that all have inherent value.

It is challenging to try to envision a society based on that principle. The implications are radical and far-reaching, because all of our present society's institutions, from the most oppressive to the most benign, are based on the authority some individuals hold that allows them to control others.

* * *

And we have reason to hope. The forces of destruction seem great, but against them we have our power to choose, our human will and imagination, our courage, our passion, our willingness to act and to love. And we are not, in truth, strangers to this world.

We are part of the circle.

When we plant, when we weave, when we write, when we give birth, when we organize, when we heal, when we run through the park while the redwoods sweat mist, when we do what we're afraid to do, we are not separate. We are of the world and of each other, and the power within us is a great, if not an invincible power. Though we can be hurt, we can heal; though each one of us can be destroyed, within us is the power of renewal.

And there is still time to choose that power.

CARTER HEYWARD
(1945–   )

One of eleven women deacons ordained to the Episcopal priesthood in 1974 in Philadelphia, Carter Heyward is a professor of theology at Episcopal Divinity School in Cambridge, Massachusetts, and the author of *Our Passion for Justice, God's Fierce Whimsy,* and *Touching Our Strength: The Erotic as Power and the Love of God,* excerpted here and of which German theologian Dorothee Sölle (see page 324) writes: "The whole book testifies to the mystical experience that is at the heart of both religious and sexual life. We have known a long time that God's power is Love and nothing else, but we forgot, often enough, that this power necessarily empowers the lovers of God. Carter Heyward brings this out with feminist anger and strength, with hilarity and clarity." As Heyward describes her version of spirituality, "I am . . . interested . . . in probing the Sacred—exploring divine terrain—through sexual experience. . . . our power in mutual relation [is] the basis of our hope for the world."

From *Touching Our Strength*

Walking with my dogs, I become aware in a fresh way of how marvelous it is to be a member of a "group"—women—which, along with blacks and animals, has been associated closely in western history with "nature." Not that wind and water and fire and earth are simply or always benign, because they are not. Nature can be cruel and deadly—human nature especially. And each of us dies in our own embodied way, which is seldom easy. But keeping slow pace with my older dog, Teraph, I know what I have in common with the trees' gnarled roots at the water's edge, the windchill whipping my cheeks, the pile of dog shit I step in, the crows harping from the fence, the joggers and other walkers, some smiling and nodding, others preoccupied and aloof. I know them all, the people and the trees. I do not know their names, but I know that our sensuality, our shared embodied participation in forming and sustaining the relational matrix that is our home on this planet, is our most common link, and that our sensuality can be trusted.

If we learn to trust our senses, our capacities to touch, taste, smell, hear, see, and thereby know, they can teach us what is good and what is bad, what is real and what is false, for us in relation to one another and to the earth and cosmos. I say to myself, as I return to campus from my outing with my dogs, that sensuality is a foundation for our authority.

Our power in relation reveals herself through our senses and feelings, the basic resources of our intelligence, a relational quality with origins in our capacities to live responsibly in relation to one another. The quality of our intelligence is embedded in feeling connected to one another. Our feelings are evoked and strengthened sensually by touching, tasting, hearing, seeing, and smelling *with* one another. Our senses and the feelings that are generated by them become primary spiritual resources. In knowing one another through our senses, feelings, and intelligence—and intuition is a form of intelligence—we come to know God.[1]

God reveals herself through our relationships not only to other people but also to other creatures and nature. This is a faith-claim that is both in continuity and discontinuity with those of traditional western christianity. Its continuity is in the emphasis on revelation through incarnation; its discontinuity is in stressing the sacred character of nature—flesh, dirt, wetness, sex, woman.[2] The erotic is known most immediately through our senses. We see, hear, touch, smell, and taste the divine, who is embodied between and among us insofar as we are moving more fully into, or toward, mutually empowering relationships in which all creatures are accorded profound respect and dignity.

The erotic fabric of our lives in relation has not been treated affirmatively in the history of christian life and thought. The incarnation is not taken seriously, even in Jesus' life, much less as the basic character structure of all creation. The incarnation of God in Jesus has been interpreted historically as an essentially spiritual act, in which Jesus' bodyself ("flesh") got spiritualized.[3] The god whom christians believe to be the source of love and justice in the universe did not materialize for long, if at all, in Jesus. "Christ" became historically the symbol by which we know that Jesus' spiritualization was accomplished as a unique and singular event: Only Jesus is Christ; he and he alone is Lord of the Universe, according to christian teachings.

The christian bible was canonized, and is used still, to support this process of spiritualization. A major problem, therefore, with using the bible as a primary resource for authority among justice-seeking christians is that it is weighted, especially in the New Testament, toward the spiritualization—trivialization and denial—of our bodyselves. The effect of this process is damaging to all people whose self-images are shaped in cultures dominated by christianity, which is all of us in the United States.

To deny the sacred power of our embodied yearnings is to be pulled away from one another and hence from ourselves. To have our bodyselves trivialized and demeaned is to be snatched out of our senses and alienated from our erotic desires. This process of alienation from our sacred power produces antierotic (or pornographic) psyches and lives, in which our bodies and feelings are jerked off by abusive power dynamics: domination, coercion, and violence.

Where then do we turn for help in healing our broken bonds and wounded lives? To whom do we look for images of sacred power, mutuality, and friendship? We come to our senses, quite literally, and we look to our people and other creatures as well. But who are they, these friends to whom we are accountable in our theologies and ethics and in living our daily lives?

To hold oneself accountable is to make a moral claim on the basis of our values (what we believe to be good); our obligations (the constraints that respect for one another set on our actions); and our vision (our images of life as we seek to create/liberate our life together on the basis of our values and obligations). It is on the basis of these foundations that we are drawn, consciously or not, toward certain people, processes, and resources, and not toward others, in framing the authority for our theological and ethical claims.

These three basic dimensions of our moral lives—forged out of our lives in relation to past, present, and future generations of people, other creatures, and our cocreative power—are the primary resource for our spiritual and theological authority. Never simply our own private opinions, our values, obligations, and visions are created and recreated constantly in our relational matrix, in which—along with our values, obligations, and visions—we are growing in relation to those whose lives we trust. We see them, hear them, learn from them, teach them, and know ourselves as connected to them in value-enhancing ways.

I am accountable to those who are committed to justice *for all*. This does not mean that I live this value very evenly or very well. Most of us do not. But the commitment is honest and strong. The promise that draws me to such people is that they will remind me of the limits of what I can know and of the fact that, even when I believe I'm being inclusive in my work, someone is being left out. To the extent that this "someone" has been left out historically, repeatedly and as a matter of course, I am helping hold unjust power in place even in my honest outpourings for justice.

I see the value of justice—right, mutual, relation—borne out in the lives of those with whom I choose to stand, those whose lives bear concrete specific witness: for example, in the efforts of antiracist workers; in the commitment of those who resist the contras; in the vitality and justice-centered issues of Jesse Jackson's 1988 campaign; in the struggles of battered women who have had enough; in liberation work in South Africa, Korea, the Soviet Union, El Salvador, Iran, the United States, Israel; in the movement of lesbians and gaymen who are coming out.

I see mutuality/justice embodied by an old man who cares for his dogs and is grateful for what they give him. I recognize mutuality in a heterosexual friend's refusal to say she is not a lesbian when asked by her bishop. I hear mutuality in music celebrating the whales and the earth. I am moved by the mutuality in the commitment of some christian feminists to expunge anti-Semitism from their worship and their lives.

I see mutuality borne out in the lives of women and men raising their children to befriend rather than fear the world, its human and other creatures, and at the same time to take care of themselves and one another in a world often hostile to gentle people. I know mutuality is lived out as one friend sits with another dying of AIDS; I watch this same commitment flash in the eyes of a woman working the streets of Spanish Harlem, giving bleach to addicts for their needles, to help protect them from the deadly HIV virus.

I experience mutuality with my students who are coming together with one another and me into new questions and clarifications of a shared vocation as teachers and preachers of good news to marginalized and oppressed persons and to those in solidarity with them. I know mutuality with my own teachers and healers who with me continue to come into our power to learn and mend together so that we can make a difference in a world that needs our friendship as testimony to a relational power that is trustworthy.

I stand with those whose politics and spirituality I have come to trust: those who know that we meet the Sacred in relation to one another, and who understand that any power that we or others use in ways that are not mutually empowering is abusive. I look to such women and men, of whatever color, religion, class, sexual preference or orientation, to confirm in me a joyful commitment to live responsibly in this world.

With these people, I envision a world/church in which the lamb and lion will be friends, a time/space in which healing and forgiveness, touching and pleasure, celebration and justice, will be far more universally available than any of these relational blessings are among us today.

These are people to whom I am accountable in discerning resources for authority in my life—for helping me separate out the wheat from the chaff, the true from the false. My people have led me to Elie Wiesel's *Night*, Adrienne Rich's *On Lies, Secrets and Silence*, Julia Esquivel's *Threatened with Resurrection*, Gloria Naylor's *Women of Brewster Place*, Audre Lorde's *Sister Outsider*, Dorothee Sölle's *Beyond Mere Obedience*, and Beverly Harrison's *Making the Connections*.[4] Such books have become staples in my canon of scripture and their authors have become my people.

My people have shown me that racism is more than wrong, it is evil— and so is what our nation is doing to the poor of the world in Guatemala, Angola, Korea, and in these United States. They suggest to me that class injury cuts to the core of our life together and leaves us wounded and hurt in ways invisible to the vast majority of United States citizens, *especially* those of us with ready access to economic survival resources.[5]

My people remind me of my roots, my limits, my gifts, and my questions. They help keep me humble—connected, that is, to others, and aware that we are a commonpeople. My people pull me toward the margins of the church, academia, and the disciplines, to the margins even of movements for justice.

My people keep me growing and expect me to be relationally aware. They ask me to be honest with them about what I am doing, what I yearn for, what my commitments are, what I delight in, what I am willing to suffer for, if need be die for—and what I am trying, therefore, to live for. My people ask me to realize and celebrate ways in which my accountability is reliable, trustworthy, and empowering to them as well as to me, which it is not consistently or always.

My people embody, for me, the real presence of sacred movement, enabling me to stand and bend not merely with the oppressed but with all who are struggling against unjust power relations. With my people—friends, *compañeras*, sisters and brothers, known and unknown—I realize that our creative power in relation, the power of our godding, is the wellspring of our sexualities: our yearnings to embody mutually empowering relations, our desire to live into our YES.

Notes

1. Coming to know, or understand, God—the business of theological education in its broadest sense—is a *relational* adventure in making, and understanding, right relation. See Paulo Freire, *Pedagogy of the Oppressed* (New York: Herder and Herder, 1970); Ira Shor and Paulo Freire, *A Pedagogy for Liberation: Dialogues on Transforming Education* (South Hadley, MA: Bergin and Garvey, 1987); Ira Shor, *Critical Teaching and Everyday Life* (Boston: South End Press, 1980); Alice Frazer Evans, Robert A. Evans, and William Bean Kennedy, *Pedagogies for the Non-Poor* (Maryknoll, NY: Orbis, 1987); Thomas P. Fenton, ed., *Education for Justice* (Maryknoll, NY: Orbis, 1975); Amanecida Collective, *Revolutionary Forgiveness: Feminist Reflections on Nicaragua* (Maryknoll, NY: Orbis, 1986); and MudFlower Collective, *God's Fierce Whimsy: Christian Feminism and Theological Education* (New York: Pilgrim, 1985).

2. When christian women have laid claim historically to sacred power, the ecclesiastical response has been punitive. Probably the most dramatic and large-scale violent response was the European witch hunt in the fifteenth and sixteenth centuries. For bone-chilling testimony to the missionary zeal with which church fathers undertook this persecution, see *Malleus Maleficarum (Hammer of Witches)*, translated with introduction by the Rev. Montague Summers (New York: Dover, 1971). *Malleus* was published in 1456. Writing his introduction in 1928, Fr. Summers began with these words: "It has been recognized even from the very earliest times, during the first gropings towards the essential conveniences of social decency and social order, that witchcraft is an evil thing, an enemy to light, an ally of the powers of darkness, disruption, and decay." (xi)

3. See Isabel Carter Heyward, "Chalcedon's Ontology," Appendix B, in *The Redemption of God: A Theology of Mutual Relation* (Washington, D.C.: University Press of America, 1982), 189–92. My thanks to Richard A. Norris, with whom I worked occasionally at Union Theological Seminary, for helping me to wrestle with philosophical nuances in the christological controversy.

4. Elie Wiesel, *Night* (New York: Avon, 1969); Adrienne Rich, *On Lies, Secrets and Silence: Selected Prose, 1966–78* (New York: W. W. Norton, 1979); Julia Esquivel, *Threatened with Resurrection: Prayers and Poems of an Exiled Guatemalan* (Elgin, IL: Brethren, 1982); Gloria Naylor, *The Women of Brewster Place* (New York: Penguin, 1982); Lorde, *Sister Outsider*; Dorothee Sölle, *Beyond Mere Obedience, Reflections on a Christian Ethic for the Future* (Minneapolis: Augsburg, 1971); Beverly Wildung Harrison, *Making the Connections: Essays in Feminist Social Ethics*, edited by Carol S. Robb (Boston: Beacon, 1985).

5. See Richard Sennett and Jonathan Cobb, *The Hidden Injuries of Class* (New York: Random, 1973); Angela Y. Davis, *Women, Race, and Class* (New York: Vintage, 1981); Lillian B. Rubin, *Worlds of Pain: Life in the Working Class Family* (New York: Basic Books, 1976); Karen Stollard, *et al.*, *Poverty in the American Dream* (Boston: South End Press, 1983); Michelle Russell, "Women, Work, and Politics in the U.S.," *Theology in the Americas*, edited by Sergio Torres (Maryknoll, NY: Orbis, 1976); Barbara H. Andolsen, "A Woman's Work Is Never Done: Unpaid Household Labor as a Social Justice Issue," in Barbara Hilkert Andolsen, Christine E. Gudorf, and Mary D. Pellauer, eds., *Women's Consciousness, Women's Conscience* (San Francisco: Harper & Row, 1985), 3–18; and Nancy Bancroft, "Women in the Cutback Economy: Ethics, Ideology, and Class," in Andolsen, *et al.*, 19–31.

JUDITH PLASKOW
(1947–   )

Professor of religious studies at Manhattan College, cofounder and coeditor of the *Journal of Feminist Studies in Religion*, theologian Judith Plaskow is also the author of the highly regarded *Standing Again at Sinai: Judaism from a Feminist Perspective*, a dynamic reevaluation of the role of women in Judaism. The following piece, which appeared in *Tikkun: A Bimonthly Jewish Critique of Politics, Culture, and Society*, elaborates on the assumptions presented in the introduction of this book. In her words, "I assume that to have been a slave in the land of Egypt is the basis of a profound religious obligation to do justice in the world. I assume that one finds God in the world, in acts of love and justice, and not beyond or outside the world." Plaskow's work and writings combine the prophetic and pragmatic spirituality that characterizes the wisdom tradition of so many historical biblical women, including Sarah, Miriam, Deborah, and Hannah.

Spirituality and Politics: Lessons from B'not Esh

One of the earliest and most important lessons I learned from my Jewish feminist spirituality collective, B'not Esh, concerned the connection between spirituality and politics. In seeking to get to know each other when we first met in 1981, we spent three sessions in small groups sharing our spiritual pasts, presents, and futures. The past and the present, we had no difficulty discussing. When it came to the future, however, my group seemed to veer from the subject into numerous digressions.

After repeatedly chiding ourselves for talking about work, community, relationships, politics—in short, everything but spirituality—we suddenly realized that, in fact, we were addressing those realities that stood between us and our ability to imagine our spiritual futures. If we wanted to live as feminist Jews, we would have to help create communities—and create a world—in which such a spirituality would be possible. For all of us, this was a key moment in understanding the relationship between our individual spiritual lives and the wider social and political contexts in which we lived. As feminists, we were committed to the notion that "the personal is political": That many of women's seemingly personal problems are a function of fundamental social inequities, and can be resolved only as those inequities are addressed.

Now we began to see that "the spiritual is political." Our difficulties in projecting our spiritual futures were likewise connected to larger structural issues. Both the ways in which Judaism as a religious tradition diminished us as women, and the demands and priorities of the larger social system constituted impediments to our relationship with the sacred. In this situation, politics, we realized, is the necessary work we do to make the world safe for our spirituality.

We made less effort to define "spirituality" precisely. The group implicitly understood it as both ongoing mindfulness of the sacred in the ordinary moments of our lives, and special moments of vision and celebration, of particularly intense connection between ourselves and the sacred.

In the aftermath of the 1994 elections and the increasing influence of the Christian Right, I keep coming back to these insights as a potential source of an alternative religious/political vision. On the one hand, it is clear that religion and spirituality are much too important to many people's lives to surrender their mantle and definition to the Right's patriarchal, authoritarian, and individualistic reading of a complex biblical tradition. On the other hand, unless we are to fall into what liberation theologian Hugo Assman aptly calls the "fundamentalism of the left"—a tendency to equate liberating texts with the whole of the "biblical message"—it must be acknowledged that progressives cannot advance the same neat and authoritative program of religious principles and injunctions that the Right pretends to offer.

Progressive spirituality is, by definition, a critical spirituality, cognizant of the oppressive strands within the Bible and tradition, and concerned about their power to shape consciousness and actions. As we tried to imagine our spiritual futures as B'not Esh, for example, we were repeatedly brought up against those aspects of Judaism that themselves impeded this process. Mindful of the tensions and contradictions within each religious tradition, a liberating spirituality must consciously ally itself with some strands against others. But this means it is unwilling to claim the absolute authority that is part of what makes the Right so attractive.

In other columns . . . I have discussed the problem of authority and laid out a feminist critique of various aspects of Jewish tradition. Here, in an effort to formulate an alternative to the right-wing version of a religious politics, I want to suggest some positive elements of the spirituality and politics I have experienced through B'not Esh as well as in other contexts.

• A progressive spirituality affirms and fosters the humanity and dignity of each and every person, in the context of community. To use biblical language, it recognizes that every person is created in the image of God, and that that image is intrinsically relational: Male and female he created them. The divine image inheres not only in those who have status according to various social hierarchies, but also in those who are of "no account" by any historical measure. Just as the Israelites in Egypt were liberated from bondage and entered into the covenant at Sinai as two moments in the same process, so various oppressed groups in contemporary society have awakened to their own value and demanded recognition and rights as persons and as partners in creation. For me, the process of discovering in community with other women the power of our individual and collective voices has also been a process of connecting with larger currents of power and energy which ground and sustain both community and self. Formed in the divine image, we also grow into that image as we claim our role as agents in naming and shaping the world.

• If all are created in the divine image, then our images of God must be fluid and multifarious.

Feminist experiments with female imagery are at once an expression of the bursting sense of "I am/we are" that accompanies liberation, a form of insistence that women are in God's image, and an invitation to seek God in overlooked places in human experience. This expansion of metaphors for the sacred is just the beginning of a process that must name the divine presence in all the corners of creation. The sea monsters and the deep, fire and hail, snow and frost also praise God (Psalm 148:7–8). The wild ass and the ostrich have a power and purpose that surpasses human understanding (Job 39:5–8, 13–18).

Because relationships among human beings are unique in containing the potential for the full mutuality and reciprocity that form the foundations of the moral life, it is important that we use anthropomorphic imagery, and that we broaden it as far as possible. But our moral responsibility extends to the entire web of creation, all of which manifests and can symbolize divine presence and activity.

• Hear, oh Israel, God is One.

These diverse images of God are not the names of multiple divinities, but guises of the One that manifests itself in and through the changing forms of the many. The notion that all of creation is taken up in a larger unity is a fundamental moral principle: Everything is connected; each of us is responsible one for another; ultimately we are more alike than different from each other. The relationship between particular images of God and the divine totality finds its analogy in human community. As each image of God is also a face of the divine whole that embraces the diversity of an infinite community, so individuals and groups within the human community also belong to a common humanity. Just as we need to lift up particular metaphors for God without forgetting that they are aspects of the One, so we desperately need to learn to value human diversity without forgetting the many things that bind us together.

• A progressive spirituality is aware of the structural injustices in both religious traditions and the world that diminish the humanity of many groups of persons. It is, therefore, critical of those elements in Judaism and other traditions that depict women as other, that call for the annihilation of idolaters and unbelievers, or even that counsel individual compassion for widows and orphans while reinforcing the structures that contribute to their marginality. It is equally critical of the profound inequality in the global distribution of resources that marginalizes and impoverishes much of the world's population, of the power of multi-national corporations to pursue profits at the expense of people, of the rise in the number of homeless or the punitive attitude toward those on welfare. In these and other arenas, a progressive spirituality seeks to resist and challenge the continual reinforcement and recreation of unequal access to power.

• *Tikkun olam* (repair of the world).

Insofar as a progressive spirituality is committed to a politics that makes the world safe for itself, such a spirituality realizes itself in action. It strives in large and small ways to provide the fundamental preconditions for human dignity and planetary survival: food, shelter, a fair share of the Earth's resources in the context of respect for the Earth; but also the right to name one's own situation and desires, and to define and participate in the shaping and healing of history and creation. Such a struggle is not separate from awareness of God or the affirmation of human dignity, but is its complement and expression. Through politics, we become responsible members of a human community rooted in a far larger community and purpose. Through spirituality, we cultivate awareness of the sacred pervading the world, a presence that continually compels us to honor it through action.

DOROTHEE SÖLLE
(1929–   )

Born in Cologne, Germany, Dorothee Sölle is an internationally recognized theologian, writer, and leader of the German peace movement. She has been visiting professor of systematic theology at Union Theological Seminary in New York City and published numerous studies that explore an inherited theological tradition from the perspectives of liberation theology and feminism. Some of her titles include *On Earth as in Heaven: A Liberation Spirituality of Sharing; Revolutionary Patience;* and *The Strength of the Weak,* from which the following essay, "Mary Is a Sympathizer," is taken. Sölle's reinterpretation of a conservative Marian tradition in the context of the late twentieth century's widening gap between the rich and the poor demonstrates the significance of an ancient story and icon to contemporary lives and feminist aspiration.

Mary Is a Sympathizer

Mary—the first image that comes to my mind is the plaster figure in the grotto at Lourdes, her eyes lowered, the outlines of her body lost in the endless folds of her robe: desexualized and humble, the feminine ideal, a symbol created to teach self-oppression to the oppressed, self-censure to the self-critical, self-exploitation to the doubly exploited.

This ploy works best if the idol appears to be elevated, raised up on a pedestal and glorified. Just as the image of the loyal, self-sacrificing Uncle Tom was an integral part of the oppression of blacks, so the image of a sublime and elevated Mary was integral to the oppression of women. She is enthroned above us. She is pure; we are filthy. She is desexualized; we have sexual needs and problems. We can never measure up to her and should therefore feel guilty and ashamed. And that, in turn, makes us feel all the more humble.

Mary's submission was voluntary. "Let it be to me according to your word" is her response to an unwanted pregnancy (Luke 1:38). She accepts deprivation and pain; she serves without complaint. She has no will of her own. She is the Lord's handmaiden. And even if we cannot be "pure" like her, we can at least be as submissive as she is.

Raising someone up on a pedestal is a strategy of domination. Women are glorified, elevated, and praised so that they can be humiliated, restricted, and blocked at every turn. The inevitable reverse image of the madonna is the whore. *Finalmente siamo donne, non piu putane, non piu madonne!* (We are women, not whores or madonnas!) This is one of the slogans of the women's movement in Italy. And it is no coincidence that the feminists of a Catholic country are so outspoken in opposing the mindless alternative of "whore or saint." But is Mary really this plaster figure, a girl from Nazareth with an illegitimate son who was later executed as a revolutionary? Was it this Mary who appeared to the peasant girl Joan of Arc and entrusted to her that most masculine of instruments, the sword?

Is submission really the theme of that passage in the Bible in which Mary celebrates her pregnancy? The passage is utterly unequivocal in its distinction between the lowly and the high and mighty, between the poor and the rich, utterly clear about the impotence of the unpropertied classes in relation to the powers that be, the helplessness of those who are without rights because they are without property.

> And Mary said,
> "My soul magnifies the Lord,
> and my spirit rejoices in God my Savior. . . .
> He has shown strength with his arm,
> he has scattered the proud in the imagination of
> their hearts,
> he has put down the mighty from their thrones,
> and exalted those of low degree;
> he has filled the hungry with good things,
> and the rich he has sent empty away."

(Luke 1:46–53)

The people who have turned to Mary—and women in particular—have thought, desired, and hoped for very different things in different periods. The desexualization that culminated in the breastless, bloodless plaster noblewoman of Lourdes is the outgrowth of a development in art history that began in the Renaissance and reached its high point in the nineteenth century. This is the bourgeois period, and it was the theology of this particular class that inspired the image of a humble, desexualized Mary.

In the Middle Ages, for example, depictions of Mary are more sensual, lively, and cheerful. She is shown nursing her baby, her breasts bared and beautiful. She is shown changing his diapers and bouncing him on her knee. She is also shown crying out with pain or numbed by grief as she mourns her son who has been tortured to death. There are paintings that show her taking leave of him as he sets out into the world. She knows perhaps better than he what lies before him. (My God, I wish that my relationship with my son were characterized by their kind of "communication without domination," by that kind of warmth, understanding of each other, closeness, pain, trust!) There are other Marys quite different from the submissive one. The one that first comes to mind, of course, is the great mother who comforts and protects. The Catholic tradition took from her her other children who are mentioned in the Bible, but the people's needs and fantasies have given these children back to her, shoving them in under her skirts, as it were, where they find shelter from hail and rain, from pestilence and war.

Very early on, Mary assumed the role as a protector not only against the forces of nature but also those of a violent society. She did not embody "justice" as our society understands it and practices it today. That is, she did not operate on the principle that everyone should get what he or she deserves, a principle that leaves inequality of opportunity intact. No, Mary embodied mercy, or what we usually call "charity." I am a bit uneasy with this word, but I cannot find a better one. What I mean to say is that Mary rejects "performance" as a measure of human value. I will not stick by you, she says, because you are handsome, clever, successful, musical, potent, or whatever. I'll stick by you without reservations or conditions. I'll stick by you because you are there, because you need me. Her unconditional acceptance is that of a mother who cannot exchange her child in the store if she finds it doesn't suit her. If we strip charity of sentimentality, the "amoral" quality it originally had becomes visible again. And it is for this kind of amorality that the Mary of legends and folk tales has a mischievous penchant.

Until well into the High Middle Ages, Mary was not a particularly popular figure in the liturgy, in dogmatic writings, and in literature under the influence of the clergy. She belonged to the poor, the unlettered, the mendicant friars, the people. She was known as the "madonna of rogues," which is to say the madonna of the impoverished rural proletariat, who could not help being at odds with the increasingly stringent laws that defined and protected property. A Polish legend tells about a robber who calls on Mary for aid just before the hangman puts the noose around his neck. Mary hastens to him, stands under the gallows, and supports the hanged man's feet for three days and three nights. Presumed dead, the robber is cut down from the gallows, only to run off, rendering thanks to the Virgin. The heroes of such legends are often thieves and robbers—or monks and nuns who have fled the rigors of monastery or cloister—people who oppose law and order and that masculine set of mind intent on domination and regulation. When a "fallen" abbess gives birth to a child, Mary attends her as a midwife. When a nun runs away from the cloister, Mary takes her place for years at the cloister's prayer services.

This kind of subversive activity is bound to bring Mary into religious conflict with God the Father and with Christ. Mary subverts the division of people into sheep and goats. This anarchistic tendency of hers has never been completely eradicated, and a Protestant encyclopedia has this indignant comment to make on such folk legends: "These stories are infused with a rather peculiar morality" (*Die Religion in Geschichte und Gegenwart*, 2d ed., 1927).

The figure of Mary, then, is as ambiguous as all religious concepts and symbols. She serves the interests of religiously glorified submissiveness but also those of consolation, protection, and the rescue of victims. Mary is submissive, but she is also subversive in the way police in Latin America use this word: She undermines the power of the ruling classes. To use a term that has been used widely in West Germany recently, we could say that Mary is a sympathizer.*

The little madonna who spoke of liberation in the passage quoted from Luke is not made of plaster or plastic. She is very much alive, alive in the history of all who are oppressed, alive in the history of women. The only reason we know so little of the dreams, visions, and stories of those who fight and resist is that history has been written by the victors.

In Latin America, the *madonna leone* rides naked on the back of a lion and—at least for our tamed and corrupted sense of religion—appears to be more witch than saint. In the late Middle Ages, the rebellious peasants who wanted to give the land back to the people who actually cultivated it gathered under the aegis of Mary.

And that brings me to a new and better image of the girl Mary: impudent as Joan of Orleans, who dared to tell an archbishop to his face that what he had just said was, "even for him, unusually stupid." Seen in this light, Mary is no longer just a tamed, subdued woman but also a rebellious girl. Militance and charity are united in her, and she becomes an image of hope for those who have been cheated of their lives.

At the same time, however, she has always been a model that repressive forces have held up to women to keep them humble and in their place. This is why Catholic cultures in particular have been so ready to cast off and forget this double-sided figure.

Personally, though, I take a rather skeptical view of any kind of throwaway society. I cannot put any trust in an existence that is presumably free of images and myths. We have seen it happen that where old images are put aside, new ones in no respect more enlightened take their place. In the niche once occupied by the untainted madonna, we now find a Mrs. Whiter-than-White from the detergent ads. Both ideologies force onto women a role that weakens and cripples them.

Like many Christians in the liberation movement, I am not ready to surrender Mary to our opponents. The suggestion that we forget Mary and religion as quickly as we can strikes me as hasty and simplistic. Contemporary liberation movements need their patron saints and models, too; they need to be rooted in history. Merely to rid ourselves of the Lourdes madonna, then, is to achieve nothing at all.

I find it hard to think that the millions of women before me who have loved Mary were simply blind or duped. They, too, must have offered resistance, resistance from which we can learn.

---

*TRANSLATORS' NOTE: The term *Sympathisant* was used widely in the German press in the mid-1970s in connection with reports on terrorist activity. The term suggested that anyone with leftist political convictions "sympathized" with terrorism and was guilty by association.

RIFFAT HASSAN
(1943–   )

Riffat Hassan was born and grew up in Pakistan, studied in England, and began her study of women's issues in Islam after moving to the United States with her young daughter. Currently professor and chairperson of religious studies at the University of Louisville, Kentucky, and the leading feminist scholar of the Qur'an, she has written numerous articles and two books on the Muslim thinker Allah Muhammad Iqbal. The following autobiographical piece reflects the conviction that grounds her devotion to Islamic studies: "['I']he more I saw the justice and compassion of God reflected in the Qur'anic teachings regarding women, the more anguished and angry I became at seeing the injustice and inhumanity to which Muslim women, in general, are subjected in actual life. I began to feel that it was my duty . . . to do as much consciousness-raising regarding the situation of Muslim women as I could," and that includes studying the Islamic tradition from a woman's perspective.

"Jihād Fī Sabīl Allah"*: A Muslim Woman's Faith Journey from Struggle to Struggle to Struggle

"We want you to be the ideologue of our movement." The earnest faces looking at me out of a world unutterably grim and dark . . . the earnest voices speaking to me in the deathly stillness of an hour of despair when one is afraid to hear even the throbbing of one's own heart. . . . I saw and heard the angry, tearful, fearful, defiant, despairing, determined, struggling, suffering women from one of the most active women's groups in my native Pakistan, and was spellbound . . . overwhelmed . . . transformed. In that moment of truth I knew with absolute clarity that I had arrived at a point of destiny . . . it seemed natural—inevitable—that the strange paths I had trodden in my life should have led me here, though I had never dreamed that I would be called upon so suddenly—so unexpectedly—to become the theoretician for a movement involved in a life-and-death struggle in a country that was mine by birth and unbreakable bonds of love, from which I had chosen to exile myself in order to be able to do my life's work.

---

*Jihād fi Sabīl Allah: striving or exerting in and for the cause of God; this is a Qur'anic imperative for all Muslims.

For years I had lived a hard and solitary life in an alien world, striving to become free and whole—returning periodically to my "homeland" only to find how alienated I was from "my people" in so many ways. Even as I saw and heard the women who wanted me to dedicate myself to their struggle for self-identification, for self-preservation, I knew how many worlds separated us. The mere fact that I lived alone with my young daughter, in a foreign land, earning my livelihood by the sweat of my brow, using every free moment of my work-filled life to pore endlessly over words, sacred and secular, to find a way to liberate millions of Muslim women from the unspeakable bondage imposed on them in the name of God, created a wide gulf between me and these women who addressed me. Would any of these women be willing to give up their lives of affluence and ease to share a day of my toil-filled life? I would have been surprised to find even one who would—and this thought saddened me. However, it did not affect my deep response to the call I had received. Whatever the distances, the differences that existed between these women and me, I knew in the hour of trial that they were my sisters and that our bond was indissoluble. I was grateful that the work I had done over so many years out of my own passionate quest for truth and justice had become profoundly relevant to the lives of my sisters. I had not hoped to see this day in my lifetime. With a heart full of tears—of joy, of sorrow—I said a silent prayer to my Creator and Sustainer who had brought me to this historic moment. I offered thanks for the opportunity to participate in such a moment and asked for strength and courage so that I might not fail in the critical task entrusted to me.

As I stood on the threshold of a new beginning, a new life, scenes from my past flashed before my eyes. I paused—to cast a look backward at the passages through which my life-journey had led me to bring me to this point of destiny. I knew that tomorrow would usher in a new phase of toil and tribulation and that then there would be no time to look back. But today I could be alone with my memories—of places and peoples and moments that had made my life-journey significant. I did not like to recall many of these memories for they are painful, but I knew that in order for me to have a clear sense of where I was and where I was to go in terms of my inner journey, I had to remember where I had been. I do not believe that it is possible to go forward without going backward, since our future is born out of our past. I closed my eyes and went back to the old house where I was born, which stood at the end of a *galee* (narrow street) adjoining Temple Road in the ancient city of Lahore in what is now Pakistan. In this house my story had begun.

My memories of the house in which I was born, where I spent the first seventeen years of my life, are heavily shaded with darkness. Even now I cannot read a passage about the joy, the beauty, the golden sunshine of childhood years without a storm of tears arising in my heart. I wish I had had a different childhood . . . my own was a nightmare that has never ceased to haunt me. What I remember most distinctly about being a child was how utterly lonely I felt in a house full of people and how unspeakably unhappy, scared, and bewildered I was most of the time.

Objectively, there were many reasons why I should have considered myself and my five brothers and three sisters as very privileged children. We were born into an upper-class Saiyyad family, and the Saiyyads, being the descendants of the Holy Prophet Muhammad, are regarded as the highest caste of Muslims, even though Muslims constantly protest against the idea that Islam has any caste system! My father and mother came from among the oldest and most distinguished families in the city and were both "good" parents in that they took care to provide us with a high quality of life. We lived in a spacious *kothee* (bungalow) and had a glamorous automobile (when only a handful of people had any) and a household full of servants who performed all the domestic duties. We went to the best English-medium schools (which to this day are regarded as status symbols), where we received a sound British education. Children in our neighborhood envied us: we were the children of "Shaah Saahib," as everyone called my father, who was the patriarch of the area and greatly respected and liked by all; all considered it an honor to come to our house to play, even though they knew about my mother's temper-tantrums and the possibility that they might be told unceremoniously to go home at any moment.

Why, when we were so blessed, was my life so full of shadows? The major reason was undoubtedly the deep conflict between my parents. Not only did they have diametrically opposing views on most matters but also radical incompatibility of temperament and character. My father was very traditional in his ways and values. Through most of my life I hated his traditionalism, because I understood it almost exclusively in terms of his belief in sex roles and his conviction that it was best for girls to be married at age sixteen to someone who had been picked out for them by the parents. It took me a long time to see that in some ways my father's traditionalism had been pure gold. He truly believed in taking care of disadvantaged people, relatives and strangers alike, and responding to every call he received for assistance. He was genuinely kind and compassionate and took joy in solving other people's problems, whether they were personal, professional, or social. Anybody could call on him at any hour, and he would receive the caller with courtesy and goodwill. My mother's ways and values differed fundamentally from my father's, even though, in her own way, she responded positively to many who sought the assistance of the "Begum Saahiba," as she was called. Her nonconformism to traditional Muslim culture consisted largely of her rejection of the hallowed cult of women's inferiority and submissiveness to men. She herself was not submissive to her husband. She treated her daughters better than her sons (with the exception of one favorite son) and believed that it was more important to educate daughters than sons because girls were born into Muslim societies with a tremendous handicap. Pre-Islamic Arabs had buried their daughters alive because they had regarded daughters not only as economic liabilities but also as potential hazards to the honor of the men in the tribe. Islam notwithstanding, the attitude of Muslims toward daughters has remained very similar to that of their nomadic forebears. My mother's repudiation of the ideals and practices of patriarchal culture and her passionate commitment to the liberation of her daughters from the *chardewari* (four walls) of the male-centered, male-dominated household put her into the category of radical feminists, which made her strangely out of place in my father's house and in the society in which we lived.

Long before I began to understand the complexities and ambiguities of the Muslim value-system, I knew that my mother would not win in any popularity contest vis-à-vis my father. She had a protected place in society because she was the daughter of the outstanding and creative artist-poet, playwright, and scholar, Hakim Ahmad Shuja'—who had also been a highly regarded educator and bureaucrat—and my father's wife, but in her own person she was viewed as a dangerous deviant. The fact that she had a biting and brutal tongue, and that she could, at times, be ruthless and unscrupulous, did not help to improve her image in many eyes. However, to me, all through my childhood, my mother was a savior-figure who protected me from being sacrificed upon the altar of blind conventionalism. And my father, who was admired and loved by so many, seemed to me through most of my early life to be a figure of dread, representing customary morality in a society that demanded that female children be discriminated against from the moment of birth.

As a child I used to be greatly troubled by the fact that my subjective perceptions of my parents differed greatly from the way in which others perceived them. I remember feeling very guilty because I could not relate to my "good" father to whom almost everyone could relate so well. I also remember feeling very angry and perplexed as to why my father, who liked everyone, seemed so averse to me. I knew that what I perceived to be his negative attitude toward me had something to do with my being one of my mother's "favorites" and belonging to her "camp." Their respective camps were the centers from where my parents conducted their cold war campaigns that enveloped us all and poisoned our family life. My parents did not yell and scream at each other. My father was too much of a gentleman to do that, and even my mother, whom many regarded as a "shrew," was conventional enough not to engage in a vociferous exchange with my father. But though physical and verbal violence did not characterize the relationship between my parents, there was no disguising the fact that they had deep-seated resentments against one another that manifested themselves in all kinds of destructive ways. I remember how the way my parents interacted with one another reminded me of Milton's words: "For never can true reconcilement grow / where wounds of deadly hate have pierced so deep," and I often wondered as a child why they continued to live together. Now I understand the reasons that made it imperative for them to live under one roof—they both came from "old" families to whom divorce was anathema, and they had nine children to raise. But the one roof under which we all lived could not be called a "home," if one defines this term as a place of love, warmth, and security. Our home was a rough sea where tempests raged incessantly. I could only deal with the unremitting hostility that pervaded the atmosphere by becoming a recluse. Before I was twelve years old I had retired from the world.

I believe that it was because I withdrew from an outer to an inner reality that I was able to survive the seemingly unending crises and calamities to which I was exposed. A hypersensitive, painfully shy, and profoundly lonely child, I hated the ugliness that surrounded me and retreated to a world made up of a child's prayers, dreams, and wishful thinking. In this world I found three things that have sustained me through the heartbreaks and hardships of my life: an unwavering belief in a just and loving God, the art of writing poetry, and a deep love for books. Unable to relate at a deep personal level to either of my two parents—such dialogue, I see now, is virtually impossible in Muslim culture, in which human beings relate to each other mainly in terms of their "functions" or roles and not in terms of who they are as persons—I learned to talk to my Creator and Preserver, who at all times seemed very close. I often asked God to reveal to me the purpose of my life and to help me fulfill this purpose. Perhaps that was a strange prayer for a child. However, I was not just any child—I was a war-ravaged child. Born female in a society in which it is customary to celebrate the birth of a son and to bemoan the birth of a daughter, and growing up in a house lacking in love and trust, I could at no time simply take it for granted that I had the right to exist, to be. I had, at all times, to find a justification for living. A very ailing child, I came quite close to dying a few times and almost wished that I were dead, but somewhere, deep within my heart and soul, I always had the assurance that God had a special purpose for my life that justified my existence, and that so long as I remained faithful to God I would be protected from the dangers and devastation that threatened me.

Alone in my inner world I discovered that, like my mother and grandfather, I could write poetry almost effortlessly. This gave me great happiness and hope. I felt as if this was a gift from God given to me so that I could create a world free of shadows, of hate, bitterness, and pain. Looking at the first poem in "My Maiden," a book of eighty-five sonnets written when I was about thirteen years old, I can recall the earnest child who wrote:

> This humble work of mine do bless my God,
> My fervent message to the world proclaim,
> I do not covet wealth or power or fame,
> I just want satisfaction for reward.
> I felt it was Your Will that I should write
> Of Beauty, Love and Joy, Eternal Peace,
> Of Sorrow, Struggle that a Death does cease,
> Of Hope, its sweet illuminating light.
>
> I've done my duty with all faithfulness,
> I strove to do Your Will, without a rest,
> I pray I have succeeded in this test,
> If I have, I can scarce my joy express.
> I am sincere that You, dear God, can see,
> I'll do Your Will, however hard may be.

How many worlds have passed away since I wrote that poem, but what I said in that poem still remains true for me. I believed then, as I believe now, that God had chosen me to be an instrument in implementing a plan that I could see only in part and understand only dimly. Since I first experienced the presence of God—powerful, healing, comforting, directing—in the solitude of my inner world, I have regarded my life as a trust that must be spent in *jihād fī sabīl Allah* (striving in the cause of Allah). As a child, there were times when I wanted to share my strong sense of being a missionary for God with my close friends. But I was afraid that they would not understand my calling and would ridicule me. I remember that once, not without trepidation, I mentioned to a friend whom I considered to be wiser than the rest that I believed God spoke to me in special moments and showed me the path I was to follow. I hoped that he would understand what I was trying to say, but he was shocked by what seemed to him to be pretentious words. I remember how his words "So you consider yourself a prophetess or something!" went through my heart like a dagger and left me speechless. After that I would not speak about what lay closest to my soul. . . .

Besides writing, my greatest joy in life in childhood was reading. One day, looking through a dusty bookcase in my house, I found a torn and tattered copy of Palgrave's "Golden Treasury" of poems. Finding that book was one of the most important things that ever happened to me, for it introduced me to many poems I grew to love deeply, including some sonnets of Shakespeare. I loved to recite poems to myself, over and over, till I knew them by heart. There was something about the measured music of poetry that captivated my heart and spirit. Though poetry was my first love, I also liked to read novels and read many "classics" by Dickens, Hardy, the Brontë sisters, Jane Austen, and many others. Of all the novels that I read in my childhood, the one that made the greatest impact on me was Emily Brontë's *Wuthering Heights*. This book had a haunting quality, and it seemed suspended between the world of reality and the world of dream, nightmare, and fantasy. The bleakness and wildness of its landscape seemed to correspond to my own psyche, and I identified with its strange characters, especially Cathy and Heathcliff. Apart from my reading of English "classics," I was also an avid reader of Agatha Christie's books, from which I learned much about human nature.

Most of my childhood I spent alone, writing and reading. I do not remember studying much for school. Despite that, I was the star pupil in my class from the beginning to the end of my scholastic career and won every honor and award there was to win. Many people, including my classmates and their parents, were very impressed with my academic success and treated me as if I were rather special. But as a child, and even as an adult, I did not crave success—perhaps because one does not crave what one does or can have. What I craved was love and peace around me and within me. I was a superachiever almost against my will. Toward the end of my high school career I became resentful of my own success and wanted to fail. My family never seemed to notice my success, or at least never mentioned it to me—I thought that perhaps if I failed they would pay some attention to me. Had it not been for a teacher who cared for me, I might have acted out my bitter, rebellious feelings, but I did not, and in future years was very grateful that I had not wrecked a record career. I learned very early in life that there is no necessary connection between success and happiness, but I have also come to know that, though many bright women are afraid to succeed, lack of success is not likely to lead to an enhancement of happiness, and I could not have found what I craved through underachieving.

The twelfth year of my life was a landmark year for me because during that year my struggle as an "activist feminist" began. Up until that time I had been a quiet child living for the most part in an inner sanctuary. But before I had turned twelve, all of a sudden the reality of the external world began to close in on me ominously, threatening to destroy my place of refuge. My second sister, who was sixteen, was married off to a man with a lot of money and very little education. She had tried to resist the arranged marriage but had succumbed, as most girls do, to the multifarious crude as well as subtle ways of "persuading" wavering girls to accept the arrangement in order to safeguard the family's "honor" and her own "happiness." Seeing her fall into the all-too-familiar trap I experienced total panic. I was the next in line. Four years later the same ritual would be reenacted, and this time I would be the sacrificial victim unless I found a way of averting the catastrophe. I knew that my mother would try to protect me from an arranged marriage, but I was not sure that she would succeed. I felt that I had to learn to fend for myself, to take a stand against my father and his rigid conventionalism. I had to learn to fight to survive in a society in which women's refusal to submit to patriarchal authority is tantamount to heresy. At twelve I had not learned how to fight. I had not wanted to learn to fight. I simply wanted to be left alone in my dream-world where I could write my poems and read my books . . . but I knew then, as I know now, that if one is born female in such a society as the one I was born in and wants to be regarded as a person and not as an object, one has no option but to fight. And so I learned to fight, and the fight continues to this day, though many battles have been won and lost. Battle-weary, I pray for the dawning of the day when it will not be required of women like myself to spend their entire lifetime fighting for their freedom each day of their life, but I also pray for strength to continue the fight until there is justice and freedom, under God, for all my sisters.

*   *   *

Much of what I am today is due to my mother's meticulous schooling, but I could never become the ruthless superwoman she wanted me to be. Even as a child I could not accept the way she discriminated against many people, including some of her own children. My earliest battle with her was over my three younger brothers, whom she frequently treated unjustly and unkindly. I protested in their behalf, and in behalf of the other "disadvantaged" persons, like domestic servants, whom my mother mistreated. Strangely enough she did not mind my protesting—in fact, she was rather amused by it and called me "leader of the opposition." Perhaps she did not mind my taking a stand against her because she liked to see me fight, even though it was against her. But my efforts to make her review her own conduct never worked. She lived, and still lives, in a world dominated by the idea of will-to-power.

While my mother wanted me to succeed, she never patted me on the back for doing well. I know that she was proud of my achievements because she told others about them, but I did not hear her tell me that she loved me. In my society there were many stories of how a mother's love was superior to all other kinds of love because it was "unconditional." I wanted so much to believe that, but I could not, since I heard my mother say repeatedly to me: "I do not love you, I love your qualities." Her words, which were meant to affirm my "qualities," made me feel very lonely and sad. I could not receive my mother's love simply because I was her child. I could receive her approval only if I proved myself worthy. I recall that as a child my mother's attitude toward me often made me very melancholy, but that as an adolescent it made me very angry. Part of this anger, which stayed with me for a long time, was directed at myself because I could not break loose of my mother's control over me. Regardless of how strongly I wished to resist her emotional manipulation, when confronted by her immensely powerful personality I felt myself relapsing into a state of juvenile behavior when I reacted to her instead of acting as an autonomous person. It took some devastating experiences to finally sever the chains that bound the little girl in me to my mother's power and make me free of the burden of living out her fantasies instead of living my own life. Free of the bondage, I have sought to reestablish the bond. I still find it very difficult to "dialogue" with my mother, and my feelings toward her remain ambivalent, but I feel a strong sense of duty toward her. My mother not only gave me life but also the strength required to live the kind of life I wanted to live, and for that I owe her more than I can give. With her egocentricity and eccentricity, my mother's indomitable spirit, reflected in her steadfastness of purpose, courage, and refusal to give up in the face of insuperable odds, makes her the most extraordinary woman I have ever known, and despite all the heartache and agony she has caused me, I am proud of the fact that I am my mother's daughter.

* * *

Terrified lest I fall somehow into the death trap of an arranged marriage, I wanted desperately to escape from the danger that stalked me. My eldest sister had gone to England on a scholarship, and I asked her to secure admission for me in her college. She did so. I expected my father to oppose the idea of my studying abroad, but he permitted me to go. Perhaps by this time he had begun to feel that I deserved to have the opportunity to study abroad. Perhaps he also hoped that once I left home I would be out of my mother's sphere of influence and he would have greater access to me. He never told me his reasons for letting me go, but he spoke to me after a number of years on the day on which my brother and I set out for England with my mother. I wept as he embraced me and felt the pain of saying goodbye to him. In that moment of farewell he was simply my father and not "the adversary."

My seven years at St. Mary's college, University of Durham, in England, were full of homesickness and hard studying. After three years I graduated with joint honors in English literature and philosophy, and then, at age 24, I became a Doctor of Philosophy specializing in the philosophy of Al-lama Muhammad Iqbal, the national poet-philosopher of Pakistan, whose work I had loved and admired since childhood. During my years in Eng-land, I did, in fact, grow closer to my father and more distant from my mother (who never liked the idea of my being on good terms with my fa-ther), but when I returned home after finishing my studies abroad, I found that I was alienated from them both in fundamental ways. I could conform neither to my father's norms nor to my mother's values. Since I was no longer a child, I did not experience a child's fears, but I felt unutterably, unbearably alone. Coming home after seven long years of exile, I was again an outcast, an outsider.

It was in that state that I decided to marry a man who seemed to need me intensely. Always having had a great need not only to receive love but also to give it, for me the heaviest part of the price I paid for being a rebel against patriarchal society was that I did not feel free to express the love I felt for my own family members. A rebel's gifts are not accepted, and no one seemed to need my love. But Dawar needed it, and for years I gave it to him—unconditionally, unreservedly. My family was not thrilled with the idea of my marrying an "unmade" man, but they did not oppose it. Per-haps they had learned from experience that opposition did not deter me; perhaps they were glad that finally I had agreed to be married at all. Any-how, as I began my married life I was aware of the social problems my hus-band and I would encounter on account of the fact that I was more educated than he and had better wage-earning prospects. These were se-rious matters in a society in which the man must always be seen to be in control and ahead of the woman, but in my joy at having found what I had always craved I did not pay much thought to them. For me, love was God's greatest gift, a miracle in a world of hate, and I believed that it could ac-complish anything and overcome any difficulty. In Dawar's eyes I saw what I had never had—the promise of sustaining love. . . .

*　　*　　*

My dream of love on which I thought our marriage was based was beauti-ful, no doubt, but it turned out to be a dream. Dawar was a typical prod-uct—victim—of the patriarchal society and had a compelling need to be the "head" of the family. He found it impossible to fulfill this need being married to a woman who was a superachiever, while he regarded himself as a loser. He was attracted by my strength but resented it at the same time. He wanted to utilize my talents but also to deny them. I tried to be a "good" wife, exemplifying the rebel's hidden desire to conform to tradition. For what seemed like a long time I was the model wife, selflessly devoted to her husband, living only for him and through him, but all my efforts to build up his confidence in himself only made him more conscious of what he lacked. A highly introverted person, he became even more withdrawn from life. I thought that perhaps if we left our complex-ridden, male-chauvinistic society and moved to a place where men were not under so much pressure to prove their superiority to women, our marriage would have a better chance of succeeding. We did, indeed, leave Pakistan and came to the United States, but the pattern of our relationship had already been set and it did not change. When I had married Dawar I had not known him well, but more importantly, I had not known myself well. Like many women through the ages I had thought that it was enough to give love without asking for anything in return, but I found out, after five years of constant giving, that I had nothing left to give. I was a hollow woman living in a wasteland. Never had my life seemed more empty, barren, or full of unspoken anguish. The times prior to my second exodus from my homeland (the first one having been for studying) and those which followed it were, in many ways, the darkest ones of my life. Much happened then that scarred me forever.

For me the decision to migrate from the land of my birth to a land I had never seen was one of the most difficult and heartbreaking decisions I have ever had to make. Through all the years that I had lived in England I had literally counted the days until my return to my beloved country. To serve "my people" had been a dream I had cherished since childhood. It is hard to describe the full measure of the disillusionment I suffered when I returned to my homeland and discovered that "my people" were enslaved by a corrupt government and that I could not live and work in my own country unless I was willing to renounce the ideals I most cherished. Torn as I was between love of my people and my commitment to God to work for truth and justice, I might have lingered in indecision had I not witnessed the dismemberment of Pakistan from very close quarters. As deputy director in the "brain-cell" of the federal information ministry, I had reason to believe that the tragedy that occurred could have been averted if the people in power had loved the country enough to let go of their own power fantasies. Traumatized by what I saw, I knew that the time for *hijrah** had come, for my homeland had become the territory of the godless. . . .

What remained alive was emotionally paralyzed for a long time when my only reason for living was my little daughter, who was born as all the skies were falling on my head. For me, my little Mona, as I call her, has always been a miracle of God's grace, a gift given to me to keep me alive. When

*Exile.

I named her Mehrunnisa I did not know that she would live up to her name, but she is, indeed, a child with a heart so full of love and sunshine that she makes me forget the sorrows of my life. Like all mothers I want my child to have a safe and happy passage through life, but I also tell her that she must understand what it means to be Mujāhida, which is her second name. I tell her that *jihād fī sabīl Allah* is the essence of being a Muslim and that I want her to commit her life to striving for truth and justice. I tell her that though she has herself known no discrimination, she must not become immune to the suffering of millions of Muslim girls who are discriminated against from the moment of birth. I tell her that my prayer for her is that she should be strong enough to be a *mujāhida* in the long struggle that lies ahead of us and to continue the efforts of her mother and grandmother.

In the last decade and a half of my life there have been other events and mishaps that have affected me significantly. Perhaps the most memorable of the mishaps was my extremely short-lived marriage to Mahmoud, an Egyptian Arab Muslim more than thirty years my senior in age, who persuaded me to marry him after I had known him only a few days, saying that he would take care of me and my child, and help me develop my talents in order to serve God better. Emotionally wrecked by the death of my brothers and the end of a marriage in which I had invested so much care, and frightened of living alone with a young child in an alien world, I was mesmerized by Mahmoud's powerful personality and believed him when he said that as a member of the Muslim Brotherhood movement in Egypt, he had suffered imprisonment and torture for the sake of God. Mahmoud called himself a man of God, but I learned very quickly that being a man of God had nothing to do with being kind and compassionate and loving. It meant only that Mahmoud could command me to do whatever he wished in the name of God and with the authority of God, and I had no right to refuse, since in Islamic culture refusal to do what is pleasing to the husband is tantamount to refusing to do what is pleasing to God. Short as the marriage was, I came near to total destruction, physically and mentally, at the hands of a man who was not only a male chauvinist par excellence but also a fanatic who could invoke the holy name of God in perpetrating acts of incredible cruelty and callousness upon other human beings. Had I not had a lifetime of struggle for survival behind me and a total faith that God was just and merciful, I could not have survived the three months I spent with Mahmoud or the three years I spent fighting the lawsuits in which he involved me in order to punish me for taking a stand against him. He ruined me financially and did serious damage to me in many ways. However, as good and evil are inextricably linked together in human life, I am grateful even for this soul-searing experience, for it was this experience more than any other that made me a feminist with a resolve to de-velop feminist theology in the framework of Islamic tradition so that other so-called men of God could not exploit other Muslim women in the name of God.

While my personal life has been filled with momentous crises and up-heavals throughout the years I have lived in this country, by the grace of God I have done well professionally. I am now a professor and chairper-son of the Religious Studies Program at the University of Louisville. My specialization is in the area of Islamic Studies, and it was due to this ex-pertise that I became involved in various ways, and at various levels, in the discussions going on around the country regarding Islam, after the Arab oil embargo of 1973 and the Iranian revolution of 1979 convinced the Western world that Islam was a living reality in the world. While I found many of these discussions, in which I was called upon to explain "Islamic revival" to Americans, interesting and stimulating, it was in another set-ting—that of interreligious dialogue among believers in the one God—that I found the community of faith I had sought all my life. In this commu-nity of faith I have found others who, like myself, are committed to creat-ing a new world in which human beings will not brutalize or victimize one another in the name of God, but will affirm, through word and action, that as God is just and loving so human beings must treat each other with jus-tice and love regardless of sex, creed, or color. I have found in my com-munity of faith what I did not find in my community of birth: the possibility of growing and healing, of becoming integrated and whole. Due to the af-firmation I have received from men and women of faith I am no longer the fragmented, mutilated woman that I once was. I know now that I am not alone in the wilderness, that there are some people in the world who understand my calling, and that their prayers are with me as I continue my struggle on behalf of the millions of nameless, voiceless, faceless Muslim women of the world who live and die unsung, uncelebrated in birth, un-mourned in death.

DIANA ECK
(1945–   )

Professor of Indian studies and comparative religion at Harvard, Diana Eck is currently directing a project that is documenting the spiritual diversity of American culture. Since 1965, when a change in the immigration laws resulted in the arrival of more people from Asia and

the Middle East than from Europe, the spiritual landscape of the United
States has broadened to include Hindu temples, Sikh gurdwaras, and
Islamic mosques. Eck, who is both a historian of religion specializing in
Hinduism and a Christian, argues that all religions "flow with living
waters I would call holy. Worlds apart, they carry currents of life and
meaning whose confluence is in me, deep in my own spiritual life." Her
book *Encountering God: A Spiritual Journey from Bozeman to Banares*,
an autobiographical, historical, and theological portrait of cross-cultural
spirituality—the first chapter is excerpted here—won the 1995
Louisville Grawemeyer Award in Religion, a $150,000 prize given by
the Louisville Presbyterian Theological Seminary and the University of
Louisville.

From *Encountering God: A Spiritual Journey from Bozeman to Banares*

QUESTIONS FROM THE PASSAGE TO INDIA

I grew up in Bozeman, Montana, in the Gallatin Valley, one of the most
beautiful mountain valleys in the Rockies. The Gallatin River cuts through
a spectacular canyon to the south, then flows like a stream of crystal through
the fertile farmlands of the valley. I had three horses stabled on our land
by the Gallatin and spent hours every week riding along the river. By the
time I was twenty, I had made my way "back East," as we called it, to Smith
College, and then much further east to India, to the Hindu sacred city of
Banaras, set on the banks of another river, the Ganges. Banaras was the first
real city I ever lived in. It was a city in the time of the Buddha, twenty-six
hundred years ago, and the guidebooks called it "older than history." Bozeman had been settled for scarcely one hundred years.

As a twenty-year-old, I found Banaras to be about as far from Bozeman
as any place on earth. The smoke of the cremation pyres rose night and
day from the "burning ghats" along the river. The Ganges is a much bigger river than the Gallatin; it is a powerful river that seemed to flow with
authority and peace as it slid along the ghats, the great stone steps of the
city, where Hindus bathed by the thousands at dawn. Today these two
places, Bozeman and Banaras, both convey the spiritual meaning of the
word *home* to me. And these two rivers, the Gallatin and the Ganges, both
flow with living waters I would call holy. Worlds apart, they carry currents
of life and meaning whose confluence is in me, deep in my own spiritual

life. All of us have such rivers deep within us, bearing the waters of joining streams.

This book is an exploration of the encounter of Bozeman and Banaras, a religious encounter that raises at the very deepest levels the question of difference, the inescapable question of our world today. The issues of race and culture, language and gender, take us into the question of difference in complex and multiple ways, but deeper still, I believe, are the issues of worldview, of religion, and of religious difference. For me, the question has its particular angularities, as it must for each of us. What does it mean, now, to be a Christian, having come to see with my own eyes the religious life of Hindu, Buddhist, and Muslim friends with whom I have lived in professional and personal relationships for many years? How has my own Christian faith been challenged and reformulated by taking seriously what I have learned in this encounter?

I begin this exploration with my own experience, not because my experience is so special but because it illustrates the kinds of personal, social, and theological encounters that are increasingly the reality of our common world. Today people of every faith meet one another, develop deep personal or professional friendships, perhaps even marry one another. Our experience with people of other faiths may be difficult or rewarding, or both. In any case, our "interfaith dialogue" does not usually begin with philosophy or theory, but with experience and relationships. Individually and collectively, our experience has now begun to challenge traditional religious thinking and to contribute decisively to the reformulation of our theologies.

For many people religion is a rigid concept, somewhat like a stone that is passed from generation to generation. We don't add to it, change it, or challenge it; we just pass it along. But even the most cursory study of the history of religions would undermine such a view. Religious traditions are far more like rivers than stones. Like the Ganges or the Gallatin, they are flowing and changing. Sometimes they dry up in arid land; sometimes they radically change course and move out to water new territory. All of us contribute to the river of our traditions. We do not know how we will change the river or be changed as we experience its currents. My task here is to articulate the questions that I know are not mine alone. As John A. T. Robinson put it in another context, that of rising secularism, some thirty years ago, "All I can do is to try to be honest—honest to God and about God—and to follow the argument wherever it leads."

When W. W. Alderson first saw the Gallatin Valley in July of 1864, just two months after Montana became a U.S. territory, he wrote:

The valley and the stream looked so pleasant and inviting that we concluded to lay over and look around. . . . The grass was tall everywhere, and as it was just heading out, the valley looked like an immense field of grain waving gracefully before the gentle breeze. . . . We had come to dig for gold and make a fortune in a year or two, but . . . the fever abating, we concluded to locate right here and engage in farming.

Today Bozeman is a thriving city with shopping malls and sprawling suburbs, but in my childhood it was a small college town of twelve thousand, a grid of tree-lined streets with Main Street running right down the middle. It was named for John Bozeman, a pioneer trail guide who, along with Alderson and two other members of the Bozeman Claim Association, had laid out the town in August of 1864. As a Girl Scout I earned a merit badge by writing the history of Bozeman's pioneer heritage: the sagebrush and gophers, the wooden sidewalks and muddy streets, the first cabins built in the summer of 1864, the Laclede Hotel on the site where the Montgomery Ward was later built. By the 1890s there was a train depot, an opera house with a ladies' parlor, and Cy Mount's Palace Saloon, with its gambling rooms lined with fine and intricately inlaid wood. And there were fine brick houses, one of which, I found, had retained its red color because the bricks had been soaked in stale beer before they were laid. There was one black man in town, Sam Lewis, who ran the barber shop. And there was an alleyway between Main and Mendenhall that was called Chinatown, with a laundry business and a restaurant.

The church I grew up in, the First Methodist Church on South Willson, was the oldest Methodist church building in the state. The foundation stone had been laid in 1873 by the first minister, the Reverend T. C. Iliff, in the days when Bozeman was still a frontier town with dirt streets and Saturday night shootouts. Mary Iliff, in her memoirs of life on the frontier as a young minister's wife, recalled her utter astonishment when she was presented with six Sioux scalps by a Nez Perce medicine man named Amos, in gratitude for a kindness she had shown in boiling a sack of eggs for him. With trembling hands she thanked him for his gift.

T. C. Iliff, along with W. W. Van Orsdel, whom we knew as the legendary Brother Van, were the charismatic circuit riders who set the stage for Montana Methodism—preaching and singing with such charisma they were called the Heavenly Twins. Brother Van had answered an appeal in the *Christian Advocate* of St. Louis at a time when there were only ninety-five Methodists in all of Montana: "Are there not half a dozen young men in our theological schools who are ready to band together and, taking their lives in their hands, emigrate to this new country and assist in giving the privilege of the gospel to its people?" Brother Van and T. C. Iliff rode horseback from town to town, tending to their congregations. Iliff eventually became the field secretary for the Methodist church and the namesake of the Iliff School of Theology in Denver. Brother Van worked for forty-seven years as a Montana preacher and was said to be the "best-loved man in Montana" when he died. the anthem of Montana Methodism was and still is "Brother Van's Song," a beautiful, rousing hymn about the faith of those who plant and sow not knowing if they will live to see the harvest. The refrain soars with the words "The tears of the sower and the songs of the reaper shall mingle together in joy, by and by." It is a song of frontier farmers, who regularly lived with the risk of losing their crops, and frontier preachers who labored in faith not knowing if the harvest would come.

Montana is a big state with a strong sense of identity. From the windows of our house just at the edge of that grid of tree-lined streets, I could look out over a field of cattle to Bear Mountain. I learned the names of all the mountains that circle the valley—the Bridger Range, the Spanish Peaks, the Madison Range, the Tobacco Roots. And the rivers, too—the Gallatin, the Madison, and the Jefferson, all given their names by Lewis and Clark, who came through the valley in 1805 and 1806 with their Shoshone guide, Sacajewea. At Three Forks, just thirty miles up the valley from Bozeman, the three rivers join to form the Missouri. It is spectacular landscape, its size and vastness somehow made comprehensible by the act of naming and the mastery of those names. I gradually learned the names of mountains and rivers all over the state, for as teenagers my friends and I thought nothing of driving four hundred miles for a weekend basketball tournament or a Methodist youth rally. I learned another Montana reality as well: that this vast landscape included lands set apart as reservations for the native peoples who had lived here and whose homeland this was long before John Bozeman or any of the settlers had come—the Crow and the Northern Cheyenne in the southeast, the Blackfoot in the north, the Flathead and the Kootenay in the west. There were invisible borders and multiple cultures.

Our Methodist church camps were summer meeting places where I got my first taste of a wide and vibrant sense of the church. Various churches built their own cabins in Luccock Park, the camp in the hills above the Paradise Valley near Livingston. Those log cabins, named for our towns "Bozeman," "Livingston," "Billings," and "Big Timber," nestled like miniatures below the towering mountains we called Faith, Hope, and Charity. There in our summer camps we teenagers in the Methodist Youth Fellowship, the M.Y.F., enacted the rites of bonding and commitment that are so formative in the adolescent experience of religion: confessing our secrets and dreams, singing round the campfire at night, sitting in silence and prayer as the fire began to die down, holding crossed hands in a circle of commitment around the glowing embers. When I became the state M.Y.F. president, I also went to the Flathead Lake camp, nearly four hundred miles away in the northwest part of the state. There the cabins were called "Kalispell," "Missoula," and "Great Falls," and there we sat on logs in the outdoor chapel at Inspiration Point for what we called "morning watch," looking out at daybreak past the wooden cross, over Flathead Lake toward the Mission Range.

I did a lot of building as a teenager in the Montana M.Y.F.—roofing, mixing cement, pounding and pulling nails. There were work camps every summer. We built a dining hall at Luccock Park under the supervision of my father, an architect and builder. We built a church at a little settlement called Babb on the Blackfoot Reservation in the grassy, windy prairie land east of Glacier National Park. We lived for a month in two spacious tepees, talking late into the night, sleeping in sleeping bags around the fire, and rising early for morning watch on the hilltop just above our campsite. We took an old schoolbus to Mexico, again with my father and mother, and built a silo on a rural-development farm near Patzcuaro. Our workdays included drilling holes for dynamite, blasting, and mixing cement for the master masons from the little village of Huecorio to use in raising the stone walls of what had to be the most elegant and durable silo in all of Mexico. There our days began with morning watch on the rooftop terrace, where the twenty of us studied the Bible and sang hymns looking out over the farmlands toward Lake Patzcuaro with its island village of Janitzio.

The most durable product of these teenage summers, at least for me, was a sturdy faith in God, a very portable sense of what constitutes the church, and a commitment to the work of the church in the world. I arrived at Smith College in the fall of 1963 straight from the March on Washington, where I had been with the national M.Y.F. delegation. I joined these friends again during the spring vacation of my freshman year to lobby in Washington, D.C., for the Civil Rights Bill. Civil rights and Vietnam War, racism and militarism, were the issues that shaped the whole context of college in the sixties, during the years I was at Smith. They came together in complex ways. One of my first summer jobs was a short stint working for the Montana Board of Health on the Northern Cheyenne Reservation out of Lame Deer in southeastern Montana. I saw at first hand the racism of my own state, where I had rarely met an African American, but had also rarely seen the real conditions in which most of the Native American peoples lived. After two weeks in Lame Deer, I was invited to an all-night prayer meeting of the Native American church. As we settled into a circle around the fire in the tepee, my host told me that the service was to pray for the Cheyenne boys who were serving in Vietnam. There were six from the tiny town of Lame Deer alone. The night was unforgettable: rounds of peyote, chanting, prayer, drumming. It was a form of worship I had never seen, among people who were virtual neighbors and yet virtual strangers to me in Montana, people whose sons and brothers were disproportionately drafted for service in Vietnam.

It was in this context of the Vietnam War that I first went to India. The move had only an indirect logic to it, a logic animated by the concern and yet the inadequacy so many American college students felt about the U.S. war in Asia. As a sophomore in college, I was aimed toward the study of Latin America. But when I saw the announcement of the University of Wisconsin's College Year in India program posted on the bulletin board in Wright Hall during midyear exams, I was immediately drawn to the possibility. Nothing and no one in my past had prepared me for an encounter with that part of the world. I knew nothing of Asia. In fact, the Vietnam War seemed a tragic testimony to how little most of us in America knew about Asia. The boys from Lame Deer were there. A few friends from my high school were there. My friends from Amherst thought of nothing but how to avoid going there. So I applied to go to India. It was Asia. Close enough. Maybe I would learn something. I took a spring term course taught by a visiting professor from Poona on the thought of two of India's most important twentieth-century thinkers, Gandhi and Aurobindo. That summer—which was for some a Mississippi summer, for some a Vietnam summer—I spent in the language labs at the University of Wisconsin learning Hindi.

In September of 1965, with a new group of friends from the summer of language study in Madison, I arrived in India. There was not much in Bozeman or Northampton, or even in Patzcuaro, that could have prepared me for Banaras, a vibrant, congested city sitting high on the banks of the River Ganges. Its intensity was overwhelming. I had been in Banaras only a few days when I wrote home, "Wandering half-scared through the side-walk narrow streets near the Chowk market today was an exhausting experience, exhausting because it was as if I had walked through all of India, seen, felt, tasted, smelled it all in three hours. There were too many people, too many faces, too many cows, too many catacomb streets and dead ends, too little air. The utter concentration of life, work, misery, odor, and filth in this area of the city was staggering."

Despite my feelings of claustrophobia and bewilderment, I was immediately impressed by the religiousness of Banaras. There religion was surely *the* most important observable fact of daily life. The whole city seemed to revolve on a ritual axis. There were temples everywhere, large and small, inhabited by images of gods and goddesses whose names I did not know, whose multiarmed forms I could not even distinguish one from the other, and whose significance was totally beyond my grasp. The bathing ghats along the Ganges were the scene of morning rituals for pilgrims. We had not been there more than a day or two when we rose before dawn and took rickshaws to the riverfront to see the sights for which Banaras is so famous. Thousands of Hindus were there at Dasashwamedh Ghat, bobbing in the water, standing waist deep their hands folded in prayer, chanting to a crescendo of bells as the sun rose over the river. Perhaps the one piece of my Montana past that I brought with me to the comprehension of that first dawn on the Ganges was "morning watch." For two miles along the ghats, Hindus bathed in the Ganges and worshiped as the sun broke the horizon. The city pulsed with the life of faith as vibrant as any I had known, and as different.

That year I came to know, for the first time, people of faith from a tradition not my own. I did not know any Jews, let alone Hindus or Muslims, when I set off from Montana for Smith College. I knew little of the faith of others, but at that point in life I was quite clear about the center of my own Christian faith: love, justice, human dignity, and the steady sense of being linked in kinship to Christ and to the Christian community. It was a faith nourished, as all faith finally is, by people—energetic, loving, committed, visionary people. The only people of that sort I knew—and I had the good fortune of knowing quite a few of them as a teenager—were Christians.

It was in Banaras that I experienced the first real challenge to my faith. Not surprisingly, it did not come in the form of ideas, even though I was enrolled in a course in Advaita Vedanta philosophy at the Banaras Hindu University. It came in the form of people—Hindus whose lives were a powerful witness to their faith. I had conceived a completely naive fieldwork project on "Hinduism and the Indian Intellectual." Knowing little about Hinduism myself, I concocted a set of questions about the gods, the meaning of *karma*, the meaning of reincarnation, and so forth, and set out on my bicycle to meet scholars, poets, and professionals in Banaras and to ask what they believed. It was not a very good project, but I couldn't have found a more interesting introduction to India.

One of those I met was Achyut Patwardhan, a former freedom fighter who had spent his share of years in prison in the service of the nonviolent movement for India's independence. He was a man of simple, self-giving love. Like the civil rights leaders I had admired at home, he had put his life on the line in the service of justice. "You see suffering," he said to me, "and you don't debate about it or make yourself act. Those who love simply act, respond naturally with the spontaneous good that is human. Perhaps all you can do is take another person's hand. This, then, is sufficient." Patwardhan was, to me as a twenty-year-old, a man of God and a great spiritual friend at a time of my life when questions were tumbling through my mind. He was a man whose life was a witness to love and justice. He was very much like the people I had most loved and admired as a teenager. But he was not a Christian. He did not find an example and a companion in Christ, as I did. To my surprise, it did not seem to me that he somehow ought to be a Christian. What did this mean about some of the biblical claims of my own tradition?

In November I met J. Krishnamurti, a man who did not fit any category at all. He was giving a series of daily talks at Rajghat in Banaras. Not only was he not a Christian, he was not a Hindu, not a Buddhist. That was just his point. "Truth is a pathless land," he said. "You cannot approach it by any path whatsoever, by any religion, by any sect." He did not say, Follow me. On the contrary, he said, "I desire those who seek to understand me to be free, not to follow me, not to make out of me a cage which will become a religion, a sect." He did not care for the labels of any religion. Indeed, he observed the way in which we fearfully, anxiously, shape our whole lives by religious, political, cultural, and personal labels and names—all of which function as a buffer zone of security between ourselves and the experience of life.

Krishnamurti posed my first real encounter with the "otherness" of a worldview. No one in my world had ever asked about the value of labeling, judging, discriminating, and categorizing experience or suggested that by doing so we distance ourselves from experience. We call it a beautiful sunrise on the Ganges and don't ever really see it because we have dispensed with it by giving it a name and label. Perhaps we write a poem about it to capture it in words or take a photograph of it and feel satisfied that we "got it." We name so-and-so as a friend or an enemy. The next time we encounter that person, the pigeonhole is ready. Are not our minds perpetually busy in these maneuvers? I must admit, at twenty it had never occurred to me to ask such questions. And what about religion? Is it really just a name? I had to ask myself about being a Christian. Did the name matter? Did the label provide me with a shelter or barrier to shield me from real encounter and questioning? What did I have invested in this name? Everywhere I turned I saw question marks.

It is possible, however, that Krishnamurti's ideas would have meant little to me had not Krishnamurti himself been so arresting. Never had I experienced the quality of presence—I suppose now I would say "spiritual presence"—that he brought into a room. It is what I then called his "existentialism," for want of a better word. He spoke without notes, simply, directly, and he continually named and challenged the nature of our attention to him. Were we taking down notes? Why? Were we hoping to seize what he had to say? Were we comparing his ideas to those of Teilhard de Chardin or Zen Buddhism? Were we judging his thoughts with our likes and dislikes? Why couldn't we just listen? Is simple presence and attention so impossible? The questions Krishnamurti asked were not about the world and its injustices, they were questions about me and my habits of apprehending the world. Though I had read some of Paul Tillich's work the year before and had especially liked *The Shaking of the Foundations,* this was the real shaking of the foundations for me.

Krishnamurti and Patwardhan were important to me precisely because they were what Christians might call "witnesses" to their faith; they somehow embodied their faith in their lives. In retrospect, it is somewhat embarrassing to articulate this as a discovery, but as a twenty-year-old it came as news to me: Christians did not have a corner on love, wisdom, and justice. Christians were not the only ones nourished by faith and empowered by their faith to work to change the world. I knew nothing of the Hindu devotional traditions of *bhakti* then, but I met people—like Krishnamurti and Patwardhan—whose very lives were a message of God-grounded love. These people, unbeknownst to them, pushed me into a life of work and inquiry, spiritual and intellectual. I became a student of comparative religion and focused my work on Hinduism and the traditions of India. And as a Christian I began to realize that to speak of Christ and the meaning of incarnation might just mean being radically open to the possibility that God really encounters us in the lives of people of other faiths.

That first year in Banaras changed the course of my life. I have been back and forth to India a dozen times now. I did doctoral work in comparative religion and wrote my thesis and then my first book on the city of Banaras—which Hindus call Kashi, the City of Light. It is a study of what the city, the Ganges, and the gods mean to Hindus. When I returned for research on my doctoral thesis, eight years after that first year in Banaras, I learned the names of all those gods, their stories, their powers. I visited as many of the city's thousand temples as any Hindu. I went up and down the ghats of the riverfront, learning their hidden shrines by heart. I circled the city on my bicycle and visited its protective guardians. I spoke to teachers and priests, scholars and pilgrims. Perhaps my teenage fieldwork along Main Street in the saloons and churches of old Bozeman had whetted my appetite for taking on one of the world's oldest and most complicated cities.

When I had finished the book on Banaras, I began a study of the Hindu temples and shrines that link the whole of India in interwoven networks of pilgrimage places. I traveled up and down the sacred rivers of India, visiting the headwaters of the Ganges in the Himalayas, the Narmada in the highlands of Madhya Pradesh, the Godavari in the hills of Maharashtra, and the Kaveri in the Coorg hills of the south. I went to major temples and wayside shrines and visited the four *dhams,* the divine abodes at the four corners of India—Badrinath in the northern Himalayas, Rameshvaram at the tip of southern India, Puri on the Bay of Bengal in the east, and Dvaraka on the Arabian Sea in the west. As a scholar and professor of religion, this kind of intellectual work is no small challenge—to glimpse the world of meaning in which people of another faith live their lives and die their deaths. But it is another question—equally important but very different— which I am pursuing here: What does all this mean to me, as a Christian?

THEOLOGY IN THE ENCOUNTER OF WORLDS

The meeting of Banaras and Bozeman, "East and West," can be duplicated in a hundred keys and a hundred languages. The encounter of worlds and worldviews is the shared experience of our times. We see it in the great movements of modern history, in colonialism and the rejection of colonialism, in the late-twentieth-century "politics of identity"—ethnic, racial, and religious. We experience our own personal versions of this encounter, all of us, whether Christian, Hindu, Jewish, or Muslim; whether Buddhist, Apache, or Kikuyu; whether religious, secular, or atheist. What do we make of the encounter with a different world, a different worldview? How will we think about the heterogeneity of our immediate world and our wider world? This is our question, our human question, at the end of the twentieth century.

My own versions of this question are How can those of us who are Christians articulate our own faith fully aware of the depth and breadth of the faith of others? How do we affirm our own holy ground even as we sojourn in the holy lands of other faith traditions, even as we find ourselves to be more than sojourners, to be at home there? How is Christian faith, or a "Christian worldview," challenged and changed when we take seriously the fact that we are not alone as religious people, when we recognize as truly religious the traditions, the lives, and the pilgrimages of our neighbors of other faiths?

Not everyone has encountered the gods of India, but in the 1990s most people have encountered something of a religion not their own and have found questions welling up, expressed or unexpressed, about the meaning of this encounter for their own faith. For Christians, it might be a Passover seder or a Sabbath meal shared with Jewish friends; it might be the Ramadan fasting of a Muslim colleague here in North America, or time spent living or traveling in an Islamic society, where prayer is so visible and natural a part of daily life. Many Christians have taken up Buddhist or Hindu meditation practices, and have wondered about the relation of these disciplines of meditation to their own faith. Many have seen the film *Gandhi* or have read Gandhi's autobiography and felt the religious challenge of the Sermon on the Mount presented more clearly in the life of this twentieth-century Hindu than in that of any contemporary Christian. Many have sensed the holiness of the Dalai Lama and asked what such holiness has to do with the things they call holy in their own tradition. Many have read the scriptures of other traditions of faith, like the Bhagavad Gita, and have wondered what the insights they have gained might have to do with their own faith.

The questions that rise from experience to challenge the real meaning of our faith are basic theological questions. They are theological because they have to do with ultimate meaning, with the one we call God, with articulating our faith in a way that makes sense both of our tradition and the world in which we live. . . .

FEMINISM, LIBERATION, AND PLURALISM

For me, this task is doubly complex because I hear not only the voices of Hindu or Buddhist friends and teachers as I write, but also the voices of women within my own tradition who have never been given much narrative space in the history and theology of Christianity. Indeed, the voices of women have not been fully heard in Hinduism, Buddhism, Islam, or Judaism either. Our voices have been suppressed in the texts and in the leadership of most of the world's religious traditions, though it is clear that women have done much to sustain the vibrance and vigor of these very traditions. So it is always with a profound sense of dissonance that I view the formalities of many world interfaith events, where the colorful male panoply of swamis, rabbis, bishops and metropolitans, monks and ministers line up together for a photograph of interfaith fellowship. They are portraits of a fading world, for women's hands and voices are reshaping all of our traditions.

The emergence of women's voices is worldwide—as priests and pastors in the Christian tradition, as rabbis and theologians in the Reform and Conservative Jewish tradition, as feminists in the Orthodox Jewish community, as Gandhian activists and scholars in India, as Muslim feminists insisting on their right to the radical justice and equality of the Qur'an. As the Buddhist tradition grows in new soil in the West, many of its finest teachers are women. As the Catholic church experiences the turmoil of our century, many of its leaders, ordained or not, are women. Even where women's voices are not yet fully heard, they sound the beginnings of real religious revolutions. In every tradition, these are revolutions happening before our very eyes.

Liberation theology, feminist theology, and pluralist theology are all major currents in the Christian tradition today. All three are about the re-definition of the *we* in theological thinking and the renegotiation of the *we* in our common political and cultural life. They are all attempts to re-construct more inclusive and more relevant forms of Christian thinking and Christian engagement. Liberation theologians articulate the Gospel as understood by the poor, the marginalized, those who speak the word of truth outside the houses of privilege and comfort and who insist that our priorities be set, not by the interests of the mighty, but by the priorities of the poor. Feminist theologians give voice to the concerns of both women and men who insist on the presence and perspective of women in Christ-ian leadership, teaching, and interpretation. Pluralist theologians insist that Christians must also listen to the voices of people of other faiths and not pretend that we can do our theological and ethical thinking in a vacuum, without engaging in energetic interreligious exchange.

Unfortunately, there has not as yet been much interrelation between these three currents of theological thinking. Many Christians who speak of the "preferential option for the poor" seem not to recognize that most of the world's poor are not Christians who will speak the Gospel in a new prophetic voice—they are Muslim poor or Hindu poor. To hear their voices necessitates interreligious dialogue. Many of those who want to lis-ten to the voices of Buddhists and Hindus pay scarcely any attention to the voices of women and reinforce in their interreligious dialogue the patri-archies of all the traditions; many who want to give voice to the perspec-tives of women within the Christian tradition don't think for a moment about Hindus and Buddhists. Everyone is busy on his or her own front. In a sense this is not a criticism, for feminist and womanist theologians, lib-eration theologians, and pluralist theologians have all, in their own ways, unleashed their respective revolutions in Christian thinking today. I be-lieve, however, that we all must begin to think of these issues together, for I am convinced that they belong together as part of our effort to rebuild a sense of community that does not make difference divisive and exclusive.

When I first went to India in 1965, I had not heard the word *feminism* or connected gender issues with theological thinking. While I was in India, Betty Friedan came to the Smith College campus to speak about *The Fem-inine Mystique.* Mary Daly was probably still at her typewriter working on *The Church and the Second Sex,* which was published in 1968. Her book *Beyond God the Father,* which so shaped the intellectual world of gradu-ate studies in the seventies, was still years away. But there in India, living and studying in Banaras, I encountered a multitude of gods and goddesses imaged in poetry, song, and stone. In India, through the rich theological imagination of Hindus, my understanding of God the Father was chal-lenged by the language of God the Mother, God the Dancer, God the

Lover, and God the Androgyne. In India I encountered the problem and the limits of my own religious language several years before I felt it surface through the currents of feminist writing in the Christian church. When I said, "Our Father, . . ."—which I still do—there began to be footnotes at the bottom of my mind, mental reservations about just what Father means and does not mean. And the list has become longer through the years.

Dialogue in which we listen as well as speak may seem so common-sensical it is scarcely worth making a fuss over. And yet dialogue, whether between women and men, black and white, Christian and Hindu, has not been our common practice as an approach to bridging differences with un-derstanding. Power and prestige make some voices louder, give some more airtime, and give the powerful the privilege of setting the terms for com-munication. We have had a long history of monologues. Much of the Christian missionary movement has been based on a one-way discourse of preaching and proclamation, with little thought to listening and little space for it. The Christian mission movement moved, for the most part, in the wake of European empires and in the company of the politically and eco-nomically powerful. The church did not have to listen—in India, in East Asia, in Africa, or in South America.

MUTUAL TRANSFORMATION

Today the language of dialogue has come to express the kind of two-way discourse that is essential to relationship, not domination. One might call it mutual witness: Christians have not only a witness to bear, but also a wit-ness to hear. In the process of mutual testimony and mutual questioning, we not only come to understand one another, we come to understand our-selves more deeply as well.

JOAN HALIFAX
(1944–   )

Joan Halifax is a Buddhist teacher, shaman, and ecologist who has long been at the forefront of spiritual exploration. She is the author of *Shaman: The Wounded Healer* and editor of the anthology *Shamanic Voices*. In *The Fruitful Darkness: Reconnecting with the Body of the Earth*, the source of the following selection, Halifax describes her years of practicing, working, and living with the traditions of shamanism and

Buddhism, which are rooted in the practicality of nonviolence. Seeking the wisdom of indigenous peoples, from Native American elders to Tibetan Buddhist meditators, she discovers her own "fruitful darkness"—the healing nature of suffering and compassion—in her quest for alternatives to the modern way of life. The Vietnamese monk Thich Nhat Hanh, an important influence on her work, called the book "a journey of compassion," "an important adventure." Peter Matthiessen praised it as "a feast of wisdom old and new."

From *The Fruitful Darkness: Reconnecting with the Body of the Earth*

THE WAY OF COMPASSION

May my body
  be a prayerstick
  for the world.

Many Buddhists have believed that Bodhisattva Avalokiteshvara* is beyond gender. According to the *Lotus Sutra*, this deity transforms the body and becomes a female, male, soldier, monk, god, or animal to save various beings from suffering. When he/she looked out into the world and saw the immense suffering of all beings, he/she shed tears of compassion. One of these tears was transformed into the Noble Mother Tara, the embodiment of wisdom and compassion in Tibet. Tara traveled across China and to southeast Asia and Japan. She syncretized with local protectresses, old Earth and Water Goddesses, who combined with the wisdom being Tara to give birth to Kuanyin (China), Kuan Seum (Korea), and Kanzeon (Japan), "Listening to the Sound of the World."

In her display as Avalokiteshvara, she has six heads with which to perceive the world in all its forms and a thousand arms and hands to help those who are suffering. She has given herself to the world to be shaped by its needs. All her hands hold instruments of effective action. Like the Mother of the World, she is outside us, but like our own mother, she lives inside each of us as well. In fact, she lives inside each thing. She can be found everywhere—in the falling rain that nourishes the Earth and eases the summer's heat, and in the starving child who awakens our compassion. She is the part of us that enters the body of communion without hesitation. She enters this body naturally and fearlessly.

*A bodhisattva ("enlightenment hero") of compassion.

*　　*　　*

The eyes of Kanzeon see into every corner of Calcutta. The ears of Kanzeon hear all the voices of suffering, whether understandable to the human ear, or the voices of felled cedar and mahogany or struggling sturgeon who no longer make their way up Mother Volga to spawn. The hands of Kanzeon reach out in their many shapes, sizes, and colors to help all forms of beings. They reach out from the ground of understanding and love. "Let the beauty we love be what we do. There are hundreds of ways to kneel and kiss the ground" (Rumi). It is understood that the craft of loving-kindness is the everyday face of wisdom and the ordinary hand of compassion. This wisdom face, this hand of mercy, is never realized alone but always with and through others. The Buddhist perspective shows us that there is no personal enlightenment, that awakening occurs in the activity of loving relationship.

*　　*　　*

Buddhism, shamanism, and deep ecology are ways for us to understand and realize that this Earth is a vast and rich network of mutual arisings, dyings, and renewings. Seeing this, we experience ourselves as part of the world around us, and the world around us is part of us. It is from this base that authentic harmlessness and helpfulness awaken.

*　　*　　*

Leaving behind the anthropocentric view that holds us away from the world and discovering how we are related to and indeed embedded in all that exists has profound political and environmental implications. The Earth is imperiled. It is suffering. Living as part of its body, we suffer with and through it. Awakening through this suffering, we might be able to help the Earth and ourselves, heal it, and thus heal ourselves. The Zen monk Dogen wrote, "You should know that the entire earth is not our temporary appearance, but our genuine human body." Earth, according to Dogen, is truth and speaks truth but not always or necessarily with a human tongue. It is our body. And its voice can be heard even in the desert silence.

We can ask ourselves, then, When will we see our True Eye? When will we discover our True Hand? Kanzeon has innumerable hands. They appear in every shape and color. She is everywhere, hearing the suffering of Earth. Kanzeon is Earth, as well, in its many forms of suffering and beauty. Her hands reach out through clear-cut forests, poisoned rivers, and hungry children to awaken us. Her hands reach back to herself through our compassionate response to victims of war, slaughtered rhinos, and grasslands that are now wastelands.

*   *   *

Some years ago at a Buddhist retreat for artists at the Ojai Foundation, we arrived under the oak tree to meditate and discovered that there was an arrangement of compost on the altar. Here were banana peels, egg shells, wood chips, and bits of dinner from the evening before. Someone asked Thich Nhat Hanh if this was disrespectful. He smiled and said, on the contrary, the arrangement was made by someone who truly understood the dharma.

In the Vietnamese form of Buddhism, there are small poems of mindfulness that can be recited to remind us of exactly what we are doing at this very moment. One of these *gathas* is for throwing out the garbage. It goes as follows:

> In the garbage I see a rose.
> In the rose, I see the garbage.
> Everything is in transformation.
> Even permanence is impermanent.

"Garbage can smell terrible," says Thich Nhat Hanh,

especially rotting organic matter. But it can also become rich compost for fertilizing the garden. The fragrant rose and the stinking garbage are two sides of the same existence. Without one, the other cannot be. Everything is in transformation. The rose that wilts after six days will become a part of the garbage. After six months the garbage is transformed into a rose. When we speak of impermanence, we understand that everything is in transformation. This becomes that, and that becomes this.

Looking deeply, we can contemplate one thing and see everything else in it. We are not disturbed by change when we see the interconnectedness and continuity of all things. It is not that the life of any individual is permanent, but that life itself continues. When we identify ourselves with life and go beyond the boundaries of a separate identity, we shall be able to see permanence in the impermanent, or the rose in the garbage.

In 1987, traveling back from Mount Kailas in western Tibet, I was delayed for several days when the old truck I was traveling in bogged down in the middle of the Brahmaputra River. I was exhausted and discouraged by the rigors of the travel. My Khampa truck companions were a rough group who exploited and fought with the local Drogpa nomads day after day. With little or nothing to eat, predawn departures, midnight encampments, and the abuse of riding in the crowded bed of this old Chinese beater, I was more than beginning to lose my enthusiasm for the high plateau of Tibet. So there we were, stuck in another river.

Not far from this scene was a group of small, ragged yak-hair tents inhabited by very old women who had long outlived their men. They had a few animals for milk and butter but little else. Seeing a solitary crone standing in an endless, bare landscape with cobalt skies hanging overhead filled me with a kind of wonder, and even fear.

On the third day of our involuntary visit to this impermanent settlement, my traveling companion unpacked our little cooking pot with great excitement, and we headed off to visit one of these bright old souls. There an old woman sat in her little smoky tent, her skin dark with years of sun combined with yak butter and dung smoke. Beside her was a bucket of the whitest yogurt I had ever seen. It was ours, she gestured, as much as we could take. She laughed as she refused my money. What good would this money do her out here?

I found it difficult to accept this gift. Clearly I was hungry, but didn't she need something in return? I was stunned and humbled. It seemed as if one of the old, dark hands of Kanzeon was ladling out nectar for all hungry beings of the three times and the four worlds.

When I look back on that moment by the river, I still can see those old female eyes burning with love. This fire is no different from the one I have seen in the eyes of Ogobara, Chan K'in Viejo, Guadalupe de la Cruz Ríos, Don José, and Maria Sabina. These old known and unknown men and women of elder cultures reside in the undifferentiated body of no-cause. This body is a wildfire and a lamp; it clears the brush and shows the way.

It is said that as we are dying, the last sense faculty to cease to function is our hearing. It is also said that things originally came into being through their vibration, through their sounding. "In the beginning was the Word," so the scriptures say. When a thing ceases to be, its sound disappears from the world. Kanzeon is the intimate presence of compassionate intelligence within all things that responds through perceiving the sound of life activity, no matter how small the voice, no matter how deep the suffering, how great the joy. I believe that Buddhism, shamanism, and deep ecology in their different ways are calling us to put our ear against the body of the Earth, to listen closely to what is really being said, and to consider the consequences of what we are hearing.

Breath, wind, and the holy Word are related through the experience of Spirit, the atmosphere of our World Psyche. Yet the atmosphere circulating through us is so polluted that hearing into, listening to, the Spirit of all things, into the World Psyche, though difficult, is a necessity for our common survival. Peoples of elder cultures often say that the survival of human beings depends on being able to hear the language of the birds and beasts, the language of the river, rock, and wind, being able to understand what is being said in all the tongues of plant, creature, and element. Listening to the garbage as well as the rose with the same ears, the ears of compassionate understanding. Who listens in this manner is Kanzcon. It is she who "abides in ultimate closeness" with all beings. It is she who embodies the principles of intimacy, simple communion, warmth, and mercy within each of us.

PHYLLIS TRIBLE

With her rereading of the Genesis story, Old Testament scholar Phyllis Trible, professor of sacred literature at Union Theological Seminary and author of *Texts of Terror: Literary-Feminist Readings of Biblical Narratives*, advances the work of feminist theology not to make women equal partners in an oppressive system of thought but rather to transform the world view that suffuses patriarchal theology. Her translation and reinterpretation of Genesis 2–3 would replace patterns of dominance and subordination with models of complementarity and mutually enhancing relationships. Trible argues that these liberating models exist linguistically in the Genesis creation story. Her exegesis turns upside down the usual reading of the Adam and Eve story, always troubling for women, as the divinely inspired origin of unequal gender identities and roles. By reinterpreting the origin story of the Judeo-Christian West, she produces a more capacious—and playful—identity for both genders, one that also figures in quantum spirituality: both reconstructions are based on the principle of complementarity (see the selection by Angela Tilby, page 367).

Eve and Adam: Genesis 2–3 Reread

On the whole, the Women's Liberation Movement is hostile to the Bible, even as it claims that the Bible is hostile to women. The Yahwist account of creation and fall in Genesis 2–3 provides a strong proof text for that claim. Accepting centuries of (male) exegesis, many feminists interpret this story as legitimating male supremacy and female subordination.[1] They read to reject. My suggestion is that we reread to understand and to appropriate. Ambiguity characterizes the meaning of *'adham* in Genesis 2–3. On the one hand, man is the first creature formed (2:7). The Lord God puts him in the garden "to till it and keep it," a job identified with the male (cf.

3:17–19). On the other hand, 'adham is a generic term for humankind. In commanding 'adham not to eat of the tree of the knowledge of good and evil, the Deity is speaking to both the man and the woman (2:16–17). Until the differentiation of female and male (2:21–23), 'adham is basically androgynous: one creature incorporating two sexes.

Concern for sexuality, specifically for the creation of woman, comes last in the story, after the making of the garden, the trees, and the animals. Some commentators allege female subordination based on this order of events.[2] They contrast it with Genesis 1:27 where God creates 'adham as male and female in one act.[3] Thereby they infer that whereas the Priests recognized the equality of the sexes, the Yahwist made woman a second, subordinate, inferior sex.[4] But the last may be first, as both the biblical theologian and the literary critic know. Thus the Yahwist account moves to its climax, not its decline, in the creation of woman.[5] She is not an afterthought; she is the culmination. Genesis 1 itself supports this interpretation, for there male and female are indeed the last and truly the crown of all creatures. The last is also first where beginnings and endings are parallel. In Hebrew literature, the central concerns of a unit often appear at the beginning and the end as an *inclusio* device.[6] Genesis 2 evinces this structure. The creation of man first and of woman last constitutes a ring composition whereby the two creatures are parallel. In no way does the order disparage woman. Content and context augment this reading.

The context for the advent of woman is a divine judgment: "It is not good that 'adham should be alone; I will make him a helper fit for him" (2:18). The phrase needing explication is "helper fit for him." In the Old Testament the word *helper ('ezer)* has many usages. It can be a proper name for a male.[7] In our story, it describes the animals and the woman. In some passages, it characterizes Deity. God is the helper of Israel. As helper Yahweh creates and saves.[8] Thus 'ezer is a relational term; it designates a beneficial relationship; and it pertains to God, people, and animals. By itself, the word does not specify positions within relationships; more particularly, it does not imply inferiority. Position results from additional content or from context. Accordingly, what kind of relationship does 'ezer entail in Genesis 2:18, 20? Our answer comes in two ways: (1) The word *neged*, which joins 'ezer, connotes equality: a helper who is a counterpart.[9] (2) The animals are helpers, but they fail to fit 'adham. There is physical, perhaps psychic, rapport between 'adham and the animals, for Yahweh forms *(yasar)* them both out of the ground *('adhamah)*. Yet their similarity is not equality. 'Adham names them and thereby exercises power over them. No fit helper is among them. And thus the narrative moves to woman. . . . God is the helper superior to man; the animals are helpers inferior to man; woman is the helper equal to man.

Let us pursue the issue by examining the account of the creation of woman ([verses] 21–22). This episode concludes the story even as the creation of man commences it. . . . The ring composition suggests an interpretation of woman and man as equals. To establish this meaning, structure and content must mesh. They do. In both episodes, Yahweh alone creates. For the last creation the Lord God "caused a deep sleep *(tardemah)* to fall upon the man." Man has no part in making woman; he is out of it. He exercises no control over her existence. He is neither participant nor spectator nor consultant at her birth. Like man, woman owes her life solely to God. For both of them, the origin of life is a divine mystery. Another parallel of equality is creation out of raw materials: dust for man and a rib for woman. Yahweh chooses these fragile materials and in both cases processes them before human beings happen. As Yahweh shapes dust and then breathes into it to form man, so Yahweh takes out the rib and then builds it into woman.[10] To call woman "Adam's rib" is to misread the text, which states carefully and clearly that the extracted bone required divine labor to become female, a datum scarcely designed to bolster the male ego. Moreover, to claim that the rib means inferiority or subordination is to assign the man qualities over the woman which are not in the narrative itself. Superiority, strength, aggressiveness, dominance, and power do not characterize man in Genesis 2. By contrast, he is formed from dirt; his life hangs by a breath which he does not control; and he himself remains silent and passive while the Deity plans and interprets his existence.

The rib means solidarity and equality. 'Adham recognizes this meaning in a poem:[11]

> This at last is bone of bones
>   and flesh of my flesh.
> She shall be called *'ishshah* [woman]
>   because she was taken out of *'ish* [man]. (2:23)

The pun proclaims both the similarity and the differentiation of female and male. Before this episode the Yahwist has used only the generic term *'adham*. No exclusively male reference has appeared. Only with the specific creation of woman (*'ishshah*) occurs the first specific terms for man as male (*'ish*). In other words, sexuality is simultaneous for woman and man. The sexes are interrelated and interdependent. Man as male does not precede woman as female but happens concurrently with her. Hence, the first act in Genesis 2 is the creation of androgyny (2:7), and the last is the creation of sexuality (2:23).[12] Male embodies female, and female embodies male. The two are neither dichotomies nor duplicates. The birth of woman corresponds to the birth of man but does not copy it. Only in responding to the female does the man discover himself as male. No longer a passive creature, *'ish* comes alive in meeting *'ishshah*.

Some read into the poem a naming motif. The man names the woman and thereby has power and authority over her.[13] But again . . . reread. Neither the verb nor the noun *name* is in the poem. We find instead the verb *gara'*, to call: "She shall be called woman." Now, in the Yahwist primeval history this verb does not function as a synonym or parallel or substitute for *name*. The typical formula for naming is the verb *to call* plus the explicit object *name*. This formula applies to Deity, people, places, and animals. For example, in Genesis 4 we read:

> Cain built a city and *called* the *name* of the city after
>   the *name* of his son Enoch. (v. 17)
> And Adam knew his wife again, and she bore a son and
>   *called* his *name* Seth. (v. 25)
> To Seth also a son was born and he *called* his *name*
>   Enoch. (v. 26a)
> At that time men began to *call* upon the *name* of the Lord.
>   (v. 26b)

Genesis 2:23 has the verb *call* but does not have the object *name*. Its absence signifies the absence of a naming motif in the poem. The presence of both the verb *call* and the noun *name* in the episode of the animals strengthens the point:

> So out of the ground the Lord God formed every beast of the field and every bird of the air, and brought them to the man to see what he would *call* them; and whatever the man *called* every living creature, that was its *name*. The man gave *names* to all cattle, and to the birds of the air, and to every beast of the field. (2:19–20)

In calling the animals by name, *'adham* establishes supremacy over them and fails to find a fit helper. In calling woman, *'adham* does not name her and does find in her a counterpart. Female and male are equal sexes. Neither has authority over the other.[14]

A further observation secures the argument: *Woman* itself is not a name. It is a common noun; it is not a proper noun. It designates gender; it does not specify person. *'Adham* recognizes sexuality by the words *'ishshah* and *'ish*. This recognition is not an act of naming to assert the power of male over female. Quite the contrary. But the true skeptic is already asking: What about Genesis 3:20, where "the man called his wife's name Eve"? We must wait to consider that question. Meanwhile, the words of the ancient poem

as well as their context proclaim sexuality originating in the unity of
'*adham*. From this one (androgynous) creature come two (female and
male). The two return to their original unity as '*ish* and '*ishshah* become
one flesh (2:24):[15] another instance of the ring composition.

Next the differences which spell harmony and equality yield to the differences of disobedience and disaster. The serpent speaks to the woman.
Why to the woman and not to the man? The simplest answer is that we do
not know. The Yahwist does not tell us anymore than he explains why the
tree of the knowledge of good and evil was in the garden. But the silence
of the text stimulates speculations, many of which only confirm the patriarchal mentality which conceived them. Cassuto identifies serpent and
woman, maintaining that the cunning of the serpent is "in reality" the cunning of the woman.[16] He impugns her further by declaring that "for the
very reason that a woman's imagination surpasses a man's, it was the woman
who was enticed first." Though more gentle in his assessment, von Rad
avers that "in the history of Yahweh religion, it has always been the women
who have shown an inclination for obscure astrological cults" (a claim
which he does not document).[17] Consequently, he holds that the woman
"confronts the obscure allurements and mysteries that beset our limited
life more directly than the man does," and then he calls her a "temptress."
Paul Ricoeur says that woman "represents the point of weakness," as the
entire story "gives evidence of a very masculine resentment."[18] McKenzie
links the "moral weakness" of the woman with her "sexual attraction" and
holds that the latter ruined both the woman and the man.[19]

But the narrative does not say any of these things. It does not sustain the
judgment that woman is weaker or more cunning or more sexual than man.
Both have the same Creator, who explicitly uses the word *good* to intro-
duce the creation of woman (2:18). Both are equal in birth. There is complete rapport, physical, psychological, sociological, and theological,
between them: bone of bone and flesh of flesh. If there be moral frailty in
one, it is moral frailty in two. Further, they are equal in responsibility and
in judgment, in shame and in guilt, in redemption and in grace. What the
narrative says about the nature of woman it also says about the nature of
man.

Why does the serpent speak to the woman and not to the man? Let a female speculate. If the serpent is "more subtle" than its fellow creatures, the
woman is more appealing than her husband. Throughout the myth, she
is the more intelligent one, the more aggressive one, and the one with
greater sensibilities.[20] Perhaps the woman elevates the animal world by con-
versing theologically with the serpent. At any rate, she understands the
hermeneutical task. In quoting God, she interprets the prohibition ("neither shall you touch it"). The woman is both theologian and translator. She

contemplates the tree, taking into account all the possibilities. The tree is good for food; it satisfies the physical drives. It pleases the eyes; it is esthetically and emotionally desirable. Above all, it is coveted as the source of wisdom *(haskîl).* Thus the woman is fully aware when she acts, her vision encompassing the gamut of life. She takes the fruit, and she eats. The initiative and the decision are hers alone. There is no consultation with her husband. She seeks neither his advice nor his permission. She acts independently.

By contrast, the man is a silent, passive, and bland recipient: "She also gave some to her husband, and he ate." The narrator makes no attempt to depict the husband as reluctant or hesitating. The man does not theologize; he does not contemplate; he does not envision the full possibilities of the occasion. His one act is belly oriented, and it is an act of quiescence, not of initiative. The man is not dominant; he is not aggressive; he is not a decision maker. Even though the prohibition not to eat of the tree appears before the female was specifically created, she knows that it applies to her. She has interpreted it, and now she struggles with the temptation to disobey. But not the man, to whom the prohibition came directly (2:16). He follows his wife without question or comment, thereby denying his own individuality. If the woman be intelligent, sensitive, and ingenious, the man is passive, brutish, and inept. These character portrayals are truly extraordinary in a culture dominated by men. I stress their contrast not to promote female chauvinism but to undercut patriarchal interpretations alien to the text.

The contrast between woman and man fades after their acts of disobedience. They are one in the new knowledge of their nakedness (3:7). They are one in hearing and in hiding. They flee from the sound of the Lord God in the Garden (3:8). First to the man come questions of responsibility (3:9, 11), but the man fails to be responsible: "The woman whom Thou gavest to be with me, she gave me fruit of the tree, and I ate" (3:12). Here the man does not blame the woman; he does not say that the woman seduced him;[21] he blames the Deity. The verb which he uses for both the Deity and the woman is *ntn* (cf. 3:6). . . . This verb neither means nor implies seduction in this context or in the lexicon. Again, if the Yahwist intended to make woman the temptress, he missed a choice opportunity. The woman's response supports the point. "The serpent beguiled me, and I ate" (3:13). Only here occurs the strong verb *nsh',* meaning to deceive, to seduce. God accepts this subject-verb combination when, immediately following the woman's accusation, Yahweh says to the serpent, "Because you have done this, cursed are you above all animals" (3:14).

Though the tempter (the serpent) is cursed,[22] the woman and the man are not. But they are judged, and the judgments are commentaries on the disastrous effects of their shared disobedience. They show how terrible human life has become as it stands between creation and grace. We misread if we assume that these judgments are mandates. They describe; they do not prescribe. They protest; they do not condone. Of special concern are the words telling the woman that her husband shall rule over her (3:16). This statement is not license for male supremacy, but rather it is condemnation of that very pattern.[23] Subjugation and supremacy are perversions of creation. Through disobedience, the woman has become slave. Her initiative and her freedom vanish. The man is corrupted also, for he has become master, ruling over the one who is his God-given equal. The subordination of female to male signifies their shared sin.[24] This sin vitiates all relationships: between animals and human beings (3:15); mothers and children (3:16); husbands and wives (3:16); people and the soil (3:17–18); humanity and its work (3:19). Whereas in creation man and woman know harmony and equality, in sin they know alienation and discord. Grace makes possible a new beginning.

A further observation about these judgments: they are culturally conditioned. Husband and work (childbearing) define the woman; wife and work (farming) define the man. A literal reading of the story limits both creatures and limits the story. To be faithful translators, we must recognize that women as well as men move beyond these culturally defined roles, even as the intentionality and function of the myth move beyond its original setting. Whatever forms stereotyping takes in our own culture, they are judgments upon our common sin and disobedience. The suffering and oppression we women and men know now are marks of our fall, not of our creation.

At this place of sin and judgment, "the man calls his wife's name Eve" (3:20), thereby asserting his rule over her. The naming itself faults the man for corrupting a relationship of mutuality and equality. And so Yahweh evicts the primeval couple from the Garden, yet with signals of grace.[25] Interestingly, the conclusion of the story does not specify the sexes in flight. Instead the narrator resumes use of the generic and androgynous term *'adham* with which the story began and thereby completes an overall ring composition (3:22–24).

Visiting the Garden of Eden in the days of the Women's Movement, we need no longer accept the traditional exegesis of Genesis 2–3. Rather than legitimating the patriarchal culture from which it comes, the myth places that culture under judgment. And thus it functions to liberate, not to enslave. This function we can recover and appropriate. The Yahwist narrative tells us who we are (creatures of equality and mutuality); it tells us who we have become (creatures of oppression); and so it opens possibilities for change, for a return to our true liberation under God. In other words, the story calls female and male to repent.

Notes

1. *See inter alia*, Kate Millett, *Sexual Politics* (New York: Doubleday, 1970), pp. 51–54; Eva Figes, *Patriarchal Attitudes* (Greenwich, Conn.: Fawcett, 1970), pp. 38f; Mary Daly, "The Courage to See," *The Christian Century*, September 22, 1971, p. 1110; Sheila D. Collins, "Toward a Feminist Theology," *The Christian Century*, August 2, 1972, p. 798; Lilly Rivlin, "Lilith: The First Woman," *Ms.*, December 1972, pp. 93, 114.

2. Cf. E. Jacob, *Theology of the Old Testament* (New York: Harper & Bros., 1958), pp. 172f; S. H. Hooke, "Genesis," *Peake's Commentary on the Bible* (London: Thomas Nelson, 1962), p. 179.

3. E.g., Elizabeth Cady Stanton observed that Genesis 1:26–28 "dignifies woman as an important factor in the creation, equal in power and glory with man," while Genesis 2 "makes her a mere afterthought" (*The Woman's Bible*, Part I [New York: European Publishing Company, 1895], p. 20). See also Elsie Adams and Mary Louise Briscoe, *Up Against the Wall, Mother . . .* (Beverly Hills: Glencoe Press, 1971), p. 4.

4. Cf. Eugene H. Maly, "Genesis," *The Jerome Biblical Commentary* (Englewood Cliffs, N.J.: Prentice-Hall, 1968), p. 12: "But woman's existence, psychologically and in the social order, is dependent on man."

5. See John L. McKenzie, "The Literary Characteristics of Gen. 2–3," *Theological Studies*, Vol. 15 (1954), p. 559; John A. Bailey, "Initiation and the Primal Woman in Gilgamesh and Genesis 2–3," *Journal of Biblical Literature*, June 1970, p. 143. Bailey writes emphatically of the remarkable importance and position of the woman in Genesis 2–3, "all the more extraordinary when one realizes that this is the only account of the creation of woman as such in ancient Near Eastern literature." He hedges, however, in seeing the themes of helper and naming (Genesis 2:18–23) as indicative of a "certain subordination" of woman to man. These reservations are unnecessary; see below. Cf. also Claus Westermann, *Genesis, Biblischer Kommentar* 1/4 (Neukerchener-Vluyn: Newkirchener Verlag, 1970), p. 312.

6. James Muilenburg, "Form Criticism and Beyond," *Journal of Biblical Literature*, March 1969, pp. 9f; Mitchell Dahood, "Psalm I," *The Anchor Bible* (New York: Doubleday, 1966), *passim* and esp. p. 5.

7. See 1 Chronicles 4:4; 12:9; Nehemiah 3:19.

8. See Psalm 121:2, 124:8; 146:5; 33:20; 115:9–11; Exodus 18:4; Deuteronomy 33:7, 26, 29.

9. L. Koehler and W. Baumgartner, *Lexicon in Veteris Testamenti Libros* (Leiden: E. J. Brill, 1958), pp. 591f.

10. The verb *bnh* (to build) suggests considerable labor. It is used of towns, towers, altars, and fortifications, as well as of the primeval woman (Koehler-Baumgartner, op. cit., p. 134). In Genesis 2:22, it may mean the fashioning of clay around the rib (Ruth Amiran, "Myths of the Creation of Man and the Jericho Statues," *BASOR*, No. 167 [October 1962], p. 24).

11. See Walter Brueggemann, "Of the Same Flesh and Bone (Gen. 2:23a)," *Catholic Biblical Quarterly*, October 1970, pp. 532–42.

12. In proposing as primary an androgynous interpretation of *'adham*, I find virtually no support from (male) biblical scholars. But my view stands as documented from the text, and I take refuge among a remnant of ancient (male) rabbis (see George Foot Moore, *Judaism* [Cambridge, Mass.: Harvard University Press, 1927]), I, 453; also Joseph Campbell, *The Hero with a Thousand Faces* (Meridian Books, The World Publishing Company, 1970), pp. 152ff., 279f.

13. See e.g., G. von Rad, *Genesis* (Philadelphia: Westminster Press, 1961), pp. 80–82; John H. Marks, "Genesis," *The Interpreter's One-Volume Commentary on the Bible* (Nashville: Abingdon Press, 1971), p. 5; Bailey, op. cit., p. 143.

14. Cf. Westermann, op. cit., pp. 316ff.

15. Verse 24 probably mirrors a matriarchal society (so Von Rad, op. cit., p. 83). If the myth were designed to support patriarchy, it is difficult to explain how this verse survived without proper alteration. Westermann contends, however, that an emphasis on matriarchy misunderstands the point of the verse, which is the total communion of woman and man (ibid., p. 317).

16. U. Cassuto, *A Commentary on the Book of Genesis*, Part I (Jerusalem: Magnes Press, n.d.), pp. 142f.

17. Von Rad, op. cit., pp. 87f.

18. Ricoeur departs from the traditional interpretation of the woman when he writes: *"Eve n'est donc pas la femme en tant que 'deuxieme sexe'; toute femme et tout homme sont Adam; tout homme et toute femme sont Eve."* But the fourth clause of his sentence obscures this complete identity of Adam and Eve: *"toute femme peche 'en Adam, tout homme est seduit 'en Eve."* By switching from an active to a passive verb, Ricoeur makes only the woman directly responsible for both sinning and seducing. (Paul Ricoeur, Finitude et Culpabilite, II. *La Symbolique du Mal*, Aubier, Editions Montaigne [Paris: 1960]. Cf. Paul Ricoeur, *The Symbolism of Evil* [Boston: Beacon Press, 1969], p. 255).

19. McKenzie, op. cit., p. 570.

20. See Bailey, op. cit., p. 148.

21. See Westermann, op. cit., p. 340.

22. For a discussion of the serpent, see Ricoeur, *The Symbolism of Evil*, op. cit., pp. 255–60.

23. Cf. Edwin M. Good, *Irony in the Old Testament* (Philadelphia: Westminster Press, 1965), p. 84, note 4: "Is it not surprising that, in a culture where the subordination of woman to man was a virtually unquestioned social principle, the etiology of the subordination should be in the context of man's primal sin? Perhaps woman's subordination was not unquestioned in Israel." Cf. also Henricus Renckens, *Israel's Concept of the Beginning* (New York: Herder & Herder, 1964), pp. 127f.

24. *Contra* Westermann, op. cit., p. 357.

25. Von Rad, op. cit., pp. 94, 148.

ANGELA TILBY
(1950–   )

Angela Tilby was born in Nigeria, grew up in North London, and studied theology at Cambridge. She has worked at the BBC in radio and documentary film production since 1973, specializing in documentaries on religious and scientific subjects. Her film *The Hidden Tradition* about women priests in early Christianity won a gold medal at the 1993 New York Film Festival. She is a lay reader and preacher in the Anglican Church and will be ordained to the deaconate in 1996. The following selection, about quantum spirituality, is taken from her recent book *Soul: God, Self, and the New Cosmology*. In the introduction, Tilby observes that "it is part of the feminist critique that science and religion are full of ways of thinking about the world which seem to belong more naturally to men than to women. . . . [I]t [seems] interesting that the emergence of a more holistic and complex view of nature should coincide with the advancement of opportunities for women both in science and religion."

from *Soul: God, Self and the New Cosmology*

QUANTUM MECHANICS: GOD'S DICE

"I have heard from my Indian friends that Shiva has a musical instrument, a drum, in one hand and a flame in another. The flame is destruction and the drum is creation."

(Ilya Prigogine)

"As was his custom when facing deep problems of science, he tried to regard things from the point of view of God. Was it likely that God would have created a probabilistic universe? Einstein felt that the answer must be no: 'God does not play dice.'"

(Banesh Hoffman)

The cosmology that is changing our attitude to nature reflects only one of the revolutions of the twentieth-century physics. The other is quantum mechanics, which is about the behaviour of sub-atomic particles. Quantum mechanics has had a transforming effect on the lives of many of the great scientists who have engaged with it. It devastated Einstein, who could never bring himself to accept its implications. Werner Heisenberg, one of its pioneers, recalls arguing for hours with his colleague Niels Bohr, and then going out and walking through a park in Copenhagen in the early hours of the morning, repeating to himself over and again: "Can nature possibly be as absurd as it seemed to us in these atomic experiments?" Bohr himself claimed that anyone who is not shocked by quantum mechanics has not understood it. Quantum mechanics has forced scientists to engage with philosophical issues in a quite new way. Like the early Christian fathers wrestling to adapt montheistic assumptions about God to take account of the revelation of God in Christ, quantum physicists are still trying to adapt their former picture of nature to take account of the new one. Relativity and quantum mechanics remain unreconciled and, in some respects, contradictory.

Why is quantum mechanics so shocking? First, because we do not know how to interpret it. Second, because if we interpret it one way it seems to suggest the end of objective science. Yet if we interpret it another way it seems to suggest that nature itself is inherently indeterminate. Neither interpretation is particularly congenial, either to scientists, who usually want to believe that nature *should be* predictable, or to religious people, who often want to believe that God has already arranged the fate of every aspect of the cosmos. Yet quantum mechanics is astonishingly successful. It works, as science. It gives a penetrating account of the small-scale structure of the world, and has been used by scientists since the middle 1920s with consistent and reliable results. Its technological applications have transformed our world. Modern electronic technology, from televisions to computers and lasers, depends on quantum mechanics. So too do nuclear power and nuclear bombs, and some of our latest theories about the origins of the universe.

Cosmology and quantum mechanics are coming together in our time as scientists try to develop quantum cosmologies in the hope that we might discover even more about our ultimate origins. Quantum mechanics is important for our psychological and spiritual formation because it fatally undermines the deterministic character that both science and theology had formerly imposed on nature and human nature.

THE DETERMINISTIC UNIVERSE

From the Newtonian revolution until the beginning of this century, physicists understood the world as being composed of separate things. Particles of matter were thought of as discrete entities, each with its own place in space and time. Particles could bump into, attract or repel one another, and the physicist could measure these interactions and account for them in terms of the forces acting on them. No one seriously doubted that the descriptions and predictions of science matched the reality of nature. The clarity of science's descriptions of nature was never in doubt. For Newton and most of his contemporaries, and for religious people since his time, the fact that nature could be understood bore witness to the character of the Creator. Nature portrayed God as a God of order and marvellous harmony, a master mathematician and engineer.

Newton's achievements set the scene for the industrial revolution, the massive reordering of natural resources to produce iron and steel, textiles and new forms of transport. The powers of nature were to be harnessed to serve human needs for industrial production. The regularity and predictability of the physical world also affected the way people thought about the rest of the living world, history, society and the self. It was natural to think of human beings as being above animals, and various grades of human being as above the rest. Woe betide those who tried to move "above their station"!

> The rich man in his castle,
> The poor man at the gate,
> God made them, high and lowly
> And ordered their estate.

GOD, NATURAL LAW AND SOCIETY

The intellectual battles of nineteenth-century Europe turned around the idea of law. On the one hand was the belief that social and natural distinctions were ordered by God. Nature was a hierarchy because God had made it so. On the other hand political and religious radicals, angered by injustice and oppression, invoked natural law in revolutionary causes. Conservatives tended to believe that nature was static. Radicals preferred the idea of evolution and change. Conservatives looked to God and the Church, radicals embraced atheism. But what united both sides was the belief in the utter domination of nature by unalterable laws. The nineteenth century saw a flowering of determinism in all the natural and social sciences. Darwin's portrayal of the evolutionary struggle, Marx's conviction that the future was already settled by the laws of history, and Freud's portrayal of the self emerging precariously from the dark and instinctual world of the id were all, as Danah Zohar points out,* extrapolations from Newton's physical theory. At the time they were all wildly controversial because they appeared to set out to overthrow the existing order in which regularity and predictability were guaranteed by God. But though Darwin, Marx and Freud replaced God with the blind mechanical laws of nature, their ideas belong none the less to a world-view in which the future is already ordained by the past. Nothing truly unpredictable can ever happen. The scientist's job, or the historian's or the psychologist's, is to read the book of nature, history and the self and to predict the direction of the forces which control them. The actual outcome of the three great revolutions in biology, history and psychology was already determined.

SPIRITUAL LIFE UNDER DETERMINISM

The spiritual problem that determinism set for human beings was how to have any real belief in free will, human or divine. How can there be a Creator who wills creation into existence for the pure delight of doing so? How

*[See page 375.]

can there be creatures who can actually make responsible choices in such a universe? How can anything new or original or spontaneous happen in a universe where every movement of every atom is predetermined from time immemorial?

*   *   *

When people became psychologically disturbed in the nineteenth century they often showed signs of hysteria, sexual anxiety or obsessions. Freud's case-books are full of these complaints. His diagnosis usually suggested that people were disturbed because they were out of touch with their instinctual lives. In Freud's psychology the instincts are controlled by the impersonal driving force of the id. Hysteria and obsessions are, perhaps, natural ways of not coping with a world in which every particle of matter behaves in a predictable and orderly way, and humans are expected to do the same. In a universe where nothing new can happen, almost every apparently free action is potentially deviant. Hence the extraordinary moralism of the nineteenth century. The perfect state was to be at rest, with one's tasks done and one's conscience clear. Victorian hymns are obsessed with rest. Rest and safety in the arms of Jesus, eternal rest in heaven, rest for the weary, rest after labour, rest in peace. The invitation of Jesus was to rest, to be at peace, to "abide." Perhaps this is why the Victorians were so obsessed with death. It was the nearest possible state to perfection, and yet—tragic irony—it was also the point at which the body was subject to decay and corruption.

So along with the sense of the vocation to progress was a hidden melancholy at the inevitable losses associated with it. Loss of spontaneity, loss of the ability to lose control. Loss of a sense of joy in nature. Perhaps the white man's burden contained a hidden envy of those inferior races who were thought to be closer to nature. Freud and Jung both believed that civilization had been bought at a heavy price, and that there was a tragic dimension to our alienation from the natural world. The Victorians knew they were powerful, but also sensed their distance from some of the most important sources of joy. Knowledge did not always bring happiness.

QUANTUM UNCERTAINTY

The quantum world turns out to be extremely tricky to interpret. Many claim that it is a world of genuine uncertainty and unpredictability. This is unnerving for those brought up on classical, Newtonian physics. Newtonian physics is about things. Things can be located in space. Things can be moved by forces acting on them. The speed at which they move can be measured. There is no basic contradiction between measuring the position of an object and the speed at which it is travelling. But in the quantum world there is a contradiction. The wave-like qualities of quantum objects can be measured, as can the particle-like qualities; but you cannot measure both at the same time.

Werner Heisenberg, one of the greatest pioneers of quantum physics, believed that the nature of the quantum world imposed fundamental limits on the accuracy of what could be measured. He argued that in the quantum world the very act of making a measurement jolts the object we are trying to measure. It is impossible, even in principle, to reduce this jolt to zero.

For example, if you try to find the position of a quantum particle very accurately you inevitably disturb its momentum rather a lot, because the more accurate you want to be the higher frequency of electromagnetic radiation you will need to use, and the higher the frequency of the radiation the more energy it contains and the more it knocks the particle about, thus disturbing its momentum. If, on the other hand, we want to discover the particle's momentum, we must try to disturb it as little as possible. This means using low-frequency radiation. But low-frequency radiation has a long wavelength and this will mean that it will be impossible to get an accurate reading of the particle's position. In other words, we can measure the position of a particle, or its momentum, but not both at the same time. The uncertainty principle is fundamental for understanding the quantum world.

When Heisenberg first articulated these ideas he was still assuming that quantum objects were things. The problem in understanding them was our problem rather than theirs, and it arose from the limitations of our own measuring instruments. Yet after argument and inner struggle, and long walks of self-interrogation in the dark, he came to abandon this position for a much more radical statement of his uncertainty principle.

What lay behind this can be explained by revisiting the two-slit experiment. We have seen how the intrusion of electromagnetic radiation destroys the interference pattern even as it reveals which slit the electrons pass through. Now comes the extraordinary suggestion. This is that when the electrons are not interfered with by light (are not being measured) they actually *pass through both slits at once*. It is only when they arrive at the detector screen and the measurement is made that their ambiguous state of being is resolved into a definite position. The effect of the light falling on them is to anticipate this resolution. What does this mean?

It might suggest that we have to decide what kind of information we want about a quantum particle and that this inevitably limits what we can know about it. On the other hand it might show that it is of the nature of the electron not to have a definite position. Its possible positions are spread out through the wave, and it is only by interfering with it that it resolves into a definite place.

This was eventually explained by the suggestion of Max Born that the waves described in quantum theory are actually probability waves. They map the possible positions at which particles might be found. When we talk about quantum objects in terms of waves, the waves are waves of probability. They convey information. They tell us where, for example, an electron is likely to be found. When we think about an electron circling an atom, it is not doing so in orbits that we can picture. In fact it was realized that the electron does not follow a definite path round the nucleus at all. Instead its possible paths are fanned out in a way that can only be pictured in patterns showing where the electron is most likely to be found. The electron does not glide smoothly from one circuit, representing one energy state, to another. It jumps. And, even odder, it jumps between high- and low-energy states, without any particular cause. We can think of it as being spread out in a way that comprises the different energy states it is likely to be in. But we cannot picture it. We can only say of an electron circling a nucleus that there is a state in which it is here and a state in which it is there. In classical physics all that is possible is a state in which an object is "here" and a state in which an object is "there." But in quantum physics it seems to be possible to add the two states together and to say of a particle that its address is "here" added to "there."

The dilemma is in knowing whether our difficulty with this arises because of the limits of our knowledge or whether it reflects an inherent fuzziness in the nature of the quantum world. Is it a problem of epistemology or ontology?

Niels Bohr insisted that we should not try to resolve the paradox. We simply cannot say what the quantum world is apart from our investigation of it. Instead he articulated the principle of complementarity; that our description of a quantum particle must include wave properties and particle properties, even though we cannot have knowledge of both simultaneously.

The golden year for quantum physics was 1925–6. This was when the best and brightest of physicists struggled to apply the new understanding to a host of different problems. There were momentous discoveries. In 1928 Paul Dirac combined what had been learned into a quantum field theory which, for the first time, presented a mathematical formula which elucidated the wave/particle duality of light without appeal to paradox or mystery.

IMPLICATIONS OF QUANTUM MECHANICS

This was the point at which it was clear to everyone that quantum physics involved a radical break with the classical past. To get a grip on reality at the quantum level you have to leave behind the familiar everyday world of objects moving along the shortest trajectories to a predetermined goal. Not only was the quantum world difficult to picture, it was also fundamentally indeterminate. It worked not in certainties, but in probabilities. The scientist's role was no longer to read the answers off the book of nature, but to lay out the betting odds. As the American writer Annie Dillard puts it, "Here is the word from a subatomic physicist: 'Everything that has already happened is particles, everything in the future is waves.' "

The problem is in interpreting what it actually means. For the first time in science it is inconceivable in principle to have a clear-cut pictorial relationship between the description of a thing and the thing described. Scientists are having to read nature like a text which could have many interpretations. The text of quantum mechanics describes what we find in nature, but it no longer says what it is that we are finding. The problem of Where am I? How am I moving? is replaced by What am I? How can I be?

INTERPRETATIONS

I had barely heard of quantum physics in the mid-1970s when I had the opportunity to make a series of radio programmes about religion and modernity which was transmitted alongside a television series about world faiths. The producer of the TV series, *The Long Search*, was a gifted filmmaker, Peter Montagnon. We had a number of fascinating conversations about religion in which he expressed his distrust of Christianity. He thought it was too rationalistic and mechanical to match our view of reality. This intrigued me, because I was used to atheists and agnostics dismissing Christianity for not being rational enough. "You must find out about quantum physics," he said. "Read about Heisenberg's uncertainty principle." I did, and I found myself astonished. Finding out about the indeterminacy of the quantum world filled me with awe. So it isn't all tied down and predetermined, I thought, without actually realizing that the thought that it could have been had been like an iron weight on the soul. I found the idea that sub-atomic particles behave unpredictably quite astonishingly funny and almost wicked. It seemed to put back into the universe something of the sense of adventure and life that had been missing in the classical picture.

Quantum mechanics did not seem to undermine the possibility of God, rather it opened up a way for the universe to be present to God in every moment of its particularity. At every moment creativity was in action, working through randomness, chance and spontaneity. I began thinking about angels and devils, and medieval manuscripts illustrated with monsters and moons and flowers. The quantum world seemed to reveal a world that was still going on, a world where being itself had fuzzy and undetermined edges.

It also provided a model for understanding some of the central paradoxes of Christian doctrine. The dual nature of Christ, as both divine and human, could be seen in the light of the principle of complementarity. The Church acclaims Christ as the God-man, putting together two terms which in everyday experience exclude one another. Yet both are necessary for a description of what the Church believes about Jesus Christ.

The most exciting thing to me was that it fundamentally subverted the notion that the universe is predictable. In one stroke the Victorian battleground where the laws of God and the laws of nature clash meaninglessly with each other was swept away. Quantum physics left us with nature as the text of possibilities, as the literary deconstructionists might say, and only with the text.

Yet this has not been at all easy for scientists to deal with. Like literary scholars, their attempts at interpretation have divided them into a number of different philosophical camps.

※　　※　　※

DANAH ZOHAR*

Danah Zohar is one of the many who has found that quantum physics has led her back to faith. Not to her old childhood orthodoxies, but to a new sense of the unity and creativity of nature and of our part in it. She does not share Capra's† fascination with Eastern faiths, but finds inspiration in the mystical traditions of Christianity and Cabbalistic Judaism.

She came across quantum physics almost by chance when she was ten years old, picking up a physics book intended for a neighbour's son in a laundromat in Toledo. When she started to read about waves and particles she became aware that there was a richness and excitement about nature that Newtonian science had not revealed. She began a series of horrific homemade experiments. She set up a cloud chamber with radioactive isotopes. She then constructed her own linear electron accelerator, all in order to see into the quantum world and discover the cosmic rays and colliding particles that she had read about. In the course of her experiments she was

*A philosophy and religion student at Harvard and a physics and philosophy graduate of MIT, Danah Zohar is the author of *The Quantum Self*, on the physics of consciousness.
†Fritjof Capra is the author of *The Tao of Physics* (1991).

exiled to the family garage, but she survived and managed not to irradiate herself or the rest of the household.

In the atom she found the mystery she was looking for, beyond everyday vision. Watching particles and cosmic rays in a more recent homemade cloud chamber, she sees a world that is "teeming with activity and creation." There is a deep mystery in the way in which "things bubble up from the quantum realm and exist for a while and then they go back to the quantum realm." For her the quantum world is, "A wonderful well of potential, filled with indeterminate relationships, sort of ebbing and flowing into each other, creating new realities, coming apart and going back to other realities. And everything is wonderfully interlinked and interrelated." Meditating on this, she has come to see the divine as the unbroken wholeness of the quantum world, which is unfolding itself constantly, creating more and more complex patterns and coherences as it does so.

She is particularly interested in the fact that the quantum world really does affect us. A single photon can be detected by the optic nerve. The uncertainty principle affects the behaviour of electrons which play a role in the way genes mutate. More speculatively, she argues that consciousness itself has emerged from the sub-atomic world and may even now have its physical base in a quantum state. This would explain why our minds are attuned to receive and understand quantum reality. She believes that the duality of wave and particle may provide us with a new metaphor for what a human being is. Not only a metaphor, either. If our consciousness does have a quantum-mechanical base, then we might expect it to exhibit wave-like qualities and particle-like qualities. What does she mean? Danah points out that most psychology—and most spirituality for that matter—assumes that we are isolated individuals. There is even a school of psychology called "object-relations" which deals with how we relate to others. The hidden image behind such a term is that of discrete particles attracting and repelling each other, but not really getting inside one another. If, she says, we are waves as well as particles, then we really can affect and be affected by each other, over huge distances of space and time.

To show how this links us back to faith, she suggests that everything that is has its roots in the divine well of being. She identifies this with the quantum vacuum out of which, in quantum cosmology, our universe has sprung. She quotes a story from the Cabbalistic Jewish mystics to the effect that there was a world before this one which became so full of light that it burst. The vessel which contained the world was smashed and scattered throughout our everyday world. The point of life for us is to go around the world gathering up the sacred shards and restoring the unity of the first world.

PEMA CHODRON
(1936–)

Pema Chodron is an American Buddhist nun in the tradition of Tibetan Buddhism and a student of the late Chogyam Trungpa, the founder of the Naropa Foundation. In 1986 he appointed her director of Gampo Abbey, a Buddhist monastery for Western men and women on Cape Breton Island, Nova Scotia. Her book *The Wisdom of No Escape*, excerpted here, is a transcription of talks given during a month-long retreat at the abbey. Down-to-earth and good-humored, Chodron teaches that meditation practice is about waking up to everything that happens rather than seeking oblivion in all the destructive forms through which people try to escape the tensions of the real. We must not only befriend ourselves, she says; we must also face rather than flee pain: "[T]he message . . . is to be with oneself without embarrassment or harshness. This is instruction on how to love oneself and one's world."

From *The Wisdom of No Escape*

JOY

Almost a year ago, a dear friend of ours, Sister Ayya Khema, a German woman who is a Theravadin nun living in Sri Lanka, came to visit us and to lead a *vipashyana* (insight meditation) retreat. The retreat for me personally was something of a revelation, because she emphasized joy. I hadn't realized how much emphasis I had put on suffering in my own practice. I had focused on coming to terms with the unpleasant, unacceptable, embarrassing, and painful things that I do. In the process, I had very subtly forgotten about joy.

In our seven-day silent retreat, Ayya Khema taught us that each of us has in our heart a joy that's accessible to us; by connecting to it and letting it flower, we allow ourselves to celebrate our practice and our lives. Joy is like a soft spring rain that allows us to lighten up, to enjoy ourselves, and therefore it's a whole new way of looking at suffering.

In a little book called *A Guide to Walking Meditation*, in the chapter "The World Contains All the Wonders of the Pure Land," Thich Nhat

Hanh says, "I don't think that all the Buddhas and Bodhisattvas of the three times will criticize me for giving you a little secret, that there is no need to go somewhere else to find the wonders of the Pure Land." That sense of wonder and delight is present in every moment, every breath, every step, every movement of our own ordinary everyday lives, if we can connect with it. The greatest obstacle to connecting with our joy is resentment.

Joy has to do with seeing how big, how completely unobstructed, and how precious things are. Resenting what happens to you and complaining about your life are like refusing to smell the wild roses when you go for a morning walk, or like being so blind that you don't see a huge black raven when it lands in the tree that you're sitting under. We can get so caught up in our own personal pain or worries that we don't notice that the wind has come up or that somebody has put flowers on the diningroom table or that when we walked out in the morning, the flags weren't up, and that when we came back, they were flying. Resentment, bitterness, and holding a grudge prevent us from seeing and hearing and tasting and delighting.

There is a story of a woman running away from tigers. She runs and runs, and the tigers are getting closer and closer. When she comes to the edge of a cliff, she sees some vines there, so she climbs down and holds on to the vines. Looking down, she sees that there are tigers below her as well. She then notices that a mouse is gnawing away at the vine to which she is clinging. She also sees a beautiful little bunch of strawberries close to her, growing out of a clump of grass. She looks up and she looks down. She looks at the mouse. Then she just takes a strawberry, puts it in her mouth, and enjoys it thoroughly.

Tigers above, tigers below. This is actually the predicament that we are always in, in terms of our birth and death. Each moment is just what it is. It might be the only moment of our life, it might be the only strawberry we'll ever eat. We could get depressed about it, or we could finally appreciate it and delight in the preciousness of every single moment of our life.

Trungpa Rinpoche always used to say, "You can do it." That was probably one of his main teachings, "You can do it." Thich Nhat Hanh, in his *Guide to Walking Meditation*, begins by talking about how everybody carries around this burden, and if you want to put it off, if you want to lay it down, you *can* do it. You *can* connect with the joy in your heart.

On a day of silence like today, when things are very still, you may find that you are feeling grim and doing everything with a grim expression: grimly opening the door, grimly drinking your tea, concentrating so hard on being quiet and still and moving slowly that you're miserable. On the other hand, you could just relax and realize that, behind all the worry, complaint, and disapproval that goes on in your mind, the sun is always coming up in the morning, moving across the sky, and going down in the evening. The birds are always out there collecting their food and making their nests and flying across the sky. The grass is always being blown by the wind or standing still. Food and flowers and trees are growing out of the earth. There's enormous richness. You could develop your passion for life and your curiosity and your interest. You could connect with your joyfulness. You could start right now.

The Navajo teach their children that every morning when the sun comes up, it's a brand-new sun. It's born each morning, it lives for the duration of one day, and in the evening it passes on, never to return again. As soon as the children are old enough to understand, the adults take them out at dawn and they say, "The sun has only one day. You must live this day in a good way, so that the sun won't have wasted precious time." Acknowledging the preciousness of each day is a good way to live, a good way to reconnect with our basic joy.

SUGGESTIONS FOR
FURTHER READING

The following books have been helpful to me as a student of spirituality and as the editor of *Wise Women*:

Adams, Carol J., ed. *Ecofeminism and the Sacred.* 1993.

Allen, Paula Gunn. *The Sacred Hoop: Recovering the Feminine in American Indian Tradition.* 1986.

Armstrong, Karen. *A History of God.* 1993.

Bachelard, Gaston. *The Poetics of Space.* 1994.

Baker, Houston A. *Workings of the Spirit: The Poetics of Afro American Women's Writing.* 1991.

Black Elk Speaks. As Told through John G. Neihardt. 1988.

Bonhoeffer, Dietrich. *Life Together.* 1954.

Buber, Martin. *Between Man & Man.* 1965.

———. *I and Thou.* 1970.

Buchmann, Christina, and Celina Spiegel, eds. *Out of the Garden: Women Writers on the Bible.* 1995.

Bynum, Caroline Walker. *Jesus as Mother.* 1982.

Camus, Albert. *The Rebel.* 1950.

Christ, Carol P., and Judith Plaskow, eds. *Womanspirit Rising: A Feminist Reader in Religion.* 1992.

Condren, Mary. *The Serpent and the Goddess.* 1989.

Craig, Robert H. *Religion and Radical Politics: An Alternative Christian Tradition in the United States.* 1992.

Daly, Mary. *Beyond God the Father.* 1973.

Doyle, Patricia Martin. "Women and Religion: Psychological and Cultural Implications." In *Religion and Sexism*, ed. Rosemary Radford Ruether. 1974.

Elshtain, Jean Bethke. *Power Trips and Other Journeys.* 1990.

Erikson, Joan Mowat. *Saint Francis Et His Four Ladies.* 1970.

Evans, Sara. *Personal Politics.* 1980.

Fiorenza, Elisabeth Schussler. "Feminist Spirituality, Christian Identity, and Catholic Vision." In Christ and Plaskow, op. cit.

Gies, Frances and Joseph. *Women in the Middle Ages.* 1978.

Guiterrez, Ramon. *When Jesus Came the Corn Mothers Went Away.* 1991.

Harding, Esther. *Woman's Mysteries.* 1971.

Harrison, Beverly Wildung. *Making the Connections.* 1985.

James, William. *The Varieties of Religious Experience.* 1961.

–––. *The Writings of William James,* ed. John J. McDermott. 1967.

Johnson, Elizabeth A. *She Who Is.* 1992.

Kates, Judith A., and Gail Reimer, eds. *Reading Ruth: Contemporary Women Reclaim a Sacred Story.* 1994.

Kieling, Jared T., ed. *The Gift of Prayer: A Treasury of Personal Prayer from the World's Spiritual Traditions.* 1995.

Kristeva, Julia. "Stabat Mater." In *The Kristeva Reader.* 1986.

Lang, Amy. *Prophetic Woman: Anne Hutchinson and the Problem of Dissent.* 1987.

Lerner, Gerda. *The Creation of Feminist Consciousness.* 1993.

Marty, Martin E. "Religion in America since Mid-Century." *Daedalus.* Winter 1982.

McKay, Nellie Y. "Nineteenth-Century Black Women's Spiritual Autobiographies: Religious Faith and Self-Empowerment." In *Interpreting Women's Lives. The Personal Narratives Group.* 1989.

Merton, Thomas. *The Hidden Ground of Love.* 1985.

Milhaven, Giles J. *Hadewijch and Her Sisters: Other Ways of Knowing and Loving.* 1993.

Morton, Nelle. *The Journey Is Home.* 1985.

Mounier, Emmanuel. *Be Not Afraid: A Denunciation of Despair.* 1946.

Murray, Michele. *The Great Mother and Other Poems.* 1974.

Nelson, Gertrude Mueller. *To Dance with God.* 1986.

Ochs, Carol. *Women and Spirituality.* 1983.

Pagels, Elaine. "What Became of God the Mother?" In Christ and Plaskow.

Petroff, Elizabeth Alvilda. *Medieval Women's Visionary Literature.* 1986.

Plaskow, Judith. *Standing Again at Sinai.* 1990.

Power, Eileen. *Medieval Women.* 1922.

Richards, M. C. *Centering.* 1962.

Ricoeur, Paul. *Oneself As Another.* 1992.

Ruddick, Sara. *Maternal Thinking: Towards a Politics of Peace.* 1989.

Ruether, Rosemary Radford, ed. *Womanguides: Readings toward a Feminist Theology.* 1985.

Smart, Ninian. *Worldviews: Crosscultural Explorations of Human Beliefs.* 1983.

Steiner, George. *Real Presences.* 1989.

Taylor, Charles. *Sources of the Self.* 1989.

Tillich, Paul. *The Shaking of the Foundations.* 1948.
Tracy, David. *The Analogical Imagination.* 1981.
Underhill, Evelyn. *Mysticism.* 1911.
Wyschogrod, Edith. *Saints and Postmodernism.* 1990.
Young, Serinity. *An Anthology of Sacred Texts by and about Women.* 1994.

PERMISSIONS
ACKNOWLEDGMENTS

———————————— 555 ————————————

Grateful acknowledgment is made to the following authors, translators, and publishers for their kind permission to reprint texts. Every effort has been made to trace the copyright holders of the material used in this book.

Testimonies of Ancient Cultures
   Excerpt from "The Goddess Isis Intervenes" from *The Golden Ass* from Apuleius, translated by Robert Graves. Copyright © 1978 by Robert Graves. Reprinted by permission of Farrar, Straus & Giroux, Inc.
   "The Creation of Spider Woman." From *Book of the Hopi* by Frank Waters. Copyright © 1963 by Frank Waters. Used by permission of Viking Penguin, a division of Penguin Books USA Inc.
   Excerpts from the Story of Ruth and Naomi; the Story of Judith; the Book of Proverbs; the Song of Songs; the Book of Wisdom. From The New Jerusalem Bible. Copyright © 1985 by Doubleday, a division of Bantam Doubleday Dell Publishing Group, Inc. and Darton, Longman & Todd, Ltd. Used by permission of Doubleday.
   "Eishet Chayil"—Proverbs 31 by E. M. Broner. Used by permission of E. M. Broner.
   Excerpt from "And One for His Mistress" from *Sappho: A Garland*, translated by Jim Powell. Copyright © 1993 by Jim Powell. Reprinted by permission of Farrar, Straus & Giroux, Inc.
   "Prayer to Aphrodite." From *Sappho's Lyre: Archaic Lyric and Women Poets of Ancient Greece*. Translation by Diane Rayor. Copyright © 1991 by Diane Rayor. Used by permission of University of California Press, Berkeley.
   Excerpt from "Antigone" in *Sophocles, the Oedipus Cycle: An English Version* by Robert Fitzgerald and Dudley Fitts, copyright 1939 by Harcourt Brace & Co. and renewed 1967 by Robert Fitzgerald and Dudley Fitts, reprinted by permission of the publishers.

INDEX

The author of the novel *Earth Angels* and co-author with her husband Thomas Cahill of *A Literary Guide to Ireland*, SUSAN CAHILL has edited many collections of writing by women, including *Desiring Italy*, *Writing Women's Lives*, *Growing Up Female*, and *Women and Fiction*. She teaches English at Fordham University in New York City.